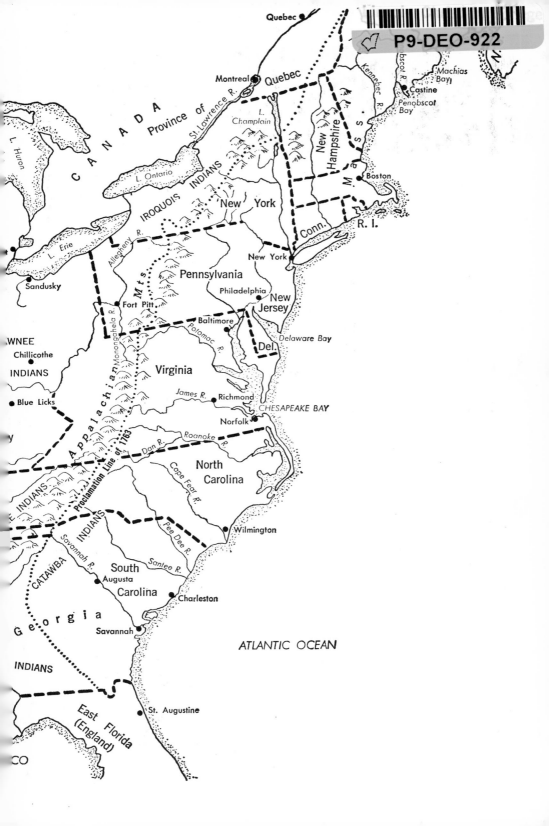

# People & Events

## of the

# American
# Revolution

# People & Events

## of the

# American Revolution

Edited by
*Trevor N. Dupuy*
*Gay M. Hammerman*

R.R. BOWKER COMPANY
New York and London

T.N. DUPUY ASSOCIATES
Dunn Loring, Virginia

1974

Published by T. N. DUPUY ASSOCIATES,
Dunn Loring, Virginia, in association with
R. R. BOWKER CO. (a Xerox company), New York, N.Y.

Printed and bound in the United States of America

**Library of Congress Cataloging in Publication Data**

Dupuy, Trevor Nevitt, 1916-
    People and events of the American Revolution.

    Bibliography: p.
    1. United States—History—Revolution, 1775-1783—
Chronology. 2. United States—History—Revolution.
1775-1783—Biography. I. Hammerman, Gay M., joint
author. II. Title.
E209.D86      973.3      74-7896
ISBN 0-8352-0777-3

This book is dedicated to
Joe and Danny Hammerman
and Fielding and Signe Dupuy
with pride and love.

# Contents

# Preface

This book is designed for two overlapping audiences. It is intended to satisfy the interest — perhaps Bicentennial-inspired — of the ordinary citizen who wants to know more about the American Revolution. It will also provide a unique and reliable reference for serious students. Until now there has been no single convenient reference presenting in simple, chronological order the principal events of our Revolution, and also including the essential available biographical information about the many people who played significant roles in those events.

We have tried to make the first section of the book — "Events of the American Revolution" — as comprehensive as possible, but we have deliberately excluded very small military actions for which no information is available except their alleged occurrence. In general the events pertain directly to the Revolution, and events are excluded that merely happened to occur during the same time span. A few exceptions are made, however, in order to provide some picture of the social and cultural background against which the Revolution took place. The reader will find an entry, for example, for the establishment of stage coach service between New York and Boston. The authors hope that readers will share their pleasure in seeing military, naval, political, and diplomatic events of the Revolution fall into place, side by side, in chronological order and in seeing them interspersed with bits of diverting, fact-based folklore — always identified as such — that were their neighbors in time.

The section on "People of the American Revolution" provides terse information about a great and motley assemblage of persons who have in common much or almost nothing, but who all share involvement in the American Revolution of 1775-1783. They include loyalists and patriots, European diplomats and American congressional delegates, Indian leaders, foreign monarchs, and men and women of entirely local fame. The only requirement for inclusion has been the playing of a remembered part in the Revolution.

Unfortunately we could not include *all* who did participate. Since we could not, for reasons of space and time, give a roster of all Revolutionary soldiers and sailors, we decided not to list any man whose Revolutionary activities were entirely military or naval unless he held at least the rank of brigadier general or naval captain, or unless he called special attention to himself in some way, whether by bravery, skill, kinship, treachery, or, in one case, longevity.

In every case where the information was available we have given the person's dates of birth and death, occupations, military rank, birthplace, and a brief biographic résumé with emphasis on Revolution-related activities. No one has been omitted, however, because any portion of this information was not available for him. We especially wanted to include here as many as possible of the half-forgotten loyalists, soldiers of fortune from overseas, and local patriot heroes, and this meant listing people for whom only fragmentary data are obtainable.

The usefulness of the "People" section of the book is increased, we believe, by Appendix A, which lists signers of the Declaration, generals of the Continental Army, and many other categories of Revolutionary people. The following additional points are mentioned here to aid the reader in using this book:

1. Use of the designation USS (United States Ship) before the Declaration of Independence is of course premature, but it has been done here for convenience.

2. British privateers and transports, and American privateers, are designated HMP, HMT, and USP for convenience.

3. The number enclosed in parentheses following the name of a ship indicates the number of guns carried by the vessel.

4. Places located in present-day Illinois, Indiana, Ohio, Kentucky, Maine, and Vermont are designated as such, even though the areas involved were not states at that time.

5. In the "People" section, military actions are identified by state (or province) and date of occurrence except for 16 especially well known battles that appear with great fre-

quency in the biographic résumés. These are listed in Appendix B, with their locations and dates.

6. The military or naval rank indicated in the brief identifying data at the beginning of a person's entry is the highest rank he held during the Revolution, up to the signing of the peace treaty on September 3, 1783.

7. The term *brevet*, often used in designations of rank, indicates that the officer was promoted to the honor of the rank, but probably not the pay, and often not to the command responsibility or authority.

8. The terms Admiral of the Blue, Rear Admiral of the Red, and so forth, are seen in biographic résumés of several British officers. These puzzling terms are explained in Appendix C.

9. The terms *patriot* and *loyalist* are used throughout simply to indicate the cause to which a man or woman gave allegiance; no laudatory or other connotations are necessarily intended in any case.

The authors have found this book in manuscript to be a most useful reference in our other Revolutionary research. It is our hope that it will be of equal use and pleasure to its readers. We were assisted in our research for this book by Edith Kilroy, Melanie Lippincott Fein, John Rabb, and Ronald G. Rago. Mary Picard typed the manuscript with skill and devotion from a very difficult draft. For help in finding sources and in checking facts and citations, we are grateful to the staffs of the Library of Congress, the Army Library, the library of the Daughters of the American Revolution, and the fine public libraries of Arlington County and Fairfax County, Virginia.

Dunn Loring, Va.

Gay M. Hammerman
Trevor N. Dupuy

# Events of the American Revolution

## *1733*

*May 17*

### The Molasses Act

This act laid a prohibitive duty on rum, molasses, and sugar imported into the American colonies from the non-British West Indies. A measure intended to protect British Indies planters, the law would have ruined the West Indian trade that was so essential to the New England merchants. They strongly opposed it. The act did not, in practice, have serious consequences on the American colonial economy, as there was much evasion by smuggling and little systematic enforcement effort by royal officials.

## *1761*

*December 2*

### Writs of assistance issued in Boston

This event was the culmination of nearly a year of fiery debate over the legality of writs of assistance (warrants issued by courts, on demand of Parliament, granting British customs authorities the right

# *1761*

to search private houses for smuggled goods). Boston merchants, represented by attorneys James Otis and Oxenbridge Thacher, had challenged the legitimacy of the writs in January, when Surveyor General Thomas Lechmere requested new authorization to replace the old authorization that would expire six months after the death of George II (October 25, 1760). The Massachusetts Superior Court had authorized customs officials to search for smuggled goods ever since 1755, but faced with the fervent protests of Otis, who charged that the writs were "against the fundamental principles of law," Chief Justice Thomas Hutchinson delayed decision until word was received from England on the matter. Finally, on November 19, the court ruled to uphold the issuance of writs of assistance.

# *1763*

*February 10*

## Treaty of Paris concludes Seven Years' War

Britain received Canada and all French claims south of the Great Lakes and east of the Mississippi except New Orleans. Britain also was left with an enormous national debt. The war had cost Britain more than £82,000,000, and it was estimated that the expense of supporting military forces to protect Britain's old and newly acquired territories in America would amount to £300,000 annually. As the burden on the British taxpayer was already great and since the military force was ostensibly for the protection of the American colonists against possible French and Indian attacks, the Grenville ministry devised a legislative program whereby the colonies would assume some of the financial burden of the war and of the subsequent military expenditures. The Sugar, Colonial Currency, Stamp, and Quartering Acts were manifestations of this program.

*October 7*

## Proclamation of 1763

This act established boundaries for Quebec, East Florida, and West Florida, barred colonial settlement or land speculation in all terri-

# *1763*

tory between the Alleghenies and the Mississippi and from Florida to the fifty degree north latitude line, and restricted trade with the Indians. Although the act was initially adopted as a temporary measure to calm the fears of the Indians, many colonists viewed it as an arbitrary and unnecessary obstacle to their natural westward expansion and development.

*November 16*

## New British commander-in-chief

General Thomas Gage, new commander-in-chief of British forces in America, arrived in New York City to assume his duties.

# *1764*

*April 5*

## Parliament passes Sugar Act (or American Revenue Act)

This measure was designed to end the smuggling of foreign molasses and to secure revenue for the purpose of "defraying the necessary expenses of defending, protection of, and securing the British colonies and plantations in America." An extension of the Molasses Act of 1733, the law reduced the tariff on foreign molasses from sixpence to threepence per gallon and raised it on imports of foreign refined sugar, wine, coffee, and other products. Importation of rum was prohibited. This was the first law passed by Parliament for the purpose of raising money in the American colonies for the crown and resulted in much opposition and debate in the colonies. The constitutionality of the act was questioned by James Otis and others, and it was denounced as taxation without representation.

*April 19*

## Colonial Currency Act passed by Parliament

This act, scheduled to take effect September 1, was aimed mainly at Virginia, which had been issuing large amounts of paper money.

# 1764

It forbade the futher use of bills of credit as legal tender. This was an extension of a similar ban which had been operating in New England since 1751. The law did not permit exercise of discretion in enforcement by colonial governors, and colonies with well-managed currencies were irritated at its harshness. Everywhere the act was regarded by colonists as a source of unnecessary hardship during the difficult times following the war.

## *May 24*

### Colonial protest against Sugar and Currency Acts

A town meeting in Boston denounced taxation without representation and appealed for united colonial protest. Later, the Massachusetts House of Representatives authorized a committee to keep contact and correspondence with other provinces (June 13).

# 1765

## *March 22*

### Stamp Act approved by Parliament

This law, to go into effect on November 1, required all legal papers and all commercial papers, including newspapers, pamphlets, almanacs, and playing cards, to bear a stamp. The intent of the act was to raise revenue to balance the debt incurred in defending the American colonies. While Parliament considered it an urgent measure to meet immediate financial obligations, the colonists viewed it rather as another violation of their constitutional rights— another instance of taxation without representation. The colonists would have preferred to be taxed by their own assemblies, but, in the opinion of Sir George Grenville, Chancellor of the Exchequer, past experience had proved that efforts to get the colonists to provide the funds for their own defense would not be successful.

# *1765*

*March 24*

## Parliament's Quartering Act takes effect

The act came in response to a January request by General Thomas Gage, commander-in-chief of British forces in America. It provided that in cases where local barracks and public lodgings were inadequate, troops could be quartered in uninhabited barns or houses. Certain rations and furniture were to be provided at the expense of the local colonial treasury. The law did not include the stipulation that soldiers could be lodged in private homes. Most colonial assemblies refused to pay the cost of quartering troops, and in New York, Gage's headquarters, opposition was particularly strong.

*May 29*

## Stamp Act Resolves in Virginia

The House of Burgesses adopted Patrick Henry's resolutions asserting the rights of the colonists as Englishmen and denouncing taxation without representation. During the debate, Henry provoked shouts of "Treason!" by saying "Caesar had his Brutus, Charles the First his Cromwell, and George the Third . . . ." He then reportedly ended the sentence ". . . may profit by their example," and added, "If *this* be treason, make the most of it." Five resolutions were introduced and passed on the 29th; the House reversed itself on the most radical resolution on the 30th. Other colonies followed suit in issuing resolutions denouncing the Stamp Act.

*June 6*

## Massachusetts proposes intercolonial congress for action against Stamp Act

The Massachusetts Assembly, at the initiative of James Otis, made the proposal and dispatched a circular letter to all the colonies (June 8) suggesting the meeting be held in October at New York City.

# *1765*

*August 14*

## Andrew Oliver, stamp distributor, hanged and burned in effigy in Boston

In response to the Stamp Act, colonists also wrecked Oliver's home and destroyed his office building. He was forced to resign and afterward fled to a fort in Boston Harbor. Many stamp distributors in other towns and colonies later resigned in fear, and only in Georgia were any stamps actually sold.

*October 7-25*

## Stamp Act Congress

In response to the appeal of the Massachusetts Assembly (June 6), 27 delegates, representing nine colonies, met in New York and framed a petition to the King and Parliament. The address declared that taxation without representation was a violation of the basic rights of Englishmen and requested the repeal of oppressive legislation. This meeting was important as the first intercolonial assembly whose acts were endorsed by most of the colonies.

*October 28*

## Colonial protest against Stamp Act

Leading citizens of New York City adopted a nonimportation agreement, resolving to ban the importation of British goods until the Stamp Act was revoked and other 1764 trade restrictions were modified. Merchants in other port cities later adopted similar nonimportation resolutions.

# *1766*

*January 17*

## London merchants petition for repeal of Stamp Act

A committee of merchants presented an appeal to Parliament expressing fear that trade was being drastically upset due to colonial protest against the Stamp Act and other oppressive laws. The decline in British exports to the American colonies, from £2,249,710 in 1764 to £1,944,108 in 1765, was testimony to the validity of their fears.

*March 18*

## Repeal of Stamp Act receives royal assent

Repeal, to take effect May 1, was in response to both colonial protest and the appeals of British merchants. Word of this legislation was received in the colonies with much rejoicing; nonimportation was abandoned and toasts were drunk to the King; the New York Assembly voted to erect statues in honor of George III and William Pitt.

*March 18*

## Declaratory Act enacted by Parliament

This was an assertion of Parliament's complete authority over the colonies, including the power to impose revenue taxes. Passed on the same date as the repeal of the Stamp Act, it was generally overlooked by the rejoicing colonists.

*November 1*

## Modification of trade restrictions

A one-penny tax on all British and non-British imports was substituted for the threepence duty on molasses, and the price of British

# *1766*

West Indian sugar was reduced. The colonists viewed these measures favorably but were much less pleased with legislation, also effective on this date, which required the clearance of all colonial products destined for Northern Europe at ports in Great Britain.

### *December 19*

### Governor prorogues (suspends) New York Assembly

This action by Governor Sir Henry Moore was the result of the Assembly's refusal to accept Parliament's Quartering Act.

# *1767*

### *June 6*

### New York Assembly Reconvened

Governor Moore recalled the Assembly when he was assured that the Quartering Act would be approved, and that costs would be met by local funds.

### *June 29*

### Townshend Acts receive royal assent

These acts, to be effective on November 20, included a revenue bill that levied duties on glass, lead, paint, tea, and paper, and—to enforce the bill—authorization of the use of writs of assistance and the trial of smugglers without juries. More outrageous to the colonists than the collection of this duty, which would in fact yield only a small revenue, was the stipulation that it would be used to pay the salaries of governors and other royal officials in the colonies, thereby making them independent of financial control by the colonial assemblies. An accompanying act, no longer necessary and the result of slow sea communications, suspended the New York Assembly for its defiance of the Quartering Act until it agreed to comply with that act's requirements. (See above, June 6.)

# *1767*

## *October 28*

### Resumption of nonimportation

In outrage against the Townshend Acts, a Boston town meeting resolved not to purchase certain British goods after December 31. Other nonimportation agreements were later adopted in Providence, Newport, and New York City.

## *November 5*

### John Dickinson writes in opposition to Townshend Acts

The first of fourteen essays, entitled "Letters from a Farmer in Pennsylvania to the Inhabitants of the British Colonies," was published. In this, as in all his widely read series of "Letters," Dickinson recognized Parliament's authority to regulate trade, but repudiated the levying of revenue taxes, denounced the Townshend Acts as unconstitutional, and called for nonconsumption resolves—that is, boycotts—in all of the colonies.

# *1768*

## *February 11*

### Massachusetts resolution against Townshend Acts

Drawn up by Samuel Adams, this was an official denunciation of the acts by the Massachusetts House of Representatives. It declared certain provisions unconstitutional and in violation of the colonists' rights as Englishmen. A circular letter carrying the resolution was sent to the other colonies with an appeal for united action against British oppression. This action was regarded as treasonable by the royal authorities, and the Assembly was dissolved by Governor Francis Bernard. Assemblies in other colonies were also threatened with dissolution by Lord Hillsborough, Secretary of State for the Colonies, if they endorsed the resolutions (April 21). Nevertheless, New Jersey, Connecticut, Maryland, Virginia, Rhode Island, Georgia, and South Carolina defied this threat and endorsed the action taken by the Massachusetts Assembly.

# *1768*

*June 10*

## *Liberty* incident

A Boston mob assaulted customs officials in protest against the seizure of John Hancock's sloop *Liberty* by HMS *Romney* (50) for evading customs payment on a cargo of Madeira wine. The customs officials fled to Castle William in Boston Harbor the following day and sent out an appeal for more troops.

*September 12*

## Boston town meeting calls people to arms

This was done for the ostensible reason that war with France was imminent. The meeting also appealed to Governor Bernard to re-open the Assembly. He refused.

*September 13*

## Boston town meeting calls provincial congress, adopts resolutions on rights of colonists

This action was taken after Governor Bernard refused to call a special session of the Assembly to discuss the arrival of British troops in Boston.

*September 23-29*

## Provincial Convention in Massachusetts

Representatives of 96 towns met informally to discuss the refusal of Governor Bernard to call the General Assembly back into session. The meeting adjourned when British troopships arrived in Boston Harbor.

# *1768*

*October 1*

## British troops land in Boston

Despite verbal threats of violent resistance by the Sons of Liberty, two regiments of British infantry with artillery were stationed in Boston.

# *1769*

*February 6*

## Nonimportation reaffirmed

Philadelphia merchants agreed to stringent nonimportation, prohibiting most British goods after April 1. Baltimore merchants took similar steps on March 30 and by the end of 1769 only New Hampshire was not involved in the boycott of British goods.

*May 16*

## Virginia Resolves against Townshend Acts adopted by House of Burgesses

Drawn up by George Mason, introduced by George Washington, and unanimously supported by the planter leadership of the colony, these resolutions asserted the sole right of Virginians to levy taxes against Virginians. They were a response to the Massachusetts circular letter of February 11, 1768. An address to the King, drafted by Patrick Henry and Richard Henry Lee, expressing these views was adopted the next day. The assembly was thereupon dissolved by Governor Botetourt.

# *1769*

*May 18*

## Virginia Association adopted

Acting as an extralegal body, the House of Burgesses met in Williamsburg, and resolved to prohibit all imports of dutiable British goods, except paper, and many nondutiable imports as well. No slaves brought into the colony after November 1 were to be purchased. This act not only flouted British authority but represented the beginnings of a new authority that could supersede it. Although the Association had no legal standing, it was to be carried into effect and adhered to more thoroughly than any official act of trade. This step was followed by similar actions in other colonies and cities throughout the following months: Maryland (June 22), Savannah, Georgia (September 19), North Carolina (November 7), Providence, Rhode Island (October 24), Newport, Rhode Island (October 30).

*December 16*

## Publication of the handbill *A Son of Liberty to the Betrayed Inhabitants of the City and Colony of New York*

Published anonymously by Alexander McDougall, a merchant and leader of the New York Sons of Liberty.

# *1770*

*January 13*

## British soldiers cut down Liberty Pole in New York City

As a result, 3,000 citizens met to discuss the Quartering Act and to protest the presence and actions of British soldiers. Liberty Poles were symbols before which the Sons of Liberty traditionally assembled.

# 1770

*January 19*

## Battle of Golden Hill, New York City

A minor clash between citizens (Sons of Liberty) using clubs, and 30-40 soldiers, using bayonets. No one was killed, although several on both sides were seriously wounded.

*January 22*

## Mayor Whitehead Hicks of New York orders British soldiers to stay in their barracks

They were not to leave barracks areas unless accompanied by officers.

*February 6*

## Sons of Libery erect their fifth Liberty Pole in New York City

The first four had been destroyed by British soldiers.

*February 8*

## Alexander McDougall imprisoned in New York for printing subversive handbills

He was pardoned and released on April 29.

*March 5*

## Lord North moves repeal of Townshend Acts

Because of colonial protest against the acts, he proposed to retain only the tax on tea. The marked decrease in colonial imports from

# *1770*

Britain (by as much as £314,743 annually in New York alone) demonstrated the impact on the British economy of the nonimportation agreements in the colonies.

*March 5*

## The Boston Massacre

A panicky redcoat guard detail under the command of Captain Thomas Preston fired on a taunting mob, killing five and injuring six. Crispus Attucks, a leader among the Negroes in the crowd, was one of those killed. A general uprising was avoided when Governor Thomas Hutchinson complied with Samuel Adams's demand and withdrew the troops from the city to harbor islands.

*March 24*

## Soldiers and citizens clash in New York City

British soldiers failed in an attempt to destroy the Liberty Pole.

*April 12*

## Parliament repeals the Townshend Acts

The tax on tea was retained.

*May 30*

## Nonimportation reaffirmed in New York City

A public meeting upheld the policy even though other colonies were violating it. There was widespread disagreement with this decision, particularly among merchants.

# 1770

*July 7*

## New York Assembly votes to resume importation of British goods except tea

New Yorkers also affirmed their determination to resume nonimportation if other colonies adopted the policy. Angry debate continued.

*July 25*

## New York Sons of Libery protest abandonment of nonimportation

Under the leadership of Alexander McDougall, they urged the New York counties to oppose the recent decision of the New York Assembly. Agitation continued.

*September 22*

## Massachusetts convention on the grievance of a standing army

Convention of delegates representing 96 towns met at Faneuil Hall, Boston.

*December 5*

## Boston Massacre soldiers acquitted

A Boston jury acquitted all but two of the redcoats after defense by John Adams and Josiah Quincy.

# 1770

## December 13

### Alexander McDougall called before New York Assembly

After an examination of his recent activities, McDougall was imprisoned for contempt until April 27, 1771.

## December 17

### Edmund Burke appointed an agent of New York in England

# 1771

## January 15

### The "Bloody" Act passed by North Carolina Assembly

Rioters would be guilty of treason. This action resulted from troubles caused by "Regulators" (frontier settlers, mostly Scotch-Irish) protesting lack of representation and tyranny of aristocratic Tidewater politicians. "Regulators" voiced defiance.

## May 16

### Battle of Alamance Creek

Governor William Tryon's force of 1,200 loyal militia defeated poorly led backwoods "Regulators" of western North Carolina under James Few and others. Few was hanged the following day on the Alamance battlefield.

## May 19

### Public hanging of six "Regulators" captured at Alamance

This followed trial for treason in Hillsboro, North Carolina.

# *1771*

*June 19*

## Massachusetts House of Representatives protests British governmental procedures

Specifically criticized were "all such doctrines, principles, and practices as tend to establish either ministerial or even royal instructions as laws within the province."

# *1772*

*June 9-10*

### *Gaspée* Incident

British revenue cutter *Gaspée*, aground in Narragansett Bay off Providence, Rhode Island, was set afire during the night by patriot raiders led by merchant John Brown and ship's captain Abraham Whipple.

*June 24*

### Stagecoach service begins from New York to Boston

*August 20*

## Royal Commission established to investigate *Gaspée* Incident

Despite a reward offered for information, the commission failed to find sufficient evidence to apprehend or try the perpetrators.

*November 2*

### Committee of Correspondence organized in Boston by Samuel Adams and Joseph Warren

This was for the purpose of communication with other towns and colonies to assure united, joint action in resistance to British oppres-

# *1772*

sion. James Otis was made chairman of the Boston committee. More than 80 such committees were established in Massachusetts within three months. Similar committees were later set up throughout the colonies.

*November 20*

## Boston Committee of Correspondence prepares and circulates "Resolves" on rights of colonists

These included Samuel Adams's "State of the Rights of the Colonists," Joseph Warren's "List of Infringements and Violation of those Rights," and Dr. Benjamin Church's "Letter of Correspondence."

# *1773*

*March 12*

## Virginia Resolution against *Gaspée* Commission

The House of Burgesses, led by Thomas Jefferson, Patrick Henry, and Richard Henry Lee, adopted a resolution which asserted that the commission threatened ancient legal rights. They also recommended a committee of correspondence for Virginia.

*April 27*

## Tea Act introduced into Parliament by Lord North

The purpose was to save the inefficient, and probably corrupt, East India Company from bankruptcy by providing a subsidized market in the colonies.

# *1773*

*May 10*

## Parliament passes the Tea Act

The East India Company was allowed to export tea to the colonies without paying regular duty, but with a small tax to be paid by colonial purchasers. This meant that the East India Company could undersell not only smuggled Dutch tea but also legally imported tea from other sources.

*June 25*

## The Hutchinson Letters Affair

The Massachusetts Assembly petitioned the King to remove Governor Thomas Hutchinson and Secretary Andrew Oliver from office. They were accused of plotting "to overthrow the constitution of the province" on the basis of evidence uncovered by Benjamin Franklin in letters written several years earlier by the two officials to friends in England.

*October 14*

## British cargo ship burned at Annapolis, Maryland

The reason for this is obscure; presumably it was a protest against the Tea Act.

*October 18*

## Philadelphia citizens protest Tea Act

A mass meeting demanded, and obtained, the resignation of the merchants who had been named agents for the East India Company tea.

# *1773*

*October 25*

### News of tea shipments to colonies reaches New York

*November 27*

### First tea ships arrive in colonies

East India Company ships carrying taxable tea entered Boston Harbor.

*November 27*

### New Yorkers organize to oppose tea shipments

New York patriots organized a committee to decide what should be done with tea arriving from Great Britain in New York. Naming themselves "the Mohawks," the patriots threatened tea agents with "an unwelcome visit."

*November 29*

### New York Sons of Liberty meet to consider the tea tax

They voted resolutions denouncing the tax and all importers of British tea.

*December 4*

### East India Company tea agents in New York refuse to receive British tea

*December 16*

### The Boston Tea Party

Boston patriots, organized by Samuel Adams and disguised as Mohawk Indians, boarded three "Tea Act" ships and dumped 342

# *1773*

chests of tea into the harbor. This episode was the first organized act of violent resistance to royal and parliamentary authority in the American colonies. It encouraged those radical leaders who favored breaking ties with the mother country and (through the Intolerable Acts and colonial response thereto) was to lead directly to the American Revolution.

*December 17*

### New York City public meeting votes that British tea shall not be landed

The meeting also organized a committee to correspond with other provinces on the tea issue.

# *1774*

*January 3*

### Governor Tryon writes that tea cannot be safely landed in New York except under the "point of the bayonet and muzzle of the cannon"

*January 12*

### Newport, Rhode Island, citizens boycott all persons buying or selling tea

*January 20*

### Colonial Assembly in New York names a Committee of Correspondence

# *1774*

*January 25*

## Boston mob attacks customs official

John Malcolm was tarred and feathered and paraded through the town.

*January 31*

## Benjamin Franklin dismissed by Parliament as postmaster general in the colonies

His patriot sympathies and his involvement in the Hutchinson Letters affair were considered subversive.

*March 5*

## John Hancock suggests a general congress of all British colonies in America

The initial concept, at this time or soon thereafter, was that Canada and the British colonies in Florida and the West Indies would also be represented.

*March 14*

## Boston Port Bill introduced in Parliament

This was the response of an outraged Parliament to the Boston Tea Party. Lord North proposed closing Boston Port until the destroyed tea was paid for.

*March 24*

## New York Committee of Correspondence agrees to cooperate with Boston in measures against the British

# *1774*

*March 25*

## Boston Port Bill passed by the House of Commons

It was the first of the so-called "Coercive" or "Intolerable" acts. The punitive measure prohibited loading or unloading of ships in Boston harbor, except for food and fuel shipped coastwise, until damages had been paid for tea destroyed in the "Tea Party."

*March 30*

## Governor Hutchinson dissolves the Massachusetts General Assembly

*March 31*

## King George III signs the Boston Port Act

It was to become effective June 1, 1774.

*April 2*

## Appointment of General Thomas Gage as governor of Massachusetts is announced

Gage was the commander-in-chief of British forces in North America.

*April 22*

## *London* Incident, or "New York's Tea Party"

A New York mob, including "Mohawks," boarded the ship and destroyed a private consignment of tea which the captain was concealing.

# *1774*

## *May 10*

### Boston learns of Boston Port Act

News also arrived that General Thomas Gage, British military commander in America, was to replace Governor Hutchinson.

## *May 12*

### The Boston Committee of Correspondence recommends that all colonies suspend trade with Great Britain

A circular letter was drafted to be sent to other committees of correspondence, appealing for united colonial action against British oppression. A town meeting, Samuel Adams presiding, in Faneuil Hall ratified the recommendation the following day, and Paul Revere was sent with the circular letter to New York, Philadelphia, and other points south.

## *May 16*

### New York's Committee of 51 is organized

This was a new committee of correspondence with broad representation, including radicals, moderates, and conservatives. Isaac Lowe was appointed chairman.

## *May 17*

### General Gage lands at Boston

He replaced Hutchinson as governor and assumed direct command of British military forces in Massachusetts; he retained his position as commander-in-chief in the colonies.

# *1774*

*May 17*

## Citizens of Providence, Rhode Island, call for an intercolonial convention

This was a first step toward a continental congress.


*May 19*

## Boston circular letter reaches Philadelphia


*May 19*

## Protest at Farmington, Connecticut

A crowd burned a copy of the Boston Port Act.


*May 20*

## Mass meeting in Philadelphia

A committee was selected to draft a letter to Boston in response to the circular letter.


*May 20*

## King George approves two more "Coercive" or "Intolerable" acts

Royal assent was given to the Administration of Justice Act, which was designed to protect royal officials. Such officials accused of a capital crime committed in pursuit of official duties would not be tried by the provincial court where the official was located, or where the act was committed, but would be sent to another colony or to England for trial.

# *1774*

The Massachusetts Government Act, also approved by the King, nullified that colony's charter and gave the governor control over town meetings.

*May 21*

### Philadelphia response to Boston circular letter

The committee selected the previous day was dominated by moderates. It expressed abhorrence of property destruction, stated that the destroyed tea should be paid for, suggested an intercolonial meeting to draft a petition to the King, and stated that nonimportation was a drastic measure to be adopted only as a last resort.

*May 23*

### The New York Committee of 51 calls for a congress of deputies from all colonies

*May 24*

### Virginia protests Boston Port Act

The House of Burgesses resolved that June 1, the day the act was to go into effect, should be a day of fasting and prayer.

*May 26*

### The Virginia House of Burgesses is dissolved

Governor Dunmore (John Murray, Earl of Dunmore), acted as a result of the vote of protest against the Boston Port Act.

# 1774

*May 27*

## Virginia Burgesses call for intercolonial Congress

Meeting unofficially, they declared that an attack on one colony was an attack on all.

*May 30*

## The New York Committee of 51 urges all counties to establish committees of correspondence

*May 31*

## Virginia Burgesses adopt a nonimportation resolution

This was an extension of the Virginia Association of 1769 to include all British goods. A meeting was to be held on August 1 to decide whether exports to England would also be suspended.

*June 1*

## Boston Port Act goes into effect

Boston harbor was closed to import and export. The day was observed in many colonies with fasting, mourning, and protest. Despite Dunmore's disapproval, the Virginia Burgesses attended church en masse as a gesture of protest.

*June 2*

## Parliament reenacts Quartering Act

This was the fourth of the "Coercive" or "Intolerable" Acts.

# *1774*

*June 5*

## Publication of Dr. Joseph Warren's "Solemn League and Covenant"

This was an agreement by Massachusetts merchants to boycott British goods.

*June 10*

## Outbreak of Lord Dunmore's War

Virginia Governor Dunmore called out the southwest Virginia militia, under the leadership of Colonel Andrew Lewis, to suppress a Shawnee uprising on the Virginia and Kentucky frontier.

*June 11*

## Meeting of freeholders at Newark, New Jersey

Essex County freeholders pledged constitutional obedience to England, condemned the Boston Port Act, approved boycott of British goods, and appointed a committee to meet with other county committees.

*June 14*

## Rhode Island General Assembly selects delegates to Continental Congress

Rhode Island was the first colony to take this action, as the movement for a Continental Congress gained strength.

*June 15*

## New York mob burns effigies of Lord North and other British leaders

# *1774*

*June 17*

## Massachusetts Assembly calls for delegates from colonies to meet in Philadelphia, September 1

In consequence, Governor Gage dissolved the Assembly the same day. It would never meet again.

*June 17*

## Philadelphia public meeting recommends congress of delegates from all colonies

Leaders of the meeting were Thomas Willing and John Dickinson.

*June 22*

## Parliament passes Quebec Act

Sometimes considered the fifth "Intolerable" act, it granted religious liberty to French Canadian Roman Catholics and was interpreted as a threat to the generally Protestant populations of the 13 colonies. The act also extended the frontier of Quebec to the Ohio and Mississippi Rivers, reaffirming the long-ignored provisions of the Proclamation of 1763 that restricted the other colonies from settlement west of the Appalachians.

*June 23*

## Windham, Connecticut, Resolution

A town meeting voted to support the Boston Committee of Correspondence in urging an intercolonial congress.

# *1774*

*June 29*

### New York Committee of 51 votes to send five deputies to Continental Congress

Controversy over appointments lasted several days thereafter.

*July 6*

### "Meeting in the Fields" in New York City

Alexander McDougall and Alexander Hamilton spoke out against British tyranny; nonimportation resolutions were passed.

*July 10*

### New York Committee of 51 asks counties to appoint delegates to the proposed Continental Congress

*July 18*

### Fairfax County, Virginia, Resolves

Drafted by George Mason and approved by a citizens' assembly, the resolutions supported nonimportation, aid to Boston, united resistance by all the colonies, an intercolonial congress, and, if the measures against Massachusetts were not removed, nonexportation and refusal to grow tobacco.

*July 22*

### Pennsylvania Assembly names delegates to the proposed Continental Congress

# *1774*

*August 1*

## Representatives from Virginia Counties meet in convention at Williamsburg

The original purpose had been to decide upon the question of non-exportation to England. However, the first order of business became the question of representation at the proposed Continental Congress in Philadelphia.

*August 5*

## Virginia Convention names delegates to Continental Congress

Seven delegates were selected, including George Washington, Patrick Henry, and Richard Henry Lee. Thomas Jefferson, who almost certainly would have been included, was left out because of illness.

*August 6*

## Virginia Association amended by Virginia Convention

The original Virginia Association of May 18, 1769, an agreement banning imports of slaves and of dutiable British goods, had been extended to all British goods on May 31, 1774. The extension was reaffirmed, and it was declared that if American grievances were not redressed earlier, all exports to England would be stopped on August 10.

*August 8*

## Rowan County, North Carolina, Resolutions

Freeholders denounced unjust taxes, advocated restriction of imports from Great Britain, and denounced the slave trade.

# *1774*

*August 20*

## Massachusetts delegates to Continental Congress welcomed in New York City

*August 23*

## Mass meeting at Edenton, North Carolina, protests the Boston Port Act

*August 25*

## Convention to form North Carolina Provincial Congress meets at New Bern

The meeting criticized the acts and policies of the King and Parliament, and resolved to boycott British tea after September 10 and all British goods after January 1, 1775. Delegates to Congress were selected.

*September 1*

## New York deputies to Congress set out for Philadelphia

They were cheered by a crowd as they left.

*September 1*

## General Gage seizes colonists' stock of powder at Charlestown, Massachusetts, across the Charles River from Boston

*September 1*

## Opening of the First Continental Congress delayed

The delegations from Virginia, North Carolina, Maryland, Georgia, and New York had not yet arrived.

# 1774

*September 5*

## First Continental Congress convenes in Philadelphia

Peyton Randolph of Virginia was elected President. All colonies but Georgia were represented. A committee was set up to prepare a declaration of rights and grievances and a nonimportation association.

*September 9*

## Suffolk Resolves

Delegates from towns in Suffolk County, Massachusetts, adopted Joseph Warren's resolutions protesting the Coercive Acts; urged Massachusetts to form a government responsive to the people and to withhold taxes from the Crown until the acts were repealed; advised the people to arm; recommended indemnities against Britain. The resolves stated that the people of Massachusetts would never submit to Parliamentary repression, but asserted that they had "no inclination to commence a war with his majesty's troops."

*September 16*

## Paul Revere arrives in Philadelphia with Suffolk Resolves

*September 17*

## Continental Congress endorses the Suffolk Resolves

Congress also voted continued help to the people of Boston.

*September 28*

## Congress rejects loyalist resolution by one vote

Joseph Galloway, conservative Pennsylvania delegate had proposed a "Plan of Proposed Union between Great Britain and the Colo-

# *1774*

nies," including a declaration of abhorrence of the idea of independence. By this close vote, Congress deferred consideration, which was tantamount to rejection.

*October 1*

## Congress establishes a committee to prepare an Address to the King

The address was to include a provision assuring that the colonies would pay just taxes.

*October 3*

## Congress agrees on amendment to Address to King

Assurance was to be given that the repeal of obnoxious laws would remove colonial grievances.

*October 5*

## Massachusetts Assembly, meeting without authority in Salem, reorganizes as a Provincial Congress

It then adjourned to Concord and elected John Hancock president (October 7).

*October 10*

## Battle of Point Pleasant, Virginia (present-day West Virginia)

Colonel Andrew Lewis and about 1,100 men from the southwest Virginian frontier were attacked in the early morning by Chief Cornstalk and a large force of Shawnee in a decisive engagement of Lord Dunmore's War. Colonel Charles Lewis and Colonel William Fleming led two divisions against the Indians, who were repulsed. Both were wounded, and Fleming died. Losses were heavy on both sides, the colonists having nearly 50 killed and about 100 wounded.

# *1774*

*October 14*

## First Continental Congress adopts a Declaration of Rights

Eleven resolutions proclaimed that Parliament had deprived the colonists of rights of Englishmen. It asserted their rights to "life, liberty, and property," to representation in Parliament and participation in legislation, to trial by peers, and the rights to assemble and to petition the King. The practice of keeping a standing army in the colonies in time of peace without consent of the legislature was denounced as a violation of rights. Control of legislative power in several colonies by a council appointed by the King was declared to be "unconstitutional, dangerous, and destructive to the freedom of American legislation".

*October 19*

## Ship *Peggy Stewart* burned at Annapolis for defiance of nonimportation agreement

Captain Anthony Stewart had paid duty on 17 packages of tea. The people of Annapolis met and resolved to destroy Stewart's vessel. To prevent public unrest that might not be allayed by the mere destruction of the vessel, and to soften public feeling against him, Stewart consented to burn his ship himself, ran her aground near Windmill Point, and set her afire. (Also known as "The *Peggy Stewart* Tea Party.")

*October 20*

## First Continental Congress adopts the "Association"

Modeled after the Virginia Association, the Continental Association was a nonimportation, nonconsumption, nonexportation agreement. It provided for enforcement by committees of correspondence, discontinuation of the slave trade, and development of American agriculture and industry. Nonimportation would be effective December 1, 1774, and nonexportation on September 10, 1775. The Association was operating in 12 colonies by April of the following year, the exception being Georgia, which later adopted a modi-

# *1774*

fied version. A decrease of over 90 percent in the value of British imports by the colonies between 1774 and 1775 showed its effectiveness.

*October 21*

## Address to the People of Great Britain

Drafted by Lee, Livingston, and Jay, the address gave a historical exposition of American grievances and warned that if the Crown was allowed to tax America at pleasure, thus becoming financially independent of Parliament, it would soon take oppressive measures against the British people.

*October 21*

## Congress approves Memorial to the Inhabitants of the British Colonies

Drafted by Lee, Livingston, and Jay, this document related the history of American grievances, expressed hope for reconciliation with Britain, and appealed for firm, united compliance with the measures recommended by Congress.

*October 25*

## Congress approves the Address to the King

This document was the result of the resolutions of October 1 and 3. The first draft, prepared by Patrick Henry, was modified before approval.

*October 25*

## "Ladies Tea Party"

Fifty housewives of Edenton, North Carolina, met and publicly declared their allegiance to principles of colonial self-government

# *1774*

by endorsing the proceedings of the Continental Congress. They also passed resolutions discouraging the drinking of tea and wearing of British goods.

*October 26*

## First Continental Congress adjourns

The delegates voted to meet again May 20, 1775, at Philadelphia, if by that time Parliament had not acted to reconcile American grievances.

*October 26*

## Massachusetts Provincial Congress recommends that the towns of Massachusetts prepare for defense

Meeting at Cambridge, it organized selected companies of the militia as "Minute Men" and took measures for the collection of stores and ammunition for public defense.

*November 5*

## Virginia militia at Fort Gower pledge loyalty to fellow countrymen rather than to the King

*November 16*

## Loyalist attack on Continental Congress

The Reverend Samuel Seabury of New York, writing as a "Westchester Farmer," published "Free Thoughts on the Proceedings of the First Continental Congress."

# *1774*

*November 17*

## Philadelphia Troop of Light Horse founded

Established by 26 Philadelphia patriots, it later became the First
Troop Philadelphia City Cavalry.

*November 22*

## Committee of 60 elected in New York City to succeed Committee of 51

*November 30*

## Thomas Paine arrives in Philadelphia

The revolutionary publicist had been given letters of introduction
by Benjamin Franklin before he left England.

*December 5*

## "A Full Vindication of the Measures of the Congress . . . ."

Alexander Hamilton's response to the attack on the Continental
Congress by Samuel Seabury was published.

*December 9-10*

## Patriots seize ordnance at Newport, Rhode Island

The weapons and ammunition were carried to Providence, where
they were guarded by the militia.

# *1774*

*December 12*

## Beginning of weekly Tory newsletter in Boston

Headed "To the Inhabitants of the Province of Massachusetts," it was by David Leonard, a Boston lawyer, writing under the pen name "Massachusettensis."

*December 14*

## New York distillers resolve to boycott molasses and syrup from the British West Indies

*December 14*

## Patriots seize Fort William and Mary, Portsmouth, New Hampshire

Warned by Paul Revere the day before of plans to garrison British troops at the fort, a band of patriots led by John Sullivan attacked and overpowered the small caretaker garrison and carried away arms and powder. No serious casualties were suffered by either side.

*December 22*

## Charleston, South Carolina "Tea Party"

A large quantity of tea was seized and sold by patriots. The resulting funds were used to promote the cause of independence.

# *1775*

*January*

### New Jersey General Assembly unanimously approves the proceedings of the First Continental Congress

It also appointed representatives to a Second Congress and issued a petition of grievances to the King. Governor Franklin expressed his adherence to the absolute authority of the King and Parliament in colonial affairs.

*January 11*

### Francis Salvador becomes first Jew to hold elective office in the New World

A plantation owner, he attended the South Carolina Provincial Congress.

*January 20*

### William Pitt proposes that British troops be withdrawn from Boston

This motion by the elder Pitt (Earl of Chatham) was defeated by a three-to-one margin in Parliament.

*January 23*

### First "Novanglus" letter by John Adams appears in Boston *Gazette*

This presented "radical" answers to the Tory "Massachusettensis." (See December 12, 1774.)

# *1775*

*January 23-28*

## Pennsylvania Provincial Convention meets in Philadelphia

It directed the Philadelphia City Committee to govern the province and call a new provincial convention if necessary.

*January 26*

## New York Assembly refuses to consider the proceedings of the Continental Congress by a vote of 11 to 10

This was a demonstration of the loyalist sympathies of a majority of the body.

*January 27*

## Gage authorized to use force to retain royal authority in Massachusetts

Lord Dartmouth, Secretary of State for the Colonies, also ordered General Gage to take any action necessary to prevent the rebellious faction from perfecting its organization.

*February 1*

## Parliament rejects William Pitt's "Plan for Conciliation with the Colonies"

The plan would have (1) recognized the Continental Congress, (2) assured the American colonies that no revenue measures would be imposed on them without their consent, and (3) endorsed means by which the Congress would vote revenue for the Crown. It was rejected at the first reading.

# *1775*

*February 1*

## Second Massachusetts Provincial Congress meets in Cambridge

John Hancock and Dr. Joseph Warren directed the organization of the defense of the colony.

*February 9*

## Massachusetts declared by Parliament to be in a state of rebellion

*February 17*

## New York Assembly votes against thanking the New York delegates to Congress, 15-9

Loyalist sentiment again prevailed.

*February 21*

## New York Assembly opposes nonimportation

By a vote of 15-10, the body rejected a motion to thank the merchants and people of New York City for their nonimportation activities.

*February 23*

## New York Assembly refuses to appoint delegates to a new Continental Congress

The motion was defeated by a vote of 17 to 9.

# 1775

*February 26*

## Confrontation at Salem, Massachusetts

British troops under Colonel Alexander Leslie, sent by General Gage to seize supplies and weapons, withdrew empty-handed and without incident, in the face of armed patriot opposition.

*February 27*

## House of Commons passes Conciliatory Resolution

It stated that Parliament, with royal approval, would refrain from imposing any but regulatory taxes upon those American colonies that taxed themselves to provide for the common defense and for the maintenance of civil government and judiciary within their respective provinces. The Resolution had been introduced by Lord North on February 17, essentially as a substitute for Pitt's "Plan for Conciliation."

*March*

## The Massachusetts Provincial Congress accepts Stockbridge Indians' offer to serve as Minute Men

*March 1*

## New York's Committee of 60 recommends forming a Provincial Congress

This was a response to loyalist measures passed by the colonial Assembly.

*March 2*

## Three hundred pounds of tea burned in Market Square, Providence, Rhode Island

# *1775*

*March 6*

## Boston commemorates Massacre Day

Dr. Joseph Warren delivered an oration at the Old South Church in the face of disapproval by British officers in the front rows. (March 5 fell on Sunday, so the meeting was scheduled for Monday the 6th.)

*March 10*

## Daniel Boone's expedition into Kentucky

Setting out from Fort Wautage, North Carolina, he went to the mouth of the Kentucky River. The purpose was to open the area for settlement, in defiance of the Quebec Act.

*March 11*

## Resolution of "Freeholders of Botetourt," Virginia

This was a pledge to defend their liberty and to support the Virginia delegation to the Continental Congress.

*March 20-27*

## Virginia Provincial Convention meets at Richmond

It was resolved to put the colony in a proper state of defense. The Convention also selected delegates to the Second Continental Congress, the same seven as the previous year.

# *1775*

*March 22*

## Edmund Burke's Address on Conciliation with America in the House of Commons

This was in part a move to discourage passage of the New England Restraint Act. (See March 30.)

*March 23*

## Patrick Henry delivers "Give me liberty or give me death" speech

Speaking before the Virginia Provincial Convention at Richmond, he predicted that news of the outbreak of hostilities in New England could soon be expected.

*March 30*

## False alarm in Massachusetts

The Provincial Congress, meeting at Concord, learned that British troops had marched out of Boston. Hasty measures to defend powder and arms at Concord were begun. The troops returned after a five-mile march, however.

*March 30*

## Royal assent given to New England Restraint Act

New England colonies were forbidden to trade with any country but Britain and the British West Indies after July 1 and were restricted from the North Atlantic fisheries after July 20. Later the act was applied also to New Jersey, Pennsylvania, Maryland, Virginia, and South Carolina.

# *1775*

*April 1*

## Boonesborough established by Daniel Boone at mouth of Kentucky River

*April 1*

## The last Militia Act passed by the New York Assembly

All males 16-50 years of age were required to enroll under penalty of fine. Royal and civil officers, professional men, firemen, slaves, and Quakers were exempt. Officers were to be appointed by the royal governor. Every man was required to supply himself with arms, ammunition, and other necessary individual equipment.

*April 3*

## Colonial Assembly of New York holds its last session and adjourns

*April 3*

## Last of David Leonard's weekly letters "To the Inhabitants of the Province of Massachusetts" published

*April 8*

## Governor Josiah Martin orders dissolution of North Carolina Assembly

*April 14*

## First abolition society organized at Philadelphia

The Pennsylvania Society for the Relief of Free Negroes Unlawfully Held in Bondage was established with Benjamin Franklin and Dr. Benjamin Rush as presidents.

# *1775*

## *April 14*

### General Gage receives Lord Dartmouth's instructions of January 27

He prepared to take action immediately rather than allow the rebel colonists time to coordinate their organizations.

## *April 17*

### Last "Novanglus" letter by John Adams appears in the Boston *Gazette*

## *April 18*

### General Gage orders expedition to Concord

Lieutenant Colonel Francis Smith was to lead 700 troops there to destroy rebel supplies. Troops began secretly embarking at 10:00 P.M. to cross the Charles River, thus avoiding the longer overland march via the Boston "neck."

## *April 18*

### "Midnight Ride" of Paul Revere and William Dawes begins

Under instructions from the Boston Committee of Safety, they set out at about 10:00 P.M., as the British were embarking, to alert patriots between Boston and Concord of the British plan for the march to Concord.

## *April 19*

### Dr. Samuel Prescott joins Revere and Dawes after midnight

Only Prescott reached Concord; Revere was seized by a British patrol and Dawes was forced to return to Lexington. But Prescott's message was received in time to permit the Concord militia to remove or destroy most supplies and prepare to fight.

# *1775*

*April 19*

## Battle of Lexington. First military action of the American Revolution

Lieutenant Colonel Francis Smith's advance guard, under Royal Marine Major John Pitcairn, arrived in Lexington at dawn and found some 70 armed Minute Men, under Captain John Parker, on the Common. The Minute Men began to disperse in response to the repeated commands of Pitcairn: "Disperse ye Rebels!" However, an unidentified shot, "the shot heard 'round the world,"* brought a series of volleys from the British. The patriots returned a few shots. After the brief action eight Americans lay dead and ten wounded. One British soldier was wounded. Pitcairn's force moved on to Concord, four miles away, followed by Smith and the main body.

*April 19*

## Battle of Concord

There were brief skirmishes between Smith's troops and militia encircling the village. After pillaging what few supplies had not already been removed or destroyed by colonists, Smith's troops returned to Boston. All along the way they were constantly harassed and attacked by militiamen. On the way back, at Lexington, they were met by reinforcements sent by Gage, a force of over 1,000 men under Brigadier General Earl Hugh Percy. The combined force returned to Boston, harassed every step of the way. At the end of the day, some 1,800 British regulars had met about 4,000 disorganized but determined American patriots; 65 British were dead, 173 wounded, and 26 missing; 49 Americans were dead and 46 were wounded or missing.

---

*Attributed to Concord by the poetic license of Ralph Waldo Emerson.

# *1775*

*April 19*

## Israel Bissel begins his ride

Postrider Israel Bissel left Watertown, Massachusetts, with news of Lexington. According to tradition, he arrived in Worcester only two hours later. He gave the news to Israel Putnam near Pomfret, Connecticut, and rode on to New London, New Haven, New York, Trenton, and Philadelphia.

*April 19*

## Siege of Boston begins after British retreat from Concord

Boston and its British garrison were besieged by a haphazard militia army which soon grew to 15,000 New England colonists. Appeals to other colonies for aid were made by the Massachusetts Provincial Congress.

*April 19*

## News of Lexington reaches Rhode Island

*April 19*

## British mail seized in Charleston, South Carolina

Patriots seized mail arriving on the British packet *Swallow*. Included were documents disclosing British intentions to suppress colonial unrest by force. The seizure was reported promptly to patriot groups in the Carolinas and Georgia, and also to the Continental Congress. This was the first clear evidence of the British determination to coerce the colonies.

*April 19*

## Opening of Provincial Convention in New York City

Nine counties sent representatives.

# *1775*

*April 20*

## General Israel Putnam arrives in Concord from Connecticut

He had ridden about 100 miles in 18 hours.

*April 20*

## News of Lexington and Concord reaches New Hampshire

*April 20*

## Royal Marines seize patriot gunpowder at Williamsburg, Virginia

The action was ordered by Governor Dunmore.

*April 21*

## New Hampshire militiamen march to Cambridge

They began a 55-mile march after learning of Lexington and Concord, and arrived in 18 hours.

*April 21*

## Patriots seize all the gunpowder in the government magazines in Charleston, South Carolina

*April 22*

## Rhode Island militia prepares to march to Boston

The Rhode Island General Assembly also ordered an army of 1,500 men to be formed (April 25).

# *1775*

*April 23*

## News of Lexington causes riot in New York

On receipt of the news carried by Israel Bissel, a mob of patriots seized the arsenal and armed themselves with 600 muskets. The customs houses and most public buildings and supplies were also seized.

*April 23*

## Massachusetts Provincial Congress raises an army

A force of 13,600 militia was to be established. General Artemas Ward was appointed commander-in-chief.

*April 24*

## News of Lexington reaches Philadelphia

Carried by Israel Bissel.

*April 25*

## Baltimore patriots seize provincial magazines

Upon receiving news of Lexington and Concord they seized nearly 1,500 stands of arms.

*April 25*

## "Associators" established at Philadelphia town meeting

About 8,000 persons resolved to associate to defend "with Arms their property, liberty and lives."

# *1775*

*April 26*

## New York Committee of 60 proposes expansion to 100 members

*April 28*

## New York Committee of 60 urges more permanent, revolutionary body to replace ineffective Provincial Congress

*April 29*

## Benedict Arnold arrives in Cambridge with New Haven militia company

He at once suggested to Massachusetts authorities an expedition to seize Fort Ticonderoga.

*April 29*

## The General Association of Orange County, New York

This group was organized to assure the execution of measures advocated by the Continental and New York Provincial Congresses.

*April 29*

## News of Lexington reaches Virginia

*April 30*

## The Massachusetts Committee of Safety authorizes expedition against Fort Ticonderoga

Benedict Arnold was to raise 400 men in western Massachusetts to carry out the operation.

# *1775*

### *May 1*

## Committee of 100 established in New York to preserve "American liberty"

It recommended that every man procure weapons and train himself in military discipline.

### *May 5*

## Naval action at Martha's Vineyard, Massachusetts

The British sloop of war *Falcon* (16) captured two American sloops; they were then reportedly recaptured by two hastily fitted out American vessels.

### *May 5*

## Benjamin Franklin returns to colonies from Europe

He had been in England and elsewhere in Europe since 1757, serving at various times as agent for Pennsylvania, Georgia, and Massachusetts, and as postmaster general of the colonies.

### *May 6*

## Benedict Arnold's leadership rejected by Vermonters

Ethan Allen and 83 Green Mountain Boys (local militia) assembled at Castleton for their own expedition against Fort Ticonderoga. Arnold decided to accompany them.

### *May 7*

## News of Lexington reaches North Carolina

# *1775*

## *May 8*

### News of Lexington reaches Charleston, South Carolina

## *May 9-10*

### Capture of Fort Ticonderoga

Ethan Allen demanded and received the surrender of the fort and its garrison of 42, "in the name of the Great Jehovah and the Continental Congress." Arnold accompanied the expedition as a private volunteer.

## *May 10*

### Loyalist President of King's (now Columbia) College threatened by New York City mob

Alexander Hamilton helped Dr. Myles Cooper escape tar and feathers.

## *May 10*

### Second Continental Congress convenes at Philadelphia

Georgia was still not represented.

## *May 11*

### Patriots seize gunpowder in royal magazines in Savannah, Georgia

# *1775*

*May 12*

## Green Mountain Boys seize Crown Point

Seth Warner commanded a detachment sent by Ethan Allen. The British post fell without resistance, yielding nine enlisted men, ten women and children, and some cannon.

*May 14*

## Benedict Arnold leads an expedition from Ticonderoga against St. Johns, Canada

He obtained 50 volunteers from local New York militia and the Green Mountain Boys.

*May 15*

## Congress instructs New York to make defensive preparations

In reply to a query from the New York Committee of 100, the Continental Congress urged that, if British troops landed, force be met with force, but that there be defensive action only.

*May 16*

## Hannastown, Pennsylvania, Resolution

Local patriots declared it was the duty of Americans to resist English oppression and formed a defense association.

# *1775*

## May 17

### New York Provincial Congress assumes functions of government

With representatives from all 14 counties, it substituted for the inactive Assembly. It was not recognized by Governor William Tryon (former governor of North Carolina).

## May 18

### Capture of St. Johns, Canada, by Benedict Arnold

Arnold and his 50 men attacked and surprised the 15-man garrison; captured the 70-ton HMS *George III* (16); destroyed five boats; evacuated prisoners, some stores, and four boats; and returned to Ticonderoga.

## May 20

### "Mecklenburg Declaration of Independence"

Tradition holds that the Mecklenburg County (North Carolina) Safety Committee drew up a declaration of independence, but there are no contemporary records to document it. It is said to have been approved by citizens of Charlotte, the county seat.

## May 23-24

### Second Provincial Congress of New Jersey confirms allegiance to Continental Congress

It also resolved that the selection of delegates to future sessions of the Continental Congress would be its responsibility rather than that of the General Assembly, and adopted measures for organizing a militia.

# *1775*

## May 24

### John Hancock elected president of the Second Continental Congress (hereafter referred to as Congress)

## May 25

### Reinforcements for British in Boston

HMS *Cerberus* arrived with British troops and Major Generals Sir William Howe, Sir Henry Clinton, and John Burgoyne. Under the overall command of General Gage, the garrison was now a force of more than 10,000 disciplined soldiers.

## May 25

### Continental Congress orders defensive posts in New York

Acting on a committee report, Congress resolved that such posts should be established at Kings Bridge, the Hudson Highlands, and on Lake George. These were to be manned by not more than 3,000 men. The New York Provincial Congress was requested to take such action as was necessary "until further order is taken by this Congress."

## May 27

### Action at Hogg [Hog] Island in Boston Harbor

Patriot forces skirmished with British foragers. When a British schooner ran aground, Americans boarded her and stripped her of everything valuable.

## May 27

### Action at Noddle's Island in Boston Harbor

Patriot forces skirmished with British foragers.

# *1775*

## *May 29*

### New York Provincial Congress orders all citizens to sign a General Association

This was similar in design and purpose to the Orange County resolution of April 29.

## *May 29*

### Congress invites the people of Canada to join the 12 colonies

There was no immediate response, and to the surprise of the Americans, predominantly Catholic French Canada eventually decided that it preferred rule by the British Crown to domination by the more populous, largely Protestant, English-speaking colonies.

## *May 31*

### Flight of the governor of North Carolina

Governor Josiah Martin of North Carolina fled from New Bern to Fort Johnston on Cape Fear. Later, on July 18, he took refuge on the British sloop HMS *Cruzier* in Cape Fear River.

## *May 31*

### Mecklenburg Resolutions

A Mecklenburg County, North Carolina, convention declared royal authority "wholly suspended" in the colonies. Henceforth all legislative and executive responsibility was to be administered by the Provincial Congress. In Mecklenburg County any person accepting a royal commission would be declared an enemy.

# *1775*

*June 2*

## Massachusetts requests Continental Congress to assume responsibility for the New England Army at Boston

The reason for this action was the fact that this army had been raised for the general defense of American rights.

*June 2*

## Army Pay Department created by Congress

In fact there was as yet no army under Congress's control, although everyone assumed that it would become responsible for the army around Boston.

*June 2*

## Arrival of HMS *Margaretta* (2) at Machias, Maine

The British armed cutter escorted two small merchant ships, bringing supplies to the village, in return for which cargoes of lumber were to be brought back to Boston.

*June 2*

## South Carolina asserts solidarity with other colonies

The Provincial Congress resolved that its citizens were "ready to sacrifice their lives and fortunes" in the patriot cause.

*June 6*

## Tory plot to remove arms foiled in New York City

Lieutenant Colonel Marinus Willett and a small group of Sons of Liberty seized five wagonloads of weapons after confronting British soldiers evacuating the arms from New York City.

# *1775*

*June 8*

## Flight of the governor of Virginia

Lord Dunmore fled to the Bitish warship HMS *Fowey* at Yorktown. This marked the beginning of open conflict between patriots and loyalists in Virginia.

*June 9*

## Massachusetts's temporary government endorsed by Congress

This action was in response to a request from the Massachusetts Provincial Congress.

*June 10*

## John Adams proposes a Continental Army

He urged Congress to declare that the militia forces besieging Boston were a Continental Army.

*June 11-12*

## Capture of HMS *Margaretta*

At Machias, Maine, a party of lumbermen led by Jeremiah O'Brien embarked on local vessels and captured the British armed cutter after a brief fight. This is usually considered the first naval action of the Revolution.

*June 12*

## General Gage proclaims martial law

He declared those in arms to be rebels and traitors, and offered pardon to all who returned to allegiance to the Crown, except Samuel Adams and John Hancock, who would be tried for treason.

*June 12*

## Rhode Island establishes naval force

The General Assembly voted to commission two sloops; they formed the first naval force to be established in America by any public authority.

*June 14*

## Birth of the United States Army

Congress authorized the raising of six companies of riflemen in Pennsylvania, Maryland, and Virginia and appointed a committee to draft rules for the administration of the Continental Army, which would include the New England Army besieging Boston, and the New York forces guarding strategic positions in that colony.

*June 15*

## Occupation of Bunker's Hill ordered by the Massachusetts Committee of Safety

This was a countermove to intelligence that Gage intended to occupy Dorchester Heights, overlooking Boston Harbor, south of Boston.

*June 15*

## George Washington chosen commander-in-chief of the Continental Army

He was elected unanimously by Congress, upon nomination of John Adams.

# *1775*

*June 15*

## Naval action in Providence River, Rhode Island

Abraham Whipple, commanding the two Rhode Island sloops, captured a tender of the British frigate HMS *Rose*.

*June 16*

## Massachusetts Provincial Congress appoints Colonel Richard Gridley as chief engineer officer

His first task was to be to design defense works at Bunker's Hill.

*June 16*

## Fortification of Breed's Hill begins

A force of 1,200 men under Colonel William Prescott had initially been sent by General Ward to fortify Bunker's Hill. By mistake, in the darkness they began to entrench Breed's Hill, a lower height, closer to Boston and more vulnerable to fire from artillery in Boston and guns of ships in the harbor.

*June 16*

## Congress appoints generals and creates supporting military services

These were to be two major generals, eight brigadier generals, an Adjutant General, Quartermaster General, Commissary General, Commissary of Musters, Paymaster General, and Chief Engineer.

# *1775*

*June 16*

## Washington accepts command at Philadelphia

He stated that he would serve without pay, except for official expenses.*

*June 17*

## George Washington commissioned commander-in-chief of the Continental Army by Congress

*June 17*

## Congress appoints senior generals

Appointed as Major Generals were Artemas Ward, Charles Lee, Philip Schuyler, and Israel Putnam.

*June 17*

## Battle of Bunker's Hill

This resulted from the British response to the patriot occupation of Breed's Hill. Gage sent General Sir William Howe with 2,200 men in an amphibious attack on Charlestown peninsula and the fortification. After being twice repelled, Howe's force, reinforced by Sir Henry Clinton, was successful in a third bayonet assault when the defenders' ammunition supply became exhausted. The British lost almost half of their starting strength, suffering 1,054 casualties. American losses numbered 100 dead (including Joseph Warren), 267 wounded, and 30 captured. Although the battle was tactically a British victory, the local situation remained unchanged. Bunker's Hill was important for its psychological impact throughout the colo-

---

*A book published in 1970, suggesting that Washington received much more by expense account than he would have by salary, ignores the fact that all of these expenses would still have been reimbursable independent of his salary. This was no mere gesture by an "expense account artist."

# *1775*

nies—Americans had been successful in repulsing assaults by British regular troops and were defeated only when their ammunition gave out. It also unfortunately suggested to most Americans, who had not considered the importance of the earthworks, that untrained colonists were a military match for British regular soldiers.

*June 20*

### Thomas Jefferson takes a seat in the Continental Congress

He replaced Peyton Randolph, who was seriously ill, and who died soon afterward.

*June 20*

### General Washington reviews the Philadelphia militia

This was the commander-in-chief's first military ceremony since his appointment.

*June 21*

### Nathanael Greene chosen brigadier general of the Rhode Island forces

*June 22*

### Congress votes to raise money to support the Continental Army

Bills of credit to the extent of $2,000,000 were issued. This was the first Continental currency.

# *1775*

*June 23*

## Washington leaves Philadelphia for Boston

He was accompanied by the Philadelphia Light Horse for the first part of his trip.

*June 24*

## New York Provincial Congress assumes power of taxation

*June 25*

## General Washington arrives in New York City

By coincidence, loyalists were that night holding a reception for Governor Tryon. A rival reception was held by patriots for the commander-in-chief.

*June 25*

## Pennsylvania Rifle Battalion organized

Nine companies of riflemen, commanded by Colonel William Thompson, were to become the First Continental Infantry on January 1, 1776, and the First Pennsylvania a year later.

*June 25*

## General Philip John Schuyler named to command "New York department" by Congress

# *1775*

*June 27*

## Congress authorizes invasion of Canada

In response to rumors of a proposed invasion of New York from Canada, General Schuyler was authorized to seize any point in Canada vital to the security of the colonies.

*June 30*

## Congress enacts Articles of War

These "rules and regulations" for the Continental Army were based on the British Articles of War.

*July 2*

## Washington arrives at Cambridge

*July 3*

## Washington assumes command of all Continental Forces on Cambridge Common

His army theoretically totaled about 14,500 men; only a small fraction of these were actually present for duty.

*July 5*

## Congress adopts Olive Branch Petition

Drafted by John Dickinson, this appeal to George III professed the attachment of the American people to the King, and their hopes for peace, and asked for a cessation of hostilities until a reconciliation could be negotiated. It was taken to London by loyalist Richard Penn.

# *1775*

*July 6*

## Congress adopts "Declaration of the Causes and Necessities of Taking up Arms"

Drafted by Dickinson and Jefferson, this resolution rejected the idea of independence but proclaimed that Americans were prepared to die rather than bear British oppression. It was, in effect, a declaration of war against Britain, but not against the British Crown.

*July 8*

## Action at Roxbury, Massachusetts

Skirmish between Americans and British foragers.

*July 10*

## Georgia's early warship

Georgia sent out one of the first patriot vessels commissioned for naval service. A schooner, it had been commissioned in June.

*July 18*

## Militia Resolution of Congress

Company officers were to be appointed by their men, and regimental officers by provincial authorities. Existing colonial militia policies could remain in effect under a committee of safety. One-fourth of the militia of each colony were to be in minute-man organizations. Each colony was to provide armed vessels to protect coasts and harbors.

# *1775*

*July 19*

## Congress appoints commissioners to negotiate treaties with the Indians

*July 20*

## Patriot raid on royal stores at Turtle Bay, New York

This was on Manhattan Island (presently East 42nd Street). The stores seized in the surprise raid were sent to Boston and Lake Champlain.

*July 21*

## American raid on Great Brewster Island, Massachusetts

Major Joseph Vose raided the island, also known as Light House Island, located a mile offshore from Nantasket Point. The raiders confiscated lamps, oil, gunpowder, and boats, and burned the wooden parts of the lighthouse. They were met by an armed British schooner and several boats of men. In the ensuing clash two Americans were wounded.

*July 21*

## New York observes Day of Fasting and Devotion

This was in accordance with the recommendation of Congress; presumably similar ceremonies took place in all or most of the colonies.

*July 25*

## First Continental Unit reaches Boston

This was a rifle company from York County, Pennsylvania, commanded by Captain Michael Doudel.

# *1775*

*July 25*

## Dr. Benjamin Church becomes the first surgeon general of the Continental Army

For his early downfall, see October 27, 1775.

*July 26*

## Congress establishes Post Office Department

Benjamin Franklin was appointed postmaster general.

*July 26*

## Maryland Convention meets at Annapolis

It voted to support measures of the Continental Congress and resolved to organize 40 companies of Minute Men.

*July 27*

## Army Medical Department established by Congress

*July 29*

## Army Chaplain Department and Judge Advocate General Department established by Congress

*July 31*

## Second American raid on Great Brewster Island

Major Benjamin Tupper led 300 men in whaleboats to halt repair work on the lighthouse, which had been damaged on July 21, and

# *1775*

to capture the British guard and workmen. The Americans were successful, killing or capturing the entire enemy force of one officer, 32 marines, and 10 carpenters. Tupper's force suffered two casualties.

*July 31*

## Congress rejects Lord North's plan for reconciliation

*August 1*

## Congress adjourns

*August 4*

## Lancaster War Dance

Captain Michael Cresap and his rifle company, en route to Cambridge, stopped in Lancaster, Pennsylvania, where, stripped to the waist and painted, they staged an Indian war dance around a fire in Court House Square.

*August 8*

## Captain Daniel Morgan and his Virginia riflemen arrive in Cambridge

This was the second Continental Army unit authorized by Congress to reach a fighting zone. Their seriousness contrasted with the antics of Captain Cresap's company, also part of the first force authorized by Congress.

# *1775*

*August 9-10*

## Naval action at Gloucester, Cape Ann, Massachusetts

Two American schooners returning to Salem from the West Indies were chased by Captain John Linzee of the sloop of war HMS *Falcon* (16) in Massachusetts Bay. Linzee captured one and pursued the other into Gloucester Harbor, where he was fired on from shore. Linzee returned fire but was driven off. During the action he lost both schooners, two barges, and 35 men.

*August 23*

## Proclamation of Rebellion

George III declared the American colonies to be in open rebellion.

*August 24*

## Action at the Battery, New York City

The New York provincial congress had resolved that the cannon in the Battery be dismantled and taken to a secure location. Just after midnight, Captain John Lamb and about 60 men set to work. British Captain George Vandeput of HMS *Asia* (64), anchored nearby, sent a barge of armed men to investigate the activity noticed at the Battery. When they learned what Lamb and his men were doing, those on the barge fired a musket shot, probably as a signal to the *Asia*. Lamb's men fired on the barge, and it returned to the *Asia* with one man killed. Meanwhile, the *Asia* fired a few shots at the Battery, whereupon the church bells were rung in alarm and drums beat the signal to arm. Several buildings near the shore were damaged, but no one was killed. Believing that the town would be sacked and burned, many families fled the area with a few belongings. This was the beginning of a general exodus of the civilian population from the city, most taking refuge in New Jersey or on Long Island.

# *1775*

*August 28*

## General Schuyler begins advance on Canada

He marched from Ticonderoga with 1,000 troops.

*August 30*

## Action at Stonington, Connecticut

HMS *Rose*, commanded by Captain Wallace, bombarded the coastal town after a foraging expedition from the ship had been repulsed. No houses were burned, as only round shot was used, but several were shattered, and some casualties were suffered by the townspeople.

*September 1*

## Congress's Olive Branch Petition refused by the King

*September 2*

## General Washington commissions a naval force to interdict British supply vessels sailing toward Boston

Colonel John Glover of Massachusetts converted merchant vessels into armed ships to execute the operation. The first ship of "Washington's Navy" was the schooner *Hannah*.

*September 5*

## Ambush of Schuyler's advance guard, near St. Johns, Canada

The ambushing force, consisting of Indians and New York loyalists, was driven off, after inflicting some casualties.

# *1775*

*September 6*

## Siege of St. Johns, Canada begins

General Schuyler's forces invested a garrison of about 600 British and Canadian troops.

*September 7*

## USS *Hannah* versus HMT *Unity*

The American schooner *Hannah* captured this British supply ship after brief resistance. This was the first prize taken by a Continental vessel.

*September 10*

## Prospect Hill Mutiny, Cambridge, Massachusetts

Disorders among poorly disciplined American riflemen led to several courts-martial; 33 men were convicted of disobedience and mutinous behavior, and were fined 20 shillings each.

*September 11*

## Start of Arnold's expedition to Quebec

With Washington's permission, Colonel Benedict Arnold with a force of about 1,100 volunteers set out from Cambridge, heading for Quebec by way of Maine. His force included Captain Daniel Morgan's company of riflemen.

*September 12*

## Brigadier General Richard Montgomery assumes command of American forces at St. Johns, Canada

Schuyler was invalided to the rear because of illness. The siege continued.

# *1775*

*September 13*

## Congress reconvenes at Philadelphia

A delegation from Georgia was present; all thirteen colonies were represented for the first time.

*September 15*

## Flight of royal governor of South Carolina

Lord William Campbell took refuge on the British sloop HMS *Tamer.*

*September 18*

## Congress establishes the Secret Committee

This committee was the governmental agency responsible for seeking and organizing foreign economic and financial assistance. Not to be confused with the Committee of Secret Correspondence (see November 29, 1775), it did in fact work closely with that committee, and was responsible for sending Silas Deane to Paris as the first American diplomatic representative abroad (March 3, 1776). In July 1777 the name was changed to Committee of Commerce.

*September 24*

## Benedict Arnold starts up the Kennebec River

He moved out from Fort Western (Augusta, Maine).

*September 25*

## Action at Montreal, Canada

Ethan Allen undertook a premature and foolhardy attack on Montreal. He and John Brown, with a combined force of less than 300

# *1775*

men, had planned to rush Montreal in a surprise attack, Allen from below the town and Brown from above. Allen reached his position and waited for Brown's signal, but when Brown failed to arrive, Allen attacked anyway. He and 40 men were captured by the British.

*September 26-October 19*

## Peace negotiations with Indians

This Indian-Virginia conference at Pittsburgh delayed the outbreak of frontier war for over a year.

*October 5*

## Congress plans interception of two British ships carrying military stores

*October 6*

## Continental Congress orders arrest of all dangerous loyalists

*October 7*

## British ships bombard Bristol, Rhode Island

A small British squadron under Captain James Wallace sent word to the town that if a delegation did not come within an hour to Wallace's ship to hear his demands on the town he would open fire. William Bradford, spokesman for the town, stated that it would be more appropriate for Wallace to come ashore and make known his demands. At about 8 P.M. Wallace opened fire on the town in a bombardment lasting an hour and a half and stopping only when a messenger was sent to the fleet to request time to select a delegation. Wallace at first asked for 200 sheep and 30 cattle but was finally satisfied with 40 sheep.

# *1775*

*October 10*

## General Sir William Howe succeeds Gage as British commander in Boston

Gage was recalled because of official displeasure at his failure to suppress the rebellion, and for allowing himself to be cooped up in Boston.

*October 13*

## Congress authorizes a Navy

It voted to outfit two ships, of which one was to carry ten guns. In November the ships *Alfred* and *Columbus* were purchased under these provisions.

*October 18*

## Falmouth (Portland, Maine) burned by the British

This action was a punitive measure resulting from Vice-Admiral Sir Samuel Graves's frustration over unsuccessful attempts to stop American privateers on the high seas and criticism directed at him from Boston. He sent two vessels, HMS *Canceau* and HMS *Halifax*, under Captain Henry Mowat to cruise the Maine coast and destroy the seaports there. After a day of vain negotiations with the town authorities, Mowat opened fire, and bombarded the town for nine hours. The townspeople and the local militia replied with ineffective, unorganized resistance, wounding two British seamen. No fatal casualties were suffered in the town, although 139 dwellings, 278 other buildings, and 11 vessels were destroyed, and four vessels captured.

# *1775*

*October 18*

## Action at Chambly, Canada

Colonel James Livingston's 300 Canadians and 50 Americans under Colonel John Brown and Colonel Timothy Bedel surrounded the fort. After a brief exchange of fire, British Major Stopford surrendered his 88-man garrison. The fort yielded 169 prisoners and large stocks of food and materiel.

*October 19*

## New York Governor Tryon retires to warship HMS *Duchess of Gordon* in New York Harbor

This was assumed by New York patriots to be an act of abdication.

*October 24-25*

## Action at Hampton Roads, Virginia

Royal Navy ships sent by Governor Dunmore bombarded Hampton; a landing attempt was repulsed and two vessels forced aground were captured by patriots.

*October 25*

## Reduction of Arnold's expedition to Quebec

Four contingents turned back because of difficult terrain and lack of provisions.

# *1775*

*October 27*

## Surgeon General Dr. Benjamin Church on trial in Massachusetts as an informer for the British

He was convicted of treason, dismissed from the Army (November 2), and jailed; later he was allowed to sail for the West Indies, but his ship was lost at sea.

*October 30*

## Congress authorizes two more ships

Two additional vessels increased the proposed Navy to four ships. The previously authorized second vessel was to carry 14 guns, and these two new vessels could carry as many as 20 and 36 respectively. The new vessels, the brigs *Andrew Doria* and *Cabot*, were purchased in November.

*October 30*

## Naval Committee appointed by Congress

This was the first executive body responsible for the administration of naval affairs. It included John Adams, Richard Henry Lee, Silas Deane, Stephen Hopkins, John Langdon, Joseph Hewes, and Christopher Gadsden.

*November 2*

## Capitulation of St. Johns, Canada

British Major Preston and 600 defenders surrendered after a 55-day siege. This left Montreal virtually unprotected.

# *1775*

*November 4*

## Congress authorizes reorganization of Continental Army at Boston

Effective on January 1, 1776, the reorganized force was to consist of 20,372 officers and men to be enlisted for one year.

*November 5*

## Esek Hopkins appointed commodore of the fleet outfitting at Philadelphia

Since this was the entire American naval force, Hopkins was in effect, but unofficially, the first commander-in-chief of the American Navy.

*November 7*

## Governor Dunmore issues proclamation declaring Virginia under martial law

He established a base at Norfolk and began to recruit a loyalist army.

*November 7*

## Congress's Olive Branch Petition rejected by House of Commons

It had already been rejected by the King (see September 1, 1775).

*November 7*

## General Assembly of Rhode Island deposes Governor Joseph Wanton

He had been suspended May 3, 1775, for unpatriotic activities.

# *1775*

*November 9*

## Arnold's expedition reaches the St. Lawrence

He had a force of 600 men opposite Quebec, including Morgan's rifle company.

*November 9*

## Action at Phipps' Farm (Lechmere Point), Massachusetts

Nine companies of British light infantry and 100 grenadiers landed to seize cattle needed for the Boston garrison. Panicky Americans, fearing that this was more than a foraging raid, staged a counter-attack led by Colonel William Thompson with his Pennsylvania riflemen. Plunging through two feet of icy water, the Americans advanced on the British, who then withdrew with 10 cows. Two Americans were wounded.

*November 9*

## Congress learns that George III rejects Olive Branch Petition

Its members also learned of the royal proclamation of rebellion of August 23.

*November 10*

## Congress resolves to raise two battalions of marines

This date is now considered the birthday of the U.S. Marine Corps.

# *1775*

*November 11-12*

## Naval action at Charleston Harbor, South Carolina

American Captain Simon Tufts, aboard the *Defence*, clashed with two British vessels, HMS *Tamer* and HMS *Cherokee*, while on a mission to blockade Hog Island Creek. Tufts was successful in sinking three of four hulks he towed to the blockade. No casualties were suffered on either side.

*November 13*

## Arnold's force crosses the St. Lawrence at Quebec

*November 13*

## Americans under General Montgomery occupy Montreal

Having only 150 regulars and a few militia to meet Montgomery, British Governor General Sir Guy Carleton had abandoned Montreal on November 11, starting to sail down the river to Quebec with his troops and valuable military stores in a small fleet led by the brigantine *Gaspee*. Adverse winds delayed the British departure.

*November 14*

## Action at Kemp's Landing, Virginia

Americans under Colonel Woodford were dispersed when they attempted to cross a bridge guarded by Lord Dunmore and 350 men. Dunmore then pursued and defeated 150 militiamen who had marched to join Woodford's force.

# *1775*

*November 15*

## Arnold occupies the Plains of Abraham

With 700 men, he unsuccessfully tried to bluff the Quebec garrison into surrender from this position.

*November 19-21*

## Action at Ninety-Six, South Carolina

Major Andrew Williamson's 600 patriots clashed with 1,800 Tories in an inconclusive action.

*November 19*

## British flotilla at Montreal surrenders to Americans

Taking advantage of the delay caused by adverse winds, the Americans set up shore batteries on the banks of the St. Lawrence and began a bombardment of the British flotilla. Upon the demand of Colonel John Brown, the British vessels surrendered; they included the *Gaspée*, two other armed vessels, eight small craft, and stores. Only Carleton and a few officers escaped ashore and reached Quebec, passing through the American blockading force.

*November 22*

## South Carolina loyalists dispersed

Patriots broke up a force assembling at Reedy River, or Cane Brake.

*November 25*

## Congress formally declares British vessels subject to capture

Admiralty courts were established to deal with prizes and prize money.

# *1775*

*November 28*

## Congress adopts "Rules for the Regulation of the Navy of the United Colonies"

*November 28*

## New Jersey General Assembly disavows colonial independence

*November 28*

## Committee of Secret Correspondence, an embryo foreign ministry, is appointed

This five-man committee was appointed by Congress. Its original members were John Dickinson, John Jay, Benjamin Franklin, Benjamin Harrison, and Thomas Johnson. On April 17, 1777, it was renamed the Committee on Foreign Affairs.

*November 29*

## American schooner USS *Lee* (14) captures British ordnance brig HMT *Nancy*

Captain John Manley commanded the *Lee*. The *Nancy* yielded a fantastic booty: 2,000 muskets, 100,000 flints, 30,000 round shot, 31 tons of musket shot, and a 13-inch, 2,700-pound brass mortar, all very useful in the siege of Boston.

*December 1*

## General Montgomery with 300 men joins Arnold at Quebec

Montgomery took command of the small force blockading Quebec.

# *1775*

## December 3

### First official American flag raised aboard USS *Alfred*

The flag was raised by Lieutenant John Paul Jones on the flagship of Commodore Esek Hopkins.

## December 6

### Congress answers the royal proclamation of rebellion of August 23

It disclaimed any intention to deny the King's sovereignty but disavowed allegiance to Parliament.

## December 6

### Governor Tryon of New York siezes public records

He transferred them to the British ship HMS *Duchess of Gordon* for safety.

## December 6

### New Jersey General Assembly dissolves itself

Governor William Franklin was assured that flight was unnecessary as he had protection under American law.

## December 8-31

### Siege of Quebec, Canada

American forces were commanded by Montgomery.

# *1775*

*December 9*

## Battle of Great Bridge, Virginia

Colonel William Woodford's patriot force defeated Tories and British under Lord Dunmore in less than 25 minutes of surprise action. There were 62 British casualties; one American was slightly wounded in the hand. The rebel colonists subsequently occupied Norfolk. Dunmore and the British took refuge on ships in the harbor.

*December 10*

## British raid at Jamestown, Rhode Island

*December 11*

## Congress votes $3,000 for support of agents abroad

The Congressional Committee of Secret Correspondence wrote the next day to Arthur Lee, agent for Massachusetts in London, requesting him to ascertain the attitude of the European powers toward the American colonies.

*December 14*

## Naval Committee organizes Marine Committee

Consisting of one representative from each colony, it was the second executive body for the administration of naval affairs, and was responsible for the outfitting and launching of armed vessels ordered by Congress.

*December 21*

## Parliament votes to confiscate all American vessels

Their crews were also to be impressed into the Royal Navy.

# *1775*

*December 22*

## Trade and intercourse with colonies prohibited by act of Parliament

*December 22*

## Action at Great Cane Brake, South Carolina

Americans under Lieutenant Colonel William Thomson (Thompson) defeated Tories under William Cunningham.

*December 23*

## Royal Proclamation closes colonies to all commerce

This was to be effective March 1, 1776.

*December 28*

## French agent Archard de Bonvouloir appears before Congress

He gave informal assurances of French interest and possible support for the American colonies.

*December 31*

## Battle of Quebec

Some 800 Americans under Montgomery and Arnold attacked Carleton's 1,800-man garrison in the midst of a snowstorm and were disastrously repulsed. American losses totaled 60 killed or wounded, including Montgomery dead and Arnold wounded, and 426 captured, including Captain Daniel Morgan. British losses were five killed and 13 wounded.

# *1776*

*January 1*

## George Washington hoists first national flag at Cambridge, Massachusetts

It bore 13 stripes and the British union.

*January 1-2*

## British naval bombardment of Norfolk, Virginia

Colonial rebels occupying Norfolk refused Lord Dunmore's demands for provisions. Dunmore opened fire on the town and sent landing parties to burn waterfront warehouses. Rebels retaliated by setting fire to the homes of prominent Tories. Flames swept through the rest of the town in a 50-hour fire. Three noncombatants were killed and seven wounded. Dunmore landed and occupied the town.

*January 5*

## New Hampshire adopts first written state constitution

*January 6*

## Founding of Alexander Hamilton's Provincial Company of Artillery of the Colony of New York

This was the beginning of the history of the oldest unit in the U.S. Army, now Battery D of the Fifth Field Artillery, the only unit of the regular armed forces tracing its history unbroken to the Revolution.

# *1776*

*January 8*

### Patriots raid Charlestown, Massachusetts

A performance of General Burgoyne's play "The Blockade of Boston" was interrupted during a successful raid by Captain Thomas Knowlton of Connecticut. One man was killed, five captured, and eight dwellings were burned.

*January 9*

### Congress requests that New York take measures to defend the entrances to her harbor

*January 10*

### North Carolina loyalists urged to join the British Army

An appeal was issued by Royal Governor Martin of North Carolina, then aboard the British sloop HMS *Scorpion*, urging loyalists to gather near Wilmington, on the Cape Fear River. They could then participate in a planned British Army offensive in the South.

*January 10*

### Thomas Paine's *Common Sense* published in Philadelphia

This pamphlet converted thousands to the idea of independence.

*January 12*

### British raid Prudence Island, Rhode Island

They were driven away the next day.

# *1776*

*January 19*

## Organization of Delaware Continentals

This was the only regiment furnished by Delaware during the war; initially it was a company.

*January 20*

## British expedition sails south from Boston

The objective of the commander, General Sir Henry Clinton, was to join North Carolina loyalists at Wilmington, which would then become a base for the reconquest of the South.

*January 20*

## General Schuyler forces the disarmament of Johnson Hall, Johnstown, New York, by Sir John Johnson

Johnson, with 700 loyalists, was forced to surrender to Schuyler and 3,000 New York militia. This ended effective loyalist resistance in the Albany area.

*January 22-23*

## British transport HMT *Blue Mountain Valley* taken by Americans off Sandy Hook, New York

The Elizabethtown, New Jersey, Committee of Safety sent an expedition of 40 to 70 volunteers under Elias Drayton and William Alexander to capture the British transport and provision ship off Sandy Hook.

# *1776*

*January 24*

## Colonel Henry Knox reaches Cambridge with 43 cannon and 16 mortars from Fort Ticonderoga

He had been sent by Washington to obtain the heavy ordnance of the fort to enable the Americans to press the siege of Boston. Most of the operation was accomplished by carrying the guns on sleds across the snow-covered Berkshire Mountains.

*February*

## Americans reoccupy Norfolk and complete its destruction

*February 4*

## Arrival of Major General Charles Lee in New York City

Many Tories fled in panic to New Jersey and Long Island when Lee and a contingent of the Continental Army arrived from Boston to occupy the city.

*February 4*

## Arrival of Sir Henry Clinton at Sandy Hook, New York, on his journey south

New York City was swept with panic and confusion, since there was uncertainty as to Clinton's objective.

*February 7*

## General William Alexander, Lord Stirling, arrives in New York

With him were 1,000 men from the Jerseys.

# *1776*

*February 14*

## Action at Dorchester Neck, Massachusetts

*February 15*

## British raid Prudence Island, Rhode Island

*February 16*

## Washington decides to seize Dorchester Heights

Because of a negative reaction by his council of war, Washington abandoned a more daring proposal, and agreed to substitute a less ambitious "strategic offensive, tactical defensive" plan which would force the British either to attack American entrenchments or to abandon their anchorage in Boston harbor. This action was possible because of the guns from Ticonderoga.

*February 17*

## First Continental Navy squadron puts to sea

Commander Esek Hopkins sailed from Philadelphia through the Delaware Bay. His objective was Nassau, in the Bahamas, although Congress had directed him to break the British blockade of Chesapeake Bay. His ships were USS *Alfred* (24), USS *Columbus* (20), USS *Andrew Doria* (14), USS *Cabot* (14), USS *Providence* (12), and USS *Wasp* (8).

*February 17*

## Congress issues more money

Expenses of war forced the issuance of $4,000,000 in additional bills.

# *1776*

*February 27*

### Battle of Moore's Creek Bridge

A force of 1,100 North Carolina militiamen, led by Colonels Richard Caswell and Alexander Lillington, defeated about 1,800 Scottish loyalists under Brigadier General Donald McDonald in a three-minute skirmish. The Tories were on their way to Wilmington, where they had planned to establish a British coastal base for Clinton's expedition. (See May 3, 1776, and following.) This action has been called the "Lexington and Concord of the South."

*February 27*

### Congress establishes military regions for the Continental Army

The Northern Department included New England, the Middle Department comprised New York through Maryland, and the Southern Department was south of the Potomac River.

*February 28*

### Washington writes to Negro poet Phyllis Wheatley

He thanked her for a poem she had written in his honor.

*March 1*

### France and Spain explore joint action to aid colonists

Both monarchies were anxious to seize the opportunity to damage Britain, but were reluctant to reach accommodation with anti-monarchical rebels.

# *1776*

*March 3*

## British expedition hesitates off Cape Fear

General Clinton, who was accompanied by the governors of North and South Carolina, decided not to land after learning of the loyalist defeat at Moore's Creek Bridge, North Carolina. He awaited the arrival of another expedition from England, under Admiral Sir Peter Parker and General Lord Charles Cornwallis.

*March 3*

## Congress votes to send a commercial agent to France

Silas Deane became, in effect, America's first ambassador.

*March 3-4*

## Hopkins's raid on the Bahamas

The first and virtually the only planned major operation of the Continental Navy. Esek Hopkins captured New Providence (Nassau) and seized its military stores.

*March 4-5*

## American occupation of Dorchester Heights

General John Thomas and 2,000 men carried out the plan which had evolved out of Washington's February 16 council of war. The plan called for the fortification of this site in one single night. The carefully planned operation was completely successful. At dawn the British fleet found itself under the guns of the American forts, made to look more formidable than they actually were by bales of hay that had been camouflaged to look like earthworks.

# *1776*

## *March 5*

### General Howe plans to assault Dorchester Heights

His plans and preparations for an attack on the 6th were ruined by heavy rain during the night. Washington, who had reserves hidden to meet the expected British assault, was probably as disappointed as Howe.

## *March 7*

### General Howe decides to evacuate Boston

The harbor and waterfront could not be protected from American fire, and the guns of British ships could not be elevated sufficiently to reach the forts. Aware of counterattack preparations, and remembering Bunker Hill, Howe decided to abandon the city.

## *March 7*

### Action at Hutchinson's Island, Georgia

Patriots routed loyalists and drove Governor Wright from the province.

## *March 9*

### Action at Nook's Hill, Massachusetts

American forces, attempting to occupy Nook's Hill, were driven off by British artillery fire from Boston.

# *1776*

*March 9-13*

## Actions in Chesapeake Bay

The British sloop of war HMS *Otter* was attacked and driven away from shore near Chariton Creek, Northampton County, Virginia, by the Maryland ship *Defence* and two Maryland militia companies.

*March 14*

## Congress advises all colonies to disarm loyalists

It also ordered the defense of New York City by 8,000 men.

*March 17*

## British evacuate Boston

All of General Howe's 6,000 troops plus some 1,000 loyalists embarked on troopships in the harbor after a siege of nearly 11 months. Washington ordered his troops to march into Boston.

*March 20*

## Continental Army completes occupation of Boston

*March 23*

## Congress authorizes privateering

It began to issue letters of marque and reprisal.

# *1776*

*March 25*

## Congress votes thanks and a gold medal to Washington

This was in recognition of his achievements during the Boston siege.

*March 25*

## Congressional diplomatic mission leaves for Canada

Benjamin Franklin, Charles Carroll, and Samuel Chase left Philadelphia as Congressional envoys to negotiate with the Canadians. No positive results were achieved.

*March 26*

## South Carolina adopts state constitution and independent government

*March 27*

## General Howe's fleet leaves Boston Harbor for Halifax, Nova Scotia

Except for scattered loyalist units, and the threatening presence of Clinton's force off the North Carolina coast, British military forces had been temporarily eliminated from the 13 colonies.

*April 1*

## General David Wooster arrives at Quebec with reinforcements

He took over command from Arnold.

# *1776*

*April 4*

## USS *Columbus* (20) versus HMS *Hawk* (6)

The American frigate, part of Hopkins's squadron, took the small British schooner with little resistance.

*April 5*

## USS *Alfred* (24) versus HMS *Bolton* (10)

Little resistance was put up by the British bomb brig, most of whose guns were designed for land bombardment.

*April 6*

## USS *Alfred* (24) versus HMS *Glagow* (20)

The *Alfred* and four of Hopkins's other Continental ships encountered Captain Tryingham Howe's British frigate off Block Island on their return from Nassau. The boldly handled lone British vessel inflicted 24 casualties while suffering only four killed and wounded herself. The *Alfred* suffered especially heavy damage. The *Glasgow*, also badly damaged, escaped.

*April 6*

## Congress declares colonial ports open to all countries except Great Britain

Only importation of slaves was forbidden.

# *1776*

*April 12*

### "Halifax Resolves"

The North Carolina Provincial Congress at Halifax, North Carolina, instructed its delegates in Congress to stand for independence. North Carolina was the first colony to take this action.

*April 13*

### Washington and main army arrive in New York from Cambridge

It was known that Howe's forces in Halifax, Nova Scotia, were to be reinforced and that another expedition was at sea from England. The Congress and Washington both expected that New York would be the next British objective.

*April 15*

### Two new American warships launched

These were USS *Warren* (32) and USS *Providence* (28), launched at Providence, Rhode Island.

*April 15*

### Congress moves toward national independence

A resolution recommended that all colonies reject all royal authority and form independent governments.

# *1776*

## *April 17*

### USS *Lexington* (16) versus HMS *Edward* (8)

Navy Captain John Barry, commanding the sloop of war (brig) *Lexington*, is credited with the first capture in actual battle of a British warship by a regularly commissioned American vessel.

## *May 1*

### General John Thomas takes over command of American forces at Quebec

He relieved inept General David Wooster.

## *May 2*

### French clandestine support to colonials begins

A million livres' worth of munitions was supplied through a fictitious company, Roderique Hortalez et Cie., administered by secret agent Pierre de Beaumarchais.

## *May 3*

### Parker and Cornwallis join Clinton off North Carolina coast

With the reinforcement of Cornwallis's troops from Britain, Clinton decided to attack Charleston, South Carolina.

# *1776*

*May 3*

## King George III appoints Admiral Lord Richard Howe and General Sir William Howe as peace commissioners

The brothers were the army and navy commanders of the expeditionary forces gathering in England and at Halifax, Nova Scotia.

*May 4*

## Rhode Island declares independence

The colony became the "State of Rhode Island and Providence Planatations" by an act of the General Assembly.

*May 6*

## Action on Plains of Abraham, Canada

A sortie from Quebec by General Carleton and 900 men routed 250 American besiegers under John Thomas. The British sortie was coordinated with the approach of a British fleet (see below).

*May 6*

## Arrival of British reinforcements at Quebec

A fleet, carrying more than 6,000 troops under General John Burgoyne, sailed up the St. Lawrence. On the appearance of the fleet, the Americans began to withdraw toward Montreal.

# *1776*

*May 8-9*

## Naval action on the Delaware River

Thirteen Pennsylvania galleys attacked two British warships near the mouth of Christiana Creek, near Wilmington, Delaware. The British were forced to withdraw down the river.

*May 10*

## John Paul Jones receives his first command

This was the sloop of war USS *Providence* (12).

*May 15*

## Virginia Convention instructs Virginia delegates in Congress to propose independence

*May 16*

## Action at The Cedars, Canada

About 30 miles downriver from Montreal a disorganized patriot force of about 500 men, retreating from Quebec, was surrounded by British troops; the Americans surrendered after slight resistance.

*May 17*

## Naval action at Nantasket Roads, Massachusetts

Captain James Mugford and a 21-man crew aboard the schooner USS *Franklin* (part of Washington's navy) captured the British transport HMS *Hope*, which was headed for Boston, unaware that the city had been evacuated by the British.

# *1776*

*May 19*

## Renewed action at The Cedars, Canada

Benedict Arnold and 900 Americans recaptured one British post and released some of the American prisoners captured on the 16th.

*May 25*

## Congress resolves to commission Indians for military service

*May 27*

## New York's Provincial Congress virtually declares independence

The Third Provincial Congress of New York took steps for the formation of a new, independent government for the province.

*May 29*

## Committee of Mechanics in New York urges New York delegates in Congress to vote for independence

*June 2*

## General John Thomas dies of smallpox at Chambly, Canada

General John Sullivan took over his command.

*June 4*

## British expeditionary force arrives off Charleston, South Carolina

Defense preparations by local militia were well advanced, due to early warning of the British ships off the North Carolina coast.

# *1776*

## June 4

### General Charles Lee arrives from New York at Charleston, South Carolina

The most experienced officer of the Continental Army, Lee had been ordered to Charleston by Congress.

## June 7

### USP *Yankee Hero* (12) versus HMS *Milford* (32?) off the coast of Massachusetts

The American privateer, under Captain Tracy and with only a third of her complement aboard, was attacked by Captain John Burr aboard the British frigate *Milford*. After a gallant fight against a crew four times her size, the *Yankee Hero* struck her colors.

## June 7

### Virginia delegate Richard Henry Lee introduces resolution for independence in Congress

"That these United Colonies are, and of right ought to be, free and independent states, and that a plan of confederation be submitted to the several colonies." The resolution was seconded by John Adams.

## June 8

### Battle of Trois Rivières

A select American force of 2,000 men under Brigadier General William Thompson was sent to seize Trois Rivières under the assumption that it was occupied by some 600-800 British and Canadians. The Americans were met by the main British army, some 6,000-8,000 men, under Carleton and Burgoyne. In a three-day running fight the Americans were dispersed. They retreated toward Sorel and Montreal, closely pursued by the British. Thompson and 235 other Americans were captured during the action.

# *1776*

*June 9*

## Americans evacuate Montreal

Arnold retreated with a force of 300 men south toward St. Johns.

*June 10*

## King Louis XVI of France approves loans to Americans

*June 11*

## New York Provincial Congress advises its delegation in the Continental Congress to abstain from voting on independence

Loyalist sentiment was still strong among New Yorkers.

*June 11*

## Riot in New York City

Tories were stripped, ridden on rails, and put in jail by a mob. This was a reaction to the hesitancy of the Provincial Congress.

*June 11*

## Congress appoints a committee to draft a Declaration of Independence

Thomas Jefferson, chairman, was to write the draft; other members were John Adams, Robert Livingston, Roger Sherman, and Benjamin Franklin.

# *1776*

*June 12-30*

## American retreat from Canada

As the British pursuit from Trois Rivières and Montreal approached Sorel, Sullivan withdrew to St. Johns, followed by Arnold and the Montreal garrison. They next evacuated St. Johns and, after a few miserable days on Isle aux Noix, withdrew to Crown Point on boats provided by Schuyler.

*June 12*

## Congress plans for a national union of the states

John Dickinson was appointed chairman of a committee to draft Articles of Confederation. At the same time a committee was appointed to consider negotiation of national treaties with foreign countries.

*June 12*

## Congress creates a Board of War and Ordnance

This resolution was the virtual beginning of a department or ministry of defense.

*June 12*

## Virginia Convention adopts George Mason's Bill of Rights

In large part it was a restatement of English principles drawn from the Magna Carta, Petition of Rights, and Bill of Rights.

# *1776*

*June 16*

### Action at Chambly, Canada

Arnold fought a rear-guard action against pursuing British.

*June 20*

### General Assembly of Connecticut absolves itself of allegiance to the King and proclaims independence

*June 21*

### Discovery of Hickey "assassination plot" against Washington, Putnam, and others

The full dimensions of this conspiracy are unknown. That there was a treasonable plot against the Continental Army and the patriot government in New York seems incontestable, as does the involvement of Thomas Hickey, one of Washington's bodyguards. Less certain is whether the plotters contemplated assassination of Washington or others, and if so, whether Hickey was involved in this aspect of the plot. He was tried for his involvement in the treasonous activities and sentenced to death by hanging as an example.

*June 21*

### Governor William Franklin of New Jersey appears under arrest before Congress

After an examination of his conduct and opinions he was removed to Connecticut under the auspices of Governor Jonathan Trumbull.

# *1776*

*June 24*

## Action at Isle aux Noix, Canada

Americans, mostly sick, barely repulsed a probe by the British advance guard. Sullivan decided to continue the retreat to Crown Point, ending the American invasion of Canada.

*June 25*

## British fleet arrives off Sandy Hook, New York

This was the fleet of Admiral Molyneux Shuldham, convoying General Howe and his forces from Halifax, Nova Scotia. Admiral Howe's fleet was already en route from England.

*June 26*

## Action at Cherokee Indian town, South Carolina

Captain James McCall, commanding the South Carolina Rangers, skirmished with Indians and was taken prisoner.

*June 28*

## Thomas Hickey hanged as a traitor

He was the first American soldier executed by verdict of a military court.

*June 28*

## Battle of Sullivan's Island, South Carolina

British fleet of eight warships under Admiral Sir Peter Parker was repulsed and severely damaged in Charleston Harbor by American

# *1776*

artillery under Colonel William Moultrie. The battle ended operations by regular British forces in the Carolinas for two years.

*June 28*

## British joint expedition sails into New York Bay

Admiral Shuldham's fleet, convoying General Howe's army, crossed the Sandy Hook bar and approached the Narrows between Long Island and Staten Island

*June 28*

## Thomas Jefferson presents his draft of the Declaration of Independence to Congress

*June 29*

## Virginia adopts state constitution

*June 30*

## British occupy Staten Island, New York

General Howe and 9,300 troops began their disembarkation, which was completed by July 7.

*July 1*

## Congress, as a committee, approves Lee's June 7 resolution on independence

# *1776*

*July 2*

## New Jersey adopts state constitution

It became the first colony to grant woman suffrage. (The action was reversed in 1807.)

*July 2*

## Congress votes for independence

The vote was 12 for, none against, New York abstaining.

*July 4*

## Declaration of Independence approved

It was signed by John Hancock, President, and Charles Thomson, Secretary.

*July 5*

## Copies of Declaration of Independence sent to the several state assemblies

*July 7*

## Silas Deane arrives in Paris

This was the beginning of his controversial career as American diplomatic representative to France.

# *1776*

### *July 7*

## American withdrawal in northern New York

General Schuyler's Northern Army withdrew from Crown Point to Ticonderoga.

### *July 8*

## Declaration of Independence publicly proclaimed in Philadelphia

### *July 8-10*

## Action at Gwyn's Island (Gwynn Island), Chesapeake Bay

Patriots captured Lord Dunmore's base camp and scattered his fleet and forces. After a brief raid up the Potomac, Dunmore withdrew to New York and then to Britain.

### *July 9*

## Declaration of Independence formally adopted by Provincial Congress in New York

New York thus joined the other 12 colonies.

### *July 9*

## Declaration of Independence read before the Army by Washington's orders

### *July 9*

## New York City patriots pull down equestrian statue of George III in Bowling Green

# *1776*

## *July 12*

### Howe brothers join forces

Admiral Lord Richard Howe arrived off Staten Island from England with over 100 ships and 11,000 soldiers.

## *July 12-18*

### British warships sail up the Hudson

Unopposed move to Tappan Zee by two frigates showed the weakness of the American defense on Manhattan.

## *July 12*

### Dickinson's Articles of Confederation and Perpetual Union presented to Congress

This was a plan for confederation of the 13 colonies.

## *July 15*

### Action at Rayborn Creek (Lyndley's Fort), South Carolina

Americans under John Downs got the better of Indians in a skirmish.

## *July 16*

### Beginning of Lord Dunmore's expedition up the Potomac River

A small British flotilla, commanded by the royal governor, attempted to seize St. George's Island, Maryland, near the mouth of the river, but the landing force was driven off by local patriot militia.

# *1776*

*July 23*

## Action on Occoquan Creek, Virginia

After the repulse at St. George's Island, Lord Dunmore's expedition sailed up the river, destroying several plantations owned by patriots. The flotilla then turned up Occoquan Creek, as far as the falls, where a landing party destroyed the mill. The expedition withdrew after the arrival of Prince William County militia.

*July 29*

## North Carolina forces invade territory of Cherokee Indians

To discourage the Indian alliance with the British, General Griffith Rutherford with 2,400 men began a long invasion which would destroy 32 Indian towns and villages. With the help of Major Andrew Williamson's South Carolina troops and Colonel William Christian's Virginia troops, Cherokee power was finally broken in North Carolina.

*August 1*

## Sir Henry Clinton and his force arrive at Staten Island from Charleston

British General Howe's expeditionary force reached a strength of about 30,000 men, with about 15,000 more sailors on Lord Howe's fleet. This was the largest overseas expedition in British history to that time.

*August 1*

## Action at Essenecca Town, South Carolina

Major Andrew Williamson led Americans in a skirmish with Indians; 13 Indians were captured. Francis Salvador (see January 11, 1775) was killed in this skirmish.

# *1776*

## August 2

### "Forks of the Tar River" becomes Washington, North Carolina

This was the first town named for the American commander-in-chief.

## August 2

### Signatures affixed to the engrossed Declaration of Independence

These men were signers of the Declaration of Independence: John Adams, Samuel Adams, Josiah Bartlett, Carter Braxton, Charles Carroll, Samuel Chase, Abraham Clark, George Clymer, William Ellery, William Floyd, Benjamin Franklin, Elbridge Gerry, Button Gwinnett, Lyman Hall, John Hancock, Benjamin Harrison, John Hart, Joseph Hewes, Thomas Heyward, William Hooper, Stephen Hopkins, Francis Hopkinson, Samuel Huntington, Thomas Jefferson, Francis Lightfoot Lee, Richard Henry Lee, Francis Lewis, Philip Livingston, Thomas Lynch, Jr., Thomas McKean, Arthur Middleton, Lewis Morris, Robert Morris, John Morton, Thomas Nelson, Jr., William Paca, Robert Treat Paine, John Penn, George Read, Caesar Rodney, George Ross, Benjamin Rush, Edward Rutledge, Roger Sherman, James Smith, Richard Stockton, Thomas Stone, George Taylor, Matthew Thornton, George Walton, William Whipple, William Williams, James Wilson, John Witherspoon, Oliver Wolcott, George Wythe. Among those who refused to sign the document were John Dickinson, James Duane, Robert R. Livingston, and John Jay. Several of those who signed were personally opposed to the document, but signed in response to instructions from provincial congresses; these included Braxton, Robert Morris, Read, and Rutledge. Five delegates were occupied elsewhere and did not have a chance to sign the document: Washington, Sullivan, George Clinton, Christopher Gadsden, and Patrick Henry.

# *1776*

*August 7*

## USP *Hancock* captures HMT *Reward*

Captain Wingate Newman, commanding the American privateer, brought his British prize into Portsmouth, New Hampshire. Her cargo included turtles destined for Lord North.

*August 8*

## Action at Oconore, South Carolina

Americans under Major Williamson killed several Indians in a skirmish.

*August 11*

## Action at Tomassy, South Carolina

Americans under Major Williamson engaged Indians in an inconclusive action.

*August 22*

## British land on Long Island

General Howe landed about 15,000 troops at Flatbush. American outposts retreated after brief skirmishing. Within the next three days the British strength on Long Island reached 20,000 men.

*August 26*

## Action at Valley Grove, Long Island

Preliminary action in the Long Island, New York, campaign.

# *1776*

*August 26-27*

## General Clinton leads night march to Jamaica Pass, Long Island

Howe's objective was to send half of his army to envelop General Israel Putnam's forces defending Brooklyn, keeping the Americans' attention focused south, toward Flatbush.

*August 27*

## Battle of Long Island

The Continental Army, under remarkably inept leadership, was disastrously defeated by the British under the masterful leadership of General Howe, whose envelopment worked perfectly. Washington, who arrived from Manhattan during the battle, did not take command from Putnam until late in the day, after the battle was irretrievably lost. This was the first pitched battle of the Revolution. The Americans lost 200 killed and nearly 1,000 captured, including General Sullivan. British losses were about 400 killed and wounded.

*August 28*

## Action at Jamaica (Brookland), Long Island

A force of about 700 British under Sir William Erskine surprised Nathaniel Woodhull's small American detachment of barely 100 men. Almost all of the American force was taken prisoner.

*August 29-30*

## Washington's evacuation of Long Island

Washington first revealed his potential as a military commander in this brilliantly planned, brilliantly executed operation.

# *1776*

*August 30*

## William Livingston elected first American governor of the state of New Jersey

*September 6*

## Congress appoints a committee to meet with British peace commission

Benjamin Franklin, John Adams, and Edward Rutledge were directed to confer with Lord Howe, in response to his peace proposals, but were to accept no terms other than recognition of independence.

*September 6-7*

## First use of the submarine in war

The "American Turtle" unsuccessfully attacked the British fleet off Staten Island.

*September 9*

## The name United States of America adopted by resolution of Congress

*September 11*

## Peace conference on Staten Island

Franklin, Adams, and Rutledge met with Lord Howe in a cordial but fruitless conference.

# *1776*

*Sepember 15*

## Battle of Kips Bay

Washington retreated from New York to Harlem Heights when the British landed on the eastern shore of Manhattan Island. The British then occupied New York City.

*September 16*

## Congress authorizes an increase in the Continental Army

The resolution provided for the enlistment of 88 battalions as soon as possible. The enlistments were to be for the duration of the war. This action was significant, since enlistments of existing Continental forces would expire at the end of 1776.

*September 16*

## Battle of Harlem Heights

Washington's forces halted General Howe's pursuit in an unexpected, limited counterattack. The success did much to restore low American morale.

*September 17*

## Congress's "Plan of 1776"

Drafted by a special committee, it proclaimed freedom of the seas and defined the rights of neutrals. It was the model for most 18th Century U.S. treaties.

# *1776*

*September 20*

## Congress adopts revised Articles of War

These new "rules and articles to govern the armies of the United States," still based upon the British articles, were drafted mainly by John Adams. Changes recommended by Washington were included.

*September 21*

## Delaware state constitution proclaimed

*September 21*

## Great fire in New York City

About 300 buildings were destroyed. Origin of the fire remains unknown.

*September 22*

## Nathan Hale executed by the British as an American spy

This was action, without a trial, partly in retaliation for presumed American responsibility for the New York fire. Captain Hale's last words were: "I only regret that I have but one life to lose for my country."

*September 23*

## Action at Montressor's Island (now Randall's Island), New York

The American surprise raid at dawn was inept and easily repulsed.

# *1776*

*September 26*

## Congress appoints three commissioners to negotiate with European nations

These were Silas Deane (already in Europe), Benjamin Franklin, and Thomas Jefferson. Jefferson declined, and in December Arthur Lee, already in Europe, was named in his place.

*September 28*

## Pennsylvania adopts state constitution

Independent Pennsylvania state government began operation.

*October 3*

## Congress authorizes domestic loan of $5,000,000 at four percent

*October 11-12*

## Battle of Valcour Island, Lake Champlain

Sir Guy Carleton's British fleet destroyed Benedict Arnold's flotilla after a hard-fought engagement and a lengthy chase.

*October 12-13*

## Battle of Throg's Neck, New York

A handful of Americans from Colonel Edward Hand's First Pennsylvania Rifle Regiment bottled up and held off a superior British force under General Cornwallis, thwarting General Howe's planned turning movement. Washington began to evacuate Manhattan Island, to avoid threatened encirclement.

# *1776*

*October 14*

## Action at Crown Point, New York

Arnold had retreated to Crown Point after the Battle of Valcour Island. After a brief skirmish with the British advance guard, he withdrew to Ticonderoga; Carleton arrived and occupied the site.

*October 18*

## Action at Pell's Point (New Rochelle), New York

General Howe finally gained a bridgehead in Westchester after resistance from John Glover's American forces. Washington expedited evacuation of Manhattan.

*October 18*

## Polish volunteer Thaddeus Kosciusko commissioned a colonel of engineers by Congress

He was one of the first, and one of the best, of the many European soldiers of fortune who volunteered to serve the American cause.

*October 22*

## Action at Mamaroneck, New York

Americans under Colonel John Haslet raided the village of Mamaroneck, occupied by Colonel Robert Rogers's recently recruited "Queen's American Rangers" (an entirely different organization from his earlier Rangers of French and Indian War fame). Americans, although delayed by Rogers's outpost, had the better of the following fire fight, but withdrew when they found that their attempt to surprise Rogers had failed.

# 1776

*October 23*

## Washington completes evacuation of Manhattan

This was necessary to avoid encirclement by Howe. Washington left a strong garrison in Fort Washington, Harlem Heights, overlooking the Hudson River. He then moved northward to White Plains.

*October 27*

## Action at Fort Washington, northern Manhattan Island, New York

The British attacked the fort by land and from the Hudson River side, but were driven off with considerable loss. One warship was badly damaged.

*October 28*

## Battle of White Plains, New York

General Howe, following Washington northward, attacked the strong American position and won a hard-fought victory by assaulting and capturing a key height which overlooked the main American position. Washington retired successfully to take up a new position about one mile farther north.

*October 30*

## Beginning of the United States Cavalry

Washington established a few units of dragoons to provide much-needed reconnaissance and screening forces. (See also December 12, 1776.)

# *1776*

*November 1*

## Washington withdraws from White Plains to North Castle, New York

This provided a better defensive position on commanding ground.


*November 3*

## British General Carleton abandons Crown Point, New York

He withdrew to Canada because of the difficulty of maintaining a line of communication from Montreal in winter.


*November 7-29*

## Siege of Fort Cumberland, Nova Scotia

A group of 180 Nova Scotia rebels led by Jonathan Eddy and John Allen made several unsuccessful attempts to wrest control from the British.


*November 11*

## Maryland adopts a state constitution


*November 16*

## First foreign salute to a United States flag (Grand Union Ensign)

A salvo of 11 guns was fired by a Dutch garrison at Fort Orange, St. Eustatius, in response to a salute from USS *Andrew Doria*, commanded by Captain Isaiah Robinson.

# *1776*

*November 16*

## Battle of Fort Washington, New York

The American garrison of 2,800 surrendered after a short, intensive British assault. This great loss of trained military manpower and valuable materiel was a serious blow to Washington.

*November 19-20*

## British night crossing of Hudson River at Closter, New Jersey

Because of this well-planned surprise move by General Cornwallis, General Nathanael Green was forced to abandon Fort Lee, which was immediately seized by Cornwallis. More badly needed materiel was lost by the Americans.

*November 21*

## Washington begins retreat across New Jersey to the Delaware River

Threatened by Cornwallis, who was closely followed by Howe's main body, Washington's weakened forces were in no condition to risk battle. He sent orders to General Charles Lee, still east of the Hudson, to follow him. Washington was closely pursued by the British.

*November 28*

## British occupy Newark, New Jersey

Washington retreated to Brunswick (New Brunswick), New Jersey.

# *1776*

*November 30*

## Howe brothers issue proclamation of pardon

Taking advantage of their successful New York campaign, Admiral Lord Richard and General Sir William promised pardon, with a few exceptions, to all who declared allegiance to the King within 60 days.

*December 1*

## Action at Brunswick, New Jersey

Washington's force barely escaped Cornwallis's pursuit. The Americans continued their retreat to the Delaware River.

*December 2*

## General Charles Lee crossed the Hudson into New Jersey at North Castle

As suggested by his slow, reluctant actions, and by letters he wrote at the time, he was hoping Washington's defeats would cause Congress to call upon him (Lee) to be commander-in-chief.

*December 3*

## Washington arrives at Trenton, New Jersey

He ordered all boats along the Delaware to be collected on the west bank of the river, as he prepared his own force to continue the retreat to the west bank.

*December 6*

## County of Kentucky incorporated by Virginia

# *1776*

*December 7*

## Action at Tappan, New York

Tories and "cowboys"—as British marauders were called in this area—pillaged the town, abused patriot citizens, and cut down the liberty pole.

*December 8*

## British reach Trenton

They arrived as the rear guard of Washington's army was still in boats crossing the Delaware into Pennsylvania.

*December 8*

## British occupy Newport, Rhode Island

Soon after this, a force of 6,000 troops under General Clinton was assembled here, in anticipation of an invasion of New England planned by General Howe for the summer of 1777.

*December 12*

## Congress vests Washington with dictatorial powers

Expecting the British to continue their advance to Philadelphia, the delegates also authorized Washington to recruit additional troops, and then fled to Baltimore.

# *1776*

*December 12*

## Congress authorizes a regiment of light dragoons

This action was based on a recommendation by Washington. Elisha Sheldon of Connecticut was appointed commander. The regiment, which incorporated units already raised by Washington, was the first cavalry in the United States Army.

*December 13*

## British army goes into winter quarters in New York

General Howe left garrisons at Trenton, Princeton, Bordentown, Perth Amboy, and Brunswick (New Brunswick) in New Jersey.

*December 13*

## British patrol captures General Charles Lee

The American general, who was spending the night at an inn some distance from his troops, was seized at Baskin's Ridge, New Jersey. Major General John Sullivan took over his command.

*December 18*

## North Carolina adopts state constitution by convention

*December 19*

## Publication of Thomas Paine's *American Crisis*

"These are the times that try men's souls."

# *1776*

*December 20*

## Congress meets at Baltimore, Maryland

Barely 25 members, less than half, were present.

*December 20*

## General Sullivan joins Washington with Lee's troops

Sullivan's 2,000 men brought Washington's forces west of the Delaware to an effective strength of about 8,000.

*December 21*

## Benjamin Franklin arrives in Paris

He joined agents Silas Deane and Arthur Lee to negotiate treaties with European nations.

*December 23*

## Congress seeks foreign loans

The diplomatic representatives in Europe were authorized to borrow up to two million pounds.

*December 24*

## Richard Caswell elected first American governor of North Carolina by the Provincial Congress

# *1776*

*December 25-26*

## Washington recrosses the Delaware

His tiny American army defied ice, cold, and sleet on its way to Trenton. Washington had about 2,400 men. Other contingents scheduled to cross with him were discouraged by bad weather.

*December 26*

## Battle of Trenton

The Hessian garrison of 1,400 men at Trenton was surprised by Washington; 22 were killed, 948 captured. American losses were 2 dead and 5 wounded. That evening Washington returned to Pennsylvania, after one of the boldest, most surprising exploits in history by a defeated general.

*December 27*

## Congress resolves to raise 16 regiments "at large"

These Continental regiments were not numbered, but were generally known by the names of their colonels.

*December 30*

## Washington again crosses Delaware to occupy Trenton

Blunders by subordinates caused him to take this risk most reluctantly, since Cornwallis was approaching from northeast New Jersey.

*December 30*

## Congress resolves to send commissioners to Austria, Prussia, Spain, and Tuscany

# *1776*

*December 31*

## Washington uses persuasion to retain an army

Although most of his men were due for discharge, he persuaded the majority to re-enlist, as British forces approached Trenton.

# *1777*

*January 1*

## Victory march in Philadelphia

Hessian prisoners taken at Trenton were marched through the streets.

*January 1*

## Cornwallis reaches Princeton to prepare advance toward Trenton

Washington sent out a brigade under Brigadier General Matthias Alexis Roche de Fermoy (a French volunteer) to delay the British advance. Sullivan's brigade took up delaying positions in Trenton.

*January 1*

## Benjamin Franklin appointed commissioner to Spain

This position was in addition to his duties with the French mission; he remained in Paris.

# *1777*

*January 2*

## Action at Trenton

The British drove back Fermoy's delaying force and contacted American lines behind Assunpink Creek, but Cornwallis decided to wait until the next day for a major attack.

*January 2-3*

## Washington's night withdrawal from Trenton

This brilliantly planned and executed operation completely deceived Cornwallis. By dawn the American advance guard was approaching Princeton.

*January 3*

## Battle of Princeton, New Jersey

Although his forces were suffering from lack of sleep, Washington overwhelmed a force supporting Cornwallis. The British were driven back with heavy losses toward Trenton and New Brunswick. Washington marched north into the Watchung Mountains, thus concluding one of the most brilliant campaigns in American military history.

*January 6*

## Georgia adopts state constitution

*January 6*

## Washington goes into winter quarters at Morristown, New Jersey

Here, secure in the Watchung Mountains, Washington could protect the approaches to northern New York and New Jersey, and

# *1777*

threaten the Brunswick-Trenton road. Cornwallis withdrew to Brunswick from Trenton.

*January 10*

## Action at East Passage, Rhode Island

An American shore battery drove away the British ship HMS *Cerberus.*

*January 14*

## British raid Prudence Island, Rhode Island

*January 16*

## New Hampshire Grants (present-day Vermont) declaration of independence

A convention at Westminister voted to seek Congressional recognition as the state of New Connecticut.

*January 17-29*

## Fiasco at Fort Independence, King's Bridge, New York

General William Heath with 3,400 men, under orders from Washington, advanced on the British-held fort, covering the approach to Manhattan Island, and demanded that the 2,000-man garrison surrender in 20 minutes or suffer the consequences. After ten days of unexpected resistance and unfavorable weather, the Americans were answered with a determined sortie that routed Heath's panicked force. Heath returned to Peekskill the laughing stock of both the British and American armies and received a personal reprimand from Washington.

# *1777*

*January 20*

## Action at Somerset Court House (Millstone), New Jersey

Indecisive skirmishing between British troops and Continentals based at Morristown.

*January 25*

## Action at West Farms, New York

A British-Tory band surprised and routed the guard at Lancey's Mill.

*January 28*

## General John Burgoyne submits a campaign plan for 1777

Burgoyne, who had returned to England, submitted his plan for a three-pronged offensive to isolate New England to Lord George Germain, Secretary of State for the Colonies, who approved it.

*February 2-9*

## Actions at Fort McIntosh (in modern Camden County), Georgia

Local patriots under Captain Richard Winn were forced to surrender the fort after several skirmishes and a two-day siege by Tories who were based on St. Augustine in British East Florida.

*February 27*

## Congress adjourns at Baltimore, Maryland

The delegates returned to Philadelphia, since Washington had disposed of the British threat.

# 1777

*March 3*

## Germain approves General Howe's campaign plan for 1777

This plan, for a sea attack on Philadelphia, which had been sent by Howe from New York, was completely inconsistent with Burgoyne's plan, which Germain had approved about a month earlier. There is no explanation for this official approval of two inconsistent campaign plans.

*March 8*

## Action at Amboy (Punk Hill), New Jersey

Brigadier General William Maxwell's American forces got the better of a British force.

*March 12*

## Congress convenes at Philadelphia, Pennsylvania

Attendance soon improved.

*March 13*

## Congress requests agents in Europe to recruit qualified foreign military experts

The result was to be an influx of European soldiers of fortune, few of whom would make any worthwhile contribution to the American cause.

*March 23*

## Action at Peekskill, New York

A British raiding party of 500 landed from ten ships to destroy magazines and storehouses. The garrison of 250 men under Briga-

# *1777*

dier General Alexander McDougall failed to take effective action. However, Lieutenant Colonel Marinus Willett, who arrived early the next day with 80 reinforcements from Fort Constitution (north of Peekskill, opposite West Point) boldly attacked. The British, having already accomplished their mission of burning supplies, then withdrew to their ships. Casualties were light on both sides.

*April 13*

## Action at Bound Brook, New Jersey

An American outpost under Major General Benjamin Lincoln was surprised by a British foraging expedition under Cornwallis. Lincoln was able to withdraw most of his 500 men, although his artillery detachment and its guns were captured by the British light horse.

*April 14*

## Congress authorizes a magazine and laboratory at Springfield, Massachusetts

This was the genesis of Springfield Arsenal.

*April 16*

## Rhode Island urged by Congress to prepare forces to drive British from Newport

*April 17*

## Congress reconstitutes Committee of Secret Correspondence as Committee for Foreign Affairs

*April 20*

## New York convention adopts a state constitution

# *1777*

*April 26*

## British raid Danbury, Connecticut

A force of about 2,000 under General William Tryon (former Governor of New York, who had been given a military commission) destroyed 19 dwellings, 22 barns and storehouses, and almost 1,700 tents.

*April 27*

## Action at Ridgefield, Connecticut

A force of about 600 Americans under Generals Benedict Arnold, David Wooster, and Gold Silliman attempted unsuccessfully to block the British withdrawal from Danbury. Wooster was killed in the action.

*April 28*

## Action at Compo Hill, Connecticut

British raiders under Tryon held off Arnold's counterattack, then continued their withdrawal to their ships on Long Island Sound.

*May 1*

## Arthur Lee named to represent the United States at the Spanish court

He replaced Benjamin Franklin.

*May 2*

## Gunpowder from New Orleans supplies western frontiersmen

Lieutenant William Linn arrived at Fort Henry (Wheeling), Virginia (present-day West Virginia), with 98 barrels of powder needed for summer fighting against Indians and Tories.

# *1777*

*May 6*

## General Burgoyne arrives in Quebec to command British forces in Canada

He carried with him orders for his planned invasion of New York.

*May 7*

## Ralph Izard appointed commissioner to the Grand Duke of Tuscany

He replaced Franklin.

*May 9*

## William Lee assigned to represent the United States at Vienna and Berlin

*May 10*

### Action at Piscataway, New Jersey

An American force under Major General Adam Stephen was repulsed in an attempt to surprise the 42nd Highlanders (Black Watch).

*May 15*

### Action at Sawpit Bluff, Florida

In a brief skirmish with Indians, Colonel John Baker retrieved 40 horses stolen from his camp. (Another source gives May 6.)

# *1777*

*May 17*

## Action at Thomas' Swamp, Florida

Indians, Rangers, and British regulars under Colonel Augustine Prevost routed Colonel John Baker's 109 Americans, killing eight and capturing 31. The Indians then began a massacre of the captives, murdering all but 16, who were saved by Prevost and his regulars with great difficulty. (Another source gives May 11.)

*May 23*

## American raid at Sag Harbor, Long Island, New York

Americans under Lieutenant Colonel Return Jonathan Meigs surprised a British foraging party, captured several vessels, and burned supplies.

*May 28*

## Washington advances from Morristown to Middlebrook Valley

This was the opening move of the campaign of 1777. In subsequent maneuvering Washington evaded efforts by General Howe to bring on a major engagement of the two armies.

*June 14*

## Stars and Stripes adopted by Congress as American flag

Its principal features were 13 stars and 13 stripes, one for each of the original states.

*June 16*

## Burgoyne's advance guard occupies Crown Point, New York

Capable Brigadier General Simon Fraser was in command of the British Advance Corps.

# *1777*

## *June 17*

### Action at Millstone (Somerset Courthouse), New Jersey

Colonel Daniel Morgan's regiment harassed an entrenching British force. (Morgan had been released by the British in a prisoner-of-war exchange, and had been given a regiment by Washington.)

## *June 17*

### Burgoyne's main body starts south from St. Johns

With Burgoyne was a force of 7,700 British and German troops, Canadians and Indians, a baggage train, and 138 pieces of artillery. Most of these were on ships and boats that sailed up Lake Champlain.

## *June 22*

### Action at Brunswick, New Jersey

Americans harassed withdrawing British.

## *June 26*

### Action at Short Hills (Metuchen), New Jersey

British harassed the American rear guard under General William Alexander, Lord Stirling.

## *June 30*

### Burgoyne's army begins disembarking near Fort Ticonderoga

The landing site was protected by Fraser's Advance Corps.

# *1777*

*June 30*

## General Howe withdraws British troops from New Jersey to New York City and Staten Island

Unable to pin Washington down in New Jersey, he prepared to carry out the approved plan for a move against Philadelphia. (See March 3, 1777.)

*July 1-4*

## General Burgoyne's troops approach Fort Ticonderoga

Americans in the area were commanded by Brigadier General Arthur St. Clair. American outposts held up the British advance.

*July 2*

## Treaty of Long Island, North Carolina

Cherokee Indians, defeated by frontier militia, ceded disputed lands to Virginia and North Carolina.

*July 5*

## British occupy undefended Mount Defiance, overlooking Fort Ticonderoga

His position no longer defensible, St. Clair immediately evacuated Ticonderoga, abandoning substantial supplies.

*July 6*

## British occupy Fort Ticonderoga, New York

Burgoyne pursued St. Clair, captured Skenesborough, and threatened the retreat of St. Clair's army.

# *1777*

*July 7*

## Battle of Hubbardton, Vermont

Americans retreating from Ticonderoga were defeated by Hessians and British under von Riedesel and Fraser, but Seth Warner's delaying action permitted St. Clair to escape the British pursuit.

*July 8*

## Vermont convention at Windsor adopts written constitution as independent republic

The constitution provided for manhood suffrage and the abolition of slavery. (The name Vermont had been substituted for New Connecticut; see January 16, 1777.)

*July 8*

## Action at Fort Anne, New York

British forces, pursuing the American rear guard retreating from Skenesboro, captured several boatloads of invalids and supplies, but failed to achieve their main objective of cutting off the retreating Americans.

*July 9*

## George Clinton elected first state governor of New York

*July 9-10*

## British General Richard Prescott captured at Newport, Rhode Island

Rhode Island militia officer William Barton surprised the general in a compromising situation with a woman.

# *1777*

## July 16

### Cruise of USS *Revenge* (14)

Captain Gustavus Conyngham sailed from Dunkirk to begin a successful two-year operation against British shipping in eastern Atlantic and European waters.

## July 23

### General Howe sails from New York with 15,000 troops

His objective was the Chesapeake Bay and Philadelphia, in accordance with the plan Lord Germain had approved. He was totally unaware of Burgoyne's advance toward Albany. Washington, however, was well aware of Burgoyne's move, and was perplexed by Howe's departure from New York, since he had expected a British offensive north, up the Hudson, to meet Burgoyne at Albany. (This, of course, was also Burgoyne's expectation, and he was unaware that Howe had received no orders from Germain.) Washington, fearing a trick, kept his army near the Hudson. Meanwhile, considering Burgoyne's invasion the main threat, Washington sent some of his best officers (including Generals Lincoln and Arnold) and best troops (including Morgan's rifle regiment) to reinforce Schuyler in northern New York.

## July 26

### Colonel Barry St. Leger advances from Oswego

In accordance with Burgoyne's plan, St. Leger was to advance toward Albany to meet Burgoyne. St. Leger's force included 875 British, Tory, and Hessian troops and 1,000 Indians under Joseph Brant.

# *1777*

*July 27*

## Murder of Jane McCrea, near Fort Edward, New York

Jane McCrea was waiting for her fiancé, Lieutenant David Jones of Burgoyne's army, when she and another woman were captured by an advance party of Burgoyne's Indians. The Indians returned to Burgoyne's main body with one woman and a scalp that was identified by Lieutenant Jones as that of his fiancée. This atrocity aroused northern settlers against the British, even though Miss McCrea was apparently a loyalist.

*July 27*

## Arrival of Marquis de Lafayette and Baron Johann de Kalb at Philadelphia

They had landed at Georgetown, South Carolina, on June 13. They were to become the most famous and among the best of foreign officers of the Revolution. Kalb, a bogus baron, but a bona fide and competent soldier, was a gigantic Bavarian soldier of fortune whose ability had brought him prominence and promotion to general in the French Army.

*July 29*

## General Philip Schuyler evacuates Fort Edward, New York

He retreated down the Hudson in the face of Burgoyne's approach.

*July 31*

## Congress commissions Lafayette a major general

He volunteered to serve without pay. Congress was charmed by the aristocratic, youthful marquis. They were less sure of de Kalb, at a time when "Philadelphia was swarming with Frenchmen" sent over by Silas Deane, and when American officers were beginning to

# *1777*

complain about the generally incompetent foreigners who were being put over them in rank and position.

*August 2*

## Action at Dutch Island, Rhode Island

A Rhode Island battery drove the British ship HMS *Renown* from Dutch Island Harbor.

*August 3*

## St. Leger invests Fort Stanwix, New York

The fort was held by a garrison of 750 men commanded by Colonel Peter Gansevoort. His second-in-command was Lt. Col. Marinus Willett.

*August 4*

## General Horatio Gates replaces General Schuyler as commander of the Continental Army of the North

Congress made the appointment without consulting Washington, who had asked be excused from this politically delicate decision.

*August 6*

## Battle of Oriskany, New York

British and Indians repulsed an American attempt to relieve Fort Stanwix, ambushing 800 militiamen under General Nicholas Herkimer. Herkimer was mortally wounded while gallantly and successfully rallying his troops. Meanwhile, Willett led a successful sortie from the fort, looting the British camp.

# *1777*

## *August 7*

### Colonel Peter Gansevoort rejects St. Leger's demand for surrender of Fort Stanwix

Despite a desperate situation, he resolutely called St. Leger's bluff that he would release his Indians to massacre civilians. Gansevoort said he would hold the fort "to the last extremity."

## *August 10*

### Benedict Arnold leads relief expedition for Fort Stanwix from Stillwater

Arnold was one of many good officers sent by Washington to help Schuyler meet the grave threat posed by the British invasion of northern New York. He volunteered to lead the expedition of about 900 men when Schuyler asked for a brigadier general.

## *August 16*

### Battle of Bennington, Vermont (fought entirely in New York)

General John Stark, of the New Hampshire militia, reinforced by Colonel Seth Warner's Green Mountain Boys, defeated a strong foraging force of British and Hessians under Lieutenant Colonel Friedrich Baum. Baum was mortally wounded and most of his command killed or taken prisoner.

## *August 21*

### Benedict Arnold's relief expedition approaches Fort Stanwix

He reached Fort Dayton, where he was disappointed in his expectation of receiving substantial local militia reinforcements. However, St. Leger's Indians, hearing of Arnold's approach, began to desert.

# *1777*

*August 21-22*

## American raid on Staten Island, New York

General Sullivan's raid was unsuccessful; he was later court-martialed and acquitted.

*August 22*

## St. Leger abandons siege of Fort Stanwix

Confronted with the approach of Benedict Arnold and the desertion of his Indians, he retreated to Canada.

*August 25*

## Howe's British army disembarks at Head of Elk, Maryland

Preparations were begun for an advance on Philadelphia. Washington, now realizing that Howe's departure from New York had been no ruse, marched rapidly through Philadelphia toward Wilmington to bar the way.

*September 1*

## Siege of Fort Henry (Wheeling), Virginia (present-day West Virginia)

400 Indians under Simon Girty besieged the fort until Major Samuel McCulloch, pursued by Indians near Fort Henry, rode his horse down a 150 ft. cliff to escape across Wheeling Creek ("McCulloch's Leap") and led reinforcements back. The Indians fled.

*September 3*

## Action at Iron Hill (Cooch's Bridge), Delaware

Brigadier General William Maxwell's Light Infantry Brigade, sent to delay Howe's advance, was driven back by German jagers.

# *1777*

*September 11*

## Battle of the Brandywine

Washington, ill served by several subordinates, and not sufficiently alert himself to a potential British envelopment, was defeated after being outmaneuvered by General Howe. He then withdrew toward Philadelphia.

*September 13*

## Burgoyne crosses the Hudson

He moved to the west bank, south of Fort Edward, unaware that neither Howe nor St. Leger would meet him at Albany.

*September 15*

## Congress commissions Baron de Kalb a major general

Kalb, who had signed a contract with Silas Deane in Paris, had threatened to sue Congress for breach of contract when it had not given him a commission. He now withdrew his threats and accepted the offered commission.

*September 16*

## Action at Warren Tavern (White Horse Tavern), Pennsylvania

A major battle was impending as Washington again blocked Howe's approach to Philadelphia. It did not materialize, however, due to torrential rain, which wet the troops' powder and kept them from firing their muskets.

# *1777*

## September 17

### Congress again grants dictatorial powers to Washington

In preparation for flight to escape the approaching British, Congress for the second time delegated to Washington full responsibility for carrying on the war.

## September 18

### Congress adjourns at Philadelphia, flees westward as British approach

Moving first to Lancaster, the members then went on westward to York, where they remained until June 1778.

## September 18

### Liberty Bell moved from Philadelphia to Allentown, Pennsylvania

It was sent in an army baggage train, to be hidden in Zion Reformed Church until June 27, 1778.

## September 18

### British capture Continental supply depot at Valley Forge

British advance elements were led by Generals Knyphausen and Cornwallis.

## September 18-24

### American raid on Lake George area

Colonel John Brown's force, heading toward Fort Ticonderoga, surprised and captured over 300 British along the west shore of Lake

# *1777*

George. They did not succeed, however, in reaching Saratoga, and posed no real threat to Burgoyne, who had abandoned his line of communications.

## *September 19*

### First Battle of Saratoga (or Freeman's Farm), New York

Burgoyne's attack on the American left was repulsed with 600 casualties; American losses numbered 300. Benedict Arnold, seizing the initiative without Gates's approval, was largely responsible for this success. He was ably assisted by Colonel Daniel Morgan and his rifle regiment, which Washington had sent north to help oppose Burgoyne's threat. Arnold requested reinforcements to counter-attack but was refused them by Gates. When Arnold scathingly rebuked Gates, implying cowardice, Gates relieved him as second-in-command.

## *September 20-21*

### Battle of Paoli, Pennsylvania ("Paoli Massacre")

A British force led by Major General Charles Grey defeated General Anthony Wayne in a surprise night attack which resulted in severe losses to the Americans. To prevent an accidental shot from giving away surprise, Grey had his men take the flints from their muskets' firing mechanisms, and was thereafter known as "No Flint" Grey. Wayne's losses have been estimated as high as 500, but 150 seems realistic. Grey lost 6 killed and about 22 wounded.

## *September 24*

### Action at Diamond Island, New York

Colonel John Brown's Continental forces concluded a semisuccessful raid against the British post 25 miles south of Ticonderoga. The raid yielded important information about the status of Burgoyne's provisions, even though the Americans failed to recapture Fort Ticonderoga. This was part of Brown's raid in the Lake George area.

# *1777*

## September 25

### Brigadier General Thomas Conway proves a troublemaker

Conway, a French volunteer officer of Irish descent, wrote to Congress disparagingly about his commanding officer, General William Alexander, Lord Stirling.

## September 26

### British occupy Philadelphia

Washington was a few miles away, near Reading and Bethlehem.

## September 27

### Congress convenes at Lancaster, Pennsylvania

After a one-day session, it adjourned to continue flight to York.

## September 30

### Congress convenes at York, Pennsylvania; adjourns immediately

However, York was to remain the seat of Congress for nearly nine months.

## October 3

### Belated British expedition from New York up the Hudson

General Clinton had been left in command of New York by Howe. He undertook a maneuver of diversion which he expected would help Burgoyne, who was now known to be north of Albany.

# 1777

## October 4

### Battle of Germantown, Pennsylvania

Mainly because of fog and a complicated plan, Washington was repulsed in a fierce assault on Howe's encampment. The Americans
had 1,100 casualties; the British lost 534. Washington withdrew to
Whitemarsh, where he entrenched his army, as a threat to Philadelphia. The battle was a psychological American success, with
Washington's boldness in defeat surprising both friend and foe.

## October 6

### Clinton captures Forts Clinton and Montgomery on the Hudson

British General Henry Clinton's superior British and Hessian force
defeated the small, 600-man garrison guarding the forts.

## October 7

### Second Battle of Saratoga (or Bemis Heights), New York

Burgoyne, attempting to drive south, was decisively repulsed by
Americans under Benedict Arnold, who assumed command of the
field forces despite Gates's orders. Morgan and his riflemen again
distinguished themselves. Gates did nothing. Arnold was wounded.

## October 7

### Congressional debate regarding proposed Articles of Confederation

In debate at York, Congress concluded that each state would have
only one vote in the new national legislature.

# *1777*

*October 8*

## Burgoyne retreats to Saratoga (Stillwater), New York

His situation was desperate, since he was short of food and ammunition. He could not expect to reach Ticonderoga without food, and no supplies could reach him from the fort or from Canada.

*October 9*

## British General Clinton receives Burgoyne's appeal for help

Despite the appeal, Clinton apparently did not realize how desperate Burgoyne's situation was. He seems never even to have considered any attempt to fight through to relieve Burgoyne.

*October 11*

## Conway Cabal begins

Thomas Conway sent Gates a letter attacking Washington, and suggesting that Gates should become commander-in-chief. There is evidence to suggest that Conway was conspiring with members of the New England faction of Congress, whose influence had declined since the war had moved away from Boston, and who hoped to regain control of the Army and of the Revolution.

*October 13*

## Burgoyne requests a cessation of hostilities

This was granted by Gates. Negotiations began for the surrender of the British army at Saratoga.

# *1777*

*October 16*

## British raid on Esopus (Kingston), New York

Troops and ships sent north by General Clinton burned the town. Clinton apparently thought such a diversion would relieve pressure on Burgoyne.

*October 17*

## Burgoyne surrenders

By the terms of the "Convention of Saratoga," agreed to the previous day, the disarmed British army of 5,700 was to be marched to Boston and shipped to England on parole. (These terms were later shamefully repudiated by the American Congress; the British and German soldiers were not permitted to sail home.) This victory assured French aid to the American cause.

*October 17*

## Congress establishes a new Board of War

This was to consist of three persons not members of Congress (later increased to five).

*October 22*

## British attack on Fort Mercer (Red Bank), New Jersey

This operation, by Hessian Troops, was the first move in Howe's campaign to open the Delaware River, up to Philadelphia, to the British fleet. The 400-man garrison of the Delaware River fort, under Colonel Christopher Greene, repelled the attack.

# *1777*

*October 22*

## General Howe requests to be relieved of command

He was bitter because of lack of reinforcements, and because of implied criticism that he had failed to cooperate with Burgoyne. (Burgoyne's surrender, of course, was not yet known to Howe.)

*October 23*

## The Royal Navy engages Fort Mifflin, Pennsylvania

The British fleet was moving up the river from Delaware Bay, in coordination with Howe's land operations on the river bank. American artillery fire inflicted severe damage on six British men-of-war. The ship of the line HMS *Augusta* (64) and the sloop of war HMS *Merlin* (16) ran aground and had to be destroyed.

*November 2*

## John Paul Jones and USS *Ranger* (18) sail from Portsmouth New Hampshire

The destination of the ship-rigged sloop of war was France and the climax of the most illustrious career in American naval annals.

*November 3*

## Washington learns of the Conway Cabal

General Alexander (Lord Stirling) informed Washington of a possible conspiracy to discredit him with Congress, and to have him displaced as commander-in-chief by General Gates.

*November 6*

## Americans capture British ship aground at Point Judith, Rhode Island

# *1777*

*November 15*

## Evacuation of Fort Mifflin, Pennsylvania

The fort had become untenable after a six-day bombardment by the British fleet. British troops occupied the fort the next day.

*November 15*

## Articles of Confederation and Perpetual Union adopted by Congress

*November 17*

## Articles of Confederation submitted to states for ratification

*November 20-22*

## Battle of Fort Mercer (Red Bank), New Jersey

After the evacuation of Fort Mifflin, Cornwallis crossed the river with 2,000 men, as the British fleet approached to begin a naval bombardment. Colonel Christopher Greene, the commander, realized that the fort was no longer tenable. He therefore abandoned the stronghold, leaving the Delaware River open to the British up to Philadelphia. The small American naval squadron upriver was burned to prevent its capture.

*November 22*

## Congress makes its first fiscal requisition upon the states

This was to be paid in paper money. By October 6, 1779, four requisitions totaling $95,000,000 had been made.

# *1777*

*November 25*

## Action at Gloucester, New Jersey

Lafayette, on a reconnaissance in force with 300 men, had the best of a skirmish with a larger force of Hessians.

*November 27*

## Confiscation of loyalist estates

Congress recommended to the states that they appropriate the property of residents who had forfeited "the right to protection."

*November 27*

## Congress names General Gates as President of the Board of War

A result of Congressional frustration over the direction of the war, and a triumph of the anti-Washington Congressional conspiracy in the Conway Cabal.

*November 28*

## John Adams appointed commissioner to France

He was to succeed Silas Deane, whose judgment—and loyalty—were being questioned (rightly, as long-secret documents eventually indicated).

*December 2*

## John Paul Jones and the USS *Ranger* reach Nantes, France

They had entered the mouth of the Loire River two days earlier.

# *1777*

*December 4*

## Word of Burgoyne's defeat at Saratoga reaches American commissioners in Paris

The information was provided to the French Foreign Minister, Comte Charles G. de Vergennes, who at once (two days later) responded positively to American overtures for negotiation of a military alliance.

*December 5-8*

## British sortie from Philadelphia

A British raiding force, carrying out a reconnaissance in force, engaged in several skirmishes at Whitemarsh, Chestnut Hill (December 6), and Edge Hill (December 7). Howe followed, with most of his army, but decided that Washington's defenses in the Whitemarsh area were too strong for a general attack, and withdrew to Philadelphia. The British failure was in large part due to the warning given Washington by Captain Allen McLane, commanding a Continental reconnaissance company.

*December 10*

## American raid on Long Island, New York

The attack was broken up by British ships; Colonel Samuel B. Webb and his regiment were captured.

*December 11*

## Washington leaves Whitemarsh for Valley Forge

He decided to go into winter quarters in a more easily defended position, a little farther away from Philadelphia.

# *1777*

## December 11

### Action at Gulph's Mills (Matson's Ford), Pennsylvania

A large British foraging force, led by Lord Cornwallis, captured over 2,000 sheep and cattle and withdrew after clashing with a major portion of the main American army, en route to Valley Forge. Expecting further action, Washington delayed his march to Valley Forge for several days.

## December 13

### Congress establishes Inspector General Department in the Continental Army

This was the result of action by adherents of Brigadier General Thomas Conway, an incident of the "Conway Cabal."

## December 14

### Conway named Inspector General by Congress

Another triumph for Washington's opponents.

## December 15

### Negotiations begin in Paris with British agent Paul Wentworth (December 15, 1777–January 6, 1778)

These culminated in a fruitless meeting with Franklin, who rightly suspected and detested the unsavory, two-faced Wentworth. The French, aware of the negotiations, hastened their decision to conclude an alliance, and so informed the American commissioners on December 17.

# *1777*

## *December 19*

### Washington goes into winter quarters at Valley Forge, Pennsylvania

This was the beginning of the most publicized of the many harsh winters suffered by the Continental Army.

# *1778*

## *January 5*

### The "Battle of the Kegs"

In a plan devised by David Bushnell, inventor of the submarine, Americans attempted to sink British ships in the Delaware River by sending downriver floating explosive and incendiary mines in kegs. Although no damage was done, the British panic when the kegs came floating down the river led to the satire "The Battle of the Kegs," a poem by Francis Hopkinson published in the *New Jersey Gazette* (January 21).

## *January 8*

### Washington condemns gambling

In general orders he directed "exemplary punishment" of any officer or soldier found gambling or playing with cards or dice in any way.

## *January 27*

### American raid on Nassau, Bahamas

Marines and seamen under Captain John Peck Rathbun seized the forts overlooking the harbor. This was the first time that the new American flag, the Stars and Stripes, had been carried ashore and raised over a captured, hostile fortification.

# *1778*

*February 6*

## Franco-American Treaty of Commerce and Treaty of Alliance signed in Paris

In an exchange of most-favored-nation status, U.S. independence was recognized by France. The alliance was to become effective if and when war broke out between Britain and France. It was ratified by Congress May 4.

*February 9*

## End of the Conway Cabal

Washington, in a firm and masterful letter to General Gates, a copy of which went to Congress, denounced Thomas Conway and rebuked Gates. Gates disavowed any participation in a conspiracy, as did several Congressmen suspected by Washington's adherents. There has been some doubt among historians as to whether there was in fact any organized plot to oust Washington, since no documents have been found to confirm it. There is no question, however, that there was connivance of some sort, in opposition to Washington, among Conway, Gates, and several members of Congress. Washington's status as the respected and trusted commander-in-chief was fully restored as a result of publication of his letter to Gates.

*February 14*

## First salute to "Stars and Stripes"

Fired by the flagship of French Admiral La Motte Picquet in response to a salute by John Paul Jones in USS *Ranger* as he sailed from Nantes to Quiberon Bay.

# *1778*

*February 17*

## Lord North presents a plan for conciliation with the colonies to Parliament

His plan called for repeal of the Tea and Coercive Acts, a promise that no revenue taxes would be imposed on the American colonies by Parliament, appointment of a commission to negotiate peace with Congress, and suspension of all acts passed since 1763 if necessary.

*February 23*

## Lieutenant General Baron Friedrich Wilhelm von Steuben arrives at Valley Forge

One of many foreign volunteers recruited by Silas Deane, the Prussian officer was a bogus general as well as a bogus baron. He was, however, a veteran of the campaigns of Frederick the Great, as he claimed, and he proved to be one of the most inspired and successful military instructors in history. Congress had accepted him as an unpaid volunteer.

*February 27*

## USS *Columbus* burned at Point Judith, Rhode Island

The Continental frigate, attempting to run the British blockade of Narragansett Bay, went aground and was destroyed to prevent her capture by the British.

*March 3*

## Elections in Vermont

A new government of the independent republic took office March 12, with Thomas Chittenden as president.

# *1778*

*March 7*

## Clinton to relieve Howe

Lord Germain signed orders appointing Sir Henry Clinton as new British commander-in-chief in the American colonies.

*March 7*

## USS *Randolph* (32) versus HMS *Yarmouth* (64)

The American ship *Randolph* was blown up after 20 minutes of fierce fighting in the West Indies. Captain Nicholas Biddle and all but four of the 315 men on board were killed.

*March 8*

## British government sends new instructions to General Howe

If unable to engage Washington in a decisive battle, he was to abandon any idea of inland operations and was to undertake raids against the New England coast.

*March 13*

## British government is informed of France's recognition of the United States

This announcement by the French ambassador was a virtual declaration of war, although hostilities did not begin at once.

*March 16*

## Lord North's plan for conciliation with the colonies is adopted

The House of Commons, alarmed by the French recognition, belatedly realized that recovery of control of the colonies by military force was far from certain.

# *1778*

*March 18*

## Action at Quintan's Bridge, New Jersey

New Jersey militia under Colonel Asher Holmes was defeated by British and Tories. (The site is also known as Quinton's, or Quintin's, Bridge.)

*March 20*

## King Louis XVI of France receives Franklin, Deane, and Lee

This was the first official French ceremony acknowledging American independence and French recognition.

*March 21*

## Action at Hancock's Bridge, New Jersey

British and Tories under Major John Simcoe surprised and killed 20 New Jersey militia.

*March 21*

## British adopt defensive strategy in the north, offensive in the south

King George signed orders to General Clinton, New British commander-in-chief, to withdraw from Philadelphia and to abandon all northern strongholds except easily defended Newport and New York City. He was to send troops to reconquer Georgia and to permit British naval forces to seize French islands in the West Indies, particularly St. Lucia.

*April 8*

## John Adams arrives in Paris

He replaced Silas Deane as one of the commissioners in Paris.

# *1778*

## April 12

### Carlisle peace commission appointed to negotiate with Congress

William Eden and George Johnstone, along with the Earl of Carlisle, were named as commissioners.

## April 17

### Action at Bristol, Pennsylvania

American foraging parties were becoming more aggressive as a result of the effects of von Steuben's training, and as Washington began to test the results of that training.

## April 22

### Congress responds to the British peace commission

It resolved that anyone coming to terms with the British commission was an enemy of the United States.

## April 22-23

### American raid on Whitehaven, England

John Paul Jones led a force from USS *Ranger*. With 30 men he spiked the guns of two forts and set three ships afire. Later that day he landed again, a few miles north on Scottish St. Mary's Isle, in a vain attempt to capture the Earl of Selkirk. These were the only American landings on British soil during the Revolution.

## April 24

### USS *Ranger* (18) versus HMS *Drake* (20)

John Paul Jones captured the British sloop of war in a one-hour, hard-fought battle off Carrickfergus, Ireland.

# *1778*

## May 1

### Action at Crooked Billet, Pennsylvania

An American outpost, so placed as to interfere with British foraging north of Philadelphia, was encircled in a surprise dawn attack by Lieutenant Colonel Robert Abercromby with 400 light infantry, Major John Simcoe's 300 Rangers, and a detachment of light horse. Brigadier General John Lacey, who had only 60 men fit for duty, skillfully extricated himself, although losing all of his baggage, and about 35 men killed or wounded. The British had nine wounded.

## May 4

### Congress ratifies treaties with France

## May 5

### Von Steuben appointed Inspector General of the Continental Army

He replaced the discredited Conway. He had been acting Inspector General, appointed as such by Washington, since early March. Von Steuben received the rank of major general.

## May 6

### Army celebrates French alliance at Valley Forge

A great review was held. The army displayed new uniforms, and new precision in drill resulting from Steuben's training. Washington ordered rum all around.

# 1778

*May 6*

## British raid up the Delaware

Some 44 American vessels were burned or sunk.

*May 8*

## Action at Bordentown, New Jersey

Some 600-700 British raiders from Philadelphia landed at Bordentown, seven miles below Philadelphia, to destroy American military
stores there. Encountering little opposition, they burned the estate
of Joseph Borden (after whom the village was named), engaged in
some minor plundering, and presumably destroyed the military
stores. They also burned two frigates and some smaller vessels at
the White Hills, a little below Bordentown.

*May 11*

## Sir Henry Clinton succeeds Sir William Howe as British commander-in-chief

He at once began to prepare plans to evacuate Philadelphia, in
accordance with the March 21 orders from King George III. General Howe departed from Philadelphia two weeks later.

*May 18*

## Extravaganza farewell to General Howe in Philadelphia

This combination of plays, exhibitions, displays, and banquets was
called "Mischianza."

# *1778*

*May 19*

## American dawn raid on British Philadelphia lines

Captain Allen McLane took advantage of British lack of alertness following the Mischianza celebration. The action was inconclusive.

*May 20*

## Exchanged prisoner-of-war General Charles Lee returns to Continental Army

Because he was next senior officer of the Continental Army, Washington immediately appointed him second-in-command.

*May 20*

## Action at Barren Hill, Pennsylvania

A Continental division under Lafayette escaped a trap set by a superior British force, planned personally by Clinton. The reconnaissance activities of Captain McLane, plus Lafayette's unquestionable talents, contributed to the American success.

*May 25*

## British raid at Bristol and Warren, Rhode Island

Several buildings were destroyed and the inhabitants abused in various ways by British marauders under Major General Prescott. Much plunder and livestock were carried off.

*May 27*

## Congress reorganizes the Continental Army

Among many changes, a Provost Corps was established and three engineer companies authorized.

# *1778*

*May 31*

## Action at Tiverton, Rhode Island

Prescott and 150 British marauders were held off by 25 defenders of the town after several mills were burned. The raiders also ravaged nearby Fall River, R.I. (now Massachusetts).

*June 1*

## Action at Cobleskill, New York

Tories and Indians under Brant pillaged and burned a settlement of about 20 families, after having dispersed Continental soldiers and militia under Captain William Patrick. Many of the settlers were massacred and Patrick was killed.

*June 6*

## British peace commission arrives in Philadelphia

The Earl of Carlisle and his fellow commissioners brought with them Lord North's proposals for negotiations, which offered the colonies autonomy under the British crown. (See April 12.)

*June 17*

## Congress's reply to British peace commission

The only acceptable terms were the withdrawal of British forces and the recognition of U.S. independence.

*June 17*

## Outbreak of war between France and England

War began with a naval clash off the coast of England, when British Admiral Keppel fired on two French frigates.

# *1778*

*June 18*

## British evacuate Philadelphia

Clinton set out overland toward New York City with about 16,000 men. Lafayette and an American advance guard pursued at once in accordance with Washington's prearranged plan.

*June 19*

## Washington and main army pursue the British from Philadelphia

Total strength, including advance guard, was about 14,500 men, of whom 12,000 were Continentals trained by von Steuben.

*June 27*

## Washington orders General Charles Lee to attack Clinton at first opportunity

Lee, as second-in-command, was placed in command of a strenthened advance guard in anticipation of Clinton's being forced to extend his column on a single road to Sandy Hook.

*June 27*

## Congress adjourns at York, Pennsylvania

The British evacuation of Philadelphia permitted a return to that city.

*June 28*

## Battle of Monmouth Courthouse (Freehold), New Jersey

In apparent disobedience of Washington's orders, General Charles Lee failed to coordinate an attack on Clinton, who counterattacked;

# *1778*

Washington saved the army from near disaster. This was the first time that American regulars fought on equal terms with British regulars on an open field. Losses on both sides were equally great in the inconclusive battle. Mary Ludwig Hays, the legendary Molly Pitcher, is said to have manned a gun in this battle.

## *June 28-29*

### British night march to escape Monmouth battlefield

Clinton marched to Sandy Hook to embark on ships for New York (June 30). By abandoning the field, he conceded victory to Washington.

## *June 30*

### Action at Alligator Bridge, Florida

American cavalry sent by General Robert Howe to surprise a party of East Florida Rangers was repulsed. Colonel Elijah Clarke was wounded in the action.

## *July*

### French ambassador arrives at Philadelphia

Conrad Alexander Gerard was the first foreign diplomatic representative accredited to the United States.

## *July 2*

### Congress convenes at Philadelphia

# *1778*

## *July 3-4*

### Wyoming Valley "Massacre"

Maj. John Butler led 900 Loyalists and Indians in a devastating sweep through Pennsylvania's Wyoming Valley. Patriot Colonel Zebulon Butler opposed them with a force of 200-300 militiamen and 60 regulars. In the resulting melee the patriots were butchered, only 60 escaping. Tory Butler reported his losses as one Indian and two Rangers killed and boasted that his force had taken 227 American scalps.

## *July 4*

### Colonel George Rogers Clark occupies Kaskaskia, Illinois

Within six weeks he organized the territory as part of Virginia.

## *July 4-12*

### Court-martial of General Charles Lee

Found guilty of disobedience and misbehavior at the Battle of Monmouth, he was suspended from command.

## *July 8*

### Arrival of Comte d'Estaing's French fleet at Delaware Bay

His fleet of 12 ships of the line represented the first French active participation in the alliance. Washington sent a message recommending a joint attack on New York.

## *July 11*

### Arrival of French fleet off New York

At the same time Washington's army blockaded the land approaches to New York.

# 1778

*July 18*

## Indian raid at Andrustown, New York

A small settlement of seven families was plundered and burned, and its inhabitants massacred, by Indians under Joseph Brant.

*July 20*

## George Rogers Clark occupies Vincennes, Indiana

The citizens of the town immediately shifted their allegiance from Great Britain to the state of Virginia.

*July 22*

## Washington and d'Estaing plan joint operation against Newport, Rhode Island

Franco-American plan of assault on New York was abandoned because French ships could not get over the bar into the harbor.

*July 27*

## Battle of Ushant

British and French fleets, under British Admiral Augustus Keppel and French Admiral Count d'Orvilliers, clashed indecisively off the coast of France.

*July 29*

## D'Estaing's fleet arrives off Newport, Rhode Island

General John Sullivan was marching toward Newport with a force of Continentals.

# *1778*

*July 30*

## Washington takes up a position at White Plains

A long-term land blockade of New York was begun.

*August 5*

## Naval action at the Sakonnet River,* Rhode Island

Crews of a British flotilla destroyed their vessels in panic to prevent capture on the approach of two French frigates under Admiral Suffren.

*August 8*

## Sullivan and d'Estaing begin joint operation against Newport, Rhode Island

Americans crossed the Sakonnet River to Newport Island. D'Estaing was incensed that the move had been made without consulting him, and was with difficulty persuaded to continue the blockade.

*August 10*

## British fleet under Admiral Lord Howe approaches Newport

D'Estaing moved out at once to fight.

*August 11*

## French and British fleets off Newport scattered by a fierce storm

D'Estaing withdrew to Boston to repair resulting damage to his fleet. Admiral Howe withdrew to New York.

*An arm of the sea also called Sakonnet (Seaconnet) Passage or Inlet.

# 1778

*August 29*

## Battle of Newport (Tiverton; Quaker Hill), Rhode Island

Without naval support, General John Sullivan had to abandon the Newport operation. On his withdrawal to the mainland he repulsed a British attack led by General Robert Pigot at Butt's Hill, opposite Tiverton. A Negro Continental regiment led by Colonel Christopher Greene particularly distinguished itself in this battle.

*August 31*

## Action at Indian field and bridge, New York

British Lieutenant Colonel Simcoe ambushed a band of Indians, under Nimham, who had been collaborating with the Americans. Although the ambuscade failed to achieve the expected results, Simcoe's troops killed nearly 40 Indians.

*September 4*

## Treaty of amity and commerce signed by representatives of Congress and the Netherlands government

The British Government was infuriated, since the Netherlands were presumably allied with Britain.

*September 5-8*

## British amphibious raids on Massachusetts coast

British Major General Charles Grey inflicted great property damage at Bedford, Fair Haven, and Martha's Vineyard.

# *1778*

*September 13*

## Indian and Tory raid at German Flats (now Herkimer), New York

Joseph Brant led 300 Tories and 150 Indians in a devastating raid against a small settlement of about 70 houses. Many buildings were burned and animals captured, although only three men (one a Negro) were killed.

*September 14*

## Congress elects Benjamin Franklin Minister to France

He replaced the commission.

*September 16*

## Action at Saw Mill River (Westchester), New York

Colonel Mordecai Gist's Americans escaped a surprise envelopment by British under Lieutenant Colonels Simcoe, Tarleton, and Emmerick when the British plan failed because of misunderstood orders.

*September 28*

## "Tappan Massacre"

A British detachment under Major General Charles Grey surprised about 100 sleeping Continental troopers. In a bayonet charge they killed about 30 and captured 50. Ten of the captives were officers.

# *1778*

## *October 3*

### British commissioners' final appeal

They urged the Americans to abandon France and make peace with Britain.

## *October 6-7*

### Action at Chestnut Creek, New Jersey

British troops, landed from ships, raided this small privateering base, pillaging houses and burning sawmills and saltworks. Captain Patrick Ferguson led a contingent of raiders.

## *October 6-8*

### American raid on Indian town of Unadilla, New York

The village was destroyed by a punitive expedition under Lieutenant Colonel William Butler.

## *October 14-15*

### British raid at Mincock Island (Egg Harbor), New Jersey

Captain Patrick Ferguson led another successful surprise night attack, this time on Count Casimir Pulaski's legion (brigade of cavalry and light infantry).

## *October 28*

### USS *Hawke* versus HMS *Pigot*

Major Silas Talbot of the Continental Army, commanding the *Hawke*, captured the British vessel on the Sakonnet River without incurring any casualties. He was afterward promoted to the rank of lieutenant colonel (November 14, 1778).

# *1778*

*November 4*

### D'Estaing leaves Boston with his fleet for the West Indies

First efforts at Franco-American military cooperation had resulted only in friction and bruised feelings.

*November 11*

### Cherry Valley Massacre

Walter Butler's Tory Rangers and Joseph Brant's Indians attacked Cherry Valley, New York, and massacred 40 survivors after their surrender.

*November 19*

### Action at Spencer's Hill (Bulltown Swamp), Georgia

Americans under Colonel John Baker, on their way to harass British Lieutenant Colonel James Mark Prevost's plundering expedition on the southern frontier of Georgia, were caught in an ambuscade set by Prevost's subordinate, Lieutenant Colonel M'Girth. The Americans retreated with Baker wounded.

*November 24*

### Action at Medway Church, Georgia

A British expedition under Lieutenant Colonel Prevost skirmished with American troops under Colonel John White and burned several buildings, including the church.

# *1778*

*November 25*

## British expedition sails for Georgia

A detachment of 3,500 men under Lieutenant Colonel Archibald Campbell embarked at New York as General Sir Henry Clinton shifted British operations to the south in accordance with his directive from the King.

*November 27*

## British commissioners leave New York for England

The Carlisle peace commission had failed.

*December 10*

## John Jay elected president of Congress

*December 11*

## Washington goes into winter quarters at Middlebrook, New Jersey

Outposts maintained the blockade of New York. The New Jersey position made it possible for Washington to move rapidly south to the Delaware in case of a surprise British move against Philadelphia.

*December 12-28*

## Action in the West Indies

The British took St. Lucia, West Indies, from the French.

# *1778*

*December 17*

## Naval action off Newport, Rhode Island

Lieutenant Seth Chapin and six other Rhode Island patriots in a whaleboat captured a British vessel.

*December 17*

## British recapture Vincennes, Indiana

Lieutenant Colonel Henry Hamilton with a force of 500-800 men, half of whom were Indians, retook the town, with little opposition.

*December 21*

## Washington leaves Middlebrook for Philadelphia

The army was left under the command of General William Alexander, Lord Stirling. Washington spent six weeks in Philadelphia, conferring with Congressional leaders.

*December 25*

## Action at Young's House, New York

A band of Tories under Major Mansfield Bearmore raided the place, burning a barn, driving off livestock, capturing Joseph Young and a number of American soldiers, and accidentally killing a Tory prisoner they had sought to rescue.

*December 29*

## British capture Savannah, Georgia

Lieutenant Colonel Archibald Campbell's British forces drove General Robert Howe across the Savannah River.

# *1779*

*January 6-9*

## Actions at Fort Morris (Sunbury), Georgia

Recently promoted General Augustine Prevost assumed command of British operations in the South and began an offensive. After a light attack on January 6 by 2,000 British against 200 Continental defenders, Major Joseph Lane surrendered the fort when Prevost put his artillery into position. There were minor casualties on both sides.

*January 11*

## Lafayette sails for France

He had earlier (October 1778) requested permission to visit and consider possibilities for service there and in Canada.

*January 29*

## Action at Augusta, Georgia

Encountering little opposition, British troops under Archibald Campbell seized the town.

*February 2*

## Washington leaves Philadelphia

He rejoined the army in New Jersey, while Mrs. Washington stayed at the house of Henry Laurens.

# 1779

*February 3*

## Pennsylvania Council brings charges against General Benedict Arnold

He was charged with several abuses of his authority as commander of American forces in Philadelphia and taking financial advantage of his position. Arnold demanded a court-martial.

*February 3*

## Action at Beaufort, Port Royal Island, South Carolina

General William Moultrie, with 300 Charleston militia and 20 Continentals, repulsed a 200-man British force under Major Gardiner, sent by General Prevost to take the island.

*February 4*

## John Paul Jones takes command of USS *Bonhomme Richard* (40)

The former French merchantman *Duc de Duras* was renamed in Benjamin Franklin's honor.

*February 6*

## Colonel George Rogers Clark advances on Vincennes

He left Kaskaskia, Illinois, with 150 men to recapture the post.

*February 10*

## Action at Car's Fort, Georgia

Inconclusive skirmish between British and local militia; preliminary to Battle of Kettle Creek (see below).

# *1779*

*February 14*

## Action at Cherokee Ford, South Carolina

Inconclusive skirmish between British and local militia; preliminary to Battle of Kettle Creek later the same day.

*February 14*

## Battle of Kettle Creek, Georgia

Colonel Andrew Pickens and local militia defeated Colonel Boyd's larger loyalist brigade. This victory boosted patriot morale and prevented any serious rallying of southern Tories for some time.

*February 15*

## Congressional Committee reports on "Guidelines for Peace"

Suggested minimum demands: independence, certain minimum boundaries, complete British evacuation of U.S. territory, rights to the North Atlantic fisheries, and free navigation of the Mississippi.

*February 18*

## Celebration of anniversary of French alliance

An "elegant entertainment and display of fireworks" was staged at Pluckemin, New Jersey, by General Knox and the officers of the artillery.

*February 23-25*

## Clark takes Vincennes, Indiana

A mere show of force caused pro-British Indians to desert. Colonel Hamilton surrendered the defending garrison.

# *1779*

*February 25*

## Congress authorizes rangers to protect frontier settlements of Pennsylvania

This was to be a corps of five companies of rangers.

*February 26*

## General Israel Putnam escapes British raid at Horseneck, Connecticut

A British landing force of about 600, under General Tryon, dispersed Putnam's 150 militia and destroyed several saltworks, a small sloop, and a store, and damaged a few patriot homes. Putnam escaped by leading or riding his horse down a steep cliff.

*March 2*

## South Carolina assumes payment of $50,000 apportioned by Congress to Rhode Island

This gesture recognized the inability of Rhode Island to pay because of British occupation.

*March 3*

## Battle of Briar Creek, Georgia

British repulsed an American force under General John Ashe attempting to recapture Augusta.

*March 11*

## Congress establishes a Corps of Engineers

Existing military engineer units were to be organized within this corps.

# 1779

## March 29

### Congress recommends mobilization of 3,000 armed Negroes for defense

South Carolina and Georgia did not comply.

## April

### Actions at Chickamauga (Indian villages), Tennessee (then in North Carolina)

A force of North Carolina and Virginia troops led by Colonel Evan Shelby struck successfully at a group of Chickamauga Indians, British allies.

## April 3

### Spanish ultimatum to Britain

Spain demanded the return of Gibraltar as her price for remaining neutral in the war. Britain rejected the proposal.

## April 8

### Benedict Arnold marries Peggy Shippen

Arnold's bride was the daughter of a wealthy, conservative citizen of Philadelphia, Edward Shippen, who had been friendly with British officers during their occupation of Philadelphia, and was suspected of Tory sympathies.

## April 12

### Convention of Aranjuez

Spain concluded a secret alliance with France. Spain hoped to get Gibraltar from England.

# *1779*

*April 20*

## American raid on Onondaga Indians, New York

A force led by Colonel Gose Van Schaick destroyed an Indian village, capturing several prisoners.

*April 23*

## Lincoln advances on Augusta, Georgia

General Benjamin Lincoln moved inland with a corps of Continental troops (detached from the northern army by Washington) for an attempt against British-held Augusta.

*April 27*

## Action at Middletown, New Jersey

British under Colonel Hyde and Captain Patrick Ferguson captured an American post which had been abandoned by its occupants the night before.

*May 9*

## British raid on Norfolk, Virginia

British under Major General Edward Mathew and Commodore George Collier chased the garrison from Fort Nelson and then raided Norfolk, Portsmouth, and Gosport Navy Yard. They captured great quantities of supplies, tobacco, and ordnance, and burned over 130 coastal vessels, a frigate, and two French merchantmen.

# *1779*

*May 10*

## Beginning of Arnold's treason

General Benedict Arnold opened negotiations with British General Sir Henry Clinton in New York. Arnold was bitter because of slowness by Congress to recognize his great accomplishments of 1775-1777, and because of charges that he had abused his authority while in command of Philadelphia (1778-1779).

*May 11*

## British General Prevost advances to threaten Charleston, South Carolina

This was a counter to the move of General Lincoln against Augusta, Georgia. Lincoln returned for the relief of Charleston and Prevost withdrew.

*May 11-13*

## Action at Coosawhatchie, South Carolina

General William Moultrie's patriot force skirmished with Prevost's British troops.

*May 23*

## Benedict Arnold sends Clinton information on Washington's movements

The intelligence helped Clinton assess American plans. It also provided evidence of Arnold's "sincerity."

# *1779*

## *June 1*

### Sir Henry Clinton starts offensive up the Hudson River, New York

With 6,000 men he captured American-held forts at Stony Point (uncompleted) and Verplanck's Point, New York.

## *June 18*

### French Admiral d'Estaing captures island of St. Vincent, West Indies

This was a preliminary to a planned expedition to capture Barbados.

## *June 20*

### Battle of Stono Ferry, South Carolina

American troops under Lincoln attacked Lieutenant Colonel John Maitland's British rear guard in a poorly conceived operation. They were repulsed and suffered heavy losses.

## *June 21*

### Spain declares war against Great Britain

France had promised to help Spain recover Gibraltar and Florida after the British rejected the Spanish ultimatum of April 3. Spain made no alliance with the United States and refused to recognize U.S. independence, but began joint naval operations in cooperation with France.

# *1779*

*June 28*

## Action at Hickory Hill, Georgia

Americans under Colonel John Twiggs killed or captured an entire British force of 40 British grenadiers under Captain Muller.

*July*

## Arnold-Clinton communications

General Clinton refused to pay Benedict Arnold £10,000 for his services or to indemnify him for any losses he might suffer if detected. Relations were broken off for a time.

*July 2*

## Actions at Bedford and Poundridge, New York

Dragoons under Banastre Tarleton burned several dwellings, a tavern, and a church after ejecting a small American contingent.

*July 4*

## French Admiral d'Estaing captures island of Grenada, West Indies

Contrary winds prevented a planned operation against Barbados; the French expedition therefore moved against Grenada, which was easily captured.

*July 5-11*

## British Connecticut Coast raid

A punitive expedition led by General Tryon plundered New Haven, Connecticut, dispersed a 150-man patriot force, and then burned ships in the harbor.

# *1779*

## *July 6*

### Naval Battle of Grenada

D'Estaing's superior force got the better of British Admiral John Byron's West Indian squadron, dismasting four British ships.

## *July 7*

### USS *Argo* (12) versus HMP *Lively* (10)

After a five-hour exchange of fire, Silas Talbot, commanding the American sloop, overpowered the British privateer and took her to Boston. Several days later he captured two British merchant vessels without resistance.

## *July 8*

### British raiders plunder and burn Fairfield, Connecticut

They destroyed 83 homes, 54 barns, 47 storehouses, two churches, two schools, the jail, and the courthouse. The inhabitants had fled before the British arrived. The next day the raiders looted and burned Green's Farms, Connecticut.

## *July 11*

### British raiders pillage and burn Norwalk, Connecticut

Fifty local militia delayed Tryon's raiding force but were driven off. Some 256 buildings were destroyed and an estimated $150,000 taken in loot.

# *1779*

## *July 16*

### Battle of Stony Point, New York

General Anthony Wayne led 1,200 men in a night bayonet attack to retake the Stony Point fortification, which the British and other Americans deemed impregnable. This bold success contributed to the legend which gave him the nickname "Mad Anthony." Although the fort was later abandoned, this operation was important in ending the British threat to West Point, key American fortress on the Hudson, because the British were unwilling to risk more large garrisons ashore.

## *July 18*

### General Wayne evacuates Stony Point, New York

The British fortifications were destroyed.

## *July 19-August 24*

### Penobscot Expedition, Maine

Without consulting Continental political or military authorities, Massachusetts sent out a joint 4,600 man expedition under Commodore Dudley Saltonstall and Generals Solomon Lovell and Peleg Wadsworth to attack a British post garrisoned by a force of 800. (The post was important to the British because it protected lumbering operations that provided masts for Royal Navy vessels.) Arriving at Penobscot Bay on July 25, the expedition was a dismal fiasco. The British fleet moved against the attackers in mid-August, dispersing them hopelessly. Losses included 49 vessels and 474 American men. The British lost only 13 men and retained the fort. Several American officers involved in the operation were later court-martialed for misconduct. One of these was Colonel Paul Revere, who was acquitted.

# *1779*

## *July 22*

### Battle of Minisink, New York

Joseph Brant, with a force of Tories and Indians, overwhelmed an outnumbered militia, massacring many.

## *July 31*

### General Sullivan leads expedition from Easton, Pennsylvania, into northwestern New York

The expedition of 2,500 men was to be joined by another contingent, under General James Clinton, to operate against the hostile Indian tribes of the region, and possibly to continue on to capture Fort Niagara.

## *August 5*

### Action at Morrisania (now known as the Bronx), New York

A cavalry detachment from Brigadier General John Glover's brigade and some local militia attacked a corps of DeLancey's loyalists and took 15 prisoners.

## *August 7*

### USS *Argo* (12) versus HMP *King George*

Silas Talbot captured the Tory privateer, commanded by Stanton Hazard, off the New England coast. Later during the month the *Argo* captured HMP *Dragoon* (14), HMP *Hannah* (12), and the British merchant brig *Elliott* (6).

# *1779*

*August 11-September 14*

## Brodhead's Allegheny River expedition

Colonel Daniel Brodhead with 600 men marched from Pittsburgh up the Allegheny River valley and destroyed ten Indian villages in northern Pennsylvania. Planned coordination with Sullivan's expedition against the New York Indians, for a joint attack on Fort Niagara, failed to materialize.

*August 19*

## American raid on Paulus Hook (Jersey City), New Jersey

An isolated British outpost was successfully attacked by a force under Major "Light Horse Harry" Lee; 150 prisoners were taken.

*August 19*

## Sullivan and Clinton meet at Tioga, New York

Clinton, who had started from the Mohawk Valley, had 1,500 men. The combined force, under Sullivan, moved northwest into Indian country on August 26.

*August 26*

## First U.S. decoration awarded to a foreign national

Congress decorated Lieutenant Colonel François L. T. de Fleury for valor at Stony Point. He was the only foreigner so honored during the Revolutionary War.

# *1779*

*August 29*

## Battle of the Chemung River (Battle of Newton), New York

Generals John Sullivan and James Clinton defeated a force of 1,200 loyalists and Indians under Captain Walter Butler and Chief Joseph Brant. For the next month the expedition terrorized the Genesee River Valley, the heartland of Six Nations territory. Many Indian villages and supplies were destroyed. However, Indian activities continued against frontier settlements, and reprisals were bloody.

*September 5*

## American raid at Lloyd's Neck, Long Island, New York

Major Benjamin Tallmadge, with 150 men, captured most of the Tory garrison of 500 without losing a man.

*September 8*

## French fleet returns to U.S. coastal waters

Admiral d'Estaing arrived off the mouth of the Savannah River with a French fleet of 35 ships and 4,000 troops.

*September 10*

## Indian village of Canandaigua, New York, burned

It was destroyed by Americans under Sullivan.

*September 14*

## Revised "Guidelines for Peace" approved by Congress

The clause entailing fisheries rights was omitted.

# *1779*

## September 14

### John Paul Jones sails from Lorient, France, with allied squadron

Two American frigates—USS *Bonhomme Richard* (40) and *Alliance* (32)—and three French vessels—frigate *Pallas* (32) and sloops of war *Cerf* (18) and *Vengeance* (12)—comprised his flotilla.

## September 14

### Burning of Indian town of Genesco, New York

This village on the Genesee River was the farthest point reached during Brodhead's expedition.

## September 15

### Naval action off Savannah, Georgia

D'Estaing captured two British frigates and two supply ships in the river. He then moved against Prevost's 3,000-man garrison in Savannah in coordination with American troops under Count Pulaski. Lincoln was marching with more Americans from Charleston.

## September 16

### Allied blockade of Savannah, Georgia

Begun by about 5,000 American troops under General Benjamin Lincoln and about 5,000 French under Count d'Estaing.

# *1779*

*September 17*

## Silas Talbot changes services

Lieutenant Colonel Silas Talbot, of the Continental Army, was named captain in the Continental Navy by Congress for his remarkable exploits aboard USS *Argo* during the summer.

*September 21*

## Spanish capture of Baton Rouge, Louisiana (then in West Florida)

Don Bernardo de Galvez, Spanish governor of Louisiana, attacked and captured the British post and garrison at Baton Rouge. The British capitulation included the surrender of Natchez and other West Florida British posts on the Mississippi River.

*September 23*

## Siege operations begin against Savannah

American and French troops began systematic approaches.

*September 23*

## USS *Bonhomme Richard* (40) versus HMS *Serapis* (44)

After one of the most remarkable and sanguinary single-ship actions in history, Captain George F. Pearson of the *Serapis* struck his flag. John Paul Jones, on the verge of defeat, had stubbornly answered Pearson's hail to surrender with his famous statement, "I have not yet begun to fight!" The following day the *Bonhomme Richard* sank and Jones transferred his crew to the battered *Serapis*.

# *1779*

*September 27*

## John Jay appointed agent to Spain

His efforts to obtain recognition, an alliance, or a substantial loan were unsuccessful.

*September 27*

## John Adams named to negotiate a peace treaty with Britain

*October 3*

## John Paul Jones brings the damaged *Serapis* to Texel, Netherlands

*October 4*

## Indian ambush at Licking River, Kentucky

Half-Indian Simon Girty led the Indians in a successful, bloody ambush of patriot frontiersmen at the junction of the Licking River with the Ohio.

*October 9*

## British repulse Allied assault on Savannah

D'Estaing was wounded and Pulaski killed. Allied casualties numbered 800 to Prevost's 155.

*October 11-25*

## British evacuate Rhode Island

Clinton withdrew his garrison from Newport to permit an increased effort in the South.

# *1779*

*October 18*

## Siege of Savannah lifted by Americans and French

*October 20*

## D'Estaing's fleet withdraws from Savannah

He felt it essential to avoid the dangers of the hurricane season.

*October 22*

## New York Act for the Forfeiture and Sale of the Property of Loyalists

Governor Lord Dunmore, Governor (General) Tryon, Oliver De-Lancey and 57 others were declared public enemies by the Provincial Congress; their estates were to be confiscated.

*October 26*

## Action at Brunswick, New Jersey

Rangers and dragoons under British Lieutenant Colonel John Simcoe were attacked by Americans in inconclusive action. Simcoe was severely wounded.

*October 28*

## Board of Admiralty established by Congress

This was comparable in administrative responsibilities to the Board of War for the Army.

# *1779*

*November 7*

## Action at Jefferd's Neck, New York

Colonel Charles Armand (Charles-Armand Tuffin; a French volunteer who had taken command of Pulaski's Legion) surprised and captured Tory Major Mansfield Bearmore and five others.

*November 21*

## 3,000 British troops leave New York for Georgia

This was the first contingent of a major expedition to the South under the personal command of General Clinton.

*November 29*

## Congress issues last paper money of the war

The total amount issued from June 1775 was $241,552,780.

*December 1*

## Washington's army into winter quarters at Morristown, New Jersey

*December 23*

## Benedict Arnold's court-martial convenes

After several postponements, the court-martial Arnold had demanded finally got under way; the charges related to his Philadelphia command. (See February 3, 1779)

# *1779*

*December 26*

## British begin expedition to South Carolina

A force of 8,000 under General Clinton sailed from New York; its first objective was to capture Charleston, South Carolina.

# *1780*

*January 1*

## Mutiny of the Massachusetts Line at West Point, New York

About 100 men who had enlisted for three years at various times after January 1777 attempted to return home. They were brought back; some were punished but most were pardoned.

*January 14-15*

## American raid on Staten Island

General William Alexander (Lord Stirling) led a badly managed effort that was hampered by subzero weather. Results were poor.

*January 16*

## "The Moonlight Battle"

Admiral George Rodney's British fleet defeated the Spanish in a night operation off Gibraltar. One Spanish ship was sunk and six were captured; no British ships were lost.

*January 18*

## Action at Eastchester, New York

An American raiding party under Captain Samuel Lockwood successfully captured Tory Colonel Isaac Hatfield near DeLancey's

# *1780*

Mills. One of Hatfield's officers and his dragoons pursued the Americans to Eastchester, where they killed or captured Lockwood's entire force.

*January 25*

## British raid on Newark and Elizabeth, New Jersey

There was an inconclusive skirmish at Newark and severe damage to buildings and property at Elizabeth.

*January 26*

## Court-martial verdict on Benedict Arnold

Arnold was found guilty of minor charges of abusing his authority as commander in Philadelphia (1778-1779). The embittered Arnold determined to press ahead with his treasonable activities. (See May 10, 1779, and July 1779.)

*February 1*

## Clinton's expedition arrives off Charleston, South Carolina

His arrival followed a rough 38-day voyage from New York.

*February 3*

## Action at Young's House (Four Corners), New York

Americans under Lieutenant Colonel Joseph Thompson were attacked and defeated by a larger British force.

# *1780*

*February 11*

## Clinton's expedition lands on John's Island, near Charleston

Preparations were at once begun for an advance against the city. General Lincoln began to prepare for defense.

*February 19*

## New York cedes claims to western lands to United States

The transfer was carried out March 11.

*February 28*

## Russia proclaims armed neutrality

Russia was soon joined by Sweden (August 1) and Denmark (July 9) in an anti-British defensive treaty for the protection of neutral shipping. The agreement was later subscribed to by the Netherlands, Prussia, Portugal, and Austria.

*March 1*

## Pennsylvania legislature provides for gradual emancipation of slaves

*March 8*

## Action at Salkahatchie, South Carolina

All members of an American force under Lieutenant James Ladson were killed or captured by troops of British General James Paterson.

# *1780*

## *March 14*

### Spanish capture Mobile, British West Florida

Louisiana Governor Bernardo de Galvez, with a small force supported by a single armed vessel, overpowered the 300 men garrisoning the post.

## *March 18*

### "Forty to One" Act passed by Congress

Continental bills would be redeemed at one-fortieth of face value.

## *March 23*

### Action at Pon Pon, South Carolina

Cavalry forces under Colonel William Washington and British Colonel Banastre Tarleton clashed inconclusively. Tarleton's Tories captured four Americans and killed ten.

## *March 27*

### Action at Rentowl, South Carolina

Forces under Colonel Washington and Tarleton clashed again. Washington took seven prisoners.

## *March 29*

### British approach Charleston

General Clinton's forces crossed the Ashley River and approached the city, which was now virtually blockaded.

# *1780*

*April 2*

## Indian raid at Harpersfield, New York

The small settlement was destroyed by Tories and Indians under Joseph Brant. Most of the inhabitants had left; several were killed or captured.

*April 3*

## De Kalb ordered to march to the relief of Charleston

Washington placed the small Maryland and Delaware Continental division under his command.

*April 3*

## Action at Rheimensnyder's Bush, New York

A party of 60 Tories and Indians burned the small settlement, a few miles north of Little Falls, and took 19 prisoners. The other inhabitants safely fled to a blockhouse nearby.

*April 6*

## Washington reprimands Arnold officially

This was as a result of the court-martial verdict of January 26, and Washington, a great admirer of Arnold, had no choice. But Arnold was further embittered.

*April 9*

## Action at Little Maquoketa River, Iowa

British and Indians attacked American, French, and Spanish traders near present-day Dubuque and took several prisoners.

# *1780*

## *April 11-May 12*

### Siege of Charleston

General Clinton completed the investment of the town with 14,000 troops. Admiral Marriot Arbuthnot's squadron bombarded the town from the harbor. A precarious water-and-swamp route for messages still remained open through Monck's Corner.

## *April 14*

### Action at Monck's Corner (Monks Corner; Biggins' Bridge), South Carolina

Tarleton's Legion surprised and destroyed an American outpost, completely cutting off Charleston. (Another source gives April 13.)

## *April 15*

### Action at New Bridge, New Jersey

American Lieutenant Samuel Bryson was forced to surrender the outpost after a gallant defense.

## *April 16*

### Action at Paramus, New Jersey

Major Thomas Langhorne Byles surrendered his Continental troops after putting up a stubborn defense against an enemy attack. Byles was mortally wounded after his surrender.

## *April 19*

### Foreign dignitaries visit Washington's headquarters

Chevalier de la Luzerne, Minister of France, and Don Juan de Miralles, Spanish grandee, were visitors. A parade was given on

# *1780*

April 24 for Luzerne, who left for Philadelphia the next day. Miralles, ill, remained at Morristown.

## *April 24*

### American sortie at Charleston, South Carolina

Lieutenant Colonel Henderson led 200 Virginians and North Carolinians in a sortie that overran the first line of works of the British but was repulsed at the second.

## *April 28*

### Congressional committee visits headquarters at Morristown

Philip Schuyler, John Mathews, and Nathaniel Peabody comprised the delegation.

## *April 29*

### Funeral of Don Juan de Miralles at Morristown

He had died April 28. His funeral was attended by Washington and the Congressional committee.

## *April 29*

### Lafayette returns from France

He landed at Boston after an absence of a year.

## *May 2*

### French expedition sails for the United States

The Comte de Rochambeau commanded a force of nearly 6,000 troops.

# *1780*

## *May 6*

### Action at Lanneau's (Lenud's) Ferry, South Carolina

Tarleton's Legion surprised and defeated Colonels Anthony White's and Abraham Buford's American force, which had been marching from Virginia and North Carolina in response to Lincoln's call for reinforcements.

## *May 7*

### Surrender of Fort Moultrie, South Carolina

The stronghold surrendered to the British without a fight. Although most of the garrison escaped, 200 were taken prisoner. The British completed the occupation of Sullivan's Island the next day.

## *May 10*

### Lafayette arrives at Morristown

He brought news that King Louis XVI was sending more ships and men.

## *May 11*

### Washington honored by France

Lafayette presented him with appointments as lieutenant general in France's Army and vice admiral in its Navy.

## *May 12*

### Surrender of Charleston to the British

General Lincoln and about 2,500 Continental soldiers were taken prisoner. The British released an equal number of militia on parole.

# *1780*

Large amounts of cannon, small arms, and ammunition were also taken. This was the greatest British victory and the worst American disaster of the war.

*May 22*

### Tory and Indian raid at Caughnawaga, New York

Joseph Brant led attackers in burning the settlement to the ground.

*May 22-23*

### Tory and Indian raid at Johnstown, New York

Sir John Johnson led attackers in burning the settlement, which had been his ancestral home.

*May 25*

### Mutiny of the Connecticut Line at Morristown, New Jersey

Two regiments paraded under arms to demand a full ration (which had been cut down to one-eighth) and immediate payment of their salaries (five months in arrears). The movement was suppressed by Pennsylvania troops.

*May 26*

### Spanish repulse British expedition at St. Louis, Missouri

Captain Don Fernando de Leyba's forces repulsed Lieutenant Governor Patrick Sinclair's troops.

# *1780*

*May 29*

## Massacre of the Waxhaws, Waxhaws Creek, South Carolina

A force of Tarleton's Legion destroyed a Virginia Continental regiment under Colonel Abraham Buford. Tarleton's troops were outnumbered two to one, but were aided by surprise.

*May 29*

## Action near Winnsboro, South Carolina

A loyalist group was defeated and dispersed by patriot irregulars, offsetting the effects of the Waxhaws Massacre, and marking the beginning of effective patriot resurgence in the Carolinas.

*June*

## Mutiny of the First New York Regiment

Some 31 deserters from Fort Stanwix, believed to be headed for the enemy camp, were caught; 13 were shot.

*June 1*

## USS *Trumbull* (28) versus HMP *Watt* (34)

The two vessels engaged in an indecisive, bitterly contested naval action 200 miles north of Bermuda.

*June 5*

## Sir Henry Clinton leaves South Carolina for New York

He took about one-third of his troops, leaving Cornwallis with about 8,345 to complete conquest of the south. This was considered an easy task because of the intimidation caused by the capture of Charleston and the Waxhaws Massacre.

# *1780*

*June 6-24*

## British raid into New Jersey

German General Wilhelm von Knyphausen led a force of over 5,000 men on an extended raid across the Hudson.

*June 6*

## Action at Elizabeth, New Jersey

American outposts and advance guard units of General Knyphausen's raiding force skirmished.

*June 7*

## Massachusetts state constitution ratified by popular vote

It was the first American constitution to be prepared by a convention specifically called for that purpose. Its Bill of Rights, containing the phrase "all men are born free and equal," was understood to forbid slavery.

*June 7-8*

## Action at Connecticut Farms (Union), New Jersey

Continentals and militia repulsed Knyphausen's raiding force, although some 30 buildings were burned by the invaders.

*June 9*

## MSS *Protector* (26) versus HMP *Admiral Duff* (32)

Captain John Foster Williams's frigate *Protector*, of the Massachusetts navy, sank the British privateer, under Captain Richard Stranger, off the Newfoundland coast.

# 1780

*June 13*

## Gates commissioned by Congress to lead Southern Army

This was done without consulting Washington, who favored Greene. Gates was provided with Continentals from Washington's command. His status as co-equal with Washington was ambiguous, in a partial success by Washington's Congressional detractors.

*June 13*

## American Daughters of Liberty established

Philadelphia women organized to provide clothing for suffering soldiers.

*June 20*

## Action at Ramsour's Mills, North Carolina

One of a series of skirmishes between bands of patriots and loyalists. Colonel John Moore led a band of inexperienced, unorganized loyalists in an unauthorized, abortive skirmish with patriot militia. Cornwallis threatened to court-martial Moore for his violation of instructions.

*June 23*

## Battle of Springfield, New Jersey

General Nathanael Greene checked Knyphausen in an indecisive action between approximately equal forces, ending the British raid in New Jersey.

# *1780*

## *July 9*

### Denmark joins the "League of Armed Neutrality" (see February 28, 1780)

## *July 10*

### Comte de Rochambeau and 6,000 French troops arrive at Newport, Rhode Island

The fleet and troops were blockaded there by a British fleet for a year.

## *July 12*

### Civil war begins in the Carolinas

The widespread actions of this date marked the beginning of a protracted, bloody civil war between patriot militia and Tories.

## *July 12*

### Action at Williamson's Plantation (Brattenville), South Carolina

About 90 patriot rebels under Captain Edward Lacey, Jr., Colonel William Hile, and Colonel Thomas Neal defeated about 115 Tories under Captain Christian Huck in a surprise dawn attack. Some 30-40 Tories, including Huck, were killed and 50 wounded. One patriot was killed.

## *July 12*

### Actions at Brandon's Camp and Stallins, South Carolina

Colonel Thomas Brandon's forces were routed from their camp, but later defeated a Tory party at Stallins.

# 1780

## July 12

### Culmination of Arnold's treason

Arnold wrote to Major John André, Clinton's adjutant, expressing his desire for a conference to plan the "disposal" of West Point.

## July 13

### Action at Cedar Springs, South Carolina, and Cherokee Town, South Carolina

Colonel John Thomas, Jr., and his men killed several British and routed the rest at Cedar Springs, after Thomas had been warned by his mother of an impending dawn attack by a superior force under Major Patrick Ferguson.

## July 14

### Action at Pacolett River, North Carolina

A party of Georgia patriots surprised and defeated a band of Tories.

## July 15-16

### Action at McDonnell's (McDowell's) Camp, South Carolina

Captain John Hampton's 52-man American force was badly beaten by loyalist Colonel Alexander Innis's force of 300.

## July 19

### Action at Tom's River (Bergen), New Jersey

General Anthony Wayne was forced to withdraw after an unsuccessful, costly attempt to overwhelm the British stronghold.

# *1780*

*July 20*

## Action at Flat Rock, South Carolina

Americans under Colonel William R. Davie were successful against loyalist Major John Carden's superior force.

*July 21*

## Action at Bull's Ferry, New Jersey

General Wayne with two Pennsylvania brigades attacked a loyalist blockhouse but failed to capture it.

*July 25*

## Gates takes command of Southern Army at Coxe's Mill, North Carolina

De Kalb turned the command over to Gates but remained with the Southern Army at the head of his division. Gates then had a half-starved force of 1,200 Continental regulars (de Kalb's troops), and an unknown number of militia (probably more than 1,500).

*July 27*

## Gates advances south

Gates moved toward Camden, South Carolina, hoping to attract militia recruits and to capture supplies for his hungry men.

*July 30*

## Capture of Fort Anderson (Thickety Fort), South Carolina

Colonel Isaac Shelby captured the loyalist post without firing a shot.

# *1780*

*July 30*

## Action at Rocky Mount, South Carolina

Thomas Sumter positioned his 600 patriot militia for attack against the Tory-held site. Preliminary to the Battle of Rocky Mount. (See August 1.)

*August*

## Clark defeats Shawnees

Kentuckians under George Rogers Clark destroyed the Shawnee towns of Chillicothe and Piqua.

*August 1*

## Sweden joins the "League of Armed Neutrality." (See February 28, 1780.)

*August 1*

## Battle of Rocky Mount, South Carolina

Tories and South Carolinia militia under Sumter engaged in indecisive action. After almost gaining the surrender of Lieutenant Colonel George Turnbull's command, Sumter was forced to retreat.

*August 1*

## Action at Green Springs, South Carolina

Major Dunlap with 60 Tory dragoons and 150 mounted riflemen was surprised to find Colonel Elijah Clarke's encampment of 186 men ready and waiting for his planned surprise attack at dawn. The Tories were routed, suffering heavy casualties.

## *1780*

*August 1*

### Action at Hunt's Bluff, South Carolina

Americans led by James Gillespie and Major Tristram Thomas captured an entire British-Tory force under Colonel William Henry Mills.

*August 2*

### Indian and Tory raid on Fort Plain, New York

First of a series of raids by Joseph Brant pillaging and burning the Canajoharie settlements in the Mohawk Valley.

*August 3*

### Gates's army crosses Peedee River

The crossing was made at Mask's Ferry, South Carolina.

*August 3*

### Arnold receives orders from Washington to take command of West Point

Arnold had sought the post so that he could turn it over to the British for £20,000 and the rank of major general in the British Army. If he failed in his effort to deliver the fort, he would be a brigadier general.

*August 5*

### Congress accepts General Greene's resignation as quartermaster general

He served until the arrival of his successor, Timothy Pickering, September 20. Greene resigned because of his desire for active field

# *1780*

command, and because of attacks on his integrity during his service as quartermaster general.

## *August 6*

### Battle of Hanging Rock, South Carolina

Major William Richardson Davie, with 80 patriots, attacked and defeated 500 loyalists in a sharp engagement.

## *August 8*

### Actions at Wofford's Iron Works (Cedar Springs), South Carolina

Militia under Elijah Clarke and Isaac Shelby skirmished twice inconclusively with a Tory force at least twice their size, under British Major Ferguson.

## *August 9*

### Action on Little Miami River, Ohio

Colonel George Rogers Clark defeated British-supported Ohio Indians and destroyed their settlement.

## *August 15*

### Action at Fort Carey (Wateree Ferry), South Carolina

An American force under Colonel Thomas Taylor surprised and captured British troops, under Colonel Carey, and many supply wagons.

# *1780*

## *August 15*

### Action at Port's Ferry, South Carolina

Militia General Francis Marion and a band of 250 patriots routed a party of Tories under Major Micajah Gainey, with a loss of only two wounded. Tory losses are unknown.

## *August 15-16*

### Action at Gum Swamp, South Carolina

This was a midnight skirmish of advance guards of Cornwallis's and Gates's armies, preliminary to the battle of Camden.

## *August 16*

### Battle of Camden, South Carolina

Gates and his army of 3,000, after proceeding on a night march against the advice of de Kalb, were overwhelmed by Cornwallis's force of 2,400 men. The patriot militia fragmented when attacked by British regulars, permitting Tarleton's cavalry to charge de Kalb's Continentals from the rear. American losses were nearly 900 killed, including de Kalb, and 1,000 captured, after a gallant struggle. Gates fled the battlefield when the militia broke, leaving de Kalb and his Continentals to continue the hopeless fight.

## *August 18*

### Battle of Fishing Creek, South Carolina

British troops under Tarleton defeated Thomas Sumter. This action, combined with the Battle of Camden, culminated British and Tory efforts to undermine the Revolutionary cause in the Carolinas and opened the way for a British invasion of North Carolina.

# *1780*

*August 18*

## Action at Musgrove's Mills, South Carolina

A loyalist attack was repulsed by militia under Elijah Clarke and Isaac Shelby.

*August 20*

## Action at Great Savannah (Nelson's Ferry), South Carolina

General Francis Marion surprised and routed a combined force of British and loyalists.

*August 26*

## First specie requisition by Congress upon the states

This was for $3,000,000; by March 16, 1781, three specie requisitions totaled $10,642,988.

*August 27*

## Action at Kingstree, South Carolina

Marion and a band of 150 patriots clashed indecisively with Major James Wemyss's force of 300 British and Tories.

*September 1*

## John Hancock elected first governor of the State of Massachusetts

# *1780*

*September 3*

## Henry Laurens captured

Commissioner Henry Laurens, on a diplomatic mission to Holland, was captured aboard the packet *Mercury* off Newfoundland by the British frigate HMS *Vestal*.

*September 4*

## Action at Blue Savannah, South Carolina

Marion routed 200 Tory militia under Captain Jesse Barefield.

*September 8*

## British invasion of North Carolina begins

Encouraged by victories at Camden and Fishing Creek, Cornwallis believed that conquest of North Carolina would be relatively easy, and that it would cut off support for the patriot partisans in South Carolina.

*September 12*

## Action at Cane Creek, North Carolina

Inconclusive skirmish between local militia and Tory troops led by Major Patrick Ferguson.

*September 14-18*

## Actions at Forts Grierson and Cornwallis (Augusta), Georgia

Troops under Colonel Elijah Clarke captured the forts but were repulsed at the Tory stronghold (White House) at Augusta.

# 1780

*September 20-24*

## Washington-Rochambeau Conference at Hartford, Connecticut

Plans were prepared for a joint operation against New York in 1781.

*September 21*

## Action at Wahab's Plantation, North Carolina

American partisans, led by Colonel William Davie, routed a British force.

*September 21*

## Arnold meets Major John André near Haverstraw, New York

He delivered plans of West Point and informed the British officer of the fort's weak points.

*September 23*

## André's capture

He was apprehended in civilian dress by three militiamen near Tarrytown, New York. Incriminating papers were discovered with him.

*September 25*

## Arnold flees

Learning of André's capture, Arnold fled to HMS *Vulture*, a British warship in the Hudson. When he arrived in New York, Clinton appointed Arnold a British brigadier general, under the terms of their agreement.

# *1780*

*September 25*

## Militia gathering at Sycamore Shoals, Tennessee

Mountain militiamen gathered on the Watauga River, near present Elizabethtown, to discuss mass opposition to the growing British-Tory threat. The gathering was preliminary to the Battle of Kings Mountain, South Carolina.

*September 26*

## Action at Charlotte, North Carolina

General Cornwallis's advance guard was engaged in a brief delaying action by American cavalry under Colonel William Davie. Pushing aside the Americans, the British occupied Charlotte.

*September 29*

## Action at Black Mingo Creek, South Carolina

Marion's force overran a Tory outpost under Colonel John C. Ball.

*September 29*

## André convicted as a spy

The court included Generals Greene (presiding), Alexander (Stirling), Lafayette, von Steuben, St. Clair, and Robert Howe.

*October 2*

## Major André hanged as spy at Tappan, New York

His courageous and calm demeanor was admired by the Americans.

# *1780*

## October 3

### Reorganization of the Continental Army

Congress reduced the authorized strength to 58 regiments (45 infantry, four artillery, four cavalry, one artificer). The resolution provided for other organizational changes, and for state contributions to the support of the Army.

## October 5

### United States accepts armed neutrality agreement between Russia, Denmark and Sweden

The dominant principle was "free ships make free goods."

## October 7

### Battle of Kings Mountain, South Carolina

An entire loyalist force of 1,100 under Major Patrick Ferguson was killed, wounded, or captured by 1,400 frontiersmen under Colonel William Campbell, assisted by Colonel Isaac Shelby and other militia commanders. All participants in the battle were Americans except Ferguson. This disaster was an important factor in Cornwallis's decision to abandon his invasion of North Carolina.

## October 10

### Resolution of Congress urges states to cede their western lands to the Union

Such lands would be settled and admitted as states. Connecticut complied immediately.

# *1780*

*October 11*

### Action at Fort George (Fort William Henry), New York

Tories recaptured the fort and held it briefly.

*October 14*

### Cornwallis withdraws into South Carolina

He established winter quarters at Winnsboro.

*October 15*

### Action at Middleburg (Middle Fort), New York

A force of 1,000 British, Tories, Indians, and Hessians under Joseph Brant and Sir John Johnson made a feeble, unsuccessful attack on Middle Fort. Although the fort was garrisoned by only 200 Continentals under Major Melancthon Lloyd Woolsey, was low in ammunition, and probably would not have withstood another attack, Brant and Johnson withdrew toward Schoharie, burning all of the houses and barns in the village, as well as a church, as they left.

*October 17*

### British, Tory, and Indian raid on Schoharie, New York

Sir John Johnson led the raiders in an attack which left the valley in flames.

*October 19*

### Battle at Fort Keyser (Palatine, or Stone Arabia), New York

Colonel John Brown was killed and his militia routed when he attempted an attack against Sir John Johnson's force ten times the size of his own. He had acted on the assurance that General Robert

# *1780*

Van Rensselaer's forces would arrive to strike the enemy's rear, which they did not.

*October 19*

## Battle of Klock's Field, New York

New York militia, under General Robert Van Rensselaer, pursuing Johnson's raiders, were ambushed by Johnson near Fort Plain. The militia successfully repulsed the attack but missed an opportunity to inflict what might have been a decisive defeat on the raiders when Van Rensselaer refused to authorize a counterattack.

*October 21*

## Congress resolves to provide army officers life pensions

*October 22*

## Congress issues instructions to Nathanael Greene, new commander of the Southern Department

General Greene had been nominated by Washington for the post. His subordination to Washington was unequivocal, Congress being remorseful about its earlier trust in General Gates.

*October 23*

## Action at Kanassoraga, New York

The settlement was raided by Johnson's marauders.

*October 26*

## Action at Black River (Tearcoat Swamp), South Carolina

Marion surprised and routed Tories in a midnight attack.

# *1780*

*October 29*

## Action at German Flats, New York

Militia forces skirmished with Johnson raiders.

*November 4*

## Congress asks states for war support quotas

These were to be provided in flour, hay, and pork.

*November 9*

## Action at Fishdam Ford (Broad River), South Carolina

British Major James Wemyss with 250 men failed in a night effort to capture General Thomas Sumter, whose 550 men drove off the attackers.

*November 15-16*

## Action at Georgetown, South Carolina

General Francis Marion attacked the Tory garrison, but was forced to withdraw after two days of inconclusive fighting because of ammunition shortage.

*November 20*

## Battle of Blackstocks (Tiger River), South Carolina

Sumter had the best of Tarleton in a hard-fought engagement.

# *1780*

*November 21-23*

## American raid on Coram (Smith Point; Fort George), Long Island, New York

Major Benjamin Tallmadge led 300 Continentals from Connecticut, captured the fort without resistance, and burned 300 tons of hay, with the loss of only one man wounded. Tallmadge was later honored by Congress for this brilliantly executed operation (December 6).

*November 30*

## Creation of Lee's Legion

Major "Light Horse Harry" Lee was promoted to lieutenant colonel and his corps of three mounted troops expanded by three companies of select infantry. His legion was one of the best equipped and best disciplined units of the Continental Army.

*December 2*

## Greene assumes command of the Southern Department

The formal transfer from Gates was at Charlotte, North Carolina. The Southern Army was barely 1,600 men strong.

*December 4*

## Action at Rugeley's Mill (or Mills), South Carolina

Colonel William Washington and his Continental dragoons gained the surrender of a loyalist force by ruse. They used the "Quaker gun trick" of making a fake cannon and threatening to annihilate the garrison if it did not surrender.

# *1780*

*December 11*

## Action at Long Cane, South Carolina

Americans under Elijah Clarke skirmished with forces under Lieutenant Colonel Isaac Allen.

*December 12-13*

## Action at Halfway Swamp, Singleton's, South Carolina

Marion's partisans and British regulars engaged in inconclusive skirmishing.

*December 18*

## Congress appoints Francis Dana minister to Russia

*December 19*

## Greene advances into South Carolina

He decided to move south with part of his army, 1,000 men, to threaten Cornwallis, who was at Winnsboro. Greene ordered Brigadier General Daniel Morgan to take the remainder of the army west of the Broad River, to rally local militia, to confuse the British, and to threaten their western outposts.

*December 20*

## Morgan leaves Charlotte for western South Carolina

He had about 600 men, and hoped to recruit more on the way.

# *1780*

*December 21*

## Great Britain declares war on the Netherlands

This was a response to the December 16 Dutch declaration of association with the "League of Armed Neutrality" (see February 28, 1780).

*December 27-31*

## American raid at Williamson's Plantation, South Carolina

Colonel William Washington and his dragoons (part of Morgan's command) routed Tories. This action (also known as Hammond's Store Raid) delayed Cornwallis's winter offensive into North Carolina and reduced his hopes for an effective Tory militia in the area.

*December 30*

## Benedict Arnold arrives at Hampton Roads with British expedition to Virginia

He had been commissioned a brigadier general in the British Army, in accordance with a secret agreement with Clinton at the outset of his treason.

# *1781*

*January 1-10*

## Mutiny of the Pennsylvania Line

About 2,000 troops (six regiments) at Morristown, New Jersey, seized arms and artillery, wounded several officers who attempted to stop them, and were led by their sergeants on a march to Philadelphia to demand back pay from Congress. They camped at

# *1781*

Princeton (January 3), where they were met by a Congressional Committee (January 7). They were granted concessions which ended the mutiny (January 10), although more than half of the troops left the service.

*January 2*

## Virginia conditionally cedes to the Union its claims to western lands north of the Ohio

The conditions were not acceptable to Congress and were rejected (September 13, 1783). A revised offer was made (October 20, 1783) and accepted on March 1, 1784.

*January 3*

## Action at Hood's Point (James River), Virginia

Americans retreated after a few artillery rounds against Arnold's advance guard.

*January 5-7*

## British raid on Richmond, Virginia

Arnold's British troops plundered and burned a number of buildings in the town after Governor Thomas Jefferson refused to allow British vessels to sail up and confiscate tobacco from warehouses.

# *1781*

*January 8*

## British raid on Charles City Court House, Virginia

A reconnaissance force under Lieutenant Colonel John Simcoe surprised and dispersed patriot militia under Colonel (Ambrose?) Dudley.

*January 17*

## Battle of the Cowpens, South Carolina

Brigadier General Daniel Morgan, with a force of about 1,000, skillfully defeated Tarleton's 1,100 in what has been described as "one of the most brilliant tactical operations ever fought on American soil." Tarleton lost 110 killed and 830 captured, to Morgan's 12 killed and 61 wounded, in Morgan's double envelopment. Realizing the British reaction would be prompt and violent, Morgan hastened eastward to join Greene.

*January 19*

## Cornwallis advances north to get between Greene's and Morgan's armies

Upon receipt of news of Tarleton's defeat, Cornwallis realized that Morgan and Greene were separated, and he rushed to seize the opportunity to destroy them piecemeal. Greene at once retreated, sending word to Morgan to join him.

*January 19*

## Action in Georgetown County, South Carolina

British Captain James De Peyster was captured by American Colonel James Postell.

# *1781*

## *January 20*

### Mutiny of the New Jersey Line at Pompton, New Jersey

It was soon quelled by General Robert Howe. Two mutineers were executed.

## *January 22*

### American raid at Morrisania, New York

Continentals, under Lieutenant Colonel William Hull, destroyed military buildings and supplies. (Thirty-one years later this same officer surrendered Detroit to the British without a struggle.)

## *January 24*

### Action at Georgetown, South Carolina

Troops under "Light Horse Harry" Lee and Francis Marion harassed a Tory stronghold.

## *January 30*

### Morgan and Greene join forces at the Catawba River

Greene decided to continue the retreat northward to escape Cornwallis.

## *February 1*

### Battle of the Catawba River (Cowan's Ford), North Carolina

British under Cornwallis overwhelmed Greene's rear guard, under General William L. Davidson, in a surprise river crossing. Davidson was killed in the action and Cornwallis's horse shot out from under him, although he emerged unscathed. The British pursuit continued.

# *1781*

### *February 1*

## British occupy Wilmington, North Carolina

British regulars under Major James Craig took the town with little opposition and began a long stay, through November 1781.

### *February 1*

## Action at Torrence's (Tarrant's) Tavern, North Carolina

Tarleton's dragoons routed local militia and just missed capturing General Greene in the ensuing pursuit.

### *February 3*

## Rodney's British fleet takes Dutch island of St. Eustatius, West Indies

Unaware that war had broken out between Great Britain and the Netherlands, the small garrison yielded with little or no resistance. £3,000,000 worth of booty and several blockade runners, loading for the United States, were captured.

### *February 6*

## Department of Finance established by Congress

It was placed under a superintendent responsible to Congress.

### *February 6*

## Action at Shallow Ford, North Carolina

A skirmish during the race to the Dan River, Virginia.

# *1781*

*February 9*

## Cornwallis enters Salem, North Carolina

The British general abandoned his baggage to permit a more rapid pursuit of Greene.

*February 10*

## Greene's army leaves Guilford, North Carolina

Greene sent a light corps under Otho Williams as a decoy to lure Cornwallis from his route. Morgan, suffering from rheumatism and other maladies to the extent of not being able to sit astride his horse, was granted a leave of absence and sent to his home in Virginia in a litter.

*February 12*

## Action at Bruce's Cross Roads, North Carolina

Lee's Legion skirmished in a delaying action with Cornwallis's advance elements.

*February 14*

## Greene crosses the Dan River to escape Cornwallis

Williams's diversionary movement had been successful; Greene had sent orders ahead to have boats waiting when his army arrived. Lacking boats and an engineer train, and having pushed his men and horses to the limit of their endurance, Cornwallis was forced to halt his pursuit and withdraw (February 17).

# *1781*

*February 17*

## Spanish seize St. Joseph, Michigan

Don Eugenio Poure commanded the expedition. This provided a basis for a Spanish claim to the Illinois country at the end of the war, even though the Spanish troops withdrew ten days after seizing the post.

*February 18*

## Lee's Legion crosses Dan River, back into North Carolina

Lee was accompanied by two companies of Maryland Continentals and followed by Colonel Otho Williams's infantry in two days. This was part of Greene's strategy to keep pressure on Cornwallis. Within a few days, Greene moved back across the Dan with the rest of his army.

*February 20*

## Robert Morris chosen Superintendent of Finance by Congress

He took office May 14.

*February 25*

## Battle of Haw River (Pyle's Defeat), North Carolina

By a ruse, Lee's Legion overwhelmed a force under loyalist Colonel John Pyle to prevent Pyle from marching to join the British at Hillsboro. Lee executed the operation without losing a man. Some 90 loyalists were killed and most of the survivors wounded.

*February 27*

## Action at Wright's Bluff, South Carolina

Skirmish between loyalist forces and local militia.

# *1781*

*February 27*

## Articles of Confederation signed by Maryland

Maryland was the last state to approve. Congress named March 1 as the day for formal ratification.

*March 1*

## New York's deed of cession of western lands presented in Congress

This was the first cession of claimed western lands by any of the states with such claims. Virginia, Massachusetts, Connecticut, the Carolinas, and Georgia had agreed to follow this example, encouraging Maryland to ratify the Articles of Confederation (see February 27, above).

*March 1*

## Ratification of Articles of Confederation

The Articles became effective when ratified by delegates of the states.

*March 2*

## The United States in Congress Assembled

Congress assumed a new title. The President of the old Continental Congress, Samuel Huntington, continued in office.

*March 2*

## Action at Clapp's Mill, North Carolina

Skirmish between Lee's and Tarleton's legions.

# *1781*

## March 6

## Action at Wiboo Swamp, South Carolina

Loyalists were routed after a brisk exchange of fire and the loss of several men in an attack by a force of Marion's militia.

## March 6

## Action at Wetzell's (or Whitsall's) Mills, North Carolina

This skirmish resulted from an American advance under Colonel Otho Williams against Cornwallis's outpost. Cornwallis moved to draw Greene into a general engagement. This maneuver failed and Cornwallis withdrew. Casualties were nearly equal—some 50 lost on each side.

## March 12

## Madison urges stronger federal authority over states in a committee report to congress

He advised that Congress be authorized to compel states by force to fulfill their federal obligations.

## March 15

## Battle of Guilford Courthouse, North Carolina

Cornwallis, with about 2,000 men, against Greene's 4,300, attacked and defeated the Americans—part Continental, part militia—in a gallant but costly battle. Greene retreated, but Cornwallis bore the most scars. He lost 93 killed and 439 wounded, to Greene's 78 killed and 183 wounded. These heavy losses forced the British to retreat to the base at Wilmington (March 18).

# *1781*

## March 16

### First Naval Battle of the Virginia Capes

A French naval force under Commodore Sochet Destouches returned to Newport, Rhode Island, after getting the better of British Admiral Arbuthnot in an evenly matched action off the entrance to the Chesapeake Bay. Destouches had been on a mission to Virginia to catch Benedict Arnold.

## March 21

### Action at Beattie's Mill, South Carolina

General Pickens detached Colonels Elijah Clarke and McCall to harass a British party under Major Dunlap on a foraging expedition from Ninety-Six. Dunlap surrendered after 34 of his men were killed and others wounded, himself included. There is conflicting evidence as to whether Dunlap died of his wound or was murdered after his capture.

## March 26

### Arrival of British Major General William Phillips in Virginia

He reached Portsmouth with 2,000 reinforcements, superseding Arnold in command of British forces in Virginia.

## April

### Action at Wiggins' Hill, Georgia

American Colonel William Harden was forced to retreat after his surprise attack on Colonel Thomas Brown's encampment was repulsed.

# *1781*

## *April 2*

### USS *Alliance* (32) versus HMP *Mars* (22) and HMP *Minerva* (10)

American Captain John Barry was attacked by two British privateers but got the better of them in the ensuing action, forcing them to surrender.

## *April 7*

### Action at Four Holes, South Carolina

Colonel William Harden captured British Captain Barton and 25 of his men. Another source gives April 15 as the date of this action.

## *April 12*

### Action at Fort Balfour, South Carolina

Americans under Colonel Harden captured this redoubt and its garrison.

## *April 15-23*

### Siege of Fort Watson, South Carolina

General Francis Marion and "Light Horse Harry" Lee captured the British stronghold without siege artillery. They seized the fort's water supply and built a high "Maham" tower—named after Colonel Hezekiah (or Hezediah) Maham, who suggested it—from which they were able to fire into the stockade.

# *1781*

*April 16*

## Naval Battle of Porto Praya

On his way to the Cape of Good Hope to protect that Dutch colony from Britain, French Admiral Pierre André de Suffren with five ships of the line encountered five ships of the line and 35 transports, en route to attack the Cape of Good Hope, under British Commodore George Johnstone, anchored in the Cape Verde Islands. Disregarding neutrality, Suffren attacked and bested the British flotilla, causing it to abandon its expedition to the Cape.

*April 16–June 5*

## Siege of Augusta, Georgia

American militia under General Andrew Pickens and Colonel Elijah Clarke surrounded and besieged the Tory stronghold, commanded by Colonel Thomas Brown. The arrival of a strong force of Continentals and militia under "Light Horse Harry" Lee resulted in a more energetic prosecution of the siege (May 23), leading to the capture of major outworks and Brown's surrender (June 5). This was part of Greene's strategy to weaken the British position in the south.

*April 25*

## Battle of Hobkirk's Hill, South Carolina

Greene was repulsed by British troops under Lord Francis Rawdon, because of poor tactics and panic in the American ranks. Losses were about equal on both sides. As Greene made preparations to renew his attack, the British withdrew toward Camden.

*April 25*

## Action at Camden, South Carolina

Colonel William Washington successfully ambushed British cavalry pursuing Americans after Hobkirk's Hill.

# *1781*

*April 25*

## Cornwallis leaves Wilmington with 1,500 men and marches northward into Virginia

While this left North Carolina to patriot control, Cornwallis expected to be able to reconquer Virginia after joining British forces already there.

*April 25*

## Action at Petersburg, Virginia

British troops, under Generals William Phillips and Benedict Arnold, destroyed tobacco and supplies after skirmishing with Virginia militia.

*April 27*

## British raid Osborne's (James River), Virginia

Benedict Arnold, marching from Petersburg, captured or destroyed vessels and much tobacco.

*April 29*

## Lafayette and 1,200 Continentals reach Richmond

Washington had sent him to establish a nucleus around which Virginia militia would be able to rally in opposition to the serious British threat posed by the force of Phillips and Arnold.

*May 9*

## Spanish under Galvez capture Pensacola

This completed the Spanish conquest of West Florida.

# *1781*

## *May 10*

### British evacuate Camden, South Carolina

Lord Rawdon withdrew toward Charleston, as Greene was preparing to attack again.

## *May 10*

### British occupy Petersburg, Virginia

Phillips and Arnold waited for the arrival of Cornwallis. Phillips died shortly thereafter, leaving Arnold again in command.

## *May 11*

### Capture of Orangeburg, South Carolina

Lee and Marion forced the surrender of a British and Tory garrison.

## *May 12*

### Capture of Fort Motte, South Carolina

Lee and Marion forced a British garrison to surrender.

## *May 14*

### Tory raid at Croton River, New York

The American outpost there was surprised, and its commander, Colonel Christopher Greene, killed.

# *1781*

## *May 14*

### Action at Nelson's Ferry, South Carolina

Americans skirmished with British evacuating the post during the siege of Augusta.

## *May 15*

### Capture of Fort Granby, South Carolina

A Tory and German garrison surrendered to Lee on condition that he allow them to keep their plunder and withdraw to Charleston as prisoners of war under parole until exchanged. No losses occurred on either side.

## *May 20*

### Washington sends Wayne and 1,000 Continentals to Virginia

This was a reflection of his increasing concern about British activities and objectives in Virginia.

## *May 20*

### Cornwallis arrives at Petersburg, Virginia

He assumed command in Virginia with a total strength of nearly 6,500 men. Reinforcements from Clinton soon brought his strength to 8,000.

## *May 21*

### Action at Silver Bluff, South Carolina

Skirmish during the siege of Augusta, Georgia.

# *1781*

## *May 21*

### Capture of Fort Galphin (Fort Dreadnought), Georgia

Lee's Legion drove out a Tory garrison and thereby deprived Colonel Thomas Brown's Tory force at Fort Cornwallis (Augusta) of a considerable body of reserves and supplies. This permitted an intensification of the siege of Augusta. Lee then marched to join Pickens's force besieging Augusta.

## *May 21–24*

### Washington-Rochambeau conference at Wethersfield, Connecticut

The two commanders agreed to join forces in an attack on New York.

## *May 22–June 19*

### Greene besieges the British stronghold at Ninety-Six, South Carolina

He had fewer than 1,000 regulars and no heavy artillery. The stronghold was garrisoned by 550 Tories under Colonel John Cruger. Lord Rawdon had sent orders for the evacuation of the post but they were intercepted by Greene's men.

## *May 23–24*

### Capture of Fort Grierson, Georgia

The post was assaulted by Lee and Pickens during the siege of Augusta. Its loss gravely imperiled the remaining Tory troops in Fort Cornwallis.

# *1781*

### May 26

## Congress approves Morris proposal (May 21) for a national bank

The Bank of North America was not actually chartered until December 31.

### May 29

## USS *Alliance* (36) versus HMS *Atlanta* (16) and HMS *Trepassy* (14)

Captain John Barry's American frigate was attacked by the two British sloops of war but it got the best of the ensuing action and forced their surrender. Barry was badly wounded in the battle.

### June

## Robert Morris receives authorization to supply the Army by contract rather than by requisition from the states

### June 4

## British raid on Charlottesville, Virginia

Tarleton almost captured Governor Jefferson and the Virginia legislature. The raiders did succeed in destroying some materiel and tobacco.

### June 4–5

## British raid at Point of Fork, Virginia

Von Steuben's main supply depot was destroyed by British troops under Lieutenant Colonel John Simcoe.

# *1781*

*June 5*

## Action at Georgetown, South Carolina

Marion occupied the place after overcoming slight resistance from the garrison there. He did not have sufficient troops to garrison it himself, however, so he removed the stores and destroyed the military works.

*June 5*

## Surrender of Augusta, Georgia, to Americans

Colonel Thomas Brown surrendered his Tory garrison to General Pickens and "Light Horse Harry" Lee. American losses during the two-week offensive that climaxed the long siege were about 40; the Tories had 52 killed and 334 taken prisoner.

*June 10*

## General Lafayette is reinforced by arrival of Wayne in Virginia

Lafayette's strength was then about 4,500 men, mostly Continentals, some of the best of Washington's army.

*June 15*

## Congress appoints peace commission

John Adams, John Jay, Benjamin Franklin, Henry Laurens, and Thomas Jefferson (who declined), were named. The minimum terms were to be U.S. independence and sovereignty.

# *1781*

*June 19*

## Americans repulsed at Ninety-Six, South Carolina

Greene was forced to withdraw after a 28-day siege when Rawdon's relieving force rescued the Tory defenders. Although Greene and his men had fought with determination, they had made too many blunders against an equally stubborn enemy. This unsuccessful operation cost the Americans 57 killed, 70 wounded, and 20 missing; the British lost 27 killed and 58 wounded.

*June 26*

## Action at Spencer's Tavern, Virginia

Simcoe's raiding party got the better of a detachment of Lafayette's Continentals in a hotly fought skirmish.

*June 26*

## Action at Rahway Meadow, New Jersey

Captain Amos Morse and about 40 Americans fell into an ambuscade prepared by Lieutenant Hutchinson and immediately surrendered.

*June 30*

## Tory and Indian raid on Currytown (Currietown), New York

The small settlement was surprised and burned by a force under John Doxtader. Most of the inhabitants were in the fields when the raid occurred and were able to flee, although a number of them were killed or captured.

# *1781*

## *July 3*

### Action at King's Bridge, New York

Americans under General Benjamin Lincoln withdrew from a proposed assault after the surprise was compromised.

## *July 5*

### French army under Rochambeau joins Washington's forces above New York

Total allied strength was then 10,600, of which 4,800 were French.

## *July 6*

### Battle of Green Spring (Jamestown Ford), Virginia

Cornwallis's entire force of 7,000 British ambushed Lafayette's advance guard of 900 under Wayne. Wayne counterattacked boldly, then withdrew in good order after severe losses.

## *July 10*

### Action at Sharon Springs Swamp, New York

Militia under Colonel Marinus Willett attacked and routed Doxtader's Tory and Indian force in response to the raid at Currytown.

## July 15

### Action at Tarrytown, New York

The British attempted a bold, but unsuccessful, raid by water from their base on Manhattan Island.

# *1781*

*July 17*

## Action at Quinby's Bridge, South Carolina

Sumter attacked strong British defenses and was repulsed, because of poor management on his part. Marion, Lee, and Colonel Thomas Taylor, whose troops had participated in the action under Sumter, were so annoyed at his blundering that they left him the next day.

*August 4*

## Cornwallis occupies Yorktown and Gloucester Point on the York River, Virginia

This was a defensible position permitting communication by sea with Clinton in New York. Cornwallis expected to be reinforced so that he could renew an offensive campaign in Virginia.

*August 5*

## Naval Battle of Dogger Bank

A British merchant convoy escorted by Sir Hyde Parker's squadron encountered a Dutch merchant convoy escorted by Rear Admiral Johann Arnold Zoutman's squadron. Parker got the better of Zoutman in an evenly matched engagement. Both suffered heavy losses: the Dutch had 550 casualties; the British, 450.

August 6

## Defense of Shell's Bush, New York

The Shell family successfully held a blockhouse against an attack by 60 Tories and Indians under Donald McDonald, who was mortally wounded in the action.

# *1781*

August 8

## USS *Trumbull* (28) versus HMS *Iris* (32) and HMS *General Monk* (20)

Although three-fourths of the *Trumbull*'s motley crew refused to fight, American Captain James Nicholson and the rest of the crew put up an hour and a half's resistance before being captured.

*August 10*

## Robert R. Livingston chosen by Congress as Secretary for Foreign Affairs

*August 13*

## Action at Parker's Ferry, Edisto River, South Carolina

Francis Marion ambushed and routed 200 British dragoons under Major Thomas Fraser; Marion claimed the British lost 100 killed or wounded.

*August 13*

## De Grasse's French fleet sails from Haiti for Chesapeake Bay

The force included 28 ships of the line and 3,500 troops. The move was in response to Washington's suggestion.

August 14

## Washington receives letter from De Grasse reporting planned movement to Chesapeake Bay

Washington prepared to march his and Rochambeau's troops for Virginia. Elaborate plans were made to conceal the projected movement from British General Clinton, in New York.

# *1781*

*August 19–26*

## Washington heads for Virginia

A feint toward Staten Island preceded his march across New Jersey. The French, then north of New York, followed.

*August 22*

## Action at Wawarsing, New York

Militia under Colonel Albert Pawling routed a Tory force.

August 25

## French squadron under Admiral de Barras sails from Newport, Rhode Island, for Chesapeake Bay

The force included eight ships of the line, 1,000 troops, and siege artillery.

*August 25*

## Rochambeau's army joins Washington's in central New Jersey

*August 25*

## Lochry's Defeat, Ohio River

Joseph Brant, with about 100 Tories and Indians, surprised and defeated about the same number of Pennsylvania militia under Colonel Archibald Lochry (Lochrey, Lochray) near the Big Miami River, in present-day Indiana. Lochry was mortally wounded in the action; about half of his command was killed and the remainder captured. (Another source gives August 24.)

# *1781*

*August 29*

## Robert Morris appointed Agent of Marine

*August 30*

## Comte de Grasse with French fleet arrives in Chesapeake Bay

De Grasse established a naval blockade of the James and York Rivers, cutting off Cornwallis's communications with Clinton.

*September 2*

## French troops land near Jamestown

De Grasse sent 3,000 troops under the Marquis de Saint-Simon to join Lafayette.

*September 5-9*

## Battle of the Capes

French Admiral de Grasse outfought a British fleet under Admiral Thomas Graves off the Chesapeake Bay, getting the better of a generally indecisive engagement. The French blockade at Yorktown was consequently strengthened. This was the most strategically decisive engagement of the war; it assured the isolation, and eventual surrender, of Cornwallis.

*September 6*

## British raid New London, Connecticut

Forces under Benedict Arnold plundered and burned the town, leaving 97 families homeless and doing an estimated $485,980 worth of damage.

# *1781*

### September 6

## Battle of Groton Heights and capture of Fort Griswold, Connecticut

Benedict Arnold and his British and Tory forces captured the fort after a determined resistance by the defenders. A melee continued in the fort after the American surrender, resulting in severe American casualties. This was the last important engagement in the north during the war.

### September 6

## USP *Congress* (24) versus HMS *Savage* (16)

The Philadelphia privateer *Congress*, commanded by Captain George Geddes, forced the surrender of the British sloop of war *Savage* after a fierce engagement off the coast of South Carolina.

### September 7

## Indian raid at Fort Plain, New York

Lieutenant Solomon Woodworth and many of his small patriot force were killed in a gallant but desperate struggle after being ambushed.

### September 8

## Washington visits Mount Vernon

He stopped overnight en route to Williamsburg to join Lafayette. This was his first visit home in six years.

# *1781*

*September 8*

## Battle of Eutaw Springs, South Carolina

British troops under Colonel Alexander Stewart repulsed Greene's forces in a see-saw engagement, one of the most hard fought of the war. British casualties were the highest percentage sustained by any force during the war. Of the initial British force of 1,800-2,000, some 693-866 men were lost. The Americans lost 139 killed, including 17 officers, and 375 wounded, including 43 officers, of a starting force of 2,000. This was the last major engagement in the South and assured the liberation of the South, since Stewart decided to retreat to Charleston, even though the British repulsed the American attack.

*September 10*

## De Barras's French squadron from Newport joins de Grasse in Chesapeake Bay

De Grasse was now assured of numerical superiority over Graves's reinforced British fleet at New York.

*September 12*

## Tory raid on Hillsboro, North Carolina

Tory leaders David Fanning and Hector McNeill, with about 500 loyalists, captured Governor Burke and 200 others in what has been called "the most brilliant exploit of any group of Loyalists in any state throughout the Revolution."

*September 12*

## Action at Crane Creek, North Carolina

A Continental force attacked the Tory raiders on their withdrawal from Hillsboro. Fanning was badly wounded but kept his prisoners and eluded his pursuers.

# *1781*

*September 14-26*

## French fleet ferries Allied armies down Chesapeake Bay

The concentration of Washington's and Rochambeau's force at Williamsburg was expedited by this water movement.

*September 17-18*

## Washington-De Grasse Conference

The leaders met aboard the French flagship *Ville de Paris* to confer about joint operations. The *Ville de Paris* was the largest warship in the world at that time.

*September 28*

## Advance on Yorktown

The Allied army (9,500 Americans and 7,800 French troops) moved forward from Williamsburg.

*September 30*

## The siege of Yorktown begins

Cornwallis's abandonment of the outer fortifications at Yorktown allowed the allies to install siege guns capable of hitting all parts of the British inner line. He did this because he considered his force of 8,000 men insufficient to man the extensive works. He was still expecting to be reinforced by Clinton.

*October 3*

## Action at Gloucester, Virginia

French troops under Marquis de Choisy invested Gloucester after a sharp skirmish with British foragers.

# *1781*

*October 9*

## Bombardment of Yorktown begins

French and American siege guns opened fire from the "first parallel."

*October 10*

## American raid at Treadwell's Neck (Fort Slongo), New York

Major Lemuel Trescott and 150 Continental troops captured Tory Fort Slongo without losing a man. After destroying the stronghold and confiscating some materiel, Trescott withdrew.

*October 14*

## Capture of Redoubts 9 and 10 outside Yorktown

French troops under Colonel de Deux-Ponts captured Redoubt No. 9 while Alexander Hamilton's American troops seized Redoubt No. 10 in a simultaneous night assault.

*October 16*

## Action at Monck's Corner (Monks Corner), South Carolina

Americans attacked a British camp and took 80 prisoners.

*October 16*

## British sortie from Yorktown

Lieutenant Colonel Robert Abercromby led 350 select British troops to silence allied guns. After ineffectually spiking six guns the British were driven back to their lines by an allied counterattack.

# 1781

*October 16-17*

## British effort to evacuate Yorktown via Glouchester fails

Insufficient boats and a raging storm aborted Cornwallis's plan for a night withdrawal.

*October 17*

## Cornwallis opens negotiations to surrender

Lieutenant Colonel Thomas Dundas and Major Alexander Ross, representing Cornwallis, and Lieutenant Colonel John Laurens and the Viscomte de Noailles, representing the allies, met at the Moore House the next day to settle conditions.

*October 19*

## "The world turned upside down"

The siege of Yorktown ended with Cornwallis's surrender. Seven thousand British soldiers became prisoners of war. Great Britain had lost her last chance to reimpose royal authority on her rebellious American colonies.

*October 20-30*

## British, Tory, and Indian raid in Mohawk Valley, New York

Led by Major John Ross, the expedition was cut short by muddy roads, failure of the Indians to show as much interest as expected, and the threat posed by militia rallying under Colonel Marinus Willett for the defense of the valley. This was the last Tory threat to Tryon County.

# 1781

*October 24*

## Clinton and British reinforcements approach
## Chesapeake Bay

The force was convoyed by Admiral Graves's fleet. Clinton ordered a return to New York after learning of Cornwallis's surrender.

*October 25*

## Action at Johnson Hall (Johnstown), New York

Major John Ross, with a Tory and Indian force, occupied several buildings and repulsed a militia attack before withdrawing.

*October 30*

## Action at Jerseyfield (West Canada Creek), New York

Colonel Willett pursued and skirmished with Ross's Tory and Indian raiders. Tory Captain Walter Butler was killed in the action. Willett continued pursuit of the raiders for 20 miles and then abandoned the chase. "The woods were strewed with the packs of the enemy," he reported, "provisions they had none. . . . In this situation to the compassion of a starving wilderness we left them in a fair way of receiving punishment better suited to their merit than a musquet ball, tomahawk, or captivity."

*October 30*

## General Benjamin Lincoln chosen Secretary at War
## by Congress

*November 7*

## Action at Cloud's Creek, South Carolina

Three hundred Tories under William ("Bloody Bill") Cunningham attacked a party of 30 patriots led by James Butler, Jr., who was

# 1781

19; his father, Captain James Butler (as an advisor); and Captain George Turner. The surrender of the small patriot party resulted in a massacre when impetuous young Butler shot a Tory during the parley. Only two Americans escaped with their lives.

*November 9*

## Action at Hayes' Station, South Carolina

Cunningham and his Tory band slaughtered patriot Colonel Joseph Hayes and his men after they resisted surrender for several hours.

*November 18*

## British evacuate Wilmington, North Carolina

Major James H. Craig abandoned the town to avoid being isolated by St. Clair's movement south to reinforce Greene.

*November 27*

## Action at Fair Lawn, South Carolina

Carolina dragoons under Colonels Isaac Shelby and Hezekiah Maham captured the British stronghold.

*December 1*

## Action at Dorchester, South Carolina

A skirmish between Greene's advance elements—approaching Charleston—and Major John Doyle's cavalry and reconnaissance force, induced the British to abandon Camp Round 0 and withdraw to a site five miles from Charleston.

# *1781*

## *December 12*

### Second Battle of Ushant

British Admiral Kempenfeldt defeated de Guichen's French and Spanish squadron on its way to the West Indies with merchantmen and supply vessels. The French had 20 transports captured.

## *December 13*

### Congress Proclaims Day of Thanksgiving and Prayer for Yorktown victory

The possibly decisive effects of the victory were recognized.

## *December 22*

### General Lafayette sails from Boston for France

This ended his participation in the Revolutionary War.

## *December 28-29*

### Action at Johns Island, South Carolina

Lee's intricate plan for invading the island was aborted. Major James Hamilton's column got lost and arrived too late for the operation to be carried out.

## December 29

### Action at Dorchester, South Carolina

British Major John Coffin captured nine members of Lee's Legion, including Captain James Armstrong, during the skirmish.

# 1781

*December 31*

## Bank of North America incorporated by Congress at Philadelphia

# 1782

*January 11*

## French begin operations against St. Kitts (St. Christopher), West Indies

Admiral de Grasse arrived at the island with a powerful fleet of 29 ships-of-the-line, and landed 6,000 troops unopposed. After capturing the town of Basseterre and driving 600-700 British regulars to a stronghold at Brimstone Hill, the French began siege operations, since the British position was too strong for assault.

*January 25-26*

## Naval action off St. Kitts

British Admiral Samuel Hood, with a fleet of 22 ships, attempted to relieve the island. After brilliant maneuvering, the British enticed de Grasse's fleet from its anchorage and occupied its former position.

*February 12*

## Surrender of St. Kitts

Despite the presence and help of Admiral Hood's fleet and troops, the British garrison, sick and weary of siege, surrendered to the French. Hood's fleet sailed away the evening of February 14.

# *1782*

### *February 14*

## Action at Wambaw Creek, South Carolina

Colonel Benjamin Thompson's loyalist forces attacked and defeated Americans under Colonel Adam McDonald, inflicting 40 fatalities while incurring none.

### *February 23*

## Sir Guy Carleton is appointed British commander-in-chief in America

He replaced Clinton, who later returned to England.

### *February 27*

## British House of Commons petitions King George to make peace

This action was the result of receiving the news of the surrender of Cornwallis at Yorktown, and was a repudiation of the North ministry's coercive policy toward the Americans.

### *March 4*

## Action at Morrisania, New York

A skirmish resulted during Lieutenant Colonel William Hull's daring raid that extended more than three miles into British lines. Hull burned a ponton bridge and barracks, destroyed quantities of forage, and withdrew with 52 prisoners and much livestock, at the cost of 25 casualties. Loyalist Lieutenant Colonel James DeLancey pursued the raiders, making their withdrawal uncomfortable.

# *1782*

## *March 7-8*

### Gnadenhuetten Massacre, Ohio

American militia, incensed by recent Indian attacks, massacred 90-100 peaceful Indian men, women, and children. The massacre touched off a series of vicious Indian reprisal raids.

## *March 22*

### Lord Rockingham becomes British Prime Minister

Lord North had resigned March 20 after strong Parliamentary opposition thwarted his colonial policies. The new government decided to open direct negotiations with the American peace commissioners in Paris.

## *April 1*

### Washington establishes headquarters at Newburgh

It would remain there for more than a year, directing the blockade of New York.

## *April 8*

### Naval action on Delaware Bay

Captain Joshua Barney, commanding the Pennsylvania Navy's sloop of war *Hyder Ally* (16), fought and captured the British sloop of war HMS *General Monk* (20) and the Tory privateer *Fair American* (16). He took them both to Philadelphia.

# *1782*

*April 12*

## Peace talks begin

Richard Oswald, British commissioner, met and began negotiations with Franklin in Paris.

*April 12*

## Battle of the Saints (passage between Guadeloupe and Dominica)

This decisive British naval victory of Admiral Rodney over French Admiral de Grasse, in the West Indies, crushed French and Spanish plans for an invasion of Jamaica. De Grasse's flagship *Ville de Paris* (110), carrying all the siege artillery for the planned invasion, and four other ships were captured.

*April 12*

## New Jersey militia officer, Captain Joshua Huddy, hanged by Tories in Monmouth County

This was an act of reprisal for the murder of loyalist Philip White.

*April 19*

## The Netherlands recognizes U.S. independence

*April 24*

## Action at Dorchester, South Carolina

Captain Ferdinand O'Neal, with part of Lee's Legion, engaged in a fierce conflict with British troops under Captain Dawkins. O'Neal was forced to retreat when Dawkins received reinforcements. Nine Americans were captured.

# *1782*

## May 8

### Spanish expedition captures New Providence (Nassau) Bahamas

The troops from Havana took prisoner the entire 600-man British garrison of the islands.

## May 9

### Sir Guy Carleton arrives in New York to take command

His mission was to prepare to carry out the withdrawal of British forces from the United States, in anticipation of a peace treaty.

## May 21

### Action at Ogechee Road, Georgia

Greene's forces skirmished with British outposts near Savannah.

## June 4-5

### Action at Sandusky, Ohio (Crawford's Defeat)

Colonel William Crawford led frontiersmen on an expedition in the upper Sandusky region to reduce bases from which Tories and Indians conducted raids along the Pennsylvania-Virginia frontier. The Americans were defeated when Tory Captain William Caldwell and Indian leader Simon Girty received reinforcements. Crawford was captured during the action and tortured to death.

## June 11

### Netherlands loan to the United States

John Adams obtained a loan of about $2,000,000 from Dutch bankers.

# *1782*

*June 20*

## Great Seal of the United States is adopted by Congress

*June 23*

## Action at Ebenezer, Georgia

General Anthony Wayne repelled a surprise Indian attack led by Chief Guristersigo, who was killed during the action; his Indian force was routed.

*June 23*

## John Jay arrives in Paris from Madrid, Spain

He was the first of the other commissioners to join Benjamin Franklin in peace negotiations.

*July 1*

## Prime Minister Rockingham dies

He was succeeded by the Earl of Shelburne as British Prime Minister. Shelburne, although long conciliatory toward America, was strongly resistant to granting unconditional independence, and it was largely for this reason that George III chose him.

*July 11*

## Savannah, Georgia, evacuated by British

Governor Sir James Wright and some British civil and military officers fled to Charleston; General Alured Clarke and a portion of the British regulars went to New York; Colonel Thomas Brown's

# *1782*

rangers and Indians headed for St. Augustine; and the remaining forces were convoyed to the West Indies aboard sloop of war HMS *Vulture* and frigate HMS *Zebra*.

*August 7*

## Origin of Purple Heart

General Washington, at Newburgh, New York, wrote an order creating the "Badge of Military Merit" (later, Order of the Purple Heart) for "meritorious action." Only three men (all from Connecticut) are known to have received the award during the Revolutionary War. (This medal is now awarded to men wounded in action.)

*August 15*

## Indian and Tory raid on Bryan's Station, Kentucky

Simon Girty led the raiders. Local militia quickly gathered and pursued the retreating raiders.

*August 19*

## Battle of Blue Licks, Kentucky

Tories and Indians under Simon Girty ambushed and slaughtered pursuing Kentucky frontiersmen under Daniel Boone and Hugh McGary. In action lasting only a few minutes about 70 of the 182 frontiersmen were killed or captured. The Kentuckians fell into the ambuscade after McGary impetuously ignored Boone's advice that they wait for the reinforcements they were expecting.

*August 27*

## Action at Combahee Ferry, South Carolina

Americans were ambushed and defeated by British forces. John Laurens was killed in the action.

# *1782*

### Siege of Fort Henry, Virginia (present-day West Virginia)

Forty Tories and 250 Indians were held off by the defenders in what has been called by some "the last battle of the Revolutionary War."

*September 13-14*

### French and Spanish assault repulsed at Gibraltar

Sir George Augustus Eliott's 7,000-man British garrison repulsed a fierce joint attack by French and Spanish forces under the Duke de Crillon, maintaining the garrison's successful three-year defense against Spanish blockade and bombardment. Eliott was successful in using red-hot shot, for the first known time in history.

*September 16*

### First use of Great Seal of the United States

It was impressed on a document granting Washington authority to consult with British representatives about prisoner exchange.

*September 20*

### Action at Lookout Mountain, Tennessee

John Sevier led frontier militia in a victory over Tories and Indians.

*September 27*

### Beginning of formal peace negotiations in Paris between American and British commissioners

The British has been authorized by Lord Shelburne, in a commission sent September 21, before he had received news of the Gibralter victory, to treat the American commissioners as representatives of the "13 United States."

# 1782

*October 8*

## Treaty of Commerce and Friendship with the Netherlands

Negotiated by John Adams, it was modeled after the Franco-American treaty of February 6, 1778, and the "Plan of 1776" of September 17, 1776, and reasserted freedom of the seas.

*October 26*

## John Adams joins American commissioners in Paris

He had remained in the Netherlands to conclude treaty negotiations with the Dutch.

*November 1*

## General Assembly of Rhode Island refuses to accept authority of Congress to levy import duties

*November 4*

## Action at Johns Island, South Carolina

Americans under Captain William Wilmot (Maryland) defeated a British foraging party. Wilmot was killed during the action.

*November 10*

## Action near Chillicothe, Ohio

George Rogers Clark and 1,100 mounted riflemen routed the Shawnee Indians and burned their villages.

# *1782*

*November 30*

## Provisional treaty of peace signed in Paris

The preliminary articles, negotiated independently of America's ally, France, later constituted the final treaty of September 3, 1783. The provisions included recognition of American independence and settlements regarding boundaries of the United States, fishing rights, debts, loyalists in the United States, and the cessation of hostilities and evacuation of forces. The treaty was to go into effect when Britain and France reached a settlement. Thus the American negotiators remained faithful to the alliance, but skillfully evaded France's efforts to use America as a pawn in its international power struggle with Britain.

*December 5*

## Birth of Martin Van Buren in Kinderhook, New York

He became the first President to have been a U.S. citizen at birth.

*December 14*

## Charleston, South Carolina, evacuated by the British

General Alexander Leslie and his forces embarked on British ships sent from New York.

*December 15*

## French protest American signing of Provisional Treaty of Peace

French Foreign Minister Vergennes criticized the U.S. peace commissioners. His desire for a speedy settlement of the war and a tactful reply by Franklin (December 17) prevented serious discord among the allies.

# 1782

## December 24

### Rochambeau's army embarks from Boston for France

He stopped at Annapolis en route, making his final departure from the United States on January 8, 1783.

## December 30

### Title to Wyoming Valley ceded to Pennsylvania

A five-man court appointed by Congress in August settled the dispute between Connecticut and Pennsylvania, both of whom had claims to the territory. This later became the cause of violence between Connecticut settlers and Pennsylvania militia.

# 1783

## January 8

### Rochambeau departs from Annapolis for France

After much ceremony and celebration, he embarked on the *L'Emeraude*.

## January 14

### General William Alexander, Lord Stirling, dies in Albany, New York

Some sources indicate that General Alexander died January 15.

## January 20

### Cessation of hostilities signed by British and U.S. commissioners

The King signed to ratify the agreement on February 14.

# *1783*

*January 20*

## Peace between Britain and France, and Britain and Spain

The provisional articles of November 30, 1782, were signed by the three countries, putting a general armistice into effect. The Netherlands was included in the armistice, although preliminary articles of peace had not yet been agreed to by Britain and the United Provinces.

*January 25*

## Congress rejects previous guarantees to Army officers

An informal association of officers had earlier (December 1782) submitted a memorial of protest. Grounds of the officers' discontent were arrears in pay, unsettled food and clothing accounts, and Congress's failure to make provision for promised pensions.

*February 4*

## Britain formally proclaims cessation of hostilities

*February 5*

## Sweden recognizes independence of the United States

*February 15*

## Portugal recognizes independence of the United States

*February 25*

## Denmark recognizes independence of the United States

# *1783*

*March 10*

## USS *Alliance* (36) versus HMS *Sybil* (32)

John Barry's Continental frigate, accompanied by the recently purchased sloop of war USS *Duc de Lauzun* (20), was sailing from
Havana with a large amount of specie for Congress. The two vessels
were engaged by two British frigates and a smaller warship. Barry
drove off the British squadron in a 45-minute action in which only
*Alliance* and *Sybil* were seriously engaged. This is generally considered the last naval engagement of the war.

*March 10*

## First of Newburgh Addresses

Major John Armstrong wrote an anonymous attack on Congress
for its failures to fulfill promises to Continental officers and called
for a meeting of officers to discuss further action the next day. Armstrong's efforts had the backing of General Gates and of Gouverneur
Morris and other civilian leaders. Washington forbade the unauthorized meeting (March 11) and scheduled an official meeting for
March 15.

*March 12*

## Second of Newburgh Addresses

This stated that Washington's action in calling for an official meeting was in fact a confirmation of the validity of the officers' claims.

*March 13*

## Congress receives the text of the provisional peace treaty from Paris

# *1783*

*March 15*

## Washington addresses the Continental officers at Newburgh

"I have grown grey in your service . . . ," he began. He condemned the defiant tone of the Newburgh Addresses, expressed his confidence that Congress would treat the officers justly, and called for patience. Afterward the officers adopted respectful resolutions, and Congress later voted them full pay for five years. This is one of the most significant events in the long American tradition of the subservience of the military to civilian political authority.

*March 24*

## Spain recognizes U.S. independence

*April 11*

## Congress proclaims end of the war

*April 15*

## Congress ratifies provisional treaty of peace

During the preceding debate some members criticized the commissioners for not consulting the nation's French allies.

*April 18*

## Congress recommends greater centralization of taxing power under the Articles of Confederation

The recommendation failed to materialize due to the opposition of one state, New York, in 1786.

# *1783*

*April 19*

## End of war announced to the army at Newburgh, New York

This was exactly eight years after the battle of Lexington.

*April 26*

## Loyalists sail from New York seeking new homes

These were the last 7,000 of almost 100,000 who left the United States for Canada and Europe.

*May 13*

## Society of the Cincinnati formed

As the army prepared to disband, commissioned army officers established this hereditary society at the suggestion of General Henry Knox.

*May 26*

## Congress permits army disbandment prior to conclusion of war

In view of a shortage of funds to meet the expenses of an army which was no longer needed, Congress voted furloughs to soldiers enlisted "for the duration," until peace ratification permitted full discharge.

*May 30*

## First daily newspaper in the United States begins publication

This was the Pennsylvania *Evening Post*, published by Benjamin Towne at Philadelphia.

# *1783*

*June 13*

## Army disbands

Most of Washington's army departed for their homes without waiting for certificates for three months' pay authorized by Congress. A small force remained in Newburgh under Washington to continue a nominal blockade of the British garrison in New York.

*June 17*

## Mutinous soldiers threaten Congress

About 80 soldiers began a march from Lancaster to Philadelphia, proclaiming their determination to obtain justice from the state government and from Congress.

*June 21*

## Mutinous demonstration in Philadelphia

About 200 soldiers from regiments in Philadelphia joined the 80-man protest group from Lancaster in a demonstration at Independence Hall. Congress and the Executive Council of Pennsylvania, both in session there, hastily adjourned.

*June 30*

## Congress convenes at Princeton, New Jersey

*July*

## Russia recognizes U.S. independence

# 1783

## July 2

### Britain closes West Indies to U.S. trade

An order in Council prohibited the importation of U.S. meats, fish, and dairy products and banned trade of all other products except when carried in British vessels.

## September 3

### Treaties of Paris and of Versailles

Definitive treaties of peace were signed by Great Britain at Paris (with the United States) and at Versailles (with France and Spain). These were restatements of the November 1782 settlement.

## September 24

### Beginning of demobilization of Continental Army

General Washington was formally authorized by Congress to discharge "such parts of the Federal Army now in service as he shall deem proper and expedient."

## October 7

### Congress approves two permament seats of government

In a compromise between northern and southern states, it was decided that these were to be on the Delaware and Potomac Rivers.

## October 18

### Congress discharges all previously furloughed Continental troops

This partial reduction of forces followed British assurances of a speedy evacuation from the New York area.

# *1783*

*November 2*

## Washington's "Farewell Address to the Army"

It was issued at Rocky Hill, New Jersey.

*November 3*

## Army disbands by Congressional order

All troops enlisted for the duration of war were discharged. The small force with Washington was retained on active duty to await the British evacuation of New York.

*November 4*

## Congress adjourns

Congress agreed to meet November 26 at Annapolis, Maryland, under a plan calling for alternate sessions there and at Trenton, New Jersey, until such time as one or two permanent seats for the government were established.

*November 21*

## The British withdrew from northern Manhattan Island

They fell back into New York City, Brooklyn, and Staten Island. Washington at once crossed the Harlem River into Manhattan, taking up positions at Harlem Heights, after an absence of slightly more than seven years.

*November 25*

## British evacuation of New York City

The last British troops moved to Staten Island. Washington, accompanied by Governor George Clinton, entered the city.

# *1783*

*November 26*

## Congress convenes at Annapolis, Maryland

*December 3*

## Washington completes demobilization of the Continental Army

He ordered the infantry to be reduced to the strength of 500 rank and file, and the artillery to "minimum" strength.

*December 4*

## British complete evacuation of Staten Island and Long Island

They embarked on a fleet which remained for a few days in New York Bay and then sailed for England.

*December 4*

## Washington bids farewell to his officers at Fraunces Tavern, New York

The emotional gathering preceded Washington's departure by boat, across the Hudson River, en route to Annapolis.

*December 23*

## Washington returns to civilian life

He resigned his commission as commander-in-chief before Congress at Annapolis.

# *1783*

*December 25*

## Washington spends Christmas with his family at Mount Vernon

*December 31*

## Foreign debt of the United States at this date

Owed to France, $6,352,500; to Spain, $174,017; to Holland, $1,304,000.

# *1784*

*January 4*

## Temporary peacetime organization of the Continental Army

It was reorganized into an infantry regiment of 500 privates, 64 noncommissioned officers, and 30 commissioned officers, and an artillery corps of about 100. However, on June 2, this residual force was disbanded by Congress, except for the artillerymen, who were retained in two caretaking detachments at West Point and Pittsburgh.

*January 14*

## Congress ratifies definitive Treaty of Peace of September 3, 1783

The War of the Revolution was formally ended.

# People of the American Revolution

he was wounded and captured (17 October 1777); was then returned to England; husband of Lady Harriet Acland.

**Adams, Andrew.** American statesman, lawyer, b. Stratford, Conn.

Delegate to the Continental Congress, Connecticut, 1777-1780, 1781-1782.

**Adams, John.** 1735-1826. American statesman, lawyer, b. Braintree (now Quincy).

Adams was active in opposition to the Stamp Act. He served as defense lawyer for the British soldiers charged in the Boston Massacre. He was a delegate to the Continental Congress, Massachusetts, 1774-1778, and a signer of the Declaration of Independence. It was he who proposed George Washington for commander-in-chief of the Continental Army. In 1778 Adams was appointed a commissioner to France to supersede Silas Deane. In 1780 he was made minister plenipotentiary to the United Provinces (the Netherlands) and succeeded in negotiating (1782) a treaty of amity and commerce. In 1782 he joined John Jay and Benjamin Franklin in Paris to work on the negotiations with the British for a final peace treaty; the treaty was signed on 3 September 1783.

In 1789 Adams was elected first Vice President of the United States, serving two terms until 1797. In 1797 he was elected second President of the Uited States, defeating Thomas Jefferson, who received the second most electoral votes and thus was elected Vice President, and Thomas Pinckney. Adams's administration was marked by the passage of the Alien and Sedition Acts, which were aimed at curbing criticism of the administration but only succeeded in generating further ill will within the country. The United States was also involved in an undeclared naval war with France (1798-1800). During this time political parties began to evolve, and the supporters of the Adams administration and Alexander Hamilton, whom many looked to for leadership rather than Adams, became the Federalists. The opposition, known first as the Anti-Federalists, later became the Jeffersonian Republican Party.

In 1800 Adams was defeated for the presidency by Thomas Jefferson. Adams then retired from public office. He was the father of John Quincy Adams, a distinguished Secretary of State, 1817-1825, and the sixth President of the United States, 1825-1829.

**Adams, Samuel.** 1722-1803. American statesman, brewer, tax collector, b. Boston, Mass.

Adams began his career in public service as tax collector of Boston, 1756-64. He became identified in the 1760's with the "popular party," which was opposed to Governor Thomas Hutchinson and the unpopular measures of the British government.

Adams served in the Massachusetts legislature from 1765 until 1774. He became the leader of the "radicals" within the legislature, and drafted both the circular letter to the assemblies of other colonies calling for united action against the

Townshend Acts in 1768 and the circular letter calling for a provincial convention in Boston the same year. A leader in the Boston Tea Party, 16 December 1773, he served as a delegate to the Continental Congress, Massachusetts, 1774-1781, and was a signer of the Declaration of Independence. Adams continued public service in Massachusetts after the Revolution, serving as lieutenant governor of the state, 1789-1793, and as governor, 1793-1797.

**Adams, Thomas.** 1730-1788. American statesman, b. New Kent Co., Va.

Delegate to the Continental Congress, Virginia, 1778-1780; county clerk.

**Addison, Daniel Delany.** d. 1808. Loyalist officer (Maj.).

Served in the Maryland Loyalist militia, 1776-1783, attaining the rank of major in 1782.

**Affleck, Edmund.** 1723?-1788. British naval officer (Adm.), b. Suffolk.

Served at the battle of Chesapeake Bay, 16 March 1781; became an admiral in 1782 and a Member of Parliament (1782-1788).

**Agnew, John.** c.1727-1812. Loyalist, clergyman, b. Nansemond Co., Va.

Minister of Suffolk Parish (Anglican or Established Church), Nansemond Co., Va.; regarded as one of the most prominent loyalists in Virginia; served as chaplain to the Queen's Rangers, a loyalist regiment.

**Alexander, Robert.** American statesman, lawyer, loyalist, b. Cecil County, Md.

Delegate to the Continental Congress, Maryland, 1775-1777; fled from Maryland (1776), joined the British, and became a member of the Associated Loyalists; in 1782, fled to Britain.

**Alexander, William (Lord Stirling).** 1726-1783. Continental officer (Maj. Gen.), merchant, b. New York, N.Y.

Served in French and Indian War; failed to gain official British recognition for his claim to the Scottish earldom of Stirling, but was known as Lord Stirling in America; brigadier general, 1776-1777; fought with distinction in the battles of Long Island, Trenton, Brandywine, and Monmouth; major general, 1777-1783; presided over the court-martial of Maj. Gen. Charles Lee, 4 July–12 August 1778.

**Allen, Andrew.** 1740-1825. American statesman, lawyer, loyalist, b. Philadelphia, Pa.

Delegate to the Continental Congress, Pennsylvania, 1775-1776; withdrew in disapproval of the Declaration of Independence, took an oath of allegiance to the King, and went to England.

**Allen, Ethan.** 1738-1790. Continental officer (Brevet Col.); militia officer (Maj. Gen.), farmer, writer, b. Litchfield, Conn.

Settled in the New Hampshire Grants (now Vermont), about 1769; organized (1770) and commanded the Green Mountain Boys, partisan fighters against New York claimants to the Grants; led his men, as a patriot unit, in the capture of Fort Ticonderoga, 10 May 1775. Lost the election as commander to Seth Warner when the Green Mountain Boys became a Continental unit; then volunteered for Maj. Gen. Philip Schuyler's Canadian expedition and was captured in a foolhardy small-unit assault on Montreal, 24 October 1775. Was exchanged, 6 May 1778, breveted a Continental colonel, 14 May, and became a major general commanding the Vermont militia, 1779. Author of a number of books and pamphlets, most of them dealing with Vermont's rights or with religious matters; was an influential deist.

**Allen, Isaac.** d. 1806. Loyalist leader.

Lieutenant colonel in 2nd Battalion of New Jersey Volunteers (loyalist); in action at Long Cane, S.C., 11 December 1780.

**Allen, John.** b. Scotland.

Led a group of 180 Nova Scotia rebels in an unsuccessful siege of Fort Cumberland, Nova Scotia, 1776.

**Allen, William (the elder).** d. 1780. Loyalist, jurist.

Chief Justice of Pennsylvania; possibly the wealthiest and most influential person in Pennsylvania before the Revolution; remained a loyalist during the Revolution, but took no overt action.

**Allen, William (the younger).** Loyalist officer.

Son of William Allen; originally a patriot, but in 1776 accepted a commission as lieutenant colonel and joined the British; raised a corps of Pennsylvania loyalists (1777).

**Allison, Patrick.** Patriot.

Pastor of the Presbyterian Church in Baltimore; chaplain of the Continental Congress; an organizer of the Sons of Liberty.

**Almodovar, Marquis de.** Spanish diplomat.

Spanish Ambassador to Great Britain; led unsuccessful Spanish efforts in 1778 to acquire Gibralter and Minorca from Britain in return for Spanish neutrality in the conflict between Britain and France.

**Alsop, John.** 1724-1794. American statesman, merchant, b. New Windsor, Orange County, N.Y.

Delegate to the Continental Congress, New York, 1774-1776.

**Ambler, Jaquelin.** 1742-1798. Patriot.

Virginia (Governor's) Council member; state treasurer.

**Amboise, Chevalier d'.** French agent.

With Julien Achard de Bonvouloir, observed battle of Lexington and made observations of American military forces, 1775; reported to French embassy in London.

**André, John.** 1751-1780. British officer (Maj.), b. London (?).

Son of a Swiss merchant who had settled in London; aide-de-camp to General Henry Clinton, British commander-in-chief in North America; corresponded with and received intelligence information from American Maj. Gen. Benedict Arnold in connection with Arnold's offer to turn the American fortress at West Point over to the British; was captured, 13 September 1780, with incriminating papers that revealed the plot; was tried and executed as a spy in 1780 by the Americans; body was later interred as that of a national hero in Westminster Abbey in London.

**Andrews, John.** 1746-1813. Loyalist, clergymen, educator, b. Cecil County, Maryland.

Remained loyal to the King during the Revolution, but was not involved in any overt action; in 1810 became provost of the University of Pennsylvania.

**Apthorp, Charles Ward.** d. 1797. Loyalist.

Member of the Council of the Colony of New York, 1763-1783.

**Aranda, Pedro, Count of.** Spanish diplomat.

Spanish ambassador to France; instrumental in the negotiations leading to the Convention of Aranjuez in 1779 and the declaration of war against Great Britain, 21 June 1779.

**Arbuthnot, Marriot.** 1711-1794. British naval officer (Adm.), b. Weymouth (?), England.

Commander-in-chief on the American station, 1779; victorious, along with Gen. Henry Clinton, at Charleston, S.C., March-May 1780; temporarily superseded as commander-in-chief in 1780 by

Admiral George Rodney; succeeded by Admiral Thomas Graves in 1781.

**Armand, Charles (Charles-Armand Tuffin, Marquis de la Rouerie).** Continental officer (Brig. Gen.).

French volunteer; was commended for defense at Short Hills, N.J., 26 June 1777; took over command of the Pulaski Legion (11 October 1779) after Pulaski's death, and led it at Camden; commanded legion (renamed Armand's Partisan Corps), in Virginia operations and, after Yorktown, in South Carolina; during the French Revolution, fought as a Royalist, leading an uprising in Brittany.

**Armstrong, John.** 1717-1795. American statesman, Continental officer (Brig. Gen.), civil engineer, b. Brookbor, County Fermanagh, Ireland.

Resident of Pennsylvania; civil engineer before Revolution; brigadier general, 1776-1777; delegate to the Continental Congress, Pennsylvania, 1778-1780, 1787-1788.

**Armstrong, John, Jr.** 1755-1843. American statesman, Continental officer (Maj), b. Carlisle, Cumberland Co., Pa.

Author of the Newburgh Addresses, 10 and 12 March 1783; son of General John Armstrong.

**Armstrong, Richard.** Loyalist officer (Maj).

Major in the Queen's Rangers; considered one of the most efficient partisan officers in the service of the King.

**Arnold, Benedict.** 1741-1801. Continental officer (Maj. Gen.), British officer (Brig. Gen.), druggist, merchant, b. Norwich, Conn.

Arnold accompanied Ethan Allen at the capture of Fort Ticonderoga, 10 May 1775. In May 1775 he also captured, and then abandoned, St. Johns, Quebec. He led an expedition, notable for its boldness and hardships, through the wilderness to Quebec, 24 September–9 November 1775, and was wounded in the unsuccessful attack on Quebec, 31 December 1775. He was promoted to brigadier general on 10 June 1776.

Arnold directed the building of a flotilla on Lake Champlain and commanded it in the battle of Valcour Island, 11 October 1776. Although Arnold's force was defeated in the battle, the delay imposed on the British prevented them from attacking down the Hudson in 1776. Arnold was promoted to major general, 17 February 1777, and played an important role in the defeat of Burgoyne at Saratoga, 19 September and 7 October 1777, despite the hostility of General Gates, his superior.

Arnold commanded the Continental forces at Philadelphia, 1778-1779, was court-martialed in January 1780 on charges of relatively minor fiscal irregularities, and was reprimanded. Embittered by the charges, and by earlier lack of recognition for his abilities and accomplishments, he began negotiations in 1779 toward deserting to the British cause, and these culminated in a plot in 1780 to turn over to the British the strategic American fort at West Point, N.Y., of which he became commander in August 1780. The plot was arranged through Major John André of the British Army with the assistance of Mrs. Arnold and loyalist Joseph Stansbury. Arnold was revealed as a traitor with the capture of André, 23 September 1780, and fled to the British Army, where he was made a brigadier general. He was sent to Virginia, December 1780, and conducted successful raids there. In 1781 he went to Britain, where he spent the rest of his life in poverty and disgrace.

**Arnold, Margaret.** *See* Shippen, Peggy.

**Arnold, Jonathan.** 1741-1793. American statesman, surgeon, farmer, b. Providence, R.I.

Delegate to the Continental Congress, Rhode Island, 1782-1784.

**Atherton, Joshua.** 1737-1809. Loyalist, lawyer, b. Harvard, Worcester Co., Mass.

Successful and prominent New Hampshire lawyer before the Revolution; a professed loyalist; was kept in custody by the state during most of the war; in 1787 was a delegate from New Hampshire to the Constitutional Convention; later served as New Hampshire state senator and state attorney general.

**Atkinson, Theodore,** d. 1779. Loyalist, lawyer, jurist.

Secretary of the province of New Hampshire, 1741; chief justice of New Hampshire, 1754; took no overt action during the Revolution.

**Atlee, Samuel J.** 1739-1786. American statesman, b. Trenton, N.J.

Delegate to the Continental Congress, Pennsylvania, 1778-1782.

**Attucks, Crispus.** c. 1723-1770. Patriot.

Active Negro patriot; leader of crowd that taunted British soldiers, 5 March 1770; killed in the ensuing Boston Massacre.

**Auchmutz, Sir Samuel.** c. 1758-1822. Loyalist, British officer.

From a prominent New York family; served under Sir William Howe in the 45th Foot; made a general in 1803; was later a Member of Parliament.

# B

**Bache, Richard.** 1737-1811. American government official, merchant, b. Settle, West Riding, Yorkshire, England.

Postmaster General, 1776-1782; son-in-law of Benjamin Franklin.

**Badge, Thomas.** Soap maker, chandler, American soldier, British spy.

Philadelphia resident; served in American Army early in war; from 1777, using his tradesman's occupation as a cover, gathered American military intelligence for British; helped guide General Howe from Head of Elk, Md., to Brandywine and Philadelphia.

**Bailey, Francis.** c. 1735-1815. Continental soldier, printer, journalist, b. Lancaster Co., Pa.

Printer who published in German; made first known reference to George Washington as "Father of His Country," 1778.

**Bakeman, Daniel.** d. 5 April 1869. Continental soldier.

Resident of Freedom, N.Y.; last pensioned soldier of the Revolution.

**Baker, John.** Militia officer (Col.).

Fought at Sawpit Bluff, Fla., 15 May 1777, where he retrieved 40 horses stolen from his camp by the Indians; defeated at Thomas' Swamp, Fla., 17 May 1777; defeated and wounded at Spencer's Hill, Ga., 19 November 1778.

**Baldwin, Abraham.** 1754-1807. American statesman, clergyman, lawyer, b. North Guilford, Conn.

Delegate to the Continental Congress, Georgia, 1785-1788; author of charter for, and president of, the University of Georgia; member of Constitutional Convention of 1787; member of the U.S. House of Representatives, 1789-1799; U.S. Senator, Georgia, 1799-1807; President Pro Tempore of the Senate, 1801-1802.

**Baldwin, Jeduthan.** 1732-1788. Continental officer (Col.), b. Woburn, Mass.

Served as a colonel and engineer in the Continental Army; kept a journal of the Boston seige of 1776.

**Baldwin, Loammi.** 1740-1807. Continental officer (Col.), cabinetmaker, b. Woburn, Mass.

Served with Washington in 1776; kept a valuable journal.

**Balfour, Nisbet (or Nesbit).** 1743-1832. British officer (Lt. Col.), b. Dunbog, Fife, Scotland.

Responsible for the execution of Isaac Hayne, American militia officer, in South Carolina, 1781.

**Bancker, Gerard.** State government official, New York.

Appointed assistant to the New York state treasurer, 1775; appointed treasurer of New York state, 1778, continuing to serve throughout the Revolution, with responsibility for raising all state funds and paying all state bills.

**Bancroft, Edward.** 1744-1820. Double agent, writer, inventor, sailor, b. Westfield, Mass.

Served as a spy for both Benjamin Franklin and Silas Deane in Paris; in December 1776 began to spy for the British while remaining in the confidence of the Americans; principal role was to spy on the American commissioners in Paris.

**Banister, John.** 1734-1788. American statesman, lawyer, planter, b. "Hatcher's Run," near Petersburg, Va.

Delegate to the Continental Congress, Virginia, 1778-1779.

**Banks, John.** Continental soldier.

Free Negro; resident of Goochland Co., Va.; served two years as cavalryman in Col. Theodorick Bland's regiment; one of very few

Negroes accepted for cavalry service.

**Bankson, Jacob.** Marine officer (Capt.), American spy.

Former marine officer when he offered to gather military information in British-occupied Philadelphia, 1778; one of few agents who reported directly to General Washington.

**Barbé-Marbois, François, Marquis de.** 1745-1837. French diplomat. Accompanied Luzerne to Philadelphia in 1779 as his secretary; wrote a history of Arnold's treason, *Complot d'Arnold* (1816).

**Barclay, Thomas.** 1753-1826. Loyalist officer (Maj.), British statesman.

Served as a captain (1775) and a major (1777-1783) in the Loyal American Regiment; after the Revolution became a prominent British diplomat, serving as a commissioner for the Treaty of Ghent (1814).

**Barker, Isaac.** b. c. 1752. Farmer, American spy.

Resident of Middletown, near Newport, R.I.; sent military intelligence to the Americans from British-occupied Rhode Island.

**Barney, Joshua.** 1759-1818. Privateer, Continental naval officer (Capt., Commodore), b. Baltimore Co., Md.

Captured three times by the British and escaped three times; commanding the privateer *Hyder Ally*, captured HMS *General Monk* and the Tory privateer *Fair Ameri-*

*can* in Delaware Bay, 8 April 1782; served with distinction in war of 1812, particularly at the battle of Bladensburg, where few other Americans distinguished themselves.

**Barras, Louis de (or Jacques-Melchior Saint-Laurent, Comte de Barras).** d. c. 1800. French naval officer (Adm.).

French commander at Newport, 1781; commanded a squadron under de Grasse in Yorktown campaign, 1781.

**Barré, Isaac.** 1762-1802. British statesman, officer. b. Dublin, Ireland.

Member of Parliament, 1761-1790; vehement champion of the Americans and exceedingly unpopular with George III; coined the expression "sons of liberty," which the American patriots later adopted; the city of Wilkes-Barre, Pa., was named after him, along with John Wilkes.

**Barrington, Samuel.** 1729-1800. British naval officer (Rear Adm.)

Served in the West Indies, 1779, as commander of the *Princess Royal*; 23 January 1778, made Rear Admiral of the White and commander-in-chief in the West Indies; served until 7 January 1779, when he was superseded by Admiral Byron.

**Barrington, William Wildman** (second Viscount). 1717-1793. British statesman.

Secretary at War, 1765-1778.

**Barron, James.** 1740-1787. State naval officer.

Commodore of the Virginia State Navy, 1780.

**Barry, John.** 1745-1803. Continental naval officer (Capt.), seaman, shipmaster, shipowner. b. Ireland.

Seaman, shipmaster and shipowner before the Revolution; called "Father of the United States Navy"; made the first capture in actual battle of a British warship, the sloop *Edward*, by a regularly commissioned American warship, the brig USS *Lexington*, 17 April 1776; commanded USS *Alliance* in a well-conducted engagement against HMS *Sybille* and two other warships in January of 1783, the last important naval encounter of the war.

**Bartlett, Josiah.** 1729-1793. American statesman, physician, b. Amesbury, Mass.

Delegate to the Continental Congress, New Hampshire, 1775-1778; signer of the Declaration of Independence.

**Barton, William.** 1748-1837. Militia officer (Capt.), hatter.

Captured British General Richard Prescott in daring raid, 9-10 July 1777; Rhode Island citizen.

**Bates (or Beats), Ann.** Teacher, storekeeper, British spy.

Philadelphia resident; wife of British soldier; spied for British, apparently with great effectiveness, 1778-1781; made repeated trips into Washington's army at White Plains and on the march,

1778, posing as a peddler and gathering detailed military data.

**Bathurst, Henry (Baron Apsley; second Earl Bathurst).** 1714-1794. British statesman.

Lord Chancellor of England, 1771-1778.

**Baum, Friedrich.** d. 1777. German (Brunswick) officer (Lt. Col.).

Commander of the Brunswick Dragoons; commanded British forces at the battle of Bennington, Vt., 15 August 1777, where he was defeated and mortally wounded.

**Bauman, Sebastian.** 1739-1803. Continental officer (Col.).

Artillery commander; made military maps for Washington; New York resident.

**Bayard, John B.** 1738-1807. American statesman, militia officer (Col.), merchant, b. Bohemia Manor, Cecil Co., Md.

Early and active patriot; member, Sons of Liberty (1766); fought at Princeton; speaker, Maryland Assembly, 1778; member, Maryland Board of War; delegate to the Continental Congress, Pennsylvania, 1785-1787.

**Baylies, Hodijah.** Continental officer (Maj.).

Aide-de-camp to General George Washington, 1782-1783; Massachusetts resident.

**Baylor, George.** 1752-1784. Continental officer (Col.), b. Newmarket, Va.

Aide to Washington; served at the battle of Trenton.

**Beach, John.** Loyalist, clergymen.

Ardent loyalist; despite threats and closing of many Anglican churches, continued to preach and pray for the King; won admiration from the patriots for his courage; Connecticut resident.

**Bearmore, Mansfield.** Tory partisan.

New York resident; led the Young's House, N.Y., raid of 25 December 1778; captured at Jefferd's Neck, N.Y., by Colonel Armand, 7 November 1779.

**Beaumarchais, Pierre Augustin Caron de.** 1732-1799. French playwright, secret agent, b. Paris.

Author of the plays *The Barber of Seville* and *The Marriage of Figaro*; advocate of French aid to the rebelling American colonies; administered the fictitious company, Roderique Hortalez et Cie., by which munitions were supplied to the Americans.

**Beckley, John.** 1757-1807. Patriot.

Clerk of Virginia State Senate, 1779; clerk of the Virginia House of Delegates, 1781.

**Beckwith, George.** 1753-1823. British officer and agent.

Aide-de-camp to Hessian commander-in-chief Knyphausen while the latter was commanding British field forces in the north, 1780-1783; later, 1787-1791, an agent for the British Government gathering information on America.

**Bedinger, George.** 1756-1843. Virginia militia officer (Capt.), pioneer, congressman, b. York Co., Pa.

Served in northern and southern campaigns under General Washington, and in expeditions against the Indians in Kentucky, 1775-1781.

**Bee, Thomas.** 1725-1812. American statesman, lawyer, planter, b. Charleston, S.C.

Delegate to the Continental Congress, South Carolina, 1780-1782.

**Belknap, Jeremy.** 1744-1798. Clergyman, historian.

Author of the *History of New Hampshire* (three volumes, 1784-1792), an excellent account, much of it first hand, of the Revolution.

**Belton, Joseph.** Inventor.

Proposed to manufacture repeating arms for the patriot forces; authorized by Congress to demonstrate his device, but no procurement was made.

**Benson, Egbert.** 1746-1833. American statesman, lawyer, jurist, b. New York.

Early and active patriot; member, New York Provincial Congress, 1776, and New York Council of Safety, 1777-1778; New York attorney general, 1777-1787; member, state Legislative Assembly, 1777; delegate to the Continental Congress, New York, 1781-1784, and to the Annapolis convention of 1786; worked for ratification of the Federal Constitution; member, U.S. House of Representatives, 1789-1792; justice of New York Supreme Court, 1794-1801; appointed chief judge, Second U.S. Circuit Court, 1801.

**Berkenhout, John.** 1730(?)-1801. British agent, writer, physician. b. Leeds, England.

Came to America in 1778 to act as a secret agent for the peace commission of Lord Carlisle.

**Bernard, Francis, Sir.** 1712-1779. Royal governor, lawyer, b. England.

Royal governor of New Jersey, 1758-1760; royal governor of Massachusetts, 1760-1769; recalled to Britain because of the Stamp Act crisis.

**Bernière, Henry De.** British officer (Ensign), British spy.

With Capt. William Brown, sent by General Gage to map roads to Worcester (February 1775) and Concord (March 1775), and to locate munitions stores in those towns; guided Lt. Col. Francis Smith toward Lexington and Concord, 19 April 1775.

**Bernstorff, A. P.** Danish diplomat, b. Hanover, Germany.

Foreign Minister of Denmark; proposed concert of neutral nations for maintenance of neutral rights against Great Britain; efforts contributed to the Armed Neutrality of 1780.

**Berthier, Louis Alexander.** 1753-1815. French officer (Lt.), b. Versailles, France.

Served under Rochambeau and Lafayette; made many maps during the war; kept a journal of the war, 1780-1781; later Marshal of France.

**Bettys, Joseph.** d. 1782. Continental officer, later Tory.

After being captured, turned his allegiance to Britain and became a notorious Tory terrorist in New York; executed, 1782.

**Biddle, Edward.** 1738-1779. American statesman, lawyer, b. Philadelphia, Pa.

Delegate to the Continental Congress, Pennsylvania, 1774-1776, 1778-1779.

**Biddle, Nicholas.** 1750-1778. Continental naval officer (Capt.).

One of the first four captains of the Continental Navy; killed in action, 7 March 1778, in West Indies; Pennsylvania resident.

**Bigelow, Timothy.** Militia officer (Capt.), blacksmith.

Commander of Worcester, Mass., minutemen; discovered the British officers William Brown and Henry de Bernière on their spying expedition to Worcester, February 1775.

**Billopp, Christopher.** d. 1778. Loyalist.

Leader of the large loyalist element on Staten Island, N.Y.; kept order until the island could be occupied by General William Howe in 1776; then assisted Howe in the management of island affairs.

**Bingham, William.** Businessman.

Trading partner of Robert Morris; agent of Congress in the French West Indies, 1779-1780, where he procured supplies for the Continental Army.

**Bird, Henry.** British partisan leader.

Led the Kentucky raid of April-June 1780.

**Bissel, Israel.** Patriot postrider.

Postrider who carried the news of Lexington to New York and Philadelphia.

**Bissell, Daniel.** d. 1824. Continental soldier (Sgt.).

Sergeant, Second Connecticut Regiment, Continental Line; received "Badge of Military Merit" (later, Purple Heart) from Washington for espionage work in British-held New York City; one of only three men known to have received this award during Revolutionary War.

**Bissell, Ozias.** 1731-1822. Continental officer (Capt.).

Captain, Continental Army, 1775-1781; raised a company and marched to Boston, 1775; had three sons in the Continental Army.

**Blair, John.** 1732-1800. Patriot, jurist, b. Williamsburg, Va.

Virginia (Governor's) Council member; judge of the General Court.

**Blanchard, Claude.** 1742-1802. French officer.

Chief commissary to General Rochambeau; kept journal of his three years in America.

**Bland, Richard.** 1710-1776. American statesman, b. Orange Co., Va.

Delegate to the Continental Congress, Virginia, 1774-1775; uncle of Theodorick Bland.

**Bland, Theodorick.** 1742-1828. American statesman, Continental officer (Col.), physician, b. Cawsons, near Petersburg, Va.

Colonel, Cavalry, Continental Army, 1776-1780; delegate to the Continental Congress, Virginia, 1776-1780; his inept reconnaissance contributed to the American defeat at Brandywine; nephew of Richard Bland.

**Bliss, Daniel.** 1742-1806. Loyalist officer.

Assistant commissary general to General Burgoyne; c. 1779, in charge of whole British commissariat.

**Blount, William.** 1749-1800. American statesman, b. Windsor, Bertie Co., N.C.

Delegate to the Continental Congress, North Carolina, 1782-1783, 1786-1787; 1790, appointed governor of the territory south of the Ohio River; 1796-1797, first U.S. Senator from Tennessee; found guilty of "high misdemeanor" and expelled from the Senate, 1797.

**Blowers, Sampson Salter.** 1741-1842. Loyalist, jurist, b. Boston, Mass.

Respected Boston attorney; 1779 (after British occupation), judge of the court of admiralty of Rhode Island; solicitor general of New York, 1780; went to Nova Scotia after the war and was in succession attorney general, judge, and chief justice.

**Boerum, Simon.** 1724-1775. American statesman, farmer, miller, clerk, b. New Lots (now Brooklyn), Long Island, N.Y.

Delegate to the Continetal Congress, New York, 1775.

**Boone, Daniel.** 1734-1820. Militia officer (Col.), frontiersman, b. near Reading, Pa.

Settled in Kentucky area of Virginia; reached what was to become Boonesborough, 1 April 1750; 1776, made a captain in the Virginia militia; later promoted to major; became a colonel in 1780; distinguished himself at the disaster of Blue Licks, Ky., 19 August 1782.

**Botetourt, Norborne Berkeley, Baron de.** 1718-1770. Royal governor.

Royal governor of Virginia, 1768-1770; dissolved the House of Burgesses, 1769, in response to its protests (Virginia Resolves) against the Townshend Acts.

**Boucher, Jonathan.** c. 1737-1804. Loyalist, clergyman, b. Cumberland Co., England.

Leading Tory minister of Maryland who boldly denounced the patriot cause in the pre-Revolutionary period, despite threats of violence against him; left America in 1775.

**Boudinot, Elias.** 1740-1821. American statesman, lawyer, b. Philadelphia, Pa.

Delegate to the Continental Congress, New Jersey, 1777-1778; President of the Continental Congress, 1782-1783; commissary general of prisoners, 1777-1778.

**Bougainville, Louis Antoine de.** 1729-1811. French explorer, naval officer (Rear Adm.), b. Paris.

Made a famous voyage around the world, 1767-1769; largest island of the Solomons chain in the South Pacific bears his name; commanded ships of the line in action in the West Indies, 1779-1782; rescued eight ships of his division in battle of the Saints (off Saints Passage), April 1782.

**Boutineau, James.** 1710-1778. Loyalist.

Member of the Council of Massachusetts, 1774-1775; resigned in 1775, seeing no prospect of reconciliation, and went to Britain.

**Bowler, Metcalf.** 1726-1789. Loyalist, merchant, b. London.

Chief justice of Rhode Island, 1776; an informer to General Henry Clinton.

**Boyd, Thomas** d. 1779. Continental officer (Lt.).

Leader of the advance guard, Sullivan's expedition; captured by Indians near Genesee, N.Y., and tortured to death.

**Brackenridge, Hugh Henry.** 1748-1816. Patriot writer, chaplain, jurist, b. Campbelton, Scotland.

Coauthored with Philip Freneau the poem "The Rising Glory of America," 1772.

**Bradford, William.** 1722-1791. Militia officer (Col.), printer, bookseller, businessman, b. New York, N.Y.

Opened printery and bookstore in Philadelphia, 1742, published widely circulated *Weekly Advertiser, or Pennsylvania Journal,* from 1742; opposed Stamp Act; Son of Liberty; saw action at Trenton; severely wounded at Princeton; called "patriot-printer of 1776."

**Brant, Joseph.** 1742-1807. Mohawk Indian leader (half-Indian), loyalist officer (Col.).

Known also as Thayendanegea; well educated; traveled to Britain; converted to the Anglican faith; served as secretary to his brother-in-law, Sir William Johnson, when the latter was superintendent of Indian affairs; commissioned a colonel by the British; saw action at the Oriskany, N.Y., ambush, 6 August 1777, which he set up, and the Cherry Valley raid and massacre, 11 November 1778; defeated at battle of the Chemung River (Newton), N.Y., 29 August 1779.

**Brant, Molly.** Mohawk Indian, loyalist.

Sister of Joseph Brant; wife, or perhaps mistress, of Sir William Johnson.

**Braxton, Carter.** 1736-1797. American statesman, b. "Newington," King and Queen Courthouse, Va.

Delegate to the Continental Congress, Virginia, 1775-1776; signer of the Declaration of Independence.

**Brewer, Jonathan.** Patriot, tavern keeper, militia officer.

Proprietor of a tavern between Waltham and Watertown, Mass., and prominent patriot of the area; fought at Bunker Hill.

**Brewster, Caleb.** Patriot, whaleboat operator, American intelligence courier.

Connecticut resident; carried intelligence reports across Long Island Sound for the important American spy ring headed by "the Culpers" (Samuel Woodhull and Robert Townsend).

**Breymann, Heinrich Christoph.** d. 1777. German officer (Lt. Col.).

Commanded a relief column to support Colonel Baum's command during the Bennington raid, 15 August 1777, and was defeated and forced to retreat; commanded a Hessian redoubt at Bemis Heights (second battle of Saratoga) and was killed in action, 7 October 1777.

**Bridge, Ebenezer.** Militia officer (Col.).

Commander of the 27th Connecticut; agreed to remain in service at Boston (December 1775) until new army organized; personally praised by Washington.

**Broadwater, Charles.** Patriot.

Member, Virginia House of Burgesses, 1775; delegate to various Virginia Revolutionary conventions.

**Brodhead, Daniel.** 1736-1809. Continental officer (Brevet Brig. Gen.), surveyor, b. Albany, N.Y.

Commanded Fort Pitt; destroyed Indian villages in Allegheny Valley expedition, 11-14 September, 1779; Pennsylvania resident.

**Broglie, Charles-François, Comte de.** French officer (General), diplomat.

Ambassador to Poland, 1752; headed "secret cabinet" which carried out private diplomacy of Louis XV; during the American Revolution, apparently had scheme to become ruler of America under an arrangement similar to the Dutch stadholderate; sent Johann de Kalb to America, 1777; was Lafayette's commanding general in France and indirectly influenced him to come to America.

**Brooks, John.** 1752-1825. Continental officer, physician, b. Medford (now Winchester), Mass.

Aide to Inspector General von Steuben; adjutant general at Monmouth; governor of Massachusetts, 1816.

**Brown, John.** 1736-1803. Patriot, merchant, b. Providence, R.I.

Led the group that burned the the customs schooner *Gaspée* off Providence, R.I., 9-10 June 1772.

**Brown, John.** 1744-1780. Continental officer (Lt. Col.), lawyer, jurist, b. Haverhill, Mass.

Participated in Fort Ticonderoga capture, 10 May 1775, attack on Montreal, 25 September 1775, and capture of Chambly, Canada, 18 October 1775; killed at Fort Keyser, 19 October 1780.

**Brown, Thomas.** d. 1825. Tory partisan leader, b. England.

Loyalist partisan leader in the south; led the King's Rangers, a Tory militia unit; took part in the capture of Fort McIntosh, Ga., February 1777; took part in the defense of Savannah, October 1779; established himself at Augusta, Ga., 1780; though he eventually had to surrender, heroically defended the city, 22 May-5 June 1781.

**Brown, William.** 1752-1792. Physician, b. Haddingtonshire, Scotland.

Born of American parents in Scotland while his father was studying theology there; educated at University of Edinburgh; practiced in Alexandria, Va., from 1770; surgeon to 2d Virginia Regiment, 1775; succeeded Benjamin Rush as surgeon general of Middle Department, c.1776-1778; served in office of Army physician general, 1778-1780; brought out, for use of Army, first pharmacopeia published in the United States, 1778.

**Brown, William.** 1761-1804. Continental soldier (Sgt.).

Served in the 5th Connecticut Regiment; received the "Badge of Military Merit" (later, Purple Heart) from Washington for gallantry at Yorktown; one of only three men known to have received this award during the Revolutionary War.

**Brown, William.** British officer (Capt.), British spy.

With Ens. Henry De Bernière, sent by General Gage to map roads to Worcester (February 1775) and Concord (March 1775), and to locate munitions stores in those towns.

**Browne, Isaac.** 1709-1787. Loyalist, clergyman.

Served for 30 years as rector of Trinity Church, Newark, N.J. (1747-1777); chaplain of the New York Volunteers (a loyalist regi-

ment), 1778-c. 1783; went to Nova Scotia after the war.

**Browne, Montfort.** Loyalist.

Governor of New Providence, Canada, 1774-1780; in 1776 raised a regiment known as the Prince of Wales Loyal American Volunteers.

**Browne, William.** 1737-1802. Loyalist, jurist, b. Salem, Mass.

Member of the General Assembly of Massachusetts, 1762-1768; judge of the Superior Court and a member of the Provincial Council, 1774; was offered the governorship of Massachusetts, but refused it because of loyalty to the King; Governor of Bermuda, 1781-1788.

**Brownson, Nathan.** 1742-1796. American statesman, physician, b. Woodbury, Conn.

Delegate to the Continental Congress, Georgia, 1776-1778; governor of Georgia, 1782.

**Bruen, Caleb.** Militia officer (Capt.), American spy.

Resident of Newark, N.J.; left military service after 1776 to become ostensibly a British spy but actually an American double agent; played an important role during the mutinies of the Pennsylvania Line, January 1781, and New Jersey Line, February 1781, sabotaging Lt. Gen. Sir Henry Clinton's efforts to communicate with the mutineers.

**Bryan, Alexander.** American spy.

New York resident, living near Saratoga; according to family tradition, was sent by General Gates into Burgoyne's lines before the first battle of Saratoga and brought back crucial military information.

**Bryson, Samuel.** d. 1799. Continental officer (Lt.)

Pennsylvania resident; forced to surrender after a gallant defense at New Bridge, N.J., 15 April 1780.

**Buford, Abraham.** 1749-1833. Continental officer (Col.), b. Culpeper Co., Va.

Served from 1775 throughout the war; defeated by Banastre Tarleton at Waxhaws Creek, S.C., 29 May 1780, in a battle whose circumstances have led to accusations against Tarleton of treachery and inhumanity; settled in Kentucky after the war.

**Bull, William, II.** 1710-1791. Loyalist, farmer, b. Ashley Hall, S.C.

Acting royal governor of South Carolina, 1760-1761, 1764-1766, 1768, 1769-1771, and 1773-1775.

**Bulloch, Archibald.** c. 1730-1777. American statesman, lawyer, b. Charleston, S.C.

Delegate to the Continental Congress, Georgia, 1775-1776; great-great-grandfather of Theodore Roosevelt.

**Burgin, Elizabeth.** Patriot.

New York resident; operated an escape line for American prisoners of war, 1776-1779.

**Burgoyne, John ("Gentleman Johnny").** 1722-1792. British officer (Lt. Gen.).

A Member of Parliament, 1761-1792, Burgoyne came to America, 25 May 1775, as an assistant to General Gage at Boston. He returned to England and then commanded a relief expedition to Canada in 1776. After returning to England again, he was chosen to lead the northern offensive known as Burgoyne's Offensive, an invasion of New York, June-October 1777, which also included St. Leger's expedition. Burgoyne captured Fort Ticonderoga, 2-5 July, 1777; fought an indecisive action at Freeman's Farm against Continental forces under General Horatio Gates (the first battle of Saratoga), was defeated in the Battle of Bemis Heights (the second battle of Saratoga), 7 October 1777; and surrendered to Gates at Saratoga (now Stillwater), 17 October 1777, a major turning point in the war. He is generally considered an enlightened commander who showed considerably more respect for his men than was the 18th Century custom. He attributed his defeat to his being undersupplied and undersupported; actually his rashness was also a significant factor.

**Burke, Edmund.** 1729-1797. British statesman, writer, b. Dublin, Ireland.

Member of Parliament (Whig), 1766-1794; a key figure in reviving the Whig party and in forming a formidable opposition to George III; considered the most eloquent spokesman for the American cause in Britain.

**Burke, Thomas.** c. 1747-1783. American statesman, lawyer, b. Galway, Ireland.

Delegate to the Continental Congress, North Carolina, 1777-1781; governor of North Carolina, 1781-1782; kidnapped by Tories, 13 September 1781, and carried to Charleston, S.C.; exchanged; resumed his duties.

**Burnet, William.** 1730-1791. American statesman, physician, b. Newark, N.J.

Delegate to the Continental Congress, New Jersey, 1780-1781.

**Burr, Aaron.** 1756-1836. Continental officer (Lt. Col.), lawyer, statesman, b. Newark, N.J.

Burr served in the Continental Army, 1774-1779, reaching the rank of lieutenant colonel. He was attorney general for New York, 1789, and served in the U.S. Senate, New York, 1791-1797. He ran for the presidency of the United States in 1800, tying with Thomas Jefferson for the largest number of electoral votes. The House of Representatives chose Jefferson President and Burr Vice President, and Burr served from 1801 to 1805. In 1804 he mortally wounded his long-time political opponent, Alexander Hamilton, in a gun duel.

In 1807 Burr apparently plotted to seize territory in the western United States and in Spanish America to form a new republic and empire, aided by Maj. Gen. James Wilkinson. The plan failed, and Burr was tried and acquitted of treason. After exile, he returned to America and remained in New York City until his death.

**Bushnell, David.** c. 1742-1824. Inventor, b. Saybrooke, Conn.

Invented the first submarine used in actual operations, the *Turtle.*

**Butler, James.** Militia officer (Capt.).

South Carolina resident; killed in "massacre" at Cloud's Creek, S.C., 9 November 1781, by a Tory unit under "Bloody Bill" Cunningham.

**Butler, James, Jr.** Militia officer.

South Carolina resident; killed in "massacre" at Cloud's Creek, 9 November 1781, by a Tory unit under "Bloody Bill" Cunningham; son of James Butler.

**Butler, John.** 1728-1796. Loyalist officer (Col.), b. New London, Conn.

Served as an assistant to Sir Guy Johnson, superintendent of Indian affairs; led Tories at Wyoming Valley, Pennsylvania, 3-4 July 1778; was defeated at Newtown, N.Y., 29 August 1779, in the only pitched battle of Sullivan's expedition; father of Walter Butler.

**Butler, Richard.** 1743-1791. Continental officer (Col.), Indian trader, Indian agent, b. Ireland.

Pennsylvania resident; Indian trader and agent before Revolution; became major, 1776, and Continental lieutenant colonel in Morgan's Rifles, 1777; fought at Saratoga and at Stony Point, N.Y., 16 July 1779; helped suppress mutiny of Pennsylvania Line, 1781; helped negotiate important treaties with Indians after the war; served as major general and second-in-command to Gen. Arthur St. Clair in Indian campaign of 1791; mortally wounded in battle.

**Butler, Walter.** 1752(?)-1781. Loyalist militia leader, farmer, b. Johnstown, N.Y.

Active in loyalist activities in the Mohawk Valley, 1775-1778; most notorious operation was the Cherry Valley "Massacre" which he led, along with Joseph Brant, 11 November 1778; defeated at Chemung River (battle of Newtown), N.Y., 29 August 1779; killed in action at Jerseyfield, N.Y., 30 October 1781; son of John Butler.

**Butler, William.** d. 1789. Continental officer (Col.).

Pennsylvania resident; led the punitive raid on the Indian town of Unadilla, N.Y., October 1778.

**Butler, Zebulon.** Militia officer (Col.), shipowner, b. Ipswich, Mass.

Patriot leader in the Wyoming Valley area of Pennsylvania.

**Buttrick, John.** Militia officer (Maj.).

Leader of the Minutemen at Concord Bridge, Mass., 19 April 1775; said to have given the famous command, "Fire, fellow soldiers, for God's sake, fire!"

**Byles, Mather.** 1726-1788. Loyalist, clergyman, b. Boston, Mass.

While disclaiming any political involvement, he was one of the most ardent loyalists, as well as one of Boston's leading clergymen.

**Byles, Thomas Langhorne.** d. 1780. Continental officer (Maj.).

Pennsylvania resident; surrendered his entire force after a stubborn defense at Paramus, N.J., 16 April 1780; mortally wounded in the action.

**Byrd, William, III.** d. 1777. Loyalist, landowner, b. Westover, Va.

Considered "the first gentleman of Virginia"; member of the Virginia (Governor's) Council; was a loyalist, but did not take any overt action.

**Byron, John.** 1723-1786. British naval officer (Vice Adm.).

Known as "Foul Weather Jack"; 1778-1779, commander-in-chief of British Navy in North America; in the most important encounter of his Revolutionary service, was saved from a severe beating at the battle of Grenada (West Indies), 6 July 1779, when d'Estaing unaccountably withdrew.

# C

**Cabell, William.** 1729-1798. Patriot, statesman.

Member of Virginia Committee of Safety, 1775-1776.

**Cadwalader, John.** 1742-1786. Militia officer (Brig. Gen.), businessman, b. Philadelphia, Pa.

Failed to make planned crossing of the Delaware with his 2,000 men Christmas night 1776 in coordination with Washington's crossing; made unauthorized crossing 27 December; fought at Princeton, Brandywine, and Germantown; supported Washington in Conway Cabel and wounded General Conway in a duel.

**Caesar.** Patriot, ship's pilot.

Negro slave from Hampton, Va.; best known of the many Negroes used by Virginia as pilots during the Revolution; served throughout most of the war, steering the schooner *Patriot* during much of his service; distinguished himself during engagements with the enemy; given his freedom by the state for his services, 1789.

**Caldwell, James.** 1734-1781. Clergyman, Continental Army chaplain, b. Charlotte Co., Va.

Known as "the fighting chaplain" of the New Jersey Brigade; minister of the First Presbyterian Church, Elizabeth, N.J.

**Cambray-Digny, Louis Antoine Jean-Baptiste, Chevalier de.** 1751-1822. Continental officer (Lt. Col.), b. Italy.

Served as an engineer, 1778-1783; French citizen.

**Camer, Henry,** c. 1699-1792. Loyalist, clergyman.

Rector of King's Chapel, Boston, 1747-1776.

**Camm, John** 1718-1779. Loyalist, clergyman, educator, b. Yorkshire, England.

President of William and Mary College; member of the Virginia (Governor's) Council; removed as college president in 1777 for not honoring American government.

**Campbell, Archibald.** 1739-1791. British officer (Lt. Col.), b. Inverneil, Scotland.

Occupied Savannah, Ga., 29 December 1778; occupied Augusta, Ga., 29 January 1779; commander of the 2nd Battalion of the new Fraser Highlanders (71st Foot); Member of Parliament, 1774-1780.

**Campbell, Arthur.** 1743-1811. Virginia militia officer (Col.), frontiersman.

Commanded expeditions against the Indians.

**Campbell, John.** 1753-1784. British officer (Maj.), b. Levenside House, near Dumbarton, Scotland.

Served in Canada, 1774-1780, with the 7th Foot (Fusiliers) and the 26th Foot.

**Campbell, John.** d. 1806. British officer (Brig. Gen.).

Commander on Staten Island, 1777-1778; successfully defended Staten Island against Sullivan's raid, 22 August 1777; sent to take command in West Florida, November 1778; was ordered to capture New Orleans when Spain entered the war, but never had adequate forces; surrendered Pensacola, 9 May 1781, to the Spanish.

**Campbell, Lord William.** d. 1778. British official.

Royal governor of South Carolina, 1773-1775; tried unsuccessfully to salvage South Carolina for the Crown; was forced to flee in 1775.

**Campbell, William.** 1745-1781. Militia officer (Brig. Gen.), frontiersman, b. Holston River valley at Aspenvale, near Abingdon, Va.

Brigadier general of Virginia militia; was elected overall American leader at the battle of Kings Mountain.

**Carden, John.** Loyalist officer (Maj.).

Defeated at Flat Rock, S.C., 20 July 1780.

**Carey, Richard.** Continental officer (Lt. Col.).

Aide-de-camp to General George Washington; Virginia resident.

**Carleton, Christopher.** d. 1787. British officer.

Aide-de-camp to Sir Guy Carleton, whose nephew he was.

**Carleton, Sir Guy.** 1724-1808. British officer, (General, local rank), b. Strahane (County Tyrone?), Ireland.

Responsible for the drafting of the Quebec Act, 20 May 1774; governor of Quebec, 1775; independent commander of the British forces in Canada, 1775; carried out a remarkable defense of the province of Quebec, 1775-1776; after a feud with Lord Germain, asked to be recalled to England, 1777; commander-in-chief in America, 1782-1783; halted hostilities while the peace was being negotiated; governor of Quebec, 1786-1796.

**Carleton, Thomas.** 1736-1817. British officer.

Quartermaster general to Sir Guy Carleton and his forces in Canada, 1775-1777; brother of Sir Guy Carleton.

**Carlisle, Frederick Howard, Earl of.** British statesman, diplomat.

Carlisle was appointed, 22 February 1778, to negotiate a possible peace with the Americans. The commission he headed was to negotiate with Congress, and could agree to suspend all colonial legislation since 1763. The commission lasted from February to December 1778 with no tangible results, despite overt and covert attempts.

**Carlyle, John.** 1720-1780. Patriot, b. Carlisle, England.

Member, Virginia Committee of Safety for Fairfax County, 1775.

**Carmichael, William.** American statesman, diplomat, lawyer, b. "Round Top," Queen Annes County, Md.

Delegate to the Continental Congress, Maryland, 1778-1780; secretary to John Jay during Jay's mission to Spain, 1780; served in Spain as an unofficial envoy, 1780-1783, and in 1783 was recognized as the official representative of the United States; became chargé d'affaires, 1790; 1792-1794, joint commissioner with William Short.

**Carrington, Edward.** 1749-1810. Continental officer (Lt. Col.), statesman, b. Goochland Co., Va.

Officer in the Continental artillery; delegate to the Continental Congress, Virginia, 1785-1786.

**Carrington, Paul.** 1733-1818. Patriot, jurist, b. Cumberland Co., Va.

Jurist; member, Virginia Committee of Safety, 1775-1776, and several other Virginia Revolutionary groups.

**Carroll, Charles ("Barrister").**
1723-1783. American statesman,
lawyer, b. Annapolis, Md.

Delegate to the Continental
Congress, Maryland, 1776-1777.

**Carroll, Charles, of Carrollton.**
1737-1832. American statesman, b.
Annapolis, Md.

Delegate to the Continental
Congress, Maryland, 1776-1777;
signer of the Declaration of Independence.

**Carroll, Daniel.** 1730-1796. Amer-
ican statesman, farmer, b. Upper
Marlborough, Prince George's
Co., Md.

Delegate to the Continental
Congress, Maryland, 1780-1784.

**Cary, Archibald.** 1721-1787.
Patriot, planter, manufacturer.

Member of Virginia Committee
of Correspondence and delegate to
all Virginia Revolutionary conventions.

**Caswell, Richard.** 1729-1789.
American militia officer (Col.),
statesman, surveyor, court clerk,
lawyer, b. Harford (now Baltimore)
Co., Md.

Served at Moore's Creek
Bridge, N.C., 21 February 1776;
delegate to the Continental Congress, North Carolina, 1774-1776;
elected by North Carolina provisional congress first American
governor of North Carolina, 1776.

**Cathcart, Sir William Schaw.**
1755-1843. British officer (Lt. Col.),
diplomat.

In Philadelphia, 1778, organized
the Caledonian Volunteers, later

known as the British Legion (commanded by Banastre Tarleton);
ambassador to Russia, 1812-1820;
represented Britain at the Congress
of Vienna, 1814.

**Catherine II ("Catherine the
Great").** 1729-1796. Empress of
Russia, b. Stettin, Pomerania.

Catherine, who had come to the
throne in 1762 by deposing her
husband, was a strong ruler and a
consummate politician and diplomat. Her policies during the
American Revolution, designed to
strengthen Russia's international
position, were coincidentally help-
ful to the United States. In 1780
she proclaimed the League of
Armed Neutrality, in which she
was joined by leaders of other non-
belligerent European maritime
nations. The League of Armed
Neutrality asserted the right of
neutrals to trade freely, except in
war materiel, and their determination to protect this right.

**Celoron de Blainville, Paul Louis.**
1753-?. Continental officer
(Capt.), b. (present-day) Detroit,
Mich.

Canadian volunteer; served
1776-1783.

**Chalmers, George.** 1742-1825.
Loyalist, writer.

Wrote several works on the
fight for American independence
from a loyalist point of view:
*Political Annals of the United
Colonies*, 1780; *Estimate of the
Strength of Great Britain*, 1782;
and *Opinions of Law and Policy
arising from American Independence*, 1784.

**Chalmers, James.** Loyalist officer.

Raised a corps of Maryland loyalists (1777).

**Chambers, Stephen.** American officer (Capt.), American spy.

Operated an intelligence service between Valley Forge and Philadelphia.

**Champe, John.** c. 1756-1796. Continental soldier (Sgt. Maj.), b. Loudoun Co., Va.

Served in Lee's Legion; as directed by Washington and Lt. Col. Henry Lee, attempted to kidnap the traitor Benedict Arnold, 1780; after the war, pioneered to Kentucky, and later to Ohio.

**Chandler, Thomas Bradbury.** 1726-1790. Loyalist, clergyman, b. Woodstock, Conn.

Rector of St. John's Church, Elizabethtown (Elizabeth), N.J., from 1751; a leader of the pre-Revolutionary movement for the naming of American Anglican bishops; firm loyalist; published pamphlet, *What Think Ye of Congress Now?* (1775); spent Revolution years in England; returned to Elizabethtown, 1785.

**Chapin, Seth.** Continental naval officer (Lt.).

Massachusetts resident; along with six other patriots, captured a British vessel using only a whaleboat, 17 December 1778.

**Chase, Samuel.** 1741-1811. American statesman, jurist, lawyer, b. Princess Anne, Somerset Co., Md.

Delegate to the Continental Congress, Maryland, 1774-1778, 1784-1785; signer of the Declaration of Independence; named to the Supreme Court, 1796; impeached by the House of Representatives in 1804 for "high-handed conduct," but acquitted by the U.S. Senate in 1805; remained on the Court until his death in 1811.

**Chastellux, Chevalier de.** 1734-1788. French officer, writer.

Wrote *Travels in North America in the Years 1780, 1781, and 1782.*

**Chatham, Earl of.** *See* Pitt, William, the elder, Earl of Chatham.

**Cheever, Ezekial.** Continental officer.

Commissary of artillery stores for the Continental Army, appointed by Washington; Massachusetts resident.

**Chew, Benjamin.** c. 1723-1810. Loyalist, jurist, b. West River, Md.

Before the Revolution, served as recorder of Philadelphia, registrar of wills, attorney-general, and chief justice of Pennsylvania; remained in Philadelphia during the Revolution with no record of any overt action; his house, "Cliveden," played an important role in the battle of Germantown; 1790, president of the High Court of Errors and Appeals in Pennsylvania.

**Chittenden, Thomas.** 1730-1797. Patriot, statesman, b. East Guilford, Conn.

President of Vermont Council of Safety and first president (governor) of Vermont, 1778.

**Choiseul, Etienne François, Comte de Stainville.** 1719-1785. French statesman.

Minister for Foreign Affairs, 1758-1770, he saw the American war for independence as an opportunity for France to profit by defeating England. As early as 1764 he maintained agents in America to make reports on possible activity, notably Baron de Kalb.

**Choisy, Marquis de.** French officer (Lt. Gen.).

Commanded allied forces in action at Gloucester, Va., 3 October 1781.

**Christian, William.** c. 1743-1786. Militia officer (Col.), frontiersman, b. Staunton, Augusta Co., Va.

Experienced border leader who fought the Tories and Indians.

**Christophe, Henri.** 1767-1820. Soldier, King of Haiti, b. Grenada, West Indies.

Apparently as a boy of 12, took part in the attack against Savannah, Ga., 9 October 1779, in a Negro legion under the Vicomte de Fontanges; King of Haiti, 1811-1820.

**Church, Benjamin.** 1734-1777. Physician, patriot, Continental Army officer, later loyalist, b. Newport, R.I.

Prominent in revolutionary politics in Massachusetts, 1770-1775; first Surgeon General of the Continental Army; in 1775 was an informer to General Gage about American intentions at Bunker Hill; in October 1775 was tried and found guilty of treason; in 1777 was allowed to go to the West Indies in exile, but was lost at sea.

**Church, Thomas.** d.1778. Continental officer (Ensign), British spy.

Pennsylvania resident; ensign, 2d Pennsylvania; went over to British and served as spy; caught and hanged, 4 June 1778.

**Churchill, Elijah.** 1755-1841. Continental soldier.

Served in 2d Continental Dragoons (Connecticut) as a sergeant; first man to receive the "Badge of Military Merit" (later, Purple Heart) created by Washington; received award for gallantry and conduct in leading troops in raids on British outposts on Long Island; one of only three men who received the award during the Revolutionary War.

**Clark, Abraham.** 1726-1794. American statesman, b. Elizabethtown (now Elizabeth), N.J.

Delegate to the Continental Congress, New Jersey, 1776-1778, 1779-1783, 1786-1789; signer of the Declaration of Independence.

**Clark, George Rogers.** 1752-1818. Militia officer (Brig. Gen.), frontiersman, surveyor, landowner, b. Charlottesville, Va.

Explored and surveyed down Ohio River, 1772-1773; militia captain in Lord Dunmore's War, 1774; as major of militia organized defense of Kentucky, 1776; as lieutenant colonel, seized Kaskaskia (Illinois) and Fort Vincennes (Indiana), 1778; when lightly-garrisoned Vincennes was recaptured by the British and Indians, he took it again after a 180-mile midwinter march, also capturing the commander, Lt. Col. Henry Hamilton, 25 February 1779; fought the British and Indians in the northwest, 1779-1783, and won the Northwest Territory for the United States; treated shamefully by the United States and Virginia after the ' war; emigrated to Spanish-owned New Orleans; elder brother of William Clark of the Lewis and Clark expedition.

**Clark, John.** Militia officer (Maj.), American spy.

Head of an effective American spy ring, 1777, which both supplied British military information to the Americans and gave false American data to the British; warned Washington of British attack on Fort Mercer, N.J., and Fort Mifflin, Pa., November 1777.

**Clarke, Alured.** 1745?-1832. British officer (Lt. Col.)

Commanded the British garrison at Savannah, Ga., until its withdrawal in July 1782; later became commander-in-chief in India (1798) succeeding Sir Robert Abercromby.

**Clarke, Elijah.** 1733-1799. Militia officer (Col.), frontiersman, adventurer, b. Edgecombe, S.C.

Georgia militia captain; took part in actions at Green Spring, S.C., 1 August 1780; Wofford's Iron Works, S.C., 8 August 1780; Musgrove's Mill, S.C., 18 August 1780; and Augusta, Ga., 11-18 September 1780.

**Clay, Joseph.** 1741-1804. American statesman, general commission agent, b. Beverly, Yorkshire, England.

Delegate to the Continental Congress, Georgia, 1778-1780.

**Clerke, Sir Francis Carr.** 1748-1777. British officer (Capt.).

Aide-de-camp to General Burgoyne; mortally wounded at Saratoga, 7 October 1777.

**Cleveland, Benjamin.** 1738-1806. Militia officer (Col.), frontiersman, scout, b. Virginia.

A patriot leader at the battle of Kings Mountain; North Carolina resident.

**Clingan, William.** d. 1790. American statesman, jurist, b. Wagontown, Chester Co., Pa.

Delegate to the Continental Congress, Pennsylvania, 1777-1779.

**Clinton, George.** 1739-1812. Continental officer (Brig. Gen.), seaman, clerk, businessman, statesman, b. Little Britain, N.Y.

Delegate to the Continental Congress, New York, 1775-1777; brigadier general, Continental Army, 1777-1783; participated in the efforts to stop General Henry Clinton's expedition to the Hudson Highlands, October 1777; first governor of New York State, 1777; served six terms, until 1795, and again was elected in 1800; strongly opposed ratification of the Federal Constitution and preferred to see New York in a more independent role; coined the nickname "Empire State" to accentuate the independence of his state; in 1804, elected Vice President for second term of Thomas Jefferson; re-elected to serve under James Madison.

**Clinton, Sir Henry.** 1738?-1795. British officer (Lt. Gen.; General, local rank), b. Newfoundland, Canada.

Member of Parliament, 1772-1784; was second-in-command to General William Howe at Boston (1775-1776) with local rank of lieutenant general; commanded the Charleston, S.C., expedition of 1776; commanded expedition to the Hudson Highlands in October 1777; commander-in-chief of British forces in North America, 1778-1782; commander at Monmouth Courthouse, 1778; commanded Charleston expedition of 1780; succeeded as commander-in-chief by Sir Guy Carleton, 5 May 1782.

**Clinton, James.** 1733-1812. Continental officer (Brig. Gen.).

Brigadier general, 1776-1783; leader at battle of Chemung River (battle of Newton), N.Y., 29 August 1779; father of De Witt Clinton (1769-1828).

**Clow, Cheney.** d. 1788. Loyalist.

Attempted unsuccessfully, April 1778, to instigate a revolt in the Delaware legislature against the patriots; also tried an unsuccessful march against the capital, Dover.

**Clymer, George.** 1739-1813. American statesman, merchant, b. Philadelphia, Pa.

Delegate to the Continental Congress, Pennsylvania, 1776-1778, 1780-1783.

**Cobb, David.** 1748-1830. Continental officer (Lt. Col.), physician, b. Attleboro, Mass.

As lieutenant colonel, aide-de-camp to General Washington, 1781-1783; breveted brigadier general, 30 September 1783.

**Cochran, John.** 1730-1807. Physician, b. Pennsylvania.

Medical director of the Continental Army, 1781-1783.

**Coffin, Isaac.** 1759-1839. Loyalist, British naval officer (Comdr.), b. Boston, Mass.

Member of prominent Massachusetts family; brother of John Coffin; served under Admiral Hood, 1775-1779; Member of Parliament, 1818-1826; knighted in 1804 and became a full admiral by 1814.

**Coffin, John.** 1756-1838. Loyalist officer (Maj.), seaman, b. Boston, Mass.

Raised and commanded the Orange Rangers, 1776; distinguished himself at Eutaw Springs, S.C., 8 September 1781; remained with the British and became a general, 1819; elder brother of Isaac Coffin.

**Coffin, Sir Thomas Aston.** 1754-1810. Loyalist, British officer, b. Boston, Mass.

Secretary to Sir Guy Carleton, 1775-1783.

**Colden, Cadwallader.** d. 1776. Loyalist official.

Lieutenant governor of New York, 1761-1775.

**Coleraine, 4th Baron.** *See* Hanger, George.

**Collier, George.** 1738-1795. British naval officer (Commodore), b. London.

Senior naval officer at Halifax, Nova Scotia, in 1776; temporary commander-in-chief on the American station to succeed Gambier, 1779; broke up the Penobscot expedition, July 1779; became an admiral in 1793.

**Collins, John.** 1717-1795. American statesman, b. Newport, R.I.

Delegate to the Continental Congress, Rhode Island, 1778-1783.

**Colomb, Pierre.** 1754-? French volunteer, b. Nîmes, France.

Aide-de-camp to Lafayette and de Kalb.

**Conant, William.** Militia officer (Col.).

Resident of Charlestown, Mass.; pre-Revolution patriot leader; associate of Paul Revere; watched for the lights in Old North Church, 18-19 April 1775, which were a signal to him.

**Condict, Silas.** 1738-1801. American statesman, landowner, b. Morristown, N.J.

Delegate to the Continental Congress, Rhode Island, 1781-1784.

**Connolly, John.** c. 1750-? Loyalist, physician, land agent, b. Lancaster Co., Pa.

Settled in the area around Fort Pitt (Pittsburgh), which was disputed between Pennsylvania and Virginia; sided against his native state in favor of Virginia; partly responsible for Lord Dunmore's War (1774); in 1775 devised a plan whereby the Queen's Rangers, a Tory unit, would start at Detroit, seize Pittsburgh, and move on to Virginia to aid Dunmore; was captured before the plan could be executed.

**Conway, Thomas.** 1733-1800? Continental officer (Maj. Gen.), b. Ireland.

Veteran of 30 years' service in French Army; involved in the "Conway Cabal" of 1777, an attempt to discredit Washington; brigadier general, Continental Army, 1777; major general, 1777-1778; dismissed by Congress, 1778.

**Conyngham, Gustavus.** 1747-1819. Continental naval officer (Capt.), shipmaster, shipper, b. Ireland.

Emigrated to Philadelphia, 1763; shipmaster before Revolution; sailed as captain of merchant vessel to Europe, 1775; sailing from Dunkirk, took many prizes in North and Irish Seas, 1776-1777, with armed lugger *Surprise* (10) and cutter *Revenge* (14), whose command he had been given by the American commissioners in Paris; known as the "Dunkirk Pirate"; successfully cruised Atlantic and Mediterranean from Spanish ports, and then took prizes in West Indies; in February 1779 had taken 60 prizes in 18 months; captured by British 27 April 1779; escaped from prison in England, November 1779, but was recaptured, March 1780; exchanged 1781.

**Cooper, Sir Grey.** d. 1801. British official, b. Newcastle-on-Tyne.
Treasury Secretary, 1765-1782.

**Cooper, John.** 1729-1785. American statesman, jurist, b. Woodbury, Gloucester Co., N.J.
Delegate to the Continental Congress, New Jersey, 1776.

**Cooper, Myles.** 1737-1785. Loyalist, clergyman, educator, b. Cumberland Co., England.
President of King's College (now Columbia University), 1763-1775; twice fled from patriot mobs during 1775; left for England, May 1775.

**Copley, John Singleton.** 1737-1815. Painter, b. Boston, Mass.
A skilled and successful portraitist from his early youth, Copley painted many prominent Americans during the pre-Revolutionary period. Although he was apparently a patriot in his sympathies, his wife's family were all Tories, and in 1774 he went to England, where he lived and painted until his death.

**Corbin, John Tayloe.** Loyalist.
Prominent landowner and loyalist; member of Virginia (Governor's) Council; member, House of Burgesses, 1769-1772, 1772-1774, 1775; not related to Richard Corbin.

**Corbin, Margaret Cochran.** 1751-1800. Patriot heroine, b. Franklin Co., Pa.
Served as a cannoneer at Fort Washington, N.Y., 16 November 1776, after her husband's death; seriously wounded; pensioned for life by Congress; known as "Captain Molly"; sometimes called "Molly Pitcher" and confused with Mary Ludwig Hays.

**Corbin, Richard.** Loyalist.
Receiver general of Virginia; member of the Virginia (Governor's) Council.

**Cornell, Ezekiel.** 1732-1800. American statesman, mechanic, b. Scituate, R.I.
Delegate to the Continental Congress, Rhode Island, 1780-1783.

**Cornstalk.** c. 1720-1777. Shawnee Indian chief.
Commanded Indians at Point Pleasant in Lord Dunmore's War, 1774; killed in 1777 in retribution for the death of a white settler; death set off wave of warfare with the Shawnee Indians that continued until 1794.

**Cornwallis, Charles (second Earl Cornwallis).** 1738-1805. British officer (Lt. Gen.), statesman, b. London.
As a member of the House of Lords (from 1762), Cornwallis was a Whig who consistently opposed both Parliament's efforts to tax the American colonies and the later coercive measures. He served with distinction, 1776-1778, notably as corps commander at Long Island, White Plains, and Brandywine; was second-in-command to Sir Henry Clinton, 1778-1780; and was in command of British forces in the south, 1780-1781. He defeated Horatio Gates at Camden, 16

August 1780; won a costly victory over Nathanael Greene at Guilford Courthouse, 15 March 1781; and was forced to surrender to Washington at Yorktown, 19 October 1781. After the war, Cornwallis served with distinction as governor-general of India (1786-1794) and viceroy of Ireland (1798-1801).

**Cornwallis, Sir William.** 1744-1819. British naval officer (Comdr.).

Played an important role in the battle of Grenada, West Indies (6 July 1779) and action at St. Kitts, West Indies (26 January 1782); brother of Charles, Lord Cornwallis.

**Corny, Dominique-Louis Ethis de.** 1736-1790. French officer.

French commissary officer who made advance preparations for Rochambeau's expeditionary force in 1780.

**Costigin, Lewis J.** Continental officer (Lt.), merchant, American spy.

Resident of New Brunswick, N.J.; spied for the Americans, 1776-1779; signed his reports "Z"; sent much valuable information from New York City, where he remained after having been detained as a prisoner of war and then having been exchanged.

**Coudray, Philippe Charles Jean Baptiste Tronson de.** *See* Tronson de Coudray.

**Coxe, Daniel.** 1741-1826. Loyalist, jurist.

Speaker of the New Jersey State Assembly; 1777-1778, raised the West Jersey Volunteers.

**Craig, Charles.** Continental officer (Capt.), American spy.

Pennsylvania resident; headed a spy network in the Philadelphia area that was especially active and effective in 1777.

**Craig, James Henry.** 1748-1812. British officer.

Commanded the garrison at Wilmington, N.C., 1781, and managed to escape and avoid capture, 18 November 1781.

**Craik, Dr. James.** 1730-1814. Physician, b. Arbigland, near Dumfries, Scotland.

Chief physician and surgeon of the Continental Army, 1780-1781; Virginia resident.

**Crane, John.** 1744-1805. Continental officer (Col.), housewright, lumberman, jurist, b. Braintree, Mass.

Fought in French and Indian War as a boy; Son of Liberty; participated in Boston Tea Party, 1773; major of artillery, 1775; colonel, 1777, fought in Rhode Island campaign, July-August 1778, and at Saratoga.

**Crane, Stephen.** 1709-1780. American statesman, jurist, b. Elizabethtown (now Elizabeth), N.J.

Delegate to the Continental Congress, New Jersey, 1774-1776.

**Crawford, William.** 1732-1782. Continental officer (Col.), frontiersman, farmer, surveyor, b. Berkeley Co., Pa.

Commanded an expedition into Ohio, 1782; defeated, captured, and tortured to death by Indians, supposedly in retaliation for the massacre of Indians at Gnadenhuetten, Ohio, 1782.

**Cresap, Michael.** 1742-1775. Continental officer (Capt.), trader, frontiersman, b. Allegany Co., Md. Co., Md.

Settled near present-day Wheeling, W.Va.; participated as a captain in Lord Dunmore's War; raised a company of volunteers from Ohio and western Maryland and brought them to aid Washington at Boston, 1775; resigned his command because of illness, October 1775, and died on the way home.

**Crillon, Louis des Balbes de Berton.** 1717-1796. French officer, Spanish officer (Lt. Gen.).

Led expedition that captured Minorca from English, summer, 1782; then led unsuccessful French and Spanish attack on Gibraltar, 13-14 September 1782.

**Cromot du Bourg, Baron de.** French officer.

Aide to Rochambeau; compiled a valuable journal during his stay in America.

**Crosby, Enoch.** Shoemaker, militiaman, Continental soldier, American counterintelligence agent, b. Harwich, Mass.

Resident of Danbury, Conn., at beginning of Revolution; served in invasion of Canada, 1775-1776; became counterspy and worked effectively to identify and have arrested recruits for Tory military units; served under John Jay; later returned to Army, serving in the 4th and then the 2d New York Continentals; spying exploits were the basis for James Fennimore Cooper's *The Spy*, although Cooper was not aware that Crosby was the real hero of the stories Cooper had heard and used.

**Cruger, John Harris.** 1738-1807. Loyalist officer, b. Westchester, N.Y.

Son-in-law of Oliver DeLancey; commanded loyalist battalions at Savannah, Ga., 29 December 1778, and in the defense of Savannah, 9 October 1779; provided relief at Augusta, Ga., 14-18 September 1780; commanded the Tory stronghold at Ninety-Six, S.C., May-June, 1781; highly regarded by the British.

**Culper, Jr.** *See* Townsend, Robert.

**Culper, Sr.** *See* Woodhull, Samuel.

**Cumberland, Richard.** 1732-1811. British diplomat.

Secretary of the Board of Trade, 1775-1781; unsuccessfully, along with Thomas Hussey, attempted to negotiate a settlement with Spain, 1780, 1781.

**Cunningham, Robert.** c. 1739-1813. Loyalist leader, jurist, b. Ireland.

Brigadier general of the South Carolina Tory militia.

**Cunningham, William.** c. 1717-1791. British official, horse trainer, b. Ireland.

British provost marshal; in charge of prisons in Philadelphia and New York City; accused of cruelty, starving prisoners, and hanging some without trial.

**Cunningham, William ("Bloody Bill").** d. 1787. Loyalist partisan.

South Carolina Tory partisan and leader of a raiding band in Georgia and the Carolinas.

**Curtenius, Peter T.** American statesman, merchant.

Served as commissary for New York, 1775-1782; became state auditor, 1782.

**Curwen, Samuel.** 1715-1802. Loyalist, jurist, b. Salem, Mass.

Judge of the Admirality Court in Boston; went to England when the Revolution began; wrote *Journal and Letters* (1845), an account of loyalist exiles in England.

**Cushing, Thomas.** 1725-1788. American statesman, lawyer, b. Boston, Mass.

Delegate to the Continental Congress, Massachusetts, 1774-1776.

**Cutter, Ammi.** Physician.

Physician general of hospitals, Eastern Department, 1777-1778; New Hampshire resident.

# D

**Dabney, Austin.** Militia soldier.

Free Negro; private, Georgia militia; severely wounded at battle of Kettle Creek, Ga., 24 February 1779; pensioned by Georgia state legislature.

**Dale, Richard.** 1756-1826. Continental naval officer (Lt.), seaman, b. Norfolk Co., Va.

Second-in-command to John Paul Jones, and a hero of the *Serapis* fight.

**Dalling, John.** d. 1798. British officer (Lt. Gen.), government official.

Governor of Jamaica, 1777-1782; responsible for sending expeditions to Honduras and Nicaragua in 1779 and 1781; was responsible for the ports of Mobile and Pensacola, probably had inadequate means with which to defend them, and lost them to the Spanish.

**Dalrymple, John.** 1749-1821. British officer.

Led a force in the daring capture of the Spanish fortification of Omoa in Honduras Bay, October 1779.

**Dalrymple, William.** d. 1807. British officer (Col.).

Commander of the Boston garrison, 1768-1772; quartermaster general to Sir Henry Clinton, 1779-1782.

**Dana, Francis.** 1743-1811. American statesman, diplomat, lawyer, b. Charlestown, Mass.

Delegate to the Continental Congress, Massachusetts, 1776-1778, 1784; American minister to Russia, 1780-1783.

**Darke, William.** 1736-1801. Militia officer (Col.), U.S. Army officer (Brig. Gen.), farmer, b. Philadelphia Co., Pa.

Grew up in western Virginia; militia captain, 1775; captured at Germantown, 1777; exchanged 1780; recruited regiment, 1781, and led it at siege of Yorktown; fought as colonel under St. Clair in Indian campaign of 1791 and was promoted to brigadier general.

**Darragh, Lydia.** American spy.

Philadelphia resident; sent military information from British-occupied Philadelphia, 1777; apparently enabled Washington to avoid surprise by the British at Whitemarsh, Pa., 7 December 1777.

**Dartmouth, William Legge, 2nd Earl of.** 1731-1801. British statesman.

Secretary of State for the American Department, 1772-1775; while believing in Parliamentary supremacy in America, was nevertheless considered a friend of the colonies; supported Moor's Indian Charity School in Lebanon, N.H., which was named in his honor Dartmouth College.

**Davidson, William Lee.** 1746-1781. Militia officer (Brig. Gen.), b. Lancaster, Pa.

Settled in North Carolina as child; major, 4th N.C. Regiment, 1776; fought at Germantown, 1777; lieutenant colonel, 1777; commanded a battalion of 300 light infantry at the victory at Ramseur's Mill, N.C., 20 June 1780; promoted to brigadier general, 1780; killed

at battle of Cowan's Ford, N.C., 1 February 1781.

**Davie, William Richardson,** 1756-1820. Militia officer (Col.), statesman, lawyer, b. Egremont, Cumberlandshire, England.

Brought as a child to South Carolina; served with Pulaski Legion, 1779; distinguished himself at Hanging Rock, S.C. (6 August 1780), Wahab's Plantation, N.C. (21 September 1780), and Charlotte, N.C. (26 September 1780); commissary general on General Greene's staff, 1781; governor of North Carolina, 1798.

**Davis, Joshua.** Patriot, whaleboatman, American spy.

Successfully carried out spy mission in New York City a few days after Nathan Hale's capture and execution there, September 1776; later worked with Caleb Brewster in carrying spy reports from New York across Long Island Sound.

**Dawes, William.** 1745-1799. Patriot, tanner, grocer, b. Boston, Mass.

Co-rider with Paul Revere, 18-19 April 1775.

**Dayton, Elias.** 1737-1807. Continental officer (Brig. Gen.), mechanic, storekeeper, b. Elizabethtown (now Elizabeth), N.J.

French and Indian War veteran; Continental colonel, 1776; fought in actions throughout war, including Brandywine, Germantown, Monmouth, Sullivan's New York expedition of 1779, and Yorktown; also headed an important American spy network; brigadier general, January 1783; member, Continental Congress, 1787-1788.

**Deane, Silas.** 1737-1789. American statesman, diplomat, lawyer, b. Groton, Conn.

Deane was a delegate to the Continental Congress from Connecticut, 1774-1776. In 1776 he went to Paris, as a commissioner, to obtain French assistance for the American cause and possible recognition of independence. He succeeded in establishing Roderique Hortalez et Cie., a secret company to give munitions to the Americans. Along with Benjamin Franklin and Arthur Lee, he aided in the 1778 alliance with France and the recognition of American independence. In 1781 he apparently began to have misgivings about the American cause, and favored an accommodation with the British; his dealings with a British agent were probably treasonous.

**Dearborn, Henry.** 1751-1829. American statesman, Continental officer, physician, customs collector, b. North Hampton, N.H.

Assistant quartermaster general, 1781-1783; member, U.S. House of Representatives, Massachusetts, 1793-1797; Secretary of War, 1801-1809; senior American Army officer, War of 1812; Minister to Portugal, 1822-1824.

**De Borre, Prudhomme.** *See* Prudhomme de Borre, Chevalier Philippe Hubert.

**De Haas, John Philip.** c. 1735-1786. Continental officer (Brig. Gen.), b. Netherlands.

Major, Pennsylvania Provincials, 1775; colonel, 1776; Continental brigadier general, 1777-1783; went to Philadelphia, 1779, and saw no active duty after that year.

**De Hart, John.** 1728-1795. American statesman, lawyer, b. Elizabethtown, (now Elizabeth) N.J.

Delegate to the Continental Congress, New Jersey, 1774-1775, 1776.

**DeLancey, James, the elder.** 1732-1800. Loyalist, landowner, merchant, statesman, British officer (Capt.), b. New York City.

Educated in England; served in British Army and fought in colonial wars until 1760, when he came into his rich inheritance; assembled fine stable of race horses and has been called "Father of the New York Turf"; political leader of the aristocratic DeLancey faction in New York politics, 1760-1775; supported colonial rights but opposed armed resistance; moved to England, 1775 or 1776; uncle of James DeLancey the younger; nephew of Oliver DeLancey the elder.

**DeLancey, James, the younger.** 1746-1804. Loyalist leader, b. Westchester Co., N.Y.

Sheriff of Westchester County, N.Y., 1770-1776; led Westchester Light Horse Brigade, the Tory "Cowboys" of the "Cowboys and (patriot) Skinners," marauding bands operating in "The Neutral Ground" just north of Manhattan Island; great-nephew of Oliver De Lancey the elder and nephew of

James DeLancey the elder; moved to Nova Scotia after the Revolution.

**DeLancey, Oliver, the elder.** 1718-1785. Loyalist officer (Brig. Gen.), landowner, merchant, b. Westchester Co., N.Y.

New York political leader before the Revolution; loyalist officer in America; raised the 1500-man brigade known as "DeLancey's Battalions," or "DeLancey's New York Volunteers," which served with distinction throughout the south as well as in Queens County, N.Y.; father of Oliver DeLancey the younger and uncle of James DeLancey the elder; went to England after the war.

**DeLancey, Oliver, the younger.** 1749-1822. British officer (Lt. Col.), loyalist, b. New York, N.Y.

Adjutant general to General Clinton, 1780-1781; adjutant general of the British Army in America, 1781-1783; had a distinguished post-Revolution British Army career; promoted to general in 1812; Member of Parliament.

**Demont, William.** American soldier, deserter.

Regimental adjutant, 5th Pennsylvania Battalion; deserted to camp of General Hugh Percy, 2 November 1776, and gave the British the plans for Fort Washington, N.Y.; his treason aided in the successful assault and capture of the fortress, 16 November 1776.

**Denison (Dennison), Nathan.** Militia officer (Col.), b. New London, Conn.

Leading member of the community of Connecticut settlers in Wyoming Valley, Pa.; commanded troops in the battle (or "massacre") of Wyoming Valley, 3-4 July 1778.

**De Peyster, Abraham.** 1753-c. 1779. Loyalist officer (Lt. Col.).

Became commander of the King's American Rangers after the battle of Kings Mountain, succeeding Patrick Ferguson, 7 October 1780; New York resident.

**De Peyster, Arent Schuyler.** 1736-1832. Loyalist officer (Col.), b. New York.

Commanded posts at Detroit and Mackinac; helped keep Indians of those areas loyal to the British cause; uncle of Abraham De Peyster.

**De Peyster, James.** Loyalist officer (Capt.).

New York resident; captured in Georgetown County, S.C., by Colonel James Postell, 19 January 1781.

**Derick, Jacob Gerhard.** Continental officer (Brevet Lt. Col.), b. Netherlands.

Dutch volunteer; captain, 9th Pennsylvania, 15 November 1776; captain, 4th Continental Artillery, 3 March 1777; breveted lieutenant colonel, 5 November 1778; probably the same man as Lt. Col. Johan G. Dircks, who wrote while on leave in Holland, 1779, suggesting that the Netherlands Government be approached for a loan.

**Despard, Edward Marcus.** 1715-1803. British naval officer (Capt.), government official, b. Ireland.

Took part in successful operations at Nicaragua and San Juan, 1779; made governor of the Mosquito Shore and the Bay of Honduras; later executed for his part in a plot to seize the Tower of London and Bank of England and to assassinate George III.

**Despard, John.** 1745-1829. British officer (Maj.).

Distinguished himself in Clinton expedition to the Hudson Highlands, 3-22 October 1777; deputy adjutant general in Lord Rawdon's Volunteers of Ireland, 1779; took part in the Charleston, S.C., expedition of Clinton in 1778, and in subsequent operations of Cornwallis, 1780-1781.

**Destouches, Charles-René-Dominique Sochet, Chevalier.** French naval officer (Commodore).

Commander of the French squadron at Newport, R.I., 1780-1781.

**Deux-Ponts, Guillaume, Comte de.** French officer (Lt. Col.), d. 1813.

Member of ruling family of German-speaking duchy of Deux-Ponts in Saar Basin; commanded the French force that captured Redoubt Nine outside Yorktown, 14 October 1781; died a general under Napoleon at Leipzig.

**Devens, Richard.** Patriot.

Resident of Boston area; associate of Paul Revere in patriot intelligence work; member of local committee of safety.

**DeWitt, Simeon.** 1756-1834. Continental officer, surveyor, b. Wawarsing, Ulster Co., N.Y.

Mapmaker; geographer-in-chief of Continental Army, 1780-1784.

**Dickinson, John.** 1732-1808. American statesman, lawyer, militia officer, b. "Crosiadore," near Trappe, Talbot Co., Md.

Author of influential newspaper writings against Townshend Acts, *Letters from a Pennsylvania Farmer*, 1767-1768; delegate to the Continental Congress, Pennsylvania, 1774-1776, and Delaware, 1776, 1777, 1779-1780; opposed Declaration of Independence; headed committee in Congress that drafted Articles of Confederation; member of Federal Constitutional Convention from Delaware, 1787, and worked in Delaware and Pennsylvania for ratification of Constitution.

**Dickinson, Philemon.** 1739-1809. American statesman, landowner, militia officer (Brig. Gen.), b. "Crosiadore," near Trappe, Talbot Co., Md.

Commander-in-chief of the New Jersey militia, 1777-1783; served in the Monmouth campaign, June-July 1778; delegate to the Continental Congress, Delaware, 1782-1783; brother of John Dickinson.

**Digby, Robert.** 1732-1814. British naval officer (Rear Adm.).

Commander-in-chief on the American station, 1781-1783.

**Diggs, Dudley.** 1718-1790. Patriot.

Member of Virginia Committee of Safety, 1775-1776; Virginia examiner of claims during the Revolution.

**Dircks, Johan G.** *See* Derick, Jacob Gerhard.

**Donelson, John.** Militia officer (Col.), frontiersman.

Virginian; led a pioneering expedition of settlers into present-day Tennessee, 1780.

**Donop, Carl Emil Kurt von.** c. 1740-1777. Hessian officer (Col.).

Commanded Hessian division on British left in New Jersey, late 1776, holding Mount Holly, Burlington, and Bordentown; withdrew to Princeton, N.J., after the battle of Trenton; mortally wounded at Fort Mercer (Red Bank), N.J., 22 October 1777.

**Downs, John.** Patriot.

Defeated Indians at Rayborn Creek (Lindley's Fort), S.C., 15 July 1776.

**Doxtader, John.** Tory raider.

Led the raid at Currytown, N.Y., 30 June 1781, burning the town; defeated at Sharon Springs Swamp, N.Y., 10 July 1781.

**Doyle, John.** 1750?-1834. British officer (Maj.), b. County Kilkenny, Ireland (probably).

Distinguished himself at Long Island; fought at Harlem Heights, N.Y. (16 September 1776), Brandywine, Germantown, Monmouth, and in the south; British commander at Dorchester, S.C., 1 December 1781; fought with distinction in the Napoleonic wars; became major general in 1802 and was created baronet in 1805.

**D'Oyley, Christian.** British government official.

Junior under secretary in the American Department.

**Drayton, William H.** 1742-1779. American statesman, lawyer, jurist, b. Drayton Hall, Ashley River, S.C.

Delegate to the Continental Congress, 1778-1779.

**Drummond, Duncan.** British officer (Maj.).

Aide to Lt. Gen. Sir Henry Clinton; intelligence officer; directed the work of British spy Ann Bates.

**Drummond, Robert.** c. 1736-1789. Loyalist officer (Maj.).

Member of the General Assembly of New Jersey, 1770-1774; deputy to the Provincial Convention, 1775-1776; voted against the adoption of the New Jersey Constitution, 2 July 1776; became a major in the 3rd Battalion of New Jersey Volunteers, 1776; served in the 2nd Battalion of New Jersey Volunteers, 1778-1780.

**Duane, James.** 1733-1797. American statesman, lawyer, district judge, b. New York, N.Y.

Delegate to the Continental Congress, New York, 1774-1784.

**Dubuysson des Hays, Charles-François, Vicomte.** 1752-1786. Continental officer, b. France.

Aide-de-camp to General de Kalb.

**Duché, Jacob.** 1738-1798. Clergyman, loyalist, b. Philadelphia, Pa.

Appointed chaplain of Congress, 6 July 1776; turned loyalist after the Declaration of Independence and resigned, October 1776; 8 October 1776, wrote a letter to Washington asking that the Americans rescind the Declaration of Independence and give up the "hopeless struggle."

**Dudley, Ambrose.** Militia officer (Col.).

Force dispersed by Colonel John Simcoe at Charles City Courthouse, Va., 8 January 1781.

**Duer, William.** 1747-1799. American statesman, jurist, businessman, b. Devonshire, England.

Came to New York, 1768; active early patriot; delegate to the Continental Congress, New York, 1777-1778; assistant Secretary of the Treasury under Alexander Hamilton; carried out much land speculation and other promotional activity; failure led to New York financial panic of 1792; died in debtors' prison.

**Dulany, Daniel.** 1722-1797. Loyalist, lawyer, b. Annapolis, Md.

Active in opposition to Stamp Act, 1765, but not a radical; became an avowed loyalist after the outbreak of the Revolution.

**Dumas, Charles William Frederick.** 1721-1796. Netherlands government official.

Unofficial Dutch observer in America, 1776-1783.

**Dunbar, Moses.** 1746-1777. Loyalist, b. Wallingford, Conn.

Only loyalist executed in Connecticut, he became something of a loyalist "Nathan Hale" as a symbol of Tory sentiment.

**Dundas, Thomas.** 1750-1794. British officer (Lt. Col.), b. Scotland (probably).

Member of Parliament; commanded a regiment and then a brigade in the campaigns of 1779-1781; represented General Cornwallis at surrender negotiations, 17 October 1781; fought in War of the First Coalition as major general; died of fever on active duty.

**Dunmore, John Murray, 4th Earl of.** 1732-1809. Royal governor, Scottish peer.

Royal governor of New York, 1770-1771; of Virginia, 1771-1776; called up 3,000 militiamen to suppress Shawnee uprising, 1774, and ensuing fighting was known as Lord Dunmore's War; dissolved House of Burgesses, May 1774, because of its protests against Boston Port Act; seized colony's store of powder, April 1775; declared Virginia under martial law, 7 November 1775, and established loyalist base at Norfolk; led successful action at Kemp's Landing, Va., 14 November 1775, but was defeated at Great Bridge, Va., 9 December, and fled to British warships; bombarded and set fire to Norfolk, 1 January 1776.

**Duportail, Louis, Chevalier (Louis le Begue de Presle, Chevalier).** 1743-1802. Continental officer (Maj. Gen.), b. Pithiviers, France.

French volunteer; one of four officers chosen by French government in response to Benjamin Franklin's request for trained military engineers; named colonel of engineers by Congress, 13 February 1777; strengthened Delaware River fortifications in Brandy-wine-Philadelphia campaign, September-December 1777; promoted to brigadier general and appointed Chief of Engineers, 17 November 1777; was at Valley Forge; sent by Washington to help Lincoln at Charleston, but arrived too late to play a significant role; taken prisoner, 12 May 1780; exchanged, 25 October 1780; played vital role in siege operations at Yorktown; promoted to major general, 1781; one of a handful of foreign volunteers who contributed significantly to American independence.

**Durkee, Robert.** Continental officer (Col.).

Resident of the Connecticut-settled Wyoming Valley of Pennsylvania; organized and led Wyoming Valley company to aid General Washington, 1776; killed in the Wyoming Valley "massacre," 3 July 1778.

**Dyer, Eliphalet.** 1721-1807. American statesman, b. Windham, Conn.

Delegate to Stamp Act Congress, 1765; delegate to the Continental Congress, Connecticut, 1774-1779, 1780-1783; chief justice of Connecticut, 1789-1793.

# E

**Eddy, Jonathan.** Nova Scotia rebel.

Led a group of 180 Nova Scotia rebels in an unsuccessful siege of Fort Cumberland, Nova Scotia, along with John Allen, in 1776.

**Eden, Robert.** 1741-1783. Royal governor.

Last royal governor of Maryland, 1767-1776; forced to flee Maryland in 1776 after the Maryland Council of Safety learned of his plan to support the British armed forces and demanded his arrest; brother of William Eden.

**Eden, William.** 1744-1814. British statesman.

Under secretary of state for the Southern Department, 1772; Member of Parliament, 1774; member of Board of Trade and Plantations; organized and went to America with the Carlisle peace commission, 1778; brother of Robert Eden.

**Edwards, Pierrepont.** 1750-1826. American statesman, lawyer, judge, b. Northampton, Mass.

Served as soldier in Revolution; named administrator of Benedict Arnold's estate after Arnold's treason; delegate to the Continental Congress, Connecticut, 1787-1788; member of Federal Constitutional Convention.

**Egleston, Joseph.** 1754-1811. Continental officer (Maj.), b. Middlesex Co., Va.

Cavalry commander, Continental army; distinguished himself at Guilford Courthouse, at Augusta, Ga. (May-June 1781), and at Eutaw Springs, S.C., 8 September 1781; member, U.S. House of Representatives, Virginia, 1798-1801.

**Elbert, Samuel.** 1743-1788. Continental officer (Col.), statesman, merchant, b. South Carolina.

Member, first Georgia Committee of Safety; Son of Liberty; Continental lieutenant colonel, 1776; colonel, 1776; commanded abortive attack on East Florida, 1777; fought well at Briar Creek, Ga., 3 March 1779, where he was captured; commanded a brigade at siege of Yorktown; governor of Georgia, 1785.

**Ellegood, Jacob.** Planter, loyalist.
Virginia resident; prominent in support of royalist cause.

**Ellery, William.** 1727-1820. American statesman, lawyer, b. Newport, R.I.
Delegate to the Continental Congress, Rhode Island, 1776-1781, 1783-1785; signer of the Declaration of Independence.

**Eliott, Sir George Augustus.** 1717-1790. British officer (Lt. Gen.), b. Scotland.
Led difficult, successful three-year (1779-1782) defense of Gibraltar against Spanish; created Lord Heathfield, Baron of Gibraltar, 1787.

**Elliot, Andrew.** d. 1830. Government official, loyalist leader.
Collector of the port of New York; superintendent of police for New York City after the British occupation.

**Elliot, John.** d. 1808. British naval officer (Commodore).
Second-in-command to Admiral Howe, June-August 1778; commanded the *Trident*, which carried the Carlisle peace commission to America.

**Ellis, Welbore.** 1713-1802. British statesman, b. Kildare, Ireland.
Secretary of State for the American Department, February-March 1782, succeeding Germain; served only one month because Rockingham became Prime Minister in March 1782.

**Ellsworth, Oliver.** 1745-1807. American statesman, lawyer, b. Windsor, Conn.
Delegate to the Continental Congress, Connecticut, 1777-1784.

**Elmer, Jonathan.** 1745-1817. American statesman, physician, jurist, b. Cedarville, Cumberland Co., N.J.
Delegate to the Continental Congress, New Jersey, 1776-1778, 1781-1784, 1787-1788.

**Elphinstone, George Keith.** 1746-1823. British naval officer (Capt.), b. Elphinstone Tower, near Stirling, Scotland.
Active in operations against American privateers and blockade runners, and in support of British Army land operations; commanded the warship *Warwick* off American waters, 1781-1783.

**Enos, Roger.** 1729-1808. Continental officer (Lt. Col.), militia officer (Brig. Gen.), b. Simsbury, Conn.
Commanded battalion on Arnold's Quebec expedition; court-martialed for turning back, but acquitted; resigned Continental commission and became militia officer; brigadier general in command of all Vermont militia, 1781; promoted to major general, 1787.

**Erskine, Robert.** 1735-1780. Continental officer, hydraulic engineer, mapmaker, b. Scotland.

Successful engineer in England; fellow of the Royal Society; geographer-in-chief, Continental Army, 1777-1780; New Jersey resident.

**Erskine, William.** 1728-1795. British officer (Maj. Gen.).

Commanded a brigade at Long Island and surprised the Americans at Jamaica, N.Y., 27-28 August 1776; second-in-command during Connecticut coast raid, April 1777; quartermaster general to General Henry Clinton, 1777-1779.

**Estaing, Jean-Baptiste Charles Henri Hector Théodat, Comte d'.** 1729-1794. French naval officer (Adm.), b. Auvergne, France.

Commanded the French fleet dispatched to fight the British fleet in American waters, 1778; missed opportunity to bottle up the British fleet in the Chesapeake Bay in 1778; missed another in the West Indies in July 1779, when, with superior forces, he retreated instead of pursuing the British under Byron; captured Grenada and won some minor successes in the West Indies, 1779; failure at Savannah, 9 October 1779, capped a generally unsuccessful tour of duty; returned to France, 1780.

**Eustis, William.** 1753-1825. Physician, statesman, b. Cambridge, Mass.

Served as a surgeon with various units of the Continental Army, 1776-1783; member of the General Court of Massachusetts, 1788;

member, U.S. House of Representatives, 1800, 1820-1823; Secretary of War, 1807-1812; governor of Massachusetts, 1824-1825.

**Evans, John.** American statesman, jurist.

Delegate to the Continenetal Congress, Delaware, 1776-1777.

**Eveleigh, Nicholas.** c. 1748-1782. American statesman, farmer, b. Charleston, S.C.

Delegate to the Continental Congress, 1781-1782, South Carolina; first comptroller of the United States Treausry, 1789-1791.

# F

**Fairfax, Bryan.** d. 1802. Loyalist, clergyman, b. Fairfax Co., Va.

An early proponent of colonists' rights, he vigorously opposed the Stamp Act of 1765; he was opposed, however, to forcible resistance to Britain. He remained in Virginia during the Revolution, and in 1789 became minister of the Fairfax Parish of the Protestant Episcopal Church, the newly organized Anglican church in the United States. In 1800 his title of Lord Fairfax of Cameron was recognized by the House of Lords, and he was allowed to sit in that body. Bryan Fairfax's father was a cousin of Thomas, Lord Fairfax.

**Fairfax, Thomas Lord (sixth Baron Fairfax of Cameron).** 1693-1781. Landowner, loyalist, b. Yorkshire, England.

Settled in Virginia, 1747, as proprietor of his extensive lands there; engaged George Washington to survey western portions of his holdings; remained loyalist.

**Fanning, David.** c. 1755-1825. Loyalist partisan, Indian trader, b. Beech Swamp, Amelia Co., Va.

North Carolina loyalist partisan; operated in Virginia, South Carolina, and North Carolina; trained by "Bloody Bill" Cunningham; from 1776 to 1781 was in and out of patriot prisons; most successful attack was the Hillsboro raid of 12 September 1781.

**Fanning, Edmund.** 1739-1818. Loyalist leader, lawyer, b. Long Island, N.Y.

Forced out of North Carolina in 1770 by the Regulators (*See* Few, James); private secretary to Governor William Tryon of New York, 1771; surveyor general of New York, 1774; became an ardent loyalist and raised Fanning's Regiment, 1776; wounded twice; moved to Nova Scotia after the war, and later to England; promoted to full general in the British Army, 1806.

**Fanning, Nathaniel.** 1755-1805. Seaman, b. Stonington, Conn.

Served under John Paul Jones, 1778-1781; became an American privateer captain.

**Fay, Jonas.** 1737-1818. Physician, b. Westborough, Mass.

Surgeon of Green Mountain Boys; Vermont representative to the Continental Congress to obtain independent status for Vermont.

**Fehiger, Christian.** 1746-1796. Continental officer (Col.), businessman, b. Denmark.

Virginia resident; brigade-major to Arnold on Quebec expedition; taken prisoner at Quebec, 31 December 1775; exchanged November 1776; served to end of war.

**Feltman, William.** Continental officer (2nd Lt.).

Pennsylvania resident; kept a valuable diary of his service, 1776-1781.

**Ferguson, Adam.** 1723-1816. British statesman, philosopher, historian, b. Perthshire, Scotland.

Professor of moral philosophy, Edinburgh; acting secretary of the Carlisle peace commission, 1778.

**Ferguson, Elizabeth Graeme (Mrs. Hugh).** 1737-1801. Loyalist, poet, translator, b. Philadelphia, Pa.

Mrs. Ferguson carried the famous Jacob Duché letter to General Washington, October 1776. She also acted as an intermediary between George Johnstone of the Carlisle peace commission and Congressmen Francis Dana, Joseph Reed, and Robert Morris. Johnstone was attempting to bribe the Congressmen, but Mrs. Ferguson did not know this.

**Ferguson, Hugh Henry.** Loyalist.

Commissary of prisoners in Pennsylvania.

**Ferguson, Patrick.** 1744-1780. British officer (Maj.), partisan leader, inventor, b. Scotland.

Commanded King's American Rangers; led British forces in the successful raid on Egg Harbor (Mincock Island), N.J., 14-15 October 1778; was defeated and killed at Kings Mountain, S.C., 7 October 1780; inventor of the Ferguson breech-loading rifle.

**Ferguson, Robert.** Loyalist, British spy.

Rhode Island resident; sent to Sir Henry Clinton a terrain study of the country around Providence, R.I., and similar information about other parts of New England.

**Fermoy, Matthias Alexis de Roche, Chevalier.** b. c. 1737. Continental officer (Brig. Gen.), b. Martinique.

French volunteer; brigadier general, Continental Army, 1776-1778; performed poorly at Trenton and in the preliminaries to Princeton; bungled his mission at Ticonderoga, July 1777; resigned, early 1778.

**Few, James.** "Regulator."

Few, commanding ineptly a force of western North Carolina Regulators, was defeated by Governor William Tryon at Almanace Creek, N.C., 16 May 1771, and was hanged on the battlefield, 17 May 1771. The Regulators were protesting control of the colony by eastern Carolinians.

**Few, William.** 1748-1828. American statesman, lawyer, b. Baltimore, Md.

Delegate to the Continental Congress, Georgia, 1780-1782, 1785-1788; member, U.S. Senate, Georgia, 1789-1793.

**Fish, Nicholas.** 1758-1833. Continental officer (Maj.), state and local government official, b. New York, N.Y.

Close college and lifetime friend of Alexander Hamilton; lieutenant, captain, and brigade major in New York militia, 1775-1776; Continental major, 1776-1783; fought at Saratoga and Monmouth and in Sullivan's expedition against the Indians, 1779; Hamilton's second-in-command during Yorktown campaign; New York state adjutant general after the war; alderman, 1806-1817; Federalist and anti-Tammany leader in politics.

**Fitzgerald, John.** Continental officer (Lt. Col.).

Virginia resident; aide-to-camp to General Washington, 1776-1778.

**Fitzhugh, Peregrine.** Continental officer (Lt. Col.).

Virginia resident; aide-to-camp to General Washington, 1781-1783.

**Fitzhugh, William.** 1741-1809. American statesman, farmer, b. King George Co., Va.

Delegate to the Continental Congress, Virginia, 1779-1780.

**Fitzsimmons (or FitzSimons), Thomas.** 1741-1811. American statesman, merchant, banker, b. Ireland.

Came to Philadelphia as young man; became successful merchant; raised and commanded patriot militia company; appointed to Pennsylvania Navy Board, to devise defense measures for Philadelphia and the Delaware River basin; delegate to Continenetal Congress, 1782-1783; served in Pennsylvania state legislature; member of Federal Constitutional Convention, 1787; member, U.S. House of Representatives, 1789-1795; Federalist; leading banker, insurance company official.

**Fleming, William.** 1736-1824. American statesman, lawyer, b. Cumberland Co., Va.

Delegate to the Continental Congress, Virginia, 1779-1781.

**Fleury, François Louis Teissedre de.** *See* Teissedre de Fleury, François Louis.

**Floridablanca, José.** 1728-1808. Spanish statesman, b. Murcia, Spain.

Spanish Foreign Minister, 1777; led Spanish diplomacy, through an alliance with France and cooperation with the Americans, to involvement in the war with Great Britain, 1779.

**Floyd, John.** d. 1783. Militia officer (Col.), frontiersman, b. Virginia.

Settled in Kentucky; served as a colonel in the Virginia militia; served with George Rogers Clark; killed in a raid, 12 April 1783.

**Floyd, William.** 1734-1821. American statesman, b. Brookhaven, Long Island, N.Y.

Delegate to the Continental Congress, New York, 1774-1777, 1778-1783; member, U.S. House of Representatives, New York, 1789-1791; signer of the Declaration of Independence.

**Folsom, Nathaniel.** 1726-1790. American statesman, jurist, militia officer (Maj. Gen ), b. Exeter, Rockingham Co., N.H.

Commanded New Hampshire militia during siege of Boston; delegate to the Continental Congress, New Hampshire, 1774-1775, 1777-1778, 1779-1780; member of two state constitutional conventions; served in state legislature; judge in court of common pleas.

**Fontanges, Vicomte de.** 1740-1822. French officer (Maj. Gen.).

Placed in command, July 1779, of Admiral d'Estaing's troops of debarkation for the planned attack on Savannah, Ga.; wounded at Savannah, October 1779.

**Forbes, James.** 1731-1780. American statesman, tax commissioner, b. Benedict, Charles County, Md.

Delegate to the Continental Congress, Maryland, 1778-1780.

**Forman, David.** 1745-1797. Militia officer (Brig. Gen.), Continental officer (Col.), judge, b. Monmouth Co., N.J.

Suppressed loyalist uprising in Monmouth Co., N.J., November 1776; made Continental colonel, 1776 or early 1777; commissioned brigadier general of New Jersey militia, 1777; commanded New Jersey militia at Germantown; major activity in war was harassment and suppression of loyalists in Monmouth County; called "Devil David" by loyalists for his alleged cruelty; also directed intelligence group that observed British ship movements and that included spies on Staten Island, 1777-1782; served as county judge after the Revolution.

**Foster, Isaac.** d. 1782. Physician.
Deputy director general of hospitals, Eastern Department.

**Fox, Charles James.** 1749-1806. British statesman, b. London.
Junior lord of the admiralty, 1770-1772; junior lord of the treasury, 1772-1774, dismissed for insubordination; sympathetic to the American cause, and in 1774 joined the Rockingham Whigs in opposition to the policies of the North ministry and George III; Secretary of State for Foreign Affairs, April-December 1783.

**Francis, Sir Philip.** *See* Junius.

**Francisco, Peter.** c. 1760-1831. Continental Army dragoon, landowner, b. Portugal (?).
Taken to Virginia as child; enlisted at 16; noted for great size and feats of strength; saw action at Brandywine, Stony Point, N.Y., 16 July 1779, and Camden; reportedly killed 11 British at battle of Guilford Courthouse with a five-foot sword that was a gift from George Washington.

**Franklin, Benjamin.** 1706-1790. American statesman, inventor, diplomat, writer, b. Boston, Mass.
Franklin began a career in publishing and writing in Philadelphia, 1730, with the publishing of *The Pennsylvania Gazette*, 1730-1748, and won a wide circle of readers by writing and publishing *Poor Richard's Almanack*, 1732-1757, under the pseudonym of Richard Sanders. He formed a discussion club, the Junto, about 1727, which developed by 1743 into the American Philosophical Society. He laid the foundations for a public library in 1731, and it was chartered the Philadelphia Library in 1742. As an inventor, he improved the heating stove in 1744, and in 1752 carried out the famous experiment that demonstrated the identity of lightning and electricity.

His career in public service spanned 53 years. In 1737 he became deputy postmaster at Philadelphia, and served until 1753. He was deputy postmaster for the colonies, 1753-1774. In 1754 he served as Pennsylvania's representative to the Albany Congress. From 1757 until 1762 he represented the Pennsylvania Assembly in efforts to enforce taxes on proprietary estates. He was in England in 1766 to explain colonial opposition to the Stamp Act, making an effective plea before the House of Commons. Appointed Pennsylvania's agent in England, he remained there until 1775 in an effort to obtain redress for colonial grievances; he returned when war seemed inevitable. He was delegate to the Second Continental Congress from Pennsylvania, 1775, and a signer of the Declaration of Independence.

Franklin was involved in peace negotiations with Lord Howe, 11 August 1776, at Staten Island, N.Y., which were cordial but fruitless. Along with Arthur Lee and Silas Deane, he was one of the three American commissioners assigned to negotiate a treaty with France. In his years in France, 1776-1785, he was immensely popular with the French, a fact which undoubtedly aided in the successful completion of his mission. A treaty of commerce and an alliance were signed with France on 6 February 1778. Franklin remained as sole plenipotentiary to France until 1781, when he was appointed along with John Jay and John Adams to serve as commissioners to negotiate with the British. On 3 September 1783 a final peace treaty was signed with Great Britain. Again Franklin remained on in France to serve as envoy.

Upon returning to Philadelphia in 1785, he was president of the Pennsylvania Executive Council, 1785-1787, the equivalent of being governor. In 1787 he was a member, the oldest one, of the Constitutional Convention, and is credited with serving as a mediator between opposing factions. In 1790 he signed a memorial to Congress for the abolition of slavery.

**Franklin, William.** 1731-1813. Loyalist official, lawyer, b. Pennsylvania.

Illegitimate son of Benjamin Franklin; educated at Cambridge; royal governor of New Jersey, 1763-1776; during the Revolution, imprisoned in Connecticut for about two years and then allowed to go to England.

**Franks, David Salisbury (or Solebury).** Continental officer (Maj.), b. Montreal, Canada.

Aide-de-camp to Benedict Arnold; innocent of participation in Arnold's treason; sent on a diplomatic mission in 1781 as a confidential courier to John Jay in Madrid, and to Benjamin Franklin in Paris; Pennsylvania resident; member of a prominent Jewish family.

**Franks, Isaac.** Militia officer (Lt. Col.).

Member of the same prominent Jewish family of England, Canada, and the United States to which David Salisbury Franks belonged.

**Fraser, Simon, Master of Lovat.** 1726-1782. British officer (Maj. Gen.), b. Scotland.

Highland leader; Jacobite; raised a regiment for the French and Indian War and ably commanded it in America; raised the 71st Regiment, or Fraser Highlanders, 1775, but did not accompany them to America.

**Fraser, Simon.** 1729-1777. British officer (Brig. Gen.), b. Scotland.

Occupied Crown Point, N.Y., 16 June 1776; distinguished himself at Hubbardton, Vt., 7 July 1777; mortally wounded at second battle of Saratoga.

**Fraser, Simon.** British officer (Capt.).

Commanded a company of Canadian irregulars and Indians in battle of Valcour Island, Lake Champlain, 11 October 1776, and in Burgoyne's invasion of New York, 1777; cousin of Maj. Gen. Simon Fraser.

**Freeman, Jordan.**

Negro orderly of Colonel William Ledyard; fought at battle of Groton Heights (New London), Conn., 6 September 1781; killed the British commander, Major Montgomery, with a spear; was himself killed in the battle.

**Frelinghuysen, Frederick.** 1753-1804. American statesman, lawyer, militia officer (Col.), b. Somerville, Somerset Co., N.J.

Saw action at Trenton, Princeton, and Monmouth; aide-de-camp to Brig. Gen. Philemon Dickinson; delegate to the Continental Congress, New Jersey, 1778-1779, 1782-1783; member, U.S. Senate, New Jersey, 1793-1796; brigadier general in Indian campaign of 1791; major general of militia in suppression of Whiskey Rebellion.

**Freneau, Philip.** 1752-1832. Poet, mariner, journalist, b. Freehold, N.J.

Coauthored with Hugh Henry Brackenridge the poem "The Rising Glory of America," 1772; wrote political satires; built and commanded the privateer *Aurora*, 1780; after the Revolution became one of the leading journalists in America, winning praise from Jefferson for his passionate democratic journalism.

**Frost, George.** 1720-1796. American statesman, jurist, b. Newcastle, N.H.

Delegate to the Continental Congress, New Hampshire, 1777-1779.

**Frost, Neptune.** Militia soldier, Continental soldier.

Negro slave of Deacon Gideon Frost of Cambridge, Mass.; served in the Cambridge militia; later, a drummer in the Continental Army.

**Frye, Joseph.** 1712-1794. Continental officer (Brig. Gen.), storekeeper, b. Andover, Mass.

Veteran of King George's War (1744-1745) and French and Indian War; brigadier general, 1776; resigned same year because of age and poor health.

# G

**Gadsden, Christopher.** 1723-1805. American statesman, merchant, planter, Continental officer (Brig. Gen.), b. Charleston, S.C.

Delegate to the Continental Congress, South Carolina, 1774-1776; brigadier general, Continental Army, 1776-1777.

**Gage, Thomas.** 1719?-1787. British officer (Lt. Gen.), government official, b. Sussex, England.

Commander-in-chief in America, 1772-1775; governor of Massachusetts, 1774-1775; sent troops to destroy military supplies at Concord, 18 April 1775, thus triggering the Revolutionary War; resigned his command, August 1775, under some pressure; was regarded as lacking the initiative and vigor needed for the job at hand.

**Gainey, Micajah.** Loyalist officer (Maj.).

Defeated by Francis Marion at Port's Ferry, S.C., 15 August 1780.

**Galloway, Joseph.** c. 1731-1803. Loyalist, lawyer, merchant, b. Maryland.

Delegate to the Continental Congress, Pennsylvania, 1774-1775; opposed to independence; offered the Galloway Plan of Union, 28 September 1774, whereby the American colonies would not break completely with Britain, but would obtain a kind of dominion status within the British Empire; spied for the British, 1776; accepted the Howes' offer of amnesty, December 1776; magistrate of police and superintendent of the port in British-occupied Philadelphia; went to England, 1778.

**Galvan, William (?) de.** Continental officer (Maj.).

French volunteer; praised by Lafayette for action at Green Spring, Va., 6 July 1781; von Steuben's division inspector at Yorktown.

**Gálvez, Bernardo de.** 1746-1786. Spanish officer and government official.

Governor of Louisiana and Florida, 1777; worked effectively covertly to weaken the British position in the area, 1777-1779; after the Spanish declaration of war, 1779, took the British river posts of Manchac, Baton Rouge, and Natchez; sent expeditions to attack British posts in upper Mississippi valley; seized the post of Mobile from the British, March 1780; forced British surrender of Pensacola, 9 May 1781; ended British control of West Florida through these victories, resulting in Spanish acquisition of both Floridas (and control of the mouth of the Mississippi) under the peace settlement of 1783; was made captain-general of Louisiana and the Floridas, and played a prominent role in diplomatic negotiations with the United States; became viceroy of New Spain, 1785, succeeding his father, but died the following year.

**Gálvez, José de.** Spanish government official.

Minister of the Indies; sent orders to governor of Havana in 1776 to dispatch secret agents to Pensacola, Jamaica, and other British-controlled areas; uncle of Bernardo de Gálvez.

**Gambier, James.** 1723-1789. British naval officer (Vice Adm.).

Commander-in-chief on the American station, 1770-1773; second-in-command to Lord Richard Howe, 1778-1779; commander-in-chief at Jamaica, 1783-1784.

**Gambier, James.** 1756-1833. British naval officer (Lt.), b. New Providence (Nassau), Bahamas.

Commanded warship *Thunder*, captured by d'Estaing, 1778; participated in the capture of Charleston, S.C., May 1780; nephew of James Gambier, admiral; later became Admiral of the Fleet (1830).

**Gansevoort, Peter.** 1749-1812. Continental officer (Col.), b. Albany, N.Y.

Distinguished himself in many campaigns in New York state, notably the long defense of Fort Stanwix against St. Leger's expedition, June-September, 1777.

**Gardoqui, Don Diego de.** Spanish agent.

Handled Spanish financial assistance to America.

**Garth, George.** d. 1819. British officer (Maj. Gen.).

Commanded a division in the Connecticut coast raid, July 1779, and was second-in-command to Governor Tryon; captured by the French, October 1779, while sailing to take command in Georgia.

**Gates, Horatio.** 1728-1806. Continental officer (Maj. Gen.), b. England.

Gates was sent to America as a young British officer and settled in Virginia after the French and Indian War. He was made adjutant general to General Washington in June 1775, with rank of brigadier general, and served effectively.

In 1776 Gates was made major general and sent to the Northern Department to serve under General Philip Schuyler as field army commander; he continually attempted to undermine Schuyler's position. In the spring of 1777 Congress upheld Schuyler, and Gates protested on the floor of Congress. In August 1777, after the fall of Ticonderoga, he was finally named commander of the Northern Department to replace Schuyler. He defeated General John Burgoyne at Saratoga, N.Y., 19 September and 7 October 1777, a crucial strategic and psychological victory, largely because of Burgoyne's errors and the aggressive leadership of Gates's subordinate, Benedict Arnold. Gates was involved in the Conway Cabal against Washington, while serving as president of the Board of War, an organization devised by Congress partly to remove some power from Washington. Appointed, despite Washington's recommendation of Greene, commander of the Southern Department, in June 1778, he was defeated at Camden, 16 August 1780, and fled, abandoning his army. He then retired to his farm. He was cleared of wrongdoing by a Congressional inquiry in 1782 and rejoined the Army at Newburgh near the end of the war.

**Geddes, George.** Privateer.

Captain of the American privateer *Congress*; forced the surrender of HMS *Savage* off the South Carolina coast, 6 September 1781.

**George III.** 1738-1820. King of Great Britain and Ireland, b. Norfolk House, St. James's Square, London.

George III was King of Great Britain and Ireland, 1760-1811; he succeeded his grandfather George II, 25 October 1760.

George saw as his role the changing of the political power structure that had dominated Britain for a number of years, and he almost immediately ousted William Pitt (later Lord Chatham) and the other Whig leaders who had been governing Britain; he was not able, however, to take immediate control of Parliament, and it was not until 1770, when Frederick North became Prime Minister, that he found a loyal lieutenant to support him and his policies.

George and Lord North used taxation of the American colonies as an issue to rally the nation; instead it divided Britain and precipitated the American Revolution. In spite of continued opposition both to the constitutionality of taxing the colonies and to the means used to carry it out in the face of American resistance, George III and Lord North pursued the policy. As the American conflict grew into warfare, George III surrounded himself with an inept trio of Lord North, Lord Germain, Secretary of State for the American Department, and Lord Sandwich, First Lord of the Admiralty; only after the defeat at Yorktown could George admit that his policy had failed, and appoint Lord Rockingham to replace Lord North.

Lord Shelburne took office when Rockingham died in July 1782, and his ministry negotiated the peace treaties. In late 1783 George appointed William Pitt the younger. In 1811, George became mentally ill, probably as a result of an inherited physical condition; his son was named regent and ruled until his father's death in 1820.

**Gérard, Conrad Alexandre.** 1729-1790. French diplomat.

First French minister to the United States, 1778-1779.

**Germain, George Sackville, first Viscourt Sackville (known as Lord George Germain during Revolution).** 1716-1785. British statesman.

Secretary of State for the American Department, 1775-1782, he also was Lord Commissioner of Trade and Plantations, 1775-1779; he supported the policies of Lord North and sought to uphold them in America in the face of strong opposition and eventually war. A former army officer, he was despised in the Army because he had displayed cowardice at the battle of Minden (1759). Germain was a difficult man to get along with, and his attempts to run the war from London are generally considered a major reason for British defeat. He feuded with his commanders, notably William Howe, Carleton, and Clinton. His support of Burgoyne and Cornwallis in their independent operations made British military cooperation very difficult; his constant interference with the Yorktown campaign also contributed to the British defeat.

**Gerry, Elbridge.** 1744-1814. American statesman, merchant, businessman, b. Marblehead, Mass.

Delegate to the Continental Congress, Massachusetts, 1776-1781, 1782-1785; signer of the Declaration of Independence; delegate to the Federal Consitutional Convention, 1787, but refused to sign the Constitution; Anti-Federalist; 1797 and 1798, aided French Foreign Minister, Talleyrand, in forestalling a break in relations between France and the United States over the "XYZ affair"; indirectly responsible for the expression "Gerrymander," which was first used in 1812 regarding a redistricting plan Gerry was thought to have devised.

**Gervais, John L.** d. 1798. American statesman, merchant, planter, landowner, b. France.

Delegate to the Continental Congress, South Carolina, 1782-1783.

**Getchell, Dennis.** 1736-1834. Continental officer (Capt.).

Guide through the Kennebec wilderness to Benedict Arnold during the march to Quebec, 1775; resident of Maine (then part of Massachusetts).

**Gibault, Pierre.** 1737-1804. French clergyman, b. Quebec, Canada.

Catholic missionary; helped the Americans during the Revolution in their operations in present-day Illinois.

**Gibson, George.** 1747-1791. Continental officer (Col.), merchant, b. Pennsylvania.

Appointed to deal with agent Oliver Pollock at New Orleans in 1776; returned with 10,000 pounds of powder.

**Gilbert, Thomas.** Loyalist officer.

Made the first concrete effort to organize Massachusetts loyalists, 1774, but patriots forced the break-up of this 300-man unit in April 1775.

**Gillespie, James.** Patriot.

A leader in the American victory at Hunt's Bluff, S.C., 1 August 1780.

**Gilman, John Taylor.** 1753-1828. American statesman, shipbuilder, farmer, b. Exeter, Rockingham Co., N.H.

Delegate to the Continental Congress, New Hampshire, 1782-1783; governor of New Hampshire, 1794-1805, 1813-1816.

**Gimat, Jean-Joseph Sourbader de.** Continental officer (Lt. Col.), b. 1741 or 1743.

French volunteer; aide-de-camp to Lafayette.

**Girty, George.** 1745-c. 1812. Loyalist partisan, Indian trader, b. Pennsylvania.

Lived among the Delaware Indians; served under Joseph Brant at Lochry's defeat, 24 or 25 August 1781. Brother of James and Simon Girty.

**Girty, James.** 1743-1817. Loyalist partisan, Indian trader, b. Pennsylvania.

Lived among the Shawnee Indians in Pennsylvania; St. Mary's, Ohio, is on site of Girty's Town, which he founded; brother of Simon and George Girty.

**Girty, Simon.** 1741-1818. Loyalist partisan, scout, interpreter, b. near Harrisburg, Pa.

Captured as boy by Senecca Indians and lived among them; scout and interpreter for the Americans, 1774-1778; deserted in 1778 to the British; ambushed Colonel David Rogers on the Ohio River and captured 600,000 Spanish dollars and other valuable supplies; took part in William Crawford's defeat, 4-5 June 1782, and was present at the torture of Crawford; participated in the raid at Blue Licks, Ky., 19 August 1782; closely involved with the Delaware Indians; brother of James and George Girty.

**Gist, Mordecai.** 1743-1792. Continental officer (Brig. Gen.), planter, b. Maryland.

Major in Smallwood's Maryland Regiment, 1776, and led it with distinction at Long Island; fought as colonel at Germantown; brigadier general, 1779, commanding 2d Maryland Brigade; fought well at Camden; settled in South Carolina after the war.

**Glover, John.** 1732-1797. Militia officer, Continental officer (Brig. Gen.), merchant, shipowner, b. Salem, Mass.

Raised and commanded regiment from Marblehead, Mass., 1775; responsible for vessels effectively transporting troops in retreat from Long Island, August 1776; fought well at Kip's Bay, N.Y., 15 September 1776, Pell's Point, N.Y., 18 October 1776, and White Plains; he and his Marblehead regiment provided transport for Delaware crossing, December 1776; brigadier general, 1777-1782.

**Goddard, John.**

Wagonmaster of the Continental Army; appointed by General Washington.

**Goddard, William.** 1740-1817. Patriot, journalist, printer, b. New London, Conn.

Published *Providence Gazette* (Rhode Island) 1762-1765, including special Stamp Act issue; published *Pennsylvania Chronicle*, 1767-1774, originally in partership with Joseph Galloway and Thomas Wharton, but later alone as their Tory sympathies caused conflict; editor of *Maryland Journal; and the Baltimore Advertiser*, 1773-1775.

**Goldsborough, Robert.** 1733-1788. American statesman, lawyer, b. "Horns Point," Dorchester Co., Md.

Delegate to the Continental Congress, Maryland, 1774, 1775.

**Gordon, William.** 1728-1807. Historian, clergyman, b. Hitchin, Hertfordshire, England.

Sympathizing with the American colonists, left his church in England, 1770, and became pastor of Third Congregational Church, Roxbury, Mass.; known as "the historian of the American Revolution"; published *History of the Rise, Progress, and Establishment of the Independence of the United States of America*, four volumes, 1788.

**Gorham, Joseph.** British official.

Lieutenant governor of Placentia, Canada; helped plan, and raise troops, for the defense of Nova Scotia and Canada, 1775.

**Gorham, Nathaniel.** 1738-1796. American statesman, merchant, b. Charlestown, Mass.

Delegate to the Continental Congress, Massachusetts, 1782-1783, 1785-1787; president of the Continental Congress, 1786-1787.

**Gould, Paston.** d. 1783. British officer (Major Gen., local rank).

Senior British officer in the south, 3 June - 8 November 1781.

**Gouvion, Jean Baptiste.** 1747-1792. Continental officer (Brevet Col.), b. France.

One of four French military engineers sent to America on request of Congress; helped plan and contruct West Point fortifications; participated in Yorktown campaign; killed in action in War of the First Coalition.

**Graaff, Johannes de.** Dutch government official.

De Graaf was governor of St. Eustatius (a Dutch island in the West Indies), 1776-1779. During this period there was clandestine trade through St. Eustatius between the rebelling American colonies and European countries. The British pressured for de Graaff's recall, which was accomplished in 1779.

**Grafton, Augustus Henry Fitzroy, Third Duke of.** 1735-1811. British statesman.

In the second Chatham ministry, 1766-1770, Grafton was the First Lord of the Treasury. The Prime Minister usually occupied the position, but Chatham had broken with precedent and chosen a lesser post. After Chatham's incapacity in 1767, Grafton was the nominal Prime Minister until 1770; he presided over an ineffective ministry.

**Graham, John.** Loyalist lieutenant governor of Georgia during the Revolution.

**Graham, Joseph.** 1759-1836. Militia officer (Maj.), businessman, b. Pennsylvania.

Distinguished himself at Charlotte, N.C., 26 September 1780, where he was wounded nine times; North Carolina resident.

**Grant, James.** d. 1776. British officer (Lt. Col.).

Led a regiment at battle of Long Island; killed in action.

**Grant, James.** 1720-1806. British officer (Lt. Gen.), b. Ballindolloch, Banffshire, Scotland.

Governor of the Floridas, 1764-1771; strongly anti-American; commanded two brigades at Long Island; commanded British outposts in New Jersey, 1776; his underrating of the Americans was a factor in the American victories at Trenton and Princeton; contributed to British victories at Germantown; unsuccessful at Barren Hill, Pa., 20 May 1778; captured and successfully defended the West Indies island of St. Lucia, 18-28 December 1778; member of Parliament before and after the war.

**Grasse, François Joseph Paul, de.** 1722-1788. French naval officer (Rear Adm.), b. Bar, Alpes-Maritimes.

Began military career as army officer; transferred to the navy; defeated Rear Adm. Samuel Hood, 1781, and captured Tobago; successfully commanded French naval force in the battle of the Capes, 5-10 September 1781, defeating British Rear Adm. Thomas Graves and assuring Allied victory at Yorktown; defeated by Adm. George Rodney at the battle of the Saints, April 1782, and taken prisoner; released on parole, August 1782; court-martialed for his defeat, 1784, but acquitted.

**Graves, Samuel.** 1713-1787. British naval officer (Adm.)

Vice admiral and commander-in-chief on the American Station, 1774-1776; first mission was to enforce the Boston Port Act; although not officially blamed for his lack of success nor for ensuing events, he was superseded, January 1776, and given no further active service; 1778, Admiral of the Blue; 1782, Admiral of the White.

**Graves, Thomas.** 1725?-1802. British naval officer (Rear Adm.).

Second-in-command to Admiral Arbuthnot on the American Station, 1780; took part in inconclusive battle off mouth of Chesapeake Bay, 16 March 1781; commanded British naval force at battle of the Capes, 5-10 September 1781, where he was defeated by Admiral de Grasse; sailed to New York after this battle and returned, with a larger fleet, too late to influence events at Yorktown.

**Gravier, Charles.** *See* Vergennes, Charles Gravier, Comte de.

**Gray, David.** b. c.1756. Militia officer (Capt.), American double agent.

Resident of Lenox, Mass., at beginning of Revolution; served in capture of Fort Ticonderoga, 10 May 1775, and in Canada invasion of 1775-1776; played the role of an American deserter and British intelligence courier, 1777-1782, while giving Washington's headquarters access to all significant messages he carried.

**Gray, Harrison.** 1711-1794. Loyalist, merchant, b. Boston, Mass.

Receiver general of Massachusetts, 1753-1774.

**Grayson, William.** 1740-1790. American statesman, Continental officer (Lt. Col.), lawyer, b. Prince William Co., Va.

Aide-de-camp to General Washington, 1776-1777; commissioner of the Board of War, 1779-1781; delegate to the Continental Congress, Virginia, 1784-1787; member, U.S. Senate, 1789-1790.

**Greaton, John.** 1741-1783. Continental officer (Brig. Gen.), trader, b. Roxbury, Mass.

Active pre-Revolution patriot; elected lieutenant of militia, November 1774; took part in battle of Lexington; promoted to colonel, July 1775; participated in Quebec expedition, 1775; commissioned Continental colonel, January 1776; commanded regiment throughout war; made brigadier general, January 1783.

**Greene, Christopher.** 1737-1781. Continental officer (Col.), businessman, b. Warwick, R.I.

Served in Quebec expedition, 1775, and was captured at Quebec; exchanged, 1777; voted a sword by Congress for his defense of Fort Mercer, N.J.; commanded a regiment of Negro troops—former slaves freed to serve in the Army—that fought gallantly in the battle of Newport, R.I., 29 August 1778; killed at Croton River, May 1781.

**Greene, Nathaneal.** 1742-1786. Continental officer (Maj. Gen.), forge owner, b. Potowomut (Warwick), R.I.

Brigadier general, 1775; major general, 1776; responsible for the loss of Fort Washington, N.Y., 16 November 1776; after that disaster, distinguished himself at Trenton, commanded a division at Brandywine, and led the column making the main effort at Germantown; quartermaster general, 1778-1780; commanded the Southern Department, 1780-1783; reputation was built on driving the British out of Georgia and the Carolinas in a strategically successful campagin devoid of tactical victories; turned what seemed to be a retreat into victory by forcing the British to chase him into Virginia in the race to the Dan River, with subsequent battles at Guilford Courthouse, N.C., 15 March 1781, and Hobkirk's Hill, S.C., 25 April 1781, the siege of Ninety-Six, 22 May-18 June 1781; and Eutaw Springs, S.C., 8 September 1781; returned to besiege Charleston, S.C., the only remaining British stronghold in the south; generally considered most distinguished American commander of the war, after Washington, whose most trusted subordinate he was.

**Grenville, George.** 1712-1770. British statesman.

Prime Minister, 1763-1765; responsible for the Grenville Acts (the Stamp Act, the Currency Act, and the American Revenue Act), which began the policy of taxation of the American colonies and were a precipitating force in the American Revolution.

**Grey, Charles ("No Flint").** 1729-1807. British officer (Lt. Gen.), b. Howick, Northumberland

Grey was victorious at Paoli, Pa., 21 September 1777, and at Tappan, N.Y., 28 September 1778. At Paoli, a night attack, to prevent any premature firing that would ruin his planned surprise, he ordered his men to remove the flints from their weapons; hence his nickname. Grey led the 3d Brigade at Germantown, 4 October 1777, and made raids on Bedford, Mass., 6 September 1778, and Martha's Vineyard, c. 8 September 1778. He fought in the War of the First Coalition against France, became a full general in 1794, and became Viscount Howick and Earl Grey in 1806.

**Grey, Thomas de.** British government official.

Junior under secretary in the American Department, 1778.

**Gribeauval, Jean Baptiste.** 1715-1789. French officer (General).

Because Gribeauval had developed a superior system of artillery for the French Army in 1776, the French had large stocks of good, although outdated and thus surplus, matériel to give to the Americans, under secret shipment before 1778.

**Gridley, Richard.** 1710-1796. Continental officer (Col.), surveyor, civil engineer, b. Boston, Mass.

Chief of engineers, first Continental chief of artillery.

**Griffin, Cyrus.** 1748-1810. American statesman, lawyer, b. Farnham, Richmond Co., Va.

Delegate to the Continental Congress, Virginia, 1778-1781; 1787-1788; president of the Continental Congress, 1788-1789.

**Grimaldi, Jerónimo.** Spanish diplomat.

Served as Foreign Minister until 1777; while willing to consider giving the Americans aid, he was opposed to recognition of American independence, seeing it as a threat to all colonial empires, including Spain's.

**Grymes, John.** 1746-1820. Loyalist officer (Maj.), b. "Brendon," Middlesex Co., Va.

Major in the Queen's Rangers; remained in Virginia after the Revolution as a prominent and wealthy citizen; when the British feared invasion by Napoleon, returned to London for a period to aid the Loyal Americans Company, composed of loyalists exiled in England.

**Guichen, Luc Urbain de Bouexic, Comte de.** 1712-1790. French naval officer (Admiral).

Fought at the battle off Ushant, France, 27 July 1779; March 1780, his squadron escaped disaster at the hands of British Admiral Rodney because the latter's captains handled their ships very poorly; lost a fleet of transports he was convoying to the West Indies, September 1780; defeated by Kempenfeldt at second battle of Ushant, 12 December 1781; generally successful in protecting French island possessions, and considered a skilled tactician despite his failures.

**Gunby, John.** Continental officer (Col.).

Commanded 1st Maryland Continentals, a crack battalion, 1781; distinguished himself at Guilford Courthouse.

**Guristersigo.** Inidan chief, loyalist.

Defeated by General Anthony Wayne at Ebenezer, Ga., 23 June 1782.

**Gwinnett, Button.** 1732-1777; American statesman, trader, b. Gloucestershire, England.

Delegate to the Continental Congress, Georgia, 1776-1777; signer of the Declaration of Independence.

# H

**Habersham, James.** 1712-1775. Loyalist official, merchant, planter, b. Yorkshire, England.

Leading merchant and planter in colonial Georgia; supported Royal Governor James Wright, whom he helped in maintaining order during the Stamp Act crisis; acting governor, 1771-1773; father of John and Joseph Habersham, prominent patriot leaders.

**Habersham, John.** 1754-1799. American statesman, merchant, militia officer (Maj.), b. "Beverly," near Savannah, Ga.

Lieutenant, then captain, of militia, 1776; major, 1778; twice captured; delegate to the Continental Congress, Georgia, 1785, 1786; later Indian agent, customs collector.

**Habersham, Joseph.** 1751-1815. American statesman, businessman.

A leader in the expulsion of Royal Governor James Wright of Georgia in 1776; Postmaster General of the United States, 1795-1801.

**Haldimand, Frederick.** 1718-1791. British general. b. Neufchâtel, Switzerland.

Distinguished himself in French and Indian War; British commander in Florida, 1766-1778; also second-in-command to General Gage, commander-in-chief of British forces in North America; commanded in New York, 1773-1775, during Gage's absence; called to England, 1775, ostensibly for consultations, but in reality because a Swiss was not wanted as commander-in-chief in America; commander-in-chief in Canada, 1778-1784, as well as governor.

**Hale, Nathan.** 1755-1776. Continental officer (Capt.), teacher, b. Coventry, Conn.

Graduate from Yale and taught school before the Revolution; lieutenant, July 1775; captain, 1 January 1776; served in Knowlton's Rangers under Lt. Col. Thomas Knowlton; volunteered in response to call from Washington for a spy to report on strength, dispositions, and plans of British in New York, setting out about 12 September 1776; captured by British, 21 September, and executed the next day; his last statement reportedly closed with the words, "I only regret that I have but one life to lose for my country."

**Hall, John.** 1729-1797. American statesman, lawyer, b. Annapolis, Md.

Delegate to the Continental Congress, Maryland, 1775, 1783-1784.

**Hall, Lyman.** 1724-1790. American statesman, clergyman, physician, b. Wallingford, Conn.

Settled in Georgia c. 1755; delegate to the Continental Congress, Georgia, 1775-1779; signer of the Declaration of Independence; governor of Georgia, 1783.

**Hallowell, Sir Benjamin (Carew).** d. 1834. Loyalist, British naval officer (Capt.).

Served under Admiral George Rodney; Massachusetts resident.

**Hambright, Frederick.** 1727-1817. Militia officer (Lt. Col.).

A leader at the battle of Kings Mountain, S.C., 7 October 1780; North Carolina resident.

**Hamilton, Alexander.** c. 1755-1804. American statesman, lawyer, Continental officer (Lt. Col.), b. Nevis, British West Indies.

Hamilton entered King's College (Columbia), New York City, in 1773. Active as a student in patriot activities, he spoke against British coercion at the "Meeting in the Fields," 6 July 1774. He wrote a widely circulated series of pamphlets supporting nonimportation, nonconsumption, and nonexportation, 1774-1775. Commissioned captain of the New York Company of Provisional Artillery, 14 March 1776, he commanded his guns at Long Island and White Plains, and helped fortify Harlem Heights, September 1776. He distinguished himself in a delaying action at Trenton,

2 January 1777 and in the capture of Princeton the next day. He then served as secretary, aide-de-camp, and adviser to Washington, March 1777-July 1781, and crowned his Revolutionary career by commanding a battalion at Yorktown, where he led a successful assault on Redoubt No. 10 on 14 October 1781.

In 1780-1781 Hamilton began to point out the defects of the Articles of Confederation, and called for the establishment of a strong central government. He displayed a remarkable grasp of fiscal and administrative problems of government. He was delegate to the Continental Congress, 1782-1783, 1787-1788, from New York. He also represented New York at the Annapolis convention of 1786, and at the Federal Constitutional Convention of 1787. Hamilton strongly supported the Constitution and was a major author of the *Federalist* papers; he was instrumental in obtaining the ratification of the Constitution by New York.

In 1789 Hamilton became the first Secretary of the Treasury in the cabinet of George Washington. The President's most trusted and influential adviser, he initiated policies establishing a national fiscal system, strengthening the federal government, and stimulating trade and commerce. Hamilton was also influential in the formation of political parties, which were at first drawn along the lines of the supporters of Hamilton and Washington (Federalists) and their opponents (Anti-Federalists).

Hamilton favored strong ties between the United States and Great Britain. During much of the Washington administration he maintained close contact with the British agent George Beckwith, and with considerable frequency disclosed to him American plans and intentions. These actions undermined the position of American Minister Gouverneur Morris and the negotiations of John Jay in 1794 as they sought to resolve continuing problems between the United States and Great Britain. In 1798 Hamilton was appointed Inspector General of the Army with the rank of major general.

In 1800 Hamilton was instrumental in defeating Aaron Burr for the presidency, and electing Jefferson, a man whose political policies were largely built upon opposition to his own; he also opposed Burr in his unsuccessful campaign for the governship of New York in 1804; the rivalry ended in tragedy for Hamilton, who was mortally wounded in a gun duel with Burr in Weehawken, N.J., in 1804.

**Hamilton, Henry ("the Hair Buyer").** d. 1796. British officer.

Commandant at Detroit, and Lieutenant Governor of Canada, 1775-1779; his task was to defend the west and to organize the Indians for attacks on the frontier; his nickname came from his supposed practice of offering money for scalps; opposed George Rogers Clark in his western operations, and was defeated and captured at Vincennes, 25 February 1779.

**Hamilton, James.** Continental officer (Maj.).

His column was lost, and the invasion of Johns Island, S.C., December 1781, had to be aborted.

**Hamilton, John.** Loyalist officer (Lt. Col.).

Active in gathering loyalist support in North Carolina; commander of the North Carolina Volunteers; also served in the Royal North Carolina Regiment.

**Hampton, John.** Militia officer (Capt.).

Captain in the South Carolina Dragoons; defeated at McDonnell's (McDowell's) Camp, S.C., 15-16 July 1780, by Colonel Alexander Innes.

**Hampton, Wade.** 1751 or 1752-1835. Militia officer (Col.), planter, statesman, b. Halifax Co., Va.

Settled in South Carolina; fought with General Thomas Sumter; distinguished himself at Eutaw Springs, S.C., 8 September 1781; served in the U.S. House of Representatives, 1795-1797, 1803-1805.

**Hancock, John.** 1737-1793. American statesman, militia officer (Maj. Gen.), merchant, b. Quincy, Norfolk Co., Mass.

Extremely wealthy; early agitator against British policies; closely associated with Samuel Adams; delegate to the Continental Congress, Massachusetts, 1775-1780, 1785-1786; president of the Continental Congress, 1775-1776, 1785-1786; signer of the Declaration of Independence; Governor of Massachusetts, 1780-1785, 1787-1793.

**Hand, Edward.** 1744-1802. Continental officer (Brig. Gen.), physician, statesman, b. Ireland.

Came to America as surgeon's mate with 18th Royal Irish Regiment, 1767; resigned to practice medicine; served as lieutenant colonel at siege of Boston, 1775; made colonel, 7 March 1776; commanded regiment effectively at Long Island, White Plains, and Princeton; promoted to brigadier general, 1 April 1777; led unsuccessful western expedition, 1778; commander at Albany, 1778-1781, playing important role in Sullivan's western New York expedition of 1779; adjutant general, 1781-1783; delegate to the Continental Congress, Pennsylvania, 1784-1785; Federalist.

**Hanger, George.** 1751?-1824. British officer (Maj.).

Prussian trained; came to America with Knyphausen in 1776; detachment commander in the Charleston campaign of 1780; commanded a Hessian battalion in General Paterson's march from Savannah to Charleston in 1780; aide-de-camp to General Clinton, 1780; second-in-command to Patrick Ferguson, 1780; commander of Tarleton's cavalry and upon the latter's death took over the British Legion; fought at Wahab's Plantation, N.C., 21 September 1780, and Charlotte, N.C., 26 September 1780.

**Hanson, Alexander.** 1749-1806. Continental officer, jurist, b. Annapolis, Md.

Assistant secretary to George Washington, 1776.

**Hanson, John.** 1715-1783. American statesman, farmer, b. Port Tobacco, Charles Co., Md.

Hanson was a delegate to the Continental Congress, 1780-1783, from Maryland, was elected president of the Continental Congress, 5 November 1781, and served for one year. Since he was the first president of the Continental Congress after the Articles of Confederation went into effect, he is sometimes referred to as "the First President of the United States."

**Haraden, Jonathan.** 1744-1803. State naval officer, privateer, seaman, b. Gloucester, Mass.

Lieutenant on Massachusetts navy sloop *Tyrannicide*, 1776; became commander of the *Tyrannicide*, 1777; after successful cruises, became privateer, 1778, and operated successfully until end of war; noted for wining against heavy odds.

**Haring, John.** 1739-1809. American statesman, lawyer, b. Tappan, Rockland Co., N.Y.

Delegate to the Continental Congress, New York, 1774-1775, 1785-1788.

**Harmar, Josiah.** 1753-1813. Continental officer (Col.), b. Philadelphia, Pa.

Second-in-command to General Wayne at Yorktown; as brigadier general and senior officer in U.S. Army, was defeated by Indians in Maumee Valley, Ohio, 1790.

**Harnett, Cornelius.** 1723-1781. American statesman, merchant, b. Edenton, N.C.

Delegate to the Continental Congress, North Carolina, 1777-1780.

**Harris, Sir James.** 1746-1820. British diplomat, b. Salisbury, England.

Ambassador to Russia; unsuccessfully attempted to secure an alliance with Empress Catherine II, 1777-1783.

**Harrison, Benjamin.** 1726-1791. American statesman, b. "Berkeley," Charles City Co., Va.

Served in House of Burgesses, 1749-1775; delegate to the Continental Congress, Virginia, 1774-1778; signer of the Declaration of Independence; governor of Virginia, 1782-1784.

**Harrison, Robert H.** Continental officer (Lt. Col.).

Aide-de-camp to George Washington, 1775-1776; secretary to George Washington, 1776-1781; Virginia resident.

**Harrod, James.** 1742-1793. Militia officer, frontiersman, b. Big Cone, in present-day Bedford Co., Pa.

Frontiersman; Virginia militia officer; founder of Harrodsburg, Ky.; a leader in the fighting against Indians and Tories.

**Hart, John.** 1709-1779. American statesman, farmer, jurist, b. Stonington, Conn.

Delegate to the Continental Congress, New Jersey, 1776; signer of the Declaration of Independence.

**Hart, Nancy Morgan.** Patriot heroine, b. Pennsylvania or North Carolina.

Scout and spy; captured six Tories; Georgia resident.

**Hartley, David.** 1732-1813. British government official.

Member of Parliament, 1774-1780, 1782-1784; opposed the American war; intimate friend and correspondent of Benjamin Franklin; selected by Charles James Fox as plenipotentiary to Paris peace negotiations in 1783, replacing Richard Oswald.

**Harvie, John.** 1742-1809. American statesman, lawyer, b. Albemarle Co., Va.

Delegate to the Continental Congress, Virginia, 1777-1779.

**Haslet, John.** d. 1777. Continental officer (Col.), physician, b. Ireland.

Commander, Delaware Regiment; killed at Princeton.

**Hatfield, Isaac.** Loyalist militia officer (Col.).

Captured at Eastchester, N.Y., 18 January 1780, by Samuel Lockwood.

**Haussegger, Nicholas.** Continental officer (Col.).

Pennsylvania resident; surrendered his regiment under suspicious circumstances at Trenton, 2 January 1777; later joined the British.

**Hawkins, Benjamin.** 1754-1816. American statesman, Indian agent, b. Granville Co. (now Warren Co.), N.C.

Delegate to the Continental Congress, North Carolina, 1781-1784, 1786-1787.

**Hayne, Isaac.** 1745-1781. Militia officer, planter, horse breeder, b. Colleton Co., S.C.

Hanged by British without a trial in Charleston, S.C., an act that resulted in a patriot uproar.

**Hays, Mary Ludwig.** 1754-1832. Patriot heroine.

Known as "Molly Pitcher"; fought at Fort Clinton, 6 October 1777, and at the battle of Monmouth; appointed sergeant by General Washington and pensioned by Congress. Pennsylvania resident.

**Hayes, Joseph.** d. 1781. Militia officer (Col.), b. South Carolina.

Killed, with his men, by "Bloody Bill" Cunningham at Hayes' Station, S.C., 9 November 1781.

**Hazard, Jonathan J.** 1744-1824. American statesman, b. Newport, R.I.

Delegate to the Continental Congress, Rhode Island, 1787-1789; Continental Army officer, 1777-1778.

**Hazard, Stanton.** Loyalist.

Commanded the privateer brig *King George*, which harassed the New England coast; captured by Silas Talbot in the *Argo*, August 1779.

**Hazelwood, John.** c. 1726-1800. Seaman, state naval officer, b. England.

Commodore, Pennsylvania state navy.

**Hazen, Moses.** 1733-1803. Continental officer (Brevet Brig. Gen.), farmer, b. Haverhill, Mass.

Served with distinction in French and Indian War; appointed colonel of the 2d Canadian Regiment, 1776; brevet brigadier general, 1781-1783.

**Heard, Nathaniel.** Militia officer (Brig. Gen.).

New Jersey resident; colonel, New Jersey militia, 1775-1777 or 1778; then made brigadier general and served to end of war.

**Heath, William.** 1737-1814. Militia officer (Maj. Gen.), Continental officer (Maj. Gen.), farmer, b. Roxbury, Mass.

Brigadier general of Massachusetts militia, February 1775; in command during militia harassment of British returning from Concord and during first dispositions for siege of Boston; appointed militia major general and then Continental brigadier general, June 1775; commanded a division in New York operations of 1776; major general, 1776-1783; attempted to capture Fort Independence, near King's Bridge, N.Y., 11-29 January 1777, and failed ignominiously; commanded Eastern Department (New England), 1777-1779; commanded in Hudson Highlands, to east of river, 1779-1783; served as judge and state senator after the war.

**Hector, Edward.** Continental soldier.

Negro resident of Pennsylvania; served in 3d Pennsylvania Artillery as one of few Negro artillerymen of war; despite orders, refused to abandon his ammunition wagon in withdrawal after battle of Brandywine; defended it, and brought it out safely.

**Heister, Leopold von (or de).** 1707-1777. Hessian officer (general).

Commander-in-chief of German forces in America; commanded the center of the British line at the battle of Long Island; led the Germans at White Plains; recalled, 1777, after German disaster at Trenton; died in November 1777.

**Hempstead, Stephen.** Continental soldier (Sgt.).

Accompanied Nathan Hale on his spying mission as far as Norwalk, Conn., where Hale embarked for Long Island, and waited for his return; left an account of the first stage of Hale's journey.

**Hemsley, William.** 1737-1812. American statesman, militia officer (Col.), planter, b. "Clover Fields Farm," Queenstown, Queen Annes Co., Md.

Colonel of 20th Battalion, Queen Annes County Militia, 1777; delegate to the Continental Congress, Maryland, 1782-1784.

**Henderson, William.** d. 1787. Continental officer (Lt. Col.), Militia officer (Brig. Gen.).

South Carolina resident; led a sortie at Charleston, S.C., 24 April 1780; captured at fall of Charleston, 12 May 1780, and exchanged; wounded at Eutaw Springs, S.C., 8 September 1781.

**Hendricks, Baker.** Continental officer (Capt.), American spy.

Leading member of Col. Elias Dayton's New York spy network; brother of John Hendricks.

**Hendricks, John.** American spy.

Leading member of Col. Elias Dayton's New York spy network; brother of Capt. Baker Hendricks.

**Henry, James.** 1731-1804. American statesman, lawyer, b. Accomac Co., Virginia.

Delegate to the Continental Congress, Virginia, 1780-1781.

**Henry, John.** 1750-1798. American statesman, lawyer, b. "Wharton," Dorchester Co., Md.

Delegate to the Continental Congress, Maryland, 1778-1781, 1784-1787; member, U.S. Senate, 1789-1797; governor of Maryland, 1797-1798.

**Henry, Patrick.** 1736-1799. Statesman, merchant, lawyer, b. Hanover Co., Va.

A gifted orator, Henry came into prominence for his eloquence in arguing a law case, the "Parson's Cause," in which he invoked the doctrine of natural rights. As a member of the Virginia House of Burgesses, 1765, he introduced a series of resolutions in opposition to the Stamp Act with a brilliant speech that reportedly ended, "If *this* be treason, make the most of it." He was a founder of the Virginia Committee of Correspondence, 1773, and a delegate to the Continental Congress, 1774-1776. As a member of the Virginia Provincial Convention, Richmond, March 1775, he pressed resolutions for putting the colonies in a state of defense with the famous speech containing the words "Give me liberty or give me death."

Henry was governor of Virginia, 1776-1779, 1784-1786, and member of the Virginia constitutional ratification convention of 1788. He opposed ratification and was instrumental in having the first ten amendments, the Bill of Rights, added to the Constitution.

After 1788 he returned to private life and declined offers of positions as Senator, 1794, and Chief Justice of the U.S. Supreme Court, 1795. In 1799 he was elected to the Virginia legislature, but died before he could assume his seat.

**Herkimer, Nicholas.** 1728-1777. Militia officer (Brig. Gen.), farmer, b. near present-day Herkimer, N.Y.

Patriot leader in Mohawk Valley, where Tory sentiment was strong; led a force of 800 to relieve besieged Fort Stanwix, N.Y.; ambushed at Oriskany, 6 August 1777; directed successful defense but died of wounds received in the ambush.

**Heron, William ("Hiram the Spy").** 1742-1819. Teacher, surveyor, state legislator, double agent, b. Cork, Ireland.

Settled at Redding Conn., a few years before the Revolution; ostensibly a patriot, serving as local offical and in Connecticut Assembly, 1778-1782; gave American military information, and secret information obtained from the Continental Congress via the Connecticut Assembly, to Maj. Oliver DeLancey, General Clinton's intelligence chief; obtained American military information from Maj. Gen. Samuel Holden Parsons, to whom he also gave British information, and who thought him an American intelligence agent; elected to Connecticut Assembly several times between 1784 and 1796; treason unknown until 20th Century.

**Hewes, Joseph.** 1730-1779. American statesman, merchant, b. Kingston, N.J.

Delegate to the Continental Congress, North Carolina, 1774-1777, 1779; signer of the Declaration of Independence; played leading role in organizing the Continental Navy.

**Heyward, Thomas, Jr.** 1746-1809. American statesman, lawyer, b. South Carolina.

Delegate to the Continental Congress. 1776-1778; signer of the Declaration of Independence.

**Hickey, Thomas.** Continental soldier.

One of Washington's bodyguards; implicated in "assassination plot" against Washington, Putnam, and others, which was discovered 21 June 1776; tried, convicted, and hanged for treason.

**Hicks, Gershom.** Militiaman, frontiersman, American spy.

Resident of Water Street, Blair Co., Pa.; captured by Delaware Indians as boy, and later by Shawnee, learning both languages; served in Pennsylvania militia from 1775; sent by Washington on successful intelligence mission through Indian territory of western Pennsylvania and New York, 1779.

**Hicks, John.** 1725-1775. Patriot.

Massachusetts resident; participated in Boston Tea Party, 1773; killed by British during their retreat from Concord, 19 April 1775.

**Higginson, Stephen.** 1743-1828. American statesman, merchant, shipmaster, b. Salem, Mass.

Delegate to the Continental Congress, Massachusetts, 1782-1783.

**Hill, William.** 1741-1816. Militia officer (Lt. Col. or Col.), ironmaster, statesman, b. Ireland.

Settled in South Carolina, 1762; leader in the victory over Tories at Williamson's Plantation, S.C., 12 July 1780; distinguished himself at Rocky Mount, S.C., 1 August 1780; served repeatedly in state legislature after the war.

**Hill, Whitmil.** 1743-1797. American statesman, farmer, b. Bertie Co., N.C.

Delegate to the Continental Congress, North Carolina, 1778-1781.

**Hillsborough, Wills Hill, Earl of.** 1718-1793. British statesman.

Secretary of State for the American Department, 1768-1772; influenced by Sir Francis Bernard, royal governor of Massachusetts; favored repressive measures toward the colonists.

**Hinrichs, Johann.** d. 1834. Hessian officer.

Served with distinction as a jäger; left a historical account of the Charleston operations of 1780.

**Hinton, John.** Militia officer (Col.).

A patriot leader at the battle of Moore's Creek Bridge, N.C., 27 February 1776; delegate to North Carolina Provincial Congress, 1775-1776.

**Hobart, John Sloss.** 1738-1805. American statesman, judge, b. Fairfield, Conn.

Resident of Suffolk Co., Long Island, N.Y.; member, New York Provincial Congress, 1775-1777; member of committees on drafting and organizing a state government for New York; New York Supreme Court justice, 1777-1798; U.S. Senator, 1798; U.S. district judge for New York, 1798-1805.

**Hogun, James.** d. 1781. Militia officer (Maj.), Continental officer (Brig. Gen.), b. Ireland.

Settled in North Carolina about 1751; Continental colonel, November 1776; fought at Brandywine and Germantown; brigadier general, 1779; led his brigade on three-month winter march to defense of Charleston, 1780; captured when

city fell, 12 May 1780; died as prisoner of war.

**Holker, Jean.** 1745-1822. French merchant, government official.

Consul to the United States, 1778-1781; engaged in profitable speculations during his stay in America.

**Holland, Stephen.** Loyalist officer (Capt.).

Captain, Prince of Wales Regiment; attempted unsuccessfully to get Maj. Gen. John Sullivan to come over to the loyalist side, 1781.

**Holten, Samuel.** 1738-1816. American statesman, physician, b. Danvers, Mass.

Delegate to the Continental Congress, Massachusetts, 1778-1780, 1782-1783, 1784-1785, 1786-1787.

**Holtzendorf, Louis-Casimir, Baron de.** b. 1728. Continental officer (Lt. Col.), b. Germany.

Became French Army officer, 1776; volunteered immediately to fight for United States; saw action at Brandywine and Germantown; later entered service of Holland (1785).

**Honeyman, John.** Weaver, butcher, American spy.

Resident of Griggstown, N.J.; performed valuable spy service during preparations for Washington's crossing into New Jersey, December 1776.

**Hood, Samuel, first Viscount.** 1724-1816. British naval officer

(Rear Adm.), b. Butleigh, Sommersetshire.

Second-in-command to George Rodney in the West Indies, 1780-1781; a subordinate to Thomas Graves at battle of the Capes; conducted an unsuccessful attempt to relieve St. Kitts, 1782; aided in defeat of De Grasse at battle of the Saints, April 1782; entered Parliament, 1784.

**Hooper, William.** 1742-1790. American statesman, lawyer, b. Boston, Mass.

Delegate to the Continental Congress, North Carolina, 1774-1777; signer of the Declaration of Independence.

**Hoovenden, Richard.** Loyalist officer (Capt.).

Pennsylvania resident; commanded Philadelphia Light Dragoons, c. 1778.

**Hopkins, Esek.** 1718-1802. Continental naval officer (Commodore), seaman, b. Scituate, R.I.

Brother of Stephen Hopkins; sea captain in pre-Revolutionary period; privateer during French and Indian War; put in command of Rhode Island state militia, October 1775; appointed first Commander-in-Chief of the Continental Navy, December 1775; commanded successful expedition to Bahamas, February 1776, but was censured for disobedience of orders; prevented by British blockade from conducting further fleet activities; dismissed January 1778.

**Hopkins, John Burroughs.** 1742-1796. Continental naval officer (Capt.), seaman, privateer. b. Providence, R.I.

Son of Esek Hopkins; participated in *Gaspée* affair, 1772; took part in father's expedition to Nassau, 1776.

**Hopkins, Stephen.** 1707-1785. American statesman, jurist, surveyor, merchant, b. Providence, R.I.

Delegate to the Continental Congress, Rhode Island, 1774-1780; signer of the Declaration of Independence; brother of Esek Hopkins.

**Hopkinson, Francis.** 1737-1791. American statesman, lawyer, writer, customs collector, shopkeeper, artist, inventor, b. Philadelphia, Pa.

Delegate to the Continental Congress, New Jersey, 1776; signer of the Declaration of Independence; author of poem "The Battle of the Kegs," many pamphlets, and an opera honoring the Franco-American alliance.

**Horry, Daniel.** Continental officer (Capt.), militia officer (Col.).

Captain, 2nd South Carolina Regiment; commanded a company in the defense of Charleston, 17 June 1775; colonel, South Carolina Dragoons, 1779; took oath of allegiance to the Crown, 1780, after Clinton's capture of Charleston.

**Horry, Hugh.** Militia officer (Lt. Col.1

Major and lieutenant colonel of a South Carolina regiment, 1779-1781; served in Francis Marion's brigade; commanded Marion's foot troops for a time; brother of Peter Horry.

**Horry, Peter.** Continental officer (Maj.), militia officer (Col. or Brig. Gen.).

Served in 2d South Carolina Regiment; promoted to major, September 1776; served in Francis Marion's Brigade, commanding Marion's mounted troops; brother of Hugh Horry.

**Hosmer, Titus.** d. 1780. American statesman, lawyer, b. West Hartford, Conn.

Delegate to the Continental Congress, Connecticut, 1775-1776, 1777-1779.

**Hotham, William.** 1736-1813. British naval officer (Commodore).

Joined Admiral Howe, 1776; supported landing at Kip's Bay, N.Y., 15 September 1776; during Philadelphia campaign remained in New York as senior naval officer; gave naval support for Clinton's expedition to the Hudson Highlands, October 1777; engaged the French off Newport, R.I., July-August, 1778; senior officer in Leeward Islands, West Indies, after Rodney went to New York.

**Houston, William C.** c. 1745-1788. American statesman, militia officer (Capt.), teacher, lawyer, b. Poplar Tent, Cabarrus Co., N.C.

Taught at Princeton, 1769-1783; militia service during Revolution; delegate to the Continen-

tal Congress, New Jersey, 1779-1781, 1784, 1785; deputy secretary of Continental Congress, 1775, 1776; delegate to Annapolis convention of 1786 and Federal Constitutional Convention, 1787.

**Houstoun, John.** 1744-1796. American statesman, b. Savannah, Ga.

Delegate to the Continental Congress, 1775-1777; governor of Georgia, 1778, 1784.

**Howard, Frederick.** *See* Carlisle, Frederick Howard, Earl of.

**Howard, John E.** 1752-1827. American statesman, Continental officer (Lt. Col.).

Saw action throughout the war; served with distinction at Camden, Cowpens, Guilford Courthouse, Hobkirk's Hill, S.C., 25 April 1781, and Eutaw Springs, S.C., 8 September 1781, where he was wounded; received one of the eight medals given by Congress throughout the war for his part in the battle of Cowpens; delegate to the Continental Congress, 1787-1788; governor of Maryland, 1789-1791; member, U.S. Senate, 1796-1803, president pro tempore of the Senate, 1800-1801.

**Howe, John.** British spy.

Carried out successful spying mission to Worcester and Concord for Lt. Gen. Thomas Gage before outbreak of Revolution, April 1775; settled in Canada; carried out spying mission in United States for Great Britain just before the War of 1812.

**Howe, Richard ("Black Dick"), Lord (Viscount Howe).** 1726-1799. British naval officer (Vice Adm.), b. London.

Howe went to America, 1776, as commander-in-chief on the American Station, and also, at his insistence, as peace commissioner, a mission which his brother William shared. Their powers to take action for peace were narrowly limited, partly because of official suspicions of their pro-American sentiments. Howe provided naval support for the New York campaign, 1776; defended New York harbor against the French, 1778; and broke up Franco-American operations against Newport, R.I., August 1778; he resigned and returned to England, late 1778. He later had a brilliant naval career in the wars of the First and Second Coalitions against republican France.

**Howe, Robert.** Continental officer (Maj. Gen.), planter, b. near Cape Fear River, N.C.

Brigadier general, 1776-1777; major general, 1777-1783; performed with distinction in Georgia, 1778-1779; played a major role in suppressing Pompton and Suffren mutinies, 1781.

**Howe, William.** 1729-1814. British officer (Lt. Gen.).

Served with distinction in the French and Indian War as battalion and brigade commander. He served as a Whig in Parliament, 1758-1780, and was sympathetic toward the Americans in the pre-Revolutionary period. He served as commander-in-chief of British forces in America, 1775-1778, succeeding General Gage, and also holding, with his brother, Lord Richard Howe, limited authority as peace commissioner. He planned and led the British attack on Bunker's Hill (Breed's Hill), 17 June 1775.

Howe won a brilliant victory at Long Island, but failed to pursue aggressively or seize opportunities to destroy Washington's vulnerable force in subsequent operations around New York. He underestimated Washington and his army in the New Jersey campaign of 1776-1777, and his forces suffered the significant defeats of Trenton and Princeton. He outmaneuvered and twice defeated Washington (Brandywine and Germantown) in the Philadelphia campaign of 1777, but failed to win a decisive victory. Although he has been criticized for slowness and lack of decisiveness, his performance was good by 18th Century standards.

**Howell, David.** 1747-1824. American statesman, lawyer, jurist, teacher, b. Morristown, N.J.

Delegate to the Continental Congress, Rhode Island, 1782-1785; played no active role in the Revolution; founder, teacher, and interim president of Rhode Island College (later Brown University).

**Howley, Richard.** 1740-1784. American statesman, lawyer, planter, b. Liberty Co., Ga.

Governor of Georgia, 1780; delegate to the Continental Congress, 1780-1781.

**Huck, Christian.** d. 1780. Loyalist officer.

Pennsylvania resident; commanded a body of calvary at Camden; led a raid destroying important iron works in York District, S.C.; killed in a raid at Williamson's Plantation, S.C., 12 July 1780.

**Huddy, Joshua.** Militia officer (Capt.).

New Jersey resident; artillery captain; taken prisoner, 24 March 1782, hanged by the Tories, 12 April 1782, in Monmouth County, N.J., in revenge for the death of a Tory partisan.

**Huger, Benjamin.** 1746-1779. Militia officer (Maj.), planter, b. South Carolina.

Member of South Carolina provincial congress, 1775; major in 5th South Carolina Rifles; friend of Lafayette; accidently killed, 1779, at Charleston, S.C., by American troops; brother of Francis and Isaac Huger.

**Huger, Francis.** 1751-1811. Continental officer (Lt. Col.), b. South Carolina.

Served in 2d South Carolina Continentals, 1775-1777; in action at defense of Charleston, June 1776; quartermaster general of the Southern Department, 1777-1778; brother of Benjamin and Isaac Huger.

**Huger, Isaac.** 1743-1797. Continental officer (Brig. Gen.), b. South Carolina.

Brigadier general, 9 January 1779; commanded Georgia and South Carolina militia at Savannah, Ga., 9 October 1779; defeated

by Tarleton at Monck's (Monk's) Corner, S.C., 16 October 1781; led one wing of Greene's army at Guilford Courthouse, and was seriously wounded; commanded the right wing at Hobkirk's Hill, S.C., 25 April 1781; brother of Benjamin and Francis Huger.

**Hull, William.** 1753-1825. Continental officer (Lt. Col.), lawyer, b. Derby, Conn.

Saw action throughout the war in New York and New Jersey; led the bold raid on Morrisania, 22-23 January 1781; led the not-so-bold defense of Detroit, 1812.

**Humphreys, Charles.** 1714-1786. American statesman, miller, b. Haverford, Delaware Co., Pa.

Delegate to the Continental Congress, Pennsylvania, 1774-1776; a Quaker; voted against the Declaration of Independence because of his opposition to war.

**Humphreys, David.** 1752-1818. Continental officer (Lt. Col.), statesman, poet, textile manufacturer, b. Derby, Conn.

Aide-de-camp to George Washington, 1780-1783; wrote life of Israel Putnam (1788); minister plenipotentiary to Spain, 1796-1801.

**Humpton, Richard.** c. 1733-1804. Continental officer (Col.), farmer, b. England.

During Washington's retreat across the Delaware, early December 1776, collected all boats in the area, successfully denying the British means of pursuit; fought at Brandywine, and served during the rest of the war as a regimental commander; breveted brigadier general, 30 September 1783.

**Hunter, Elijah.** Militia officer (Capt.), American double agent.

Served in 2d New York Militia; left Army in December 1776 and became American spy, moving in and out of New York; posed as British spy, giving the British false and misleading information; received certificate of service from General Washington after the war.

**Huntington, Benjamin.** 1735-1800. American statesman, surveyor, lawyer, b. Norwich, Conn.

Delegate to the Continental Congress, 1780-1784, 1787-1788; member, U.S. House of Representatives, 1789-1791.

**Huntington, Jabez.** 1719-1786. Militia officer (Maj. Gen.), trader, merchant, legislator, b. Norwich, Conn.

Commander of Connecticut state militia, 1777-1779.

**Huntington, Jedediah.** 1748-1818. Continental officer (Brig. Gen.), trader, b. Norwich, Conn.

Active pre-Revolution patriot; member, Sons of Liberty; was colonel commanding regiment at siege of Boston, 1775; served throughout war but saw little action.

**Huntington, Samuel.** 1731-1796. American statesman, cooper, lawyer, judge, b. Windham, Conn.

Delegate to the Continental Congress, 1776-1784; president of the Continental Congress, 1779;

signer of the Declaration of Independence; governor of Connecticut, 1786-1796.

**Hutchinson, Thomas.** 1711-1780. Loyalist, royal governor, historian, b. Boston, Mass.

Hutchinson was royal governor of Massachusetts, 1771-1774. Letters he wrote in 1767-1769 urged more severe policies toward the colonies, and when they found their way, by a circuitous route, into public print in 1773, they brought demands for his impeachment. His inept handling of the tea shipments under the Tea Act of 1773 precipitated the Boston Tea Party, December 1773. He dissolved the Massachusetts Assembly, March 1774, to forestall impeachment proceedings. He went to England, June 1774, was replaced by General Gage as royal governor, and never returned to America.

**Hussey, Thomas.** 1741-1803. Irish priest, British diplomat, b. Ireland.

In 1780 Hussey accompanied British diplomat Richard Cumberland to Spain to attempt to negotiate a peace, but since their instructions precluded discussion of Gibraltar and the American colonies, the effort was unsuccessful.

**Hutson, Richard.** 1748-1795. American statesman, lawyer, b. Prince William Parish, S.C.

Delegate to the Continental Congress, South Carolina, 1778-1779.

**Hyler, Adam.** Patriot.

Whaleboat guerilla; harassed British and Tories in coastal waters of northern New Jersey.


# I


**Ingersoll, Jared.** 1749-1822. American statesman, lawyer, jurist, b. New Haven, Conn.

Son of a leading loyalist of the same name; delegate to the Continental Congress, Pennsylvania, 1780-1781; unsuccessful Federalist candidate for Vice President, 1812.


**Inglis, Charles.** c. 1734-1816. Loyalist, clergyman, b. Ireland.

Answered Thomas Paine's *Common Sense* with a pamphlet called *The Deceiver Unmasked or Loyalty and Interest United, in Answer to a Pamphlet Falsely Called "Common Sense"*; New York resident.


**Innes, Alexander.** Loyalist officer.

Inspector general of provincial troops, 1776; victorious at McDonnell's (McDowell's) Camp, S.C., 15-16 July 1780.


**Irvine, William.** 1741-1804. American statesman, physician, Continental officer (Brig. Gen.), b. Ireland.

Brigadier general, 1779-1783; delegate to the Continental Congress, Pennsylvania, 1786-1788; member, U.S. House of Representatives, 1793-1795.


**Izard, Ralph.** 1742-1804. American statesman, landowner, b. "The Elms," near Charleston, S.C.

Delegate to the Continental Congress, 1782-1783; member, U.S. Senate, 1789-1795; president pro tempore of the Senate, 1794-1795.


# J


**Jackson, Jonathan.** 1743-1810. American statesman, merchant, b. Boston, Mass.

Delegate to the Continental Congress, Massachusetts, 1782.


**Jackson, Richard.** d. 1787. British statesman, lawyer.

Refused to serve on Carlisle's peace commission, 1778; favored giving independence to the American colonies to avoid war with France.


**Jackson, Robert.** 1750-1827. British officer (ensign), surgeon's mate, b. Scotland.

Served with 71st Highlanders; persuaded Daniel Morgan to parole British wounded into his care after battle of Cowpens; instrumental in reforming British Army medical service during 1790's.


**James, Jacob.** Loyalist officer (Capt.).

Commanded a troop of Pennsylvania dragoons, c. 1778.


**Jamieson, Neil.** Loyalist, trader.

Virginia resident, trader who aided the British; went to New York, where he continued his trading throughout the Revolution.

**Jasper, William.** c. 1750-1779. Continental sergeant, b. Georgetown, S.C.

Fought under Francis Marion; cited for bravery at Charleston, 1776; successful scout for Marion and Maj. Gen. Benjamin Lincoln; killed while raising the flag at Savannah, 1779.

**Jay, Sir James.** Physician.

Brother of John Jay, living and practicing medicine in England; developed effective invisible ink, made visible by use of a developer solution, which his brother adopted for use by the spies whose work he directed.

**Jay, John.** 1745-1829. American statesman, lawyer, jurist, diplomat, b. New York, N.Y.

Jay was a delegate to the Continental Congress from New York, 1774-1777 and 1778-1779, and president of the Continental Congress, 1778-1779. He was a member of the Committee of Secret Correspondence, 1775-1777; in 1777 it became known as the Committee for Foreign Affairs, the embryo of the later Department of State. Jay also, with Nathaniel Sackett, headed patriot intelligence activities in New York during the Revolution. He served on a special mission to Spain, 1780-1782, to negotiate recognition of American independence and the issue of Mississippi River trade; the mission failed because the Spanish were unwilling to negotiate these points. He also served, with Benjamin Franklin and others, as one of the plenipotentiaries to the peace negotiations with the British which culminated in the Treaty of Paris, 3 September 1783. Along with James Madison and Alexander Hamilton, Jay was an author of the *Federalist Papers*, influential writings presenting arguments for adoption of the Federal Constitution. He was first Chief Justice of the U.S. Supreme Court, 1789-1795, and governor of New York, 1795-1801.

While Chief Justice, Jay led a mission to Britain to negotiate outstanding grievances arising from British troops on the frontier, the prohibition of American trade with the West Indies, and Indian problems. He negotiated what is known as the Jay Treaty of 1794, a very controversial document that brought the Washington administration much criticism and is considered one factor in the formation of American political parties.

**Jefferson, Thomas.** 1743-1826. American statesman, lawyer, diplomat, inventor, writer, b. "Shadwell," Goochland (now Albemarle) Co., Va.

Jefferson was a member of the Virginia House of Burgesses, 1769-1774; was prominent in pre-Revoluntionary movements; and in 1773, along with Patrick Henry and Richard Henry Lee, started the Virginia Committee of Correspondence. He was a delegate to the Continental Congress from Virginia, 1775-1776, and 1783-1785. As chairman of the committee to prepare the Declaration of Independence, he wrote the first draft which, after some changes, was approved by Congress, 2 July 1776.

Jefferson was governor of Virginia, 1779-1781; was appointed and served as minister plenipotentiary to France, 1784; and from 1785 to 1789 was minister to the King of France; he resigned to accept appointment to President Washington's first Cabinet.

Jefferson served as the first Secretary of State, 1789-1793, but was in disagreement with the principal themes of the Washington administration, chiefly the emphasis on increased centralization of the government and the financial policies of Alexander Hamilton. After 1795 Jefferson became increasingly identified with the opposition to Hamilton and the administration, and became its first national leader; since the faction of Washington, Hamilton, and Adams became known as the Federalists, the opposition was known as the Anti-Federalists.

Jefferson was elected Vice President in 1796, after finishing second to Adams in the Presidential balloting, and served until 1801. He was President from 1801 until 1809.

The presidency of Thomas Jefferson was marked by both success and failure. In 1803 the Louisiana Purchase was made, beginning the westward expansion of the United States that was to continue through the 19th century. Grave diplomatic problems resulted from British and French violations of American neutrality on the seas, especially the impressment of American seamen by the British; in retaliation, Jefferson initiated an embargo on all British and French shipping (1807-1809), but the policy was not successful.

By the beginning of Jefferson's administration, the two political factions had become distinct political parties. The Anti-Federalists had taken the name Democratic-Republican or Republican, and this Republican Party of Jefferson and Madison (from which has evolved the modern Democratic Party) controlled the Presidency from 1801 until 1824.

After leaving the presidency, Jefferson retired to his home, Monticello, in Charlottesville, where he was instrumental in founding the University of Virginia in 1819.

**Jenifer, Daniel.** 1723-1790. American statesman, b. Charles Co., Md.

Member, Governor's Council, 1773-1775; president, Maryland Council of Safety, 1775; delegate to the Continental Congress, Maryland, 1778-1782; delegate to Federal Constitutional Convention, 1787.

**Jerry.** d.1775. Loyalist, ship's pilot.

Free Negro; South Carolina resident; hanged by patriot South Carolina authorities, August 1775, for giving arms to slaves and encouraging them to join the British.

**Johnson, George.** Continental officer (Lt. Col.).

Virginia resident; aide-de-camp to George Washington, 1777.

**Johnson, Guy.** c. 1740-1788. Loyalist, Indian agent, b. Ireland.

A leading loyalist in New York state; superintendent of Indian affairs, 1774-1782; succeeded in winning support of four tribes of the Iroquois nation to the loyalist cause; may have been nephew of Sir William Johnson.

**Johnson, Sir John.** 1742-1830. Loyalist, British government offical, b. Johnstown, N.Y.

Superintendent of Indian affairs, 1782; led Indian and Tory raid at Johnstown, N.Y., 22-23 May 1780; son of Sir William Johnson.

**Johnson, Thomas.** 1732-1819. American statesman, militia officer (Brig. Gen.), lawyer, jurist, b. St. Leonard's Creek, Calvert Co., Md.

Delegate to the Continental Congress, Maryland, 1774-1777; as commander of Maryland militia, raised about 1,800 recruits and led them to Washington's headquarters in New Jersey, 1777; served as first governor of New Jersey after independence, 1777-1779; worked for ratification of Federal Constitution; appointed to U.S. Supreme Court, 1791.

**Johnson, Sir William.** 1715-1774. Loyalist, British government official, b. Ireland.

Superintendent of Indian affairs, 1756-1774; brother-in-law of Joseph Brant; father of Sir John Johnson, and possibly uncle of Guy Johnson.

**Johnson, William S.** 1727-1819. American statesman, lawyer, b. Stratford, Conn.

Had early loyalist sentiments; elected to the Continental Congress in 1774 but refused to serve; later became a patriot; delegate to the Continental Congress, 1784-1787; delegate to Federal Constitutional Convention, where he made significant contributions; first president of Columbia College (University), formerly King's College, 1787.

**Johnston, Samuel.** 1733-1816. American statesman, lawyer, b. Dundee, Scotland.

Came to North Carolina as young child; delegate to the Continental Congress, North Carolina, 1780-1782; member, U.S. Senate, 1789-1793; Federalist.

**Johnstone, George.** 1730-1787. British naval officer.

Member of Carlisle's peace commission, 1778; attempted to bribe Congressmen Joseph Reed, Robert Morris, and Francis Dana; forced to resign when Congress resolved on 11 August 1778 that it could not deal with him.

**Jones, Allen.** 1739-1798. Militia officer (Brig. Gen.), statesman, b. Edgecombe (now Halifax) Co., N.C.

Member of five provincial congresses, 1774-1776; brigadier general commanding Halifax district militia; delegate to the Continental Congress, 1779-1780; supported ratification of Federal Constitution.

**Jones, Isaac.** Loyalist, tavern keeper.

Keeper of Golden Ball Tavern, Weston, Mass.; harbored British agents on spying missions during weeks before Lexington and Concord.

**Jones, John Paul.** 1747-1792. Continental naval officer (Commodore), b. Kircudbrightshire, Scotland.

A seaman from the age of 12, Jones became a Virginia resident, was commissioned a lieutenant in 1775, served on the *Alfred* in the Bahamas expedition, and was given command of the *Providence* in 1776. He brought in 16 prizes in one cruise. Commanding the *Ranger* (18), with the rank of captain, he terrorized British shipping in the English Channel and Irish Sea, successfully raided the port of Whitehaven, England, 22-23 April 1778, and defeated HMS *Drake* (20) on 24 April 1778. Later, as captain of a merchant ship converted to a frigate, which he named *Bonhomme Richard* (40), he led a small squadron in a dramatic cruise around the British Isles. In one of the most hard-fought single-ship battles in history, he defeated HMS *Serapis* (44) by superior seamanship and determination, 23 September 1779; his own battered ship sank the next day. Disbandment of the American Navy after the war led him to volunteer for the Russian Navy, where he served with comparable distinction.

**Jones, Joesph.** 1727-1805. American statesman, lawyer, judge, b. King George Co. Va.

Active pre-Revolution patriot; delegate to the Continental Congress, Virginia, 1777-1778, 1780-1783; uncle of James Monroe.

**Jones, Thomas.** 1731-1792. Loyalist, jurist, historian, b. New York, N.Y.

Judge of the Supreme Court of New York, 1773-1776; wrote a history of the Revoultion, 1776-1780, *A History of New York During the Revolutionary War*; moved to England, 1781.

**Jones, Noble Wymberly.** 1723-1805. American statesman, physician, b. Lambeth, near London, England.

Delegate to the Continental Congress, Georgia, 1775-1776, 1781-1783.

**Jones, Willie.** 1740-1801. American statesman, farmer, b. Northampton Co., N.C.

Delegate to the Continental Congress, North Carolina, 1780-1781.

**Jouett, John (Jack).** 1754-1822. Patriot, b. Albemarle Co., Va.

Rode all night to warn Governor Jefferson and the Virginia legislature, meeting in Charlottesville, of the British raid under Tarleton, 4 June 1781; called "the Paul Revere of Virginia."

**Jungkenn, Friedrich Christian Arnold, Baron von, Münzer von Mohrenstamm.** 1732-1806. German government official (Hessian), b. Hesse.

Baron von Jungkenn was Minister of State for Hesse-Cassel, 1780-1789. Letters and reports from his officers in America are included in his papers, which are printed in *The Siege of Charleston*, edited by Bernard A. Uhlendorf, Ann Arbor, Mich., 1938.

**Junius.** British writer.

Pen name for a much-read Whig political writer in Britain who attacked George III and several of his ministers, and defended John Wilkes; identity never definitely established; probably Sir Philip Francis, first clerk, War Office.


# K

**Kalb, Johann ("Baron de Kalb").** Continental officer (Maj. Gen.), French agent, b. Hüttendorf, Germany.

Of peasant background, became a soldier of fortune, took an assumed title, and thus gained the success in the French Army to which his talents and courage entitled him; served as an agent to America for French Foreign Minister Choiseul, 1768; when the Revolution broke out, volunteered for service in American, 1776, and became a major general in the Continental Army, 1777-1780; was second-in-command to Lafayette for the proposed Canada invasion, 1778; served in the southern campaign of 1780; fought with especial skill and gallantry at Camden, where he was mortally wounded, 16 August 1780.

**Kelly, Hugh.** Loyalist officer.

Maryland resident; with the support of Lord Dunmore, raised a force of 3,000 loyalists.

**Kemble, Peter.** 1704-1789. Loyalist, merchant, b. Smyrna, Turkey.

Leading citizen of New Jersey; widely respected, even by patriots during the Revolution; his manor at Morristown, N.J., was used as winter headquarters by Washington in 1779-1780 and 1780-1781; father-in-law of General Thomas Gage; father of Stephen Kemble.

**Kemble, Stephen.** c. 1730-1822. Loyalist, British officer (Col.).

Adjutant general in charge of intelligence service under General Gage, 1712; remained adjutant general to both General Howe and General Clinton; resigned in 1779 to make room for John André.

**Kempenfelt, Richard.** 1718-1782. British naval officer (Rear Adm.), b. Westminster, London.

Commanding British naval forces in the English Channel, 1781, overtook and defeated De Guichen's somewhat larger squadron and convoy bound for the West Indies in second battle of Ushant, 12 December 1781; died in *Royal George* disaster, a freak accident, 1782.

**Kenton, Simon.** 1755-1836. Frontiersman, b. Fauquier Co., Va.

Scout for Daniel Boone, 1775; scout for George Rogers Clark, 1778; raided Indian town at Chillicothe with Daniel Boone, 1778; captured by Indians at Ohio River, 1778, and taken to Detroit;

escaped, June 1779; scouted for Clark, 1780, 1782; settled in Maysville, Ky.; fought in War of 1812.

**Keppel, Augustus, Viscount Keppel.** 1725-1786. British naval officer (Adm.).

Did not favor the war against America; did not get along well with Lord Sandwich, First Lord of the Admiralty; commander of the English Channel fleet; courtmartialed and acquitted after unsuccessful battle with French fleet off Ushant, 27 July 1778.

**Kinloch, Francis.** 1755-1826. American statesman, lawyer, author, b. Charleston, S.C.

Delegate to the Continental Congress, South Carolina, 1780-1781.

**Kinsey, James.** 1731-1775. American statesman, lawyer, b. Philadelphia, Pa.

Delegate to the Continental Congress, New Jersey, 1774-1775.

**Kirkland, Moses.** Loyalist officer (Col.).

South Carolina resident; deserted from the patriot militia; served as deputy commissioner to the Seminole Indians in St. Augustine, Fla., and worked to keep them on the British side.

**Kirkwood, Robert.** 1730-1791. Continental officer (Capt.), farmer, b. New Castle Co., Del.

Commanded a Delaware company throughout the war; distinguished himself in the southern campaigns of General Greene; settled in Ohio after the war;

killed in St. Clair's defeat by Indians, 4 November 1791.

**Knowlton, Thomas.** 1740-1776. Militia officer (Capt.), Continental officer (Lt. Col.), farmer, b. West Boxford, Mass.

Distinguished himself at Bunker Hill; carried out daring raid on Charlestown, Mass., 8 January 1776; leader of a body of Connecticut Rangers at battle of Harlem Heights, N.Y., 16 September 1776, in which he was killed.

**Knox, Henry.** 1750-1806. Continental officer (Maj. Gen.), bookstore proprietor, b. Boston, Mass.

Chief of Artillery for the Continental Army; responsible for the "noble train of artillery," brought from Ticonderoga to Boston, January 1776, which forced the British to evacuate the city; brigadier general, 1776; played important role in Delaware crossing, 26 December 1776, and at battles of Princeton, Brandywine, Germantown, Monmouth, and Yorktown; major general, 1781; commanded West Point, 1782; after the Revolution became Secretary at War under the Articles of Confederation and the Continental Congress; was the first Secretary of War under Washington, 1789-1795.

**Knox, William.** 1732-1810. British government official, b. Ireland.

Under secretary of state for the American Department, 1770-1782.

**Knyphausen, Whilhelm, Baron von.** 1716-1800. German officer (Lt Gen.; eqivalent of U.S. Maj. Gen.), b. Prussia.

An extremely able soldier; came to America as commander of Hesse-Kassel contingent, 1776; played a major role in battles of Brandywine, Monmouth, and Springfield (23 June 1780); commanded New York garrison in absence of Clinton, 1779-1780; after return to Germany became military governor of Kassel.

**Kosciusko, Thaddeus.** 1746-1817. Polish patriot, Continental officer (Brevet Brig. Gen.), b. Lithuania.

Volunteered services to America, 1776; fortified Saratoga battlefield; served at West Point, N.Y., 1778-1780, where he planned and supervised construction of the defenses; chief engineer of the Southern Department under General Gates; after the Revolution, worked and fought for Polish independence the rest of his life.

# L

**Lacey, Edward, Jr.** d. 1813. Militia officer (Capt.).

South Carolina resident; leader in victory over the Tories at Williamson's Plantation, S.C., 12 July 1780.

**Lacey, John.** 1755-1814. Militia officer (Brig. Gen.), iron manufacturer, statesman, b. Buckingham, Bucks County, Pa.

Brigadier general, Pennsylvania militia; defeated at Crooked Billet, Pa., 1 May 1778, by Lt. Col. Robert Abercromby; served in Pennsylvania State Assembly and on Supreme Executive Council during late 1770's; was iron manufacturer

after the war, also serving as justice of the peace and Assembly member.

**Ladson, James.** d. 1812. Militia officer (Lt. Col.).

South Carolina resident; lost his entire force at Salkahatchie, S.C., to General James Paterson, 8 March 1780.

**Lafayette, James.** American spy.

Virginia Negro slave living in New Kent Co., Va.; effective spy for General Lafayette; given his freedom by state of Virginia in 1786 as reward for his services; took Lafayette's name for his surname.

**Lafayette, Marquis de (Marie Joseph Paul Yves Roch Gilbert du Motier).** 1757-1834. French officer, Continental officer (Maj. Gen.), b. Chevaniac Chateau, Auvergne.

An extremely wealthy nobleman; resigned from French Army in 1776 and became a volunteer in the Continental Army, serving at his own expense; commissioned a major general, 1 July 1777, by the Continental Congress; became an intimate of Washington's; fought well at Brandywine and in operations near Valley Forge, Pa., 1777-1778; was appointed commander of proposed, but never enacted, Canada invasion, 1778; figured prominently in the Monmouth campaign and at Newport, R.I., July-August, 1778; returned to France in 1779 and 1780 to plead the cause of the Americans; his plan for an invasion of England was not approved, but he laid the groundwork for the expeditionary force sent to America under Rochambeau, 1780; returned to America in 1781; was sent by Washington to command in Virginia, where he proved himself to be a competent strategist and tactician; distinguished himself at Green Spring, Va., 6 July 1781, and at Yorktown; returned to France in 1781 and assisted American Minister Thomas Jefferson in many political and economic matters; was a republican leader in the early stages of the French Revolution, 1789-1791.

**Lamb, John.** 1735-1780. Continental officer (Col.), merchant, customs collector, b. New York, N.Y.

Active pre-Revolution patriot; artilleryman; with Arnold at Quebec, 31 December 1775; wounded and captured; exchanged January 1777; participated in Danbury (Conn.) raid, April 1777, and Yorktown campaign; served at West Point, N.Y., 1779-1780.

**Lamb, Roger.** British soldier, writer.

Served as a sergeant in the Royal Welsh Fusiliers (23rd Foot); author of two valuable works on the American Revolution: *An Original and Authentic Journal of Occurences During the Late American War from its Commencement to the Year 1783* and *Memoirs of His Own Life.*

**Landais, Pierre.** 1731-1820. French naval officer, Continental naval officer (Capt.), b. Normandy.

After an undistinguished French naval career, named a captain in the Continental Navy, 1777; given command of the *Alliance*, 1778; served under John Paul Jones in his circumnavigation of Great Britain; was repeatedly insubordinate, and actually fired upon Jones's ship, the *Bonhomme Richard*, in the *Serapis* battle, 23 September 1779; relieved of command by Jones; regained control over the *Alliance* by trickery and sailed back to the United States, where he was immediately court-martialed and dismissed from the service; later went back to France; joined the French Republican Navy in 1789 or 1790; retired, 1793, and returned to New York, where he died.

**Langdon, John.** 1741-1819. American statesman, merchant, b. Portsmouth, N.H.

Delegate to the Continental Congress, New Hampshire, 1775-1777, 1786-1787; governor of New Hampshire, 1788, 1805, 1809-1811; member, U.S. Senate, New Hampshire, 1789-1801; first president pro tempore of the U.S. Senate, 1789.

**Langdon, Woodbury.** 1739-1805. American statesman, merchant, b. Portsmouth, N.H.

Delegate to the Continental Congress, New Hampshire, 1779-1780; brother of John Langdon.

**Langlade, Charles Michael de.** c. 1729-1801. Indian leader, landowner, b. Canada.

Of Indian and French ancestry; allied with the French in the French and Indian War, but shifted to the British in Pontiac's War;

supported the British, especially Carleton and Burgoyne, during the Revolution.

**Langworthy, Edward.** 1738-1802. American statesman, newspaperman, teacher, writer, b. Savannah, Ga.

Delegate to the Continental Congress, Georgia, 1777-1790.

**Laumoy, Jean Baptiste Joseph, Chevalier de.** 1750-1832. French officer, Continental officer (Col.), b. France.

Engineer in the Continental Army; active in early stages of French Revolution.

**Laurance, John.** 1750-1810. Continental officer, statesman, lawyer, b. Cornwall, England.

Judge Advocate General of the Continental Army, 1777-1782; prosecuted John André; delegate to the Continental Congress, New York, 1785-1786; member, U.S. Senate, New York, 1796-1800; president pro tempore, 1798.

**Laurens, Henry.** 1724-1792. American statesman, merchant, planter, diplomat, b. Charleston, S.C.

Delegate to the Continental Congress, South Carolina, 1777-1780; president of the Continental Congress, 1777; captured by the British off the coast of Newfoundland while going to Holland on a diplomatic mission, 3 September 1780; commissioner at the negotiations for peace in Paris, 1783; father of John Laurens.

**Laurens, John.** c. 1754-1782. Continental officer (Lt. Col.), b. South Carolina.

Aide-de-camp to George Washington; fought at Brandywine, Germantown, Monmouth, Yorktown; represented the Americans in the surrender negotiations at Yorktown, 17 October 1781; killed at Combahee Ferry, S.C., 27 August 1782; son of Henry Laurens.

**Law, Richard.** 1733-1806. American statesman, lawyer, jurist, b. Milford, Conn.

Justice of the peace, 1765; clerk of the General Court; active pre-Revolution patriot; delegate to the Continental Congress, Connecticut, 1777, 1781, 1782; U.S. district judge, 1789-1806; mayor of New London, 1784-1806; with Roger Sherman, codified Connecticut statute law.

**Lawson, Robert.** Continental officer (Col.), militia officer (Brig. Gen.).

Brigadier general in the Virginia militia; fought at Guilford Courthouse and in the Yorktown campaign of 1781.

**Learned, Ebenezer.** Militia officer (Capt.), Continental officer (Brig. Gen.), b. Oxford, Mass.

Active pre-Revolution patriot; led company of minutemen to Cambridge, 19 April 1775; played active but relatively minor role until resignation for reasons of health, March 1778.

**Le Begue de Presle Duportail, Louis.** *See* Duportail, Louis, Chevalier.

**Lee, Andrew.** Continental or militia officer (Capt.), American spy.

Resident of Paxtang, Pa.; disguised as an escaping British prisoner of war, early 1781, exposed a chain of "safe houses" from Lancaster, Pa., to the Delaware River where British spies and escaping prisoners were sheltered.

**Lee, Ann ("Mother Ann").** 1736-1784. Religious leader, b. Manchester, England.

Converted to Shaker faith in Manchester and became one of its leaders; came to America with small group of followers, 1774; and settled near Albany, N.Y.; imprisoned by patriot authorities, 1780, because pacifist Shaker teachings led to suspicions that the group was pro-British; released after six months and made preaching tour through New England, 1781-1783.

**Lee, Arthur.** 1740-1792. American statesman, physician, diplomat, b. "Stratford," Westmoreland Co., Va.

Diplomatic agent for the United States in Paris, 1775-1780; was responsible for the establishment of Roderique Hortalez et Cie., a secret firm organized to give military aid to the Americans; caused dissension among the American commissioners in Paris; delegate to the Continental Congress, Virginia, 1781-1784; brother of Francis Lightfoot, Richard Henry, Thomas Ludwell, and William Lee.

**Lee, Charles.** 1731-1782. Continental officer (Maj. Gen.), b. England.

Emigrated to America, 1773; was an experienced British Army officer and was made Continental major general, 17 June 1775; served well in defense of Charleston, 1776; insubordinate to Washington in New Jersey retreat, November-December, 1776; captured, 13 December 1776; apparently acted treasonably during capture; exchanged April 1778; dismissed as a result of his disgraceful conduct during and after the Monmouth campaign.

**Lee, Ezra.** Continental soldier (Sgt.).

Soldier of the Connecticut Line; operator of the *Turtle*, a submarine, which unsuccessfully attacked a British warship, 7 September 1776.

**Lee, Francis Lightfoot.** 1734-1797. American statesman, b. "Stratford," Westmoreland Co., Va.

Active pre-Revolution patriot; delegate to the Continental Congress, Virginia, 1775-1780; signer of the Declaration of Independence; brother of Arthur, Richard Henry, Thomas Ludwell, and William Lee.

**Lee, Henry ("Light-Horse Harry").** 1756-1818. Continental officer (Lt. Col.), statesman, b. "Leesylvania," Prince William Co., Va.

Cavalry leader; commanded daring raid on Paulus Hook, N.J., 19 August 1779; commander of Lee's Legion, which he led with distinction in Greene's southern campaigns, 1781-1782; participated in action against Dorchester, S.C., 1 December 1781, and conceived the idea of the invasion of Johns Island, South Carolina, 28-29 December 1781; delegate to the Continental Congress, Virginia, 1785-1788; governor of Virginia, 1792-1795; member, U.S. House of Representatives, 1799-1801; eulogized George Washington as "first in war, first in peace, and first in the hearts of his countrymen"; father of Robert E. Lee; cousin of Lees of "Stratford."

**Lee, Richard Henry.** 1732-1794. American statesman, jurist, b. "Stratford," Westmoreland Co., Va.

Delegate to the Continental Congress, Virginia, 1774-1780, 1784-1787; president of Continental Congress, 1784; signer of the Declaration of Independence; member, U.S. Senate, 1789-1792; president pro tempore of the Senate, 1792; brother of Arthur, Francis Lightfoot, Thomas Ludwell, and William Lee.

**Lee, Thomas Ludwell.** 1730-1778. Patriot, jurist, b. "Stratford," Westmoreland Co., Va.

Member of the Virginia Committee of Safety, 1775-1776, and other Virginia Revolutionary groups; brother of Arthur, Francis Lightfoot, Richard Henry, and William Lee.

**Lee, Thomas Sim.** 1745-1819. American statesman, landowner, b. Upper Marlboro, Prince Georges Co., Md.

Delegate to the Continental Congress, Maryland, 1783-1784; governor of Maryland, 1779-1783, 1792-1794.

**Lee, William.** 1739-1795. American merchant, diplomat, b. "Stratford," Westmoreland Co., Va.

Commercial agent in France; worked closely with his brother Arthur; appointed commissioner to Prussia and Austria, 1777, but did not serve because neither country had any intention of granting recognition to the United States; brother also of Francis Lightfoot, Richard Henry, and Thomas Ludwell Lee.

**Legge, Francis.** Governor of Nova Scotia.

Raised and commanded 1,000 men from Nova Scotia and Newfoundland in the defense of Canada, 1775.

**Leigh, Sir Egerton.** Loyalist government official.

Attorney general, surveyor general, and member of the Council of South Carolina.

**L'Enfant, Pierre Charles.** 1754-1825. Continental officer (Capt.), b. Paris.

Continental Army engineer and architect; later designed the city of Washington, D.C.

**Leonard, David.** 1740-1829. Loyalist, attorney, writer.

Published a weekly Loyalist newsletter, *To the Inhabitants of the Province of Massachusetts*, under the pen name "Massachusettensis," 12 December 1774 3 April 1775.

**Leslie, Alexander.** c. 1740-1794. British officer (Brig. Gen.; local rank, Lt. Gen.).

Commanded expedition to Salem, Mass., 26 February 1775, that almost became the first battle of the Revolution; served in Boston, 1775-1776, at battle of Long Island, at Kip's Bay, N.Y., 15 September 1776, at Harlem Heights, N.Y., 16 September 1776, and in Trenton-Princeton campaign; participated in southern campaign, 1781; fought at Cowan's Ford, N.C., 1 February 1781, and commanded the British right at Guilford Courthouse; succeeded Cornwallis as commander in the Southern Theater, October 1781; withdrew from Savannah, Ga., 11 July 1782, and Charleston, S.C., 14 December 1782.

**Levy, Aaron.** Financier, patriot, b. Netherlands.

Pennsylvania resident; made a loan of considerable size to the Continental Congress.

**Lewis, Andrew.** 1720-1781. Continental officer (Brig. Gen.), b. Ireland.

Settled in Virginia as child; fought in French and Indian War; led 1,000 men at battle of Point Pleasant, Va., in Lord Dunmore's War, 10 October 1774; appointed brigadier general, Continental Army, 1776; resigned 1777.

**Lewis, Fielding.** 1725-1782. Militia officer (Brig. Gen.), b. "Warner Hall," Gloucester Co., Va.

Active pre-Revolution patriot; prevented by bad health from active military service; superintended and supported financially a patriot small-arms factory at Fredericksburg, Va.; brother-in-law of George Washington.

**Lewis, Francis.** 1713-1803. American statesman, merchant, b. Llandaff, Wales.

Delegate to the Continental Congress, New York, 1774-1779; signer of the Declaration of Independence.

**Lewis, Morgan.** 1754-1844. Continental officer (Col.), statesman, b. New York.

Deputy quartermaster general of the Northern Army; chief of staff to General Gates, 1777; governor of New York, 1804; son of Francis Lewis.

**Leyba, Don Fernando de.** Spanish officer (Capt.).

Repulsed the British expedition at St. Louis, Mo., 26 May 1780.

**L'Hommedieu, Ezra.** 1734-1811. American statesman, lawyer, b. Southold, Long Island, N.Y.

Member of all New York provincial congresses; member, state Assembly, 1777-1783, and state Senate, 1784-1809; delegate to the Continental Congress, New York, 1779-1783, 1787-1788; instrumental in founding University of the State of New York; conducted agricultural experiments.

**Lillington, John Alexander.** d. 1786. Militia officer (Brig. Gen.), landowner.

Fought in various Carolina actions, most notably at Moore's Creek Bridge, 27 February 1776, where he led a force of 150 minutemen; participated in Camden campaign, August 1780.

**Lincoln, Benjamin.** 1733-1810. Militia officer (Maj. Gen.), Continental officer (Maj. Gen.), local official, farmer, b. Massachusetts.

Militia officer, 1755-1777; major general, Continental Army, 1777-1783; distinguished himself in defense against the Bennington (Vt.) raid, August 1777, and at the battles of Saratoga; commanded the southern Department, 1778-1780; commanded American troops in siege of Savannah, September-October, 1779; surrendered Charleston, 12 May 1780; served at Yorktown, where he accepted British surrender as Washington's representative; Secretary at War, 1781-1783.

**Linn, William.** Continental officer (Lt.).

Brought gunpowder from New Orleans to Wheeling, Va. (now W.Va.), to fight the Indians and Tories, 2 May 1777.

**Lippincott, Richard.** 1745-1826. Loyalist officer.

New Jersey resident; member of the "Associated Loyalists"; officer responsible for hanging U.S. Capt. Joshua Huddy at Middletown, N.J., 12 April 1782.

**Lisle, John.** Militia officer (Lt. Col.).

South Carolina resident; deserted to the British with his entire battalion of militia, July 1781.

**Livemore, Samuel.** 1732-1803. American statesman, lawyer, b. Middlesex Co., Mass.

Delegate to the Continental Congress, New Hampshire, 1780-1783, 1785-1786; member, U.S. House of Representatives, 1789-1793; member, U.S. Senate, 1793-1801; president pro tempore of the Senate, 1796-1797.

**Livingston, Henry Beekman.** 1750-1831. Continental officer (Col.).

Aide-de-camp to Maj. Gen. Richard Montgomery in his march to Montreal and Quebec, July-December, 1775; given a sword of honor by Congress for his part in the capture of Chambly, Canada, 18 October 1775; aide-de-camp to Maj. Gen. Philip Schuyler, 1776; distinguished himself at Monmouth, N.J., 28 June 1778.

**Livingston, Henry Brockholst.** 1757-1823. Continental officer (Lt. Col.), jurist, b. New York, N.Y.

Aide-de-camp to Maj. Gen. Philip Schuyler, 1775; on the staff of Brig. Gen. Benedict Arnold, 1776; sided with Arnold against Gates at Saratoga, September 1777; distinguished himself at Newport, R.I., 29 August 1778; became an Associate Justice of the Supreme Court, 1807; son of William Livingston.

**Livingston, James.** 1747-1832. Continental officer (Col.), b. Montreal, Canada.

Raised a body of Canadians and refugees for the American cause, 1775, which was later known as the 1st Canadian Regiment; served at Chambly, Canada, 18 October 1775.

**Livingston, Philip.** 1716-1778. American statesman, merchant, b. Albany, N.Y.

Delegate to the Stamp Act Congress, 1765; delegate to the Continental Congress, New York, 1774-1778; signer of the Declaration of Independence; brother of William Livingston.

**Livingston, Robert R.** 1718-1775. Patriot, lawyer, jurist, b. New York.

Wealthy landowner; member, New York Provincial Assembly, 1758-1768; appointed judge of Admiralty Court, 1759; appointed associate judge of New York Supreme Court, 1763; chairman, New York Committee of Correspondence during Stamp Act crisis; member of Stamp Act Congress, 1765, where he proposed a plan for confederation of the colonies; favored conciliation with Britain but did not rule out possible necessity for independence; father of Robert R. Livingston, b. 1746.

**Livingston, Robert R.** 1746-1813. American statesman, lawyer, b. New York, N.Y.

Delegate to the Continental Congress, New York, 1775-1777, 1779-1781; secretary of the Department of Foreign Affairs, 1781-1783; chancellor of New York, 1777-1801; administered oath of office to George Washington, April 1789;

minister to France, 1801-1804; instrumental in the Louisiana Purchase, 1803; worked with Robert Fulton on development of steamboat and financed his efforts; son of Robert R. Livingston, b. 1718.

**Livingston, William.** 1723-1790. American statesman, militia officer (Brig. Gen.), lawyer, b. Albany, N.Y.

Delegate to the Continental Congress, New Jersey, 1774-1776; brigadier general, New Jersey militia, 1775-1776; governor of New Jersey, 1776-1790; delegate to Federal Constitutional Convention; worked effectively for ratification; brother of Philip Livingston, father of Henry Brockholst Livingston.

**Livius, Peter.** 1729-1795. Loyalist, jurist, b. England.

Left New Hampshire as a loyalist early in the Revolution; Chief Justice of Canada, 1777-1778; dismissed by Carleton in 1778, but restored the following year, and served until 1786.

**Lochry (or Lochrey), Archibald.** d. 1781. Militia officer (Col.).

Colonel, Pennsylvania Rangers; defeated and killed by Joseph Brant while on a mission to join George Rogers Clark on the Ohio River, 24 or 25 August 1781.

**Locke, John.** 1632-1704. British philosopher, b. Wrington, Somerset, near Bristol.

Author of *Two Treatises on Government* (London, 1689); his theories and writings on government and political philosophy formed much of the intellectual foundation of the American Revolution.

**Lockwood, Samuel.** Continental officer (Capt.).

Captured Tory Col. Isaac Hatfield at Eastchester, N.Y., 18 January 1780; however, his force was pursued and all were either killed or captured.

**Logan.** c. 1725-1780. Indian leader, loyalist.

Became bitter toward settlers at the time of Lord Dunmore's War, 1774, when members of his family were murdered by a raiding party; favored British during Revolution; saved life of frontier scout Simon Kenton.

**Loring, Joshua.** 1744-1789. Loyalist official, b. Hingham, Mass.

Appointed commissary of prisoners, 1777, by General Howe; husband of the alleged mistress of General Howe; hated by the patriots for his alleged mistreatment of prisoners.

**Lossberg, Friedrich Wilhelm von.** German officer (Lt. Gen.).

Succeeded Knyphausen as commander-in-chief of German troops in America, 1782.

**Lotbinière, Louis.** Catholic chaplain.

Canadian; chaplain, 1st Canadian (Livingston's) Regiment; only Catholic chaplain in the Continental Army.

**Lott, Abraham.** c. 1726-1794. Loyalist official.

Treasurer of the colony of New York.

**Louis XVI.** 1754-1793. King of France, b. Versailles.

Louis reigned from 1774 to 1792. He and his ministers were instrumental in the success of the American cause through military aid, the alliance, and direct military support. It is believed that the American Revolution may have hastened the French Revolution, 1789-1799, by overextending French resources and thus worsening the later financial crisis, as well as by stimulating some Frenchmen to follow the American example. Louis was beheaded in 1793.

**Lovell, James.** 1737-1814. American statesman, teacher, customs collector, b. Boston, Mass.

Delivered address on first anniversery of Boston Massacre, 1771; delegate to the Continental Congress, Massachusetts, 1776-1782; admired Gates and criticized Washington; involved in Conway Cabal.

**Lovell, John.** 1710-1778. Loylist, school headmaster, b. Boston, Mass.

Headmaster of South Grammar School, Boston (now Boston Latin); father of James Lovell; taught many who became leading citizens, including John Hancock and Henry Knox; went to live in Nova Scotia, 1776.

**Lovell, Solomon.** d. 1801. Militia officer (Brig. Gen.).

Brigadier general, Massachusetts militia, 1779-1782; a leader of the ill-fated Penobscot (Me.) expedition, 22 July–14 August 1779.

**Low, Isaac.** 1735-1791. American statesman, loyalist, merchant, b. Raritan Landing, near New Brunswick, N.J.

Delegate to the Continental Congress, New York, 1774-1775; opposed an armed conflict with Great Britain, and in 1776, after the Declaration of Independence, abandoned the patriot cause; arrested for treason in 1776; went to England in 1783.

**Lowell, John.** 1743-1802. American statesman, lawyer, b. Newburyport, Mass.

Delegate to the Continental Congress, Massachusetts, 1782-1783.

**Ludlow, George Duncan.** 1734-1808. Loyalist, jurist.

New York Supreme Court judge; master of the rolls and superintendent of police on Long Island, 1780.

**Ludwick, Christopher.** 1720-1801. Baker, soldier, seaman, American secret agent, b. Giessen, Hesse-Darmstadt.

As boy, enlisted as soldier and fought in the Hapsburg armies against the Turks, 1736-1740; shipped as sailor, 1745-1752; learned baker's craft in England and settled in Philadelphia as baker, 1753; soon became prosperous and prominent; successfully encouraged desertions by Hessian troops during the Revolution; made superintendant of bakers for the Continental Army, 1777; probably spied for Americans, reporting directly to General Washington.

**Luzerne, Anne-César de la, Chevalier.** French diplomat.

Second French minister to the United States, 1779-1784.

**Lynch, Charles.** 1736-1796. Militia officer (Col.), b. Lynchburg, Va.

Lynch was a justice of the peace from 1766; a member of the House of Burgesses, 1769-1775; and a member of the Virginia House of Delegates, 1776-1778. He became a colonel of militia, February 1778, and fought well at Guilford Courthouse. Etymologists trace the term "lynch law" to Lynch's summary ordering of punishment for Tories. His extralegal sentences did not exceed flogging, however. It was after the Civil War that the term came to mean murder by a group as punishment for alleged crimes.

**Lynch, Thomas.** 1727-1776. American statesman, planter, b. St. James' Parish, Berkeley Co., S.C.

Delegate to the Continental Congress, South Carolina, 1774-1776.

**Lynch, Thomas, Jr.** 1749-1779. American statesman, planter, b. Prince George's Parish, S.C.

Delegate to the Continental Congress, South Carolina, 1776-1777; signer of the Declaration of Independence.

# M

**McAllister, Archibald.** d. 1781. Continental officer (Brevet Capt.).

Maryland resident; breveted captain for conduct at Paulus Hook, N.J., August 1779.

**McArthur, Archibald.** British officer (Lt. Col.).

Served at Cowpens; lieutenant colonel of the 3rd Battalion, 60th Foot ("Royal Americans"), 1781.

**McCall, James.** d. 1781. Militia officer (Lt. Col.).

Captured as captain with South Carolina Rangers in skirmish with Indians at Cherokee Town, S.C., 26 June 1776; lieutenant colonel of South Carolina troops at Rugley's Mill, S.C., 4 December 1780, and Long Cane, S.C., 11 December 1780.

**McClene, James.** 1730-1806. American statesman, b. New London, Chester Co., Pa.

Delegate to the Continental Congress, Pennsylvania, 1779-1780.

**MacCleod, Donald.** d. 1776. Tory militia officer.

Took command of militia from ailing Donald McDonald at Moore's Creek Bridge, N.C., 27 February 1776; killed in action.

**McComb, Eleazer.** d. 1798. American statesman.

Delegate to the Continental Congress, Delaware, 1782-1784.

**McCrea, Jane (Jenny).** c. 1754-1777.

Miss McCrea was killed and scalped by some of General Burgoyne's Indian allies near Fort Edward, N.Y., July 1777, while she was trying to arrange a meeting with her Tory officer fiance. General Burgoyne felt that he could not punish his allies, and the patriots exploited the affair.

**McCulloch, Samuel.** Militia officer (Maj.).

Reinforced Wheeling, Va. (now West Virginia), September 1777, and reportedly escaped from the pursuing Indians by leaping his horse down a 150-foot precipice.

**McDonald, Adam.** Continental officer (Col.).

Defeated by Sir Benjamin Thompson at Wambaw Creek, S.C., 14 February 1782.

**McDonald, Allan.** Loyalist officer (Brig. Gen.), b. Scotland.

Captured at Moore's Creek Bridge, N.C., 27 February 1776; husband of Flora McDonald.

**McDonald, Donald.** b. 1712. Loyalist officer (Maj. Gen.?), b. Scotland.

Led 1,500 loyalists, mostly Highland Scots, to confrontation with 1,000 Continentals and militia at Moore's Creek Bridge, N.C., where he was defeated and captured, 27 February 1776.

**McDonald, Flora.** 1722-1790. Loyalist, b. Scotland.

Jacobin heroine who, as a young girl, helped "Bonnie Prince Charlie" escape capture; settled in North Carolina with her husband

Allan McDonald, did much to arouse the Scots in North Carolina to rally behind Donald McDonald and the loyalist cause.

**McDougall, Alexander.** 1732-1786. Continental officer (Maj. Gen.), statesman, privateer, b. Islay, Innes, Hebrides, Scotland.

Came to America as a child; commanded a privateer in the French and Indian War; was a prominent pre-Revolutionary radical leader in New York; wrote *A Son of Liberty to the Betrayed Inhabitants of the City and Colony of New York*, 16 December 1769; presided at the "Meeting in the Fields," 6 July 1774, where Alexander Hamilton also spoke; brigadier general, Continental Army, 1776-1777; major general, 1777-1783; commander at West Point, N.Y., 1780, succeeding Benedict Arnold; court-martialed in 1782 for insubordination to Maj. Gen. William Heath; delegate to the Continental Congress, New York, 1781-1782, 1784-1785.

**McDowell, Joseph.** 1756-1811. Militia officer.

North Carolina resident; leader in the battles at Kings Mountain and Cowpens.

**McFarlan, Robert.** British spy.

Carried copies of Lt. Gen. Sir Henry Clinton's proclamation to the mutineers of the Pennsylvania Line, January 1781; possibly an American double agent.

**McGary, Hugh.** Frontiersman, militia officer (Maj.).

Kentucky settler; ambushed by loyalists and Indians at Blue Licks, Ky., 19 August 1782, along with Daniel Boone, who had reluctantly accompanied McGary's rash pursuit.

**McHenry, James.** 1753-1816. Continental officer (Maj.), statesman.

Assistant secretary to George Washington, 1778-1780; delegate to the Continental Congress, Maryland, 1783-1786; Secretary of War, 1796-1800.

**McIntosh, John.** 1755-1826. Continental officer (Lt. Col.), b. McIntosh Co., Ga.

Refused to surrender Fort Morris (Sunbury), Ga. with phrase, "Come and take it"; nephew of Lachlan McIntosh.

**McIntosh, Lachlan.** 1725-1806. Continental officer (Brig. Gen.), clerk, b. Inverness, Scotland.

Brigadier general, Continental Army, 1776-1783; mortally wounded Button Gwinnet in a duel, May 1777; not aggressive in western operations against Indians; 1778, participated in allied attack on Savannah, 9 October 1779; captured at Charleston, May 1780.

**McKean, Thomas.** 1734-1817. American statesman, clerk, lawyer, b. New London, Chester Co., Pa.

Opposed Stamp Act as a judge, 1765; delegate to Stamp Act Congress, 1765; delegate to the Continental Congress, Delaware, 1774-1776, 1778-1783; signer of the Declaration of Independence; president of the Continental Congress, 1781; held office in both Pennsylvania and Delaware, 1777-1783; chief justice of Pennsylvania Supreme Court, 1777-1789; Jeffersonian Republican after 1792; governor of Pennsylvania, 1800-1809.

**McKee, Alexander.** Loyalist offical.

Deputy superintendent of Indian affairs, at Pittsburgh, 1775; raised Indian auxiliaries for the British.

**McKinly, John.** 1721-1796. American statesman, physician, b. Ireland.

Sheriff and chief burgess of Wilmington, Del., pre-Revolutionary period; chosen president and commander-in-chief of Delaware, 1777, for a three-year term; captured by the British in September 1777 and exchanged for William Franklin, 1778.

**McLane, Allen (or Allan).** 1746-1829. Continental officer (Col.), partisan leader, merchant, b. Philadelphia, Pa. (probably).

Participated in early actions in Virginia, 1774 and 1775; fought with Delaware militia at Long Island, N.Y., 27 August 1776, and White Plains, N.Y., 28 October 1776; distinguished himself at Princeton, 3 January 1777; immediately commissioned Continental captain; carried out numerous harassing, reconnaissance, and foraging missions; saved Lafayette from surprise at Barren Hill, Pa., 20 May 1778.

**MacLean, Allan.** c. 1725-1784. British officer (Lt. Col.), b. Torloish, Scotland.

Led Royal Highland Emigrants; unsuccessful in effort to relieve siege of St. Johns, Canada, 5 September–2 November 1775.

**MacLean, Francis.** British officer (Col.; local rank, Brig. Gen.).

Commandant of British forces in Nova Scotia; launched the operation that resulted in the Penobscot (Me.) expedition, July-August 1779.

**Madison, James.** 1729-1812. Clergyman, educator, militia officer (Capt.), b. Port Republic, Rockingham Co., Va.

Chaplain, House of Delegates, 1777; saw action as captain of militia; president of the College of William and Mary, 1777-1812; first bishop of Protestant Episcopal Church in Virginia, 1790-1812.

**Madison, James.** 1751-1836. American statesman, lawyer, b. Port Conway, Prince George Co., Va.

Madison was a member of the Orange County Committee of Safety, 1775; a delegate to the Virginia provinicial convention of 1776, serving on the committee that drafted the state constitution and bill of rights; and a member of the state Assembly, 1776. He was elected to the Governor's Council, 1777, and was a delegate to the Continental Congress, 1780-1783, 1786-1788. Credited with drawing up the instructions for John Jay's mission to Spain, 1780, he also worked out a compromise regarding the Northwest Territory, September 1783, that allowed the establishment of the Northwest Ordinance.

Madison was a delegate to the Federal Convention of 1787, and was instrumental in developing the final form of the Constitution. During the ratification debates of 1787 and 1788 he wrote the Bill of Rights in order to assure ratification by Virginia. He was co-author, along with John Jay and Alexander Hamilton, of the *Federalist Papers.*

A member of the U.S. House of Representatives, 1789-1797, Madison was a leader in the opposition to Hamilton's financial policies; he was active in the formation of the Anti-Federalists, and later of the Republican (Democratic-Republican) Party.

Madison was Secretary of State during the administrations of Jefferson, 1801-1809, and was the fourth President of the United States (1809-1817). His terms included the War of 1812, for which the United States was basically unprepared, and which is sometimes called "Mr. Madison's War." He retired in 1817 to his home, "Montpelier," in Orange County, Virginia.

**Maham, Hezekiah (or Hezediah).** 1739-1789. Militia officer (Col.), b. St. Stephen's Parish, S.C.

Active pre-Revolution patriot; fought at Savannah, Ga., 29 December 1778, and Stono Ferry, S.C., 20 June 1779; colonel of an independent dragoon regiment, 1780; served at Fort Watson, S.C., 15-23 April 1781, where the type of siege tower named for him was first used; participated in actions at

Quinby Bridge, S.C., 17 July 1781, and Fair Lawn, S.C., 27 November 1781.

**Maitland, John.** d. 1779. British officer (Lt. Col.).

Defeated Maj. Gen. Benjamin Lincoln at Stono Ferry, S.C., 20 June 1779; lieutenant colonel commanding the 1st Battalion, 71st Highlanders.

**Malcolm, John.** Customs official.

Tarred, feathered, and paraded through Boston, 25 January 1773.

**Malcolm, William.** d. 1792. Continental officer (Col.).

New York resident; colonel of one of the 16 "additional Continental regiments"; deputy adjutant general, Northern Department, 1778.

**Malmady (or Malmedy), Francis, Marquis de.** Continental officer (Col.), b. France.

French volunteer; brigadier general of Rhode Island troops, 1776-1777; colonel, Continental Army, 1777-1780.

**Manley, John.** c. 1734-1793. Seaman, Continental naval officer (Capt.), privateer, b. Boston, Mass.

Captain of various vessels; took the first important prize of the war, the British warship *Nancy*, 29 November 1775.

**Marchant, Henry.** 1741-1796. American statesman, lawyer, jurist, b. Martha's Vineyard, Mass.

Member, Sons of Liberty; attorney general of Rhode Island,

1771-1776; member, Rhode Island Committee of Correspondence, 1773; delegate to the Continental Congress, Rhode Island, 1777-1780, 1783-1784; worked for ratification of the Federal Constitution, 1790; U.S. district judge, 1790-1796.

**Marion, Francis.** c. 1732-1795. Continental officer (Lt. Col.), militia officer (Brig. Gen.), statesman, planter, b. St. John's Parish (now Berkeley Co.), S.C.

Served as Continental officer at Charleston and Savannah, 1775-1780; commanded South Carolina militia (also known as Marion's Brigade), 1780-1783; distinguished himself at Parker's Ferry, S.C., 13 August 1781, and Eutaw Springs, S.C., 8 September 1781; known as "the Swamp Fox," for his effective partisan hit-and-run tactics, especially in 1780-1781; elected to state Senate, 1781, 1782, 1784.

**Marjoribanks, John.** d. 1781. British officer (Maj.).

Hero of Eutaw Springs, S.C., 8 September 1781, where he led the flank battalion; mortally wounded in the battle.

**Marks, Nehemiah.** British spy, b. Derby, Conn.

Son of a prominent Derby merchant; went to New York at outbreak of Revolution to serve as British courier and spy, gathering data in Connecticut and crossing Long Island Sound to report to the British.

**Marriner, William.** Whaleboat guerrilla, b. New Brunswick, N.J.

Operating with Adam Hyler, harassed the British in coastal waters of New Jersey.

**Marshall, Christopher.** 1709-1797. Pharmacist, diarist, b. Ireland (probably).

Settled in Philadelphia at 18; successful pharmacist; patriot; kept dairy of the Revolution that is a valuable source.

**Marshall, John.** 1755-1835. American statesman, lawyer, jurist, Continental officer (Capt.), b. Germantown, Fauquier Co., Va.

Marshall grew up on the frontier. He was a captain in the Continental Army, 1777-1781, serving with the 7th Virginia Regiment, and saw action at Brandywine, Germantown, and Monmouth, and at Stony Point, N.Y., 16 July 1779. He served with Baron von Steuben in the defense of Virginia, 1780-1781.

He was a member of the Virginia Assembly, 1782-1788, member of the Virginia Executive Council, 1782-1795, and member of the state constitutional convention for the ratification of the Federal Constitution, 1788. He served in the U.S. House of Representatives, 1799-1800, and as Secretary of State, 1800-1801. In a somewhat unpopular move, President John Adams appointed John Marshall Chief Justice of the U.S. Supreme Court in the late days of his administration. Marshall served in this capacity for 34 years and must be considered one of the most outstanding men ever to occupy the Chief Justiceship. Among the major decision that were handed down under Marshall were *Marbury vs. Madison*, 1803, *Fletcher vs. Peck*, 1810, *McCulloch vs. Maryland*, 1819, and *Gibbons vs. Ogden*, 1824.

He was at odds with his cousin, Thomas Jefferson, over interpretation of the Constitution; Marshall established the Federalist tradition of broad construction.

**Martin, Josiah.** 1737-1786. British official, b. Antigua, West Indies.

Served as royal governor of North Carolina, 1771-1783, succeeding William Tryon; his miscalulations led to the ill-fated Charleston expedition of 1776, and to the loyalist defeat at Moore's Creek Bridge, N.C., 14 February 1776.

**Mason, George.** 1725-1792. American statesman, landowner, b. Virginia.

Mason was active in local government before the Revolution; was a member of the House of Burgesses, 1759; devised a method for circumventing the Stamp Act; and was responsible for the drafting of the Virginia Resolves of May 1768, which asserted that only the governor and provincial legislature had the power to lay taxes in Virginia. He was also responsible for the Fairfax Resolves of 1774.

In 1776 Mason drew up the Virginia bill of rights and constitution; the bill of rights was the basis for the first part of the Declaration of Independence and the Bill of Rights of the U.S. Constitution.

Mason was on the committee that authorized the western operations of George Rogers Clark; was largely responsible for the boundary of the United States extending to the Great Lakes in 1783; and devised a plan for Virginia to cede its western lands to the central government.

Mason, along with Elbridge Gerry and John Randolph, refused to sign the final draft of the Federal Constitution, 1787; his views were expressed in *Objections to the Proposed Federal Constitution*. Mason objected to the compromise positions on slavery and tariffs, and consistently, in his public career, opposed slavery. He also objected to the absence of a bill of rights in the Constitution as it originally stood.

Mason was chosen, but refused to serve, as the first Senator from Virginia in 1789.

**Mason, John.** Loyalist.

Emissary of General Henry Clinton who tried to exploit the mutiny of the Pennsylvania Line, January 1781, by offering pardon, money equivalent to what the men were owed by Congress, and the privilege of declining military service; arrested; hanged as a spy, January 1781.

**Mason, Thomson.** 1733-1785. Lawyer, legislator, b. Prince William Co., Va.

Younger brother of George Mason; member, House of Burgesses, 1758-1761, 1765-1774; member, Virginia General Assembly, 1777-1778, 1783; early patriot; author of nine letters of a "British American," arguing the invalidity of Parliament's enacting laws for the colonies.

**Mathew, Edward.** British officer (Brig. Gen.?).

Led, with Commodore George Collier, a raid on Norfolk, Va., 9 May 1779.

**Mathews, George.** 1739-1812. Continental officer (Col.), statesman, b. Augusta Co., Va.

Served with distinction in Greene's southern campaigns; governor of Georgia, 1787, 1793-1796; member, U.S. House of Representatives, Georgia, 1789-1791.

**Mathews, John.** 1744-1802. American statesman, b. Charleston, S.C.

Delegate to the Continental Congress, South Carolina, 1778-1782; governor of South Carolina, 1782, 1783.

**Matlack, Timothy.** c. 1730-1829. American statesman, militia officer (Col.), merchant, b. Haddonfield, Camden Co., N.J.

Moved with parents to Philadelphia, c. 1745; participated in Trenton-Princeton actions of 1776-1777; delegate to the Continental Congress, Pennsylvania, 1780-1781.

**Matthews, David.** Loyalist official.

Mayor of New York City; arrested by patriots in 1776 and sent to Connecticut; after the war, president of the Council and commander-in-chief of the colony of Cape Breton Island, off Canada.

**Mauduit, Israel.** 1708-1787. Political pamphleteer; colonial agent, b. London (probably).

Englishman; agent in England for Massachusetts, 1763-1781; favored granting full independence to America.

**Maurepas, Jean Frédéric, Comte de.** 1701-1781. French statesman.

Principal minister to Louis XV, and confidential adviser of Louis XVI.

**Maussac de La Marquisie, Bernard.** Continental officer (Maj.), b. Bordeaux, France.

French volunteer; served in the 4th New York Regiment.

**Mawhood, Charles.** d. 1780. British officer (Col.).

Led British forces at battles of Princeton, Quintain's Bridge, N.J., 18 March 1778, and Hancock's Bridge, N.J., 21 March 1778.

**Maxwell, Hugh.** d. 1799. Continental officer (Lt. Col.).

Massachusetts resident; commanded a company of minutemen at Lexington; wounded at Bunker Hill.

**Maxwell, William.** c. 1733-1796. Continental officer (Brig. Gen.), statesman, b. Ireland.

Served in the French and Indian War; as colonel, participated in Canada invasion of 1776; brigadier general, Continental Army, 1776-1780; commanded Maxwell's Light Infantry, 1777; fought at Cooch's Bridge, Del., 3 September 1777; commanded a division at Brandywine; after Germantown, was charged with misconduct and excessive drinking, November 1777, but not convicted; served at battle of Monmouth; retired, 1780.

**Mazzei, Philip.** 1730-1816. Patriot, diplomat, physician, horticulturist, merchant, writer, b. Italy.

Came to Virginia, 1773, to introduce grape and olive culture; neighbor and friend of Thomas Jefferson; diplomatic agent to Italy.

**Meade, George.** Patriot, privateer.

Pennsylvania resident; traded with the West Indies for American and French forces.

**Meade, Richard Kidder.** Continental officer (Lt. Col.).

Virginia resident; aide-de-camp to George Washington, 1777-1783.

**Mease, James.** Financier.

Pennsylvania resident; aided Washington's army financially, but was involved in a plot to defraud the government.

**Meigs, Return Jonathan.** 1740-1823. Continental officer (Col.), b. Middletown, Conn.

Participated in Arnold's Quebec expedition, including the assault on the city; voted a sword by Congress for leading the Sag Harbor, N.Y. raid, 23 May 1777; stopped the mutiny of the Connecticut Line, 1780; moved west after the war and served as Indian agent to the Cherokees, 1801-1823.

**Mercer, Hugh.** c. 1725-1777. Continental officer (Brig. Gen.), physician, b. Scotland.

Emigrated to America after defeat of Jacobites at Culloden; Virginia resident; brigadier general, 1776-1777; reportedly suggested the strategy leading to the victory at Princeton; mortally wounded in the battle.

**Mercer, James.** 1736-1793. American statesman, lawyer, b. "Marlborough," Stafford Co., Va.

Fought in French and Indian War; active pre-Revolution patriot; delegate to the Continental Congress, Virginia, 1779-1780; judge of the state Court of Appeals, 1789-1793; half-brother of John Francis Mercer.

**Mercer, John Francis.** 1759-1821. Continental officer (Maj.), militia officer (Lt. Col.), statesman, lawyer, b. "Marlborough," Stafford Co., Va.

Lieutenant, 3d Virginia Regiment, 1776; captain, 1777; wounded at Brandywine; major, aide-de-camp to Maj. Gen. Charles Lee, 1778-1779; resigned after Lee's court-martial, but joined Virginia militia as lieutenant colonel, 1780; commanded cavalry unit under Lafayette; commanded corps of militia grenadiers at Yorktown; delegate to the Continental Congress, Virginia, 1782-1785; moved to Maryland, his wife's home, c. 1785; member, Federal Constitutional Convention, but left early to protest against proposed strong central government; worked against ratification; strong Jeffersonian Republican during most of his political career; member, U.S. House of Representatives, Maryland, 1792-1794; governor of Maryland, 1801-1803.

**Mergann, Maurice.** British agent.

Served in New York, reporting on loyalist and other activities to

Lord Shelburne, British Secretary of State.

**Mersereau, John, the elder.** American spy.

Resident of Staten Island, N.Y., at beginning of Revolution; worked as spy, along with his brother, Joshua Mersereau, and his nephew, John Mersereau the younger, in the important spy network headed by Col. Elias Dayton.

**Mersereau, John, the younger (John LaGrange Mersereau).** American spy.

Resident of Staten Island, N.Y., at beginning of Revolution; moved with his father, Joshua Mersereau, and his uncle, John Mersereau the elder, to New Brunswick, N.J., 1776, to escape the advancing British; at Washington's request, remained in New Brunswick when British occupied it, and then moved within British lines to Staten Island and Manhattan; spent 18 months gathering and transmitting British military information; worked with his father and uncle in important spy network headed by Col. Elias Dayton from 1777 until at least 1780 and probably throughout the war; physically handicapped by defective right arm.

**Mersereau, Joshua.** Shipbuilder, businessman, American spy.

Left Staten Island, N.Y., 1776, to escape British; worked with his son and brother, both named John Mersereau, in the important spy network headed by Col. Elias Dayton, from 1777 to 1780 and probably throughout the war; after the war, served as surrogate (a judicial officer) of Tioga Co., N.Y., and later of Chenango Co., N.Y.

**Middleton, Arthur.** 1742-1787. American statesman, planter, b. "Middleton Place" on Ashley River, near Charleston, S.C.

Delegate to the Continental Congress, South Carolina, 1776-1778, 1781-1783; signer of the Declaration of Independence; son of Henry Middleton.

**Middleton, Henry.** 1717-1784. American statesman, b. "The Oaks," near Charleston, S.C.

Delegate to the Continental Congress, South Carolina, 1774-1776; president of the Continental Congress, 1774; father of Arthur Middleton.

**Mifflin, Thomas.** 1744-1800. Continental officer (Maj. Gen.), statesman, b. Philadelphia, Pa.

Quartermaster general, Continental Army, 1776-1777; brigadier general, 1776-1777; major general, 1777-1779; delegate to the Continental Congress, 1774-1776, 1782-1784; implicated in Conway Cabal, 1777-1778; a poor and possibly corrupt quartermaster general in 1777 and largely responsible for the suffering at Valley Forge; governor of Pennsylvania, 1790-1799; commanded Pennsylvania militia (reluctantly) during Whiskey Rebellion, 1794.

**Mills, William Henry.** Loyalist officer (Col.).

Defeated at Hunt's Bluff, S.C., 1 August 1780.

**Miralles, Don Juan de.** d. 1780. Spanish official.

Unofficial observer in the United States for Spain, 1778-1780; died 28 April 1780 in Morristown, N.J.

**Mitchell, Stephen M.** 1743-1835. American statesman, lawyer, jurist, b. Wethersfield, Hartford Co., Conn.

Delegate to the Continental Congress, Connecticut, 1781-1784, 1785-1786, 1787-1788; member U.S. Senate, Connecticut, 1793-1795; held various judicial posts throughout his career, culminating in chief justiceship of Connecticut, 1807-1814.

**Monckton, Henry.** 1740-1778. British officer (Col.).

Commanded the 45th Foot, also known as "Sherwood Foresters," 1771-1772; commanded the 2nd Battalion of Grenadiers at Monmouth, where he was mortally wounded.

**Moncrieff, James.** 1744-1793. British officer (Brevet Lt. Col.), b. Scotland.

Highly regarded engineer officer; helped lead well-fought rearguard action at Stono Ferry, S.C., 20 June 1779; planned and built effective fortifications for the defense of Savannah, Ga., 1779; in charge of defenses of Charleston, S.C., 1780; later became deputy quartermaster general and acting chief engineer of the British Army; mortally wounded in combat in War of the First Coalition.

**Monroe, James.** 1758-1831. Continental officer (Maj. or Lt. Col.), lawyer, statesman, b. Westmoreland Co., Va.

Monroe served with the 3d Virginia Regiment at Harlem Heights, N.Y., 16 September 1776, and served at White Plains and Trenton. He was appointed major and aide-de-camp to Maj. Gen. William Alexander in 1777, and fought at Brandywine, Germantown, and Monmouth. He resigned from the Army in 1778 and returned to Virginia.

In 1780 Monroe studied law under Thomas Jefferson, then governor of Virginia. He was a member of the Virginia House of Delegates, 1782; delegate to the Continental Congress, Virginia, 1783-1786; delegate to the Virginia convention for the ratification of the Federal Constitution, 1788; and a member of the U.S. Senate from Virginia, 1790-1794. He also served as minister plenipotentiary to France, 1794-1796, 1803, and minister plenipotentiary to Britain, 1803-1807. During this period he also headed a diplomatic mission to Spain. He was governor of Virginia, 1799-1802; member of the state Assembly, 1810-1811; U.S. Secretary of State, 1811-1814; and U.S. Secretary of War, 1814-1815.

A Republican (Democratic Republican), Monroe was fifth President of the United States, 1817-1825. The period of his presidency is often characterized as the "Era of Good Feeling"; his administrations also saw great diplomatic accomplishments under

Secretary of State John Quincy Adams.

**Montgomery, Richard.** 1738-1775. Continental officer (Maj. Gen.), farmer, b. Ireland.

Fought as British officer in French and Indian War; settled in New York, 1773; Continental brigadier general, 1775; major general, 1775; participated in the Canada invasion of 1775-1776; successfully besieged St. Johns, 5 September–2 November 1775; seized Montreal, 13 November 1775; killed in action at Quebec, 31 December 1775.

**Montmorin, Armand, Comte de.** French diplomat.

French ambassador to Spain; negotiated Convention of Aranjuez, 1779, a Spanish-French alliance against Great Britain.

**Montresor, John.** 1736-1799. British officer (Capt.), military engineer, surveyor, b. Gibraltar.

Served in French and Indian War; British chief engineer in America, 1775-1778.

**Moody, James.** Loyalist soldier, farmer, British spy.

Resident of Sussex Co., N.J.; enlisted in Skinner's Brigade, 1777, along with more than 70 other loyalists he had recruited; continued secret recruiting and began spying missions for Lt. Gen. Sir Henry Clinton, 1778; unusually daring and effective spy; failed, however, in efforts to explode American powder magazine at Suckasanna, N.J., and to kidnap Governor William Livingston of New Jersey; captured by Americans, 1780, but escaped; continued to spy successfully, repeatedly stealing American dispatches, until late 1781; settled in Nova Scotia after the war; brother of John Moody.

**Moody, John.** d.1781. Loyalist, British spy.

Brother of James Moody; entrapped by an American double agent and hanged, 13 November 1781.

**Moore, Alfred.** 1755-1810. Continental officer (Capt.), militia officer (Col.), jurist, b. New Hanover Co., N.C.

Took part in the battle at Moore's Creek Bridge, N.C., 27 February 1776, and the defense of Charleston, S.C., June 1776; became a colonel in the North Carolina militia, 1777; harassed the British at Wilmington, N.C., 1781; Associate Justice of the U.S. Supreme Court, 1797-1804; son of Maurice Moore.

**Moore, James.** 1737-1777. Continental officer (Brig. Gen.), b. Brunswick, N.C.

Active pre-Revolution patriot; fought against the Regulators at Alamance, 16 May 1771; placed in command of the 1st North Carolina Continentals, September 1775; directed the campaign that ended in the victory at Moores Creek Bridge, 27 February 1776; brigadier general, 1776-1777; brother of Maurice Moore.

**Moore, John.** Loyalist officer (Col.).

North Carolina resident; aided in the defense of Savannah, Ga., 1779.

**Moore, Maurice.** 1735-1777. Patriot, jurist, b. Brunswick, N.C.

Prominent pre-Revolutionary North Carolina political leader and judge; advocated reconciliation; brother of James Moore; father of Alfred Moore.

**Morgan, Daniel.** 1736-1802. Continental officer (Brig. Gen.), farmer, b. Bucks Co., Pa., or Hunterdon Co., N.J.

Settled in Shenandoah Valley of Virginia at 17; raised a Continental rifle company, June 1775, and took it to Boston; led the van in Arnold's march to Quebec, September-November 1775; was captured in attack on Quebec, 31 December; exchanged 1776; played crucial part in Saratoga victories; resigned because of lack of recognition by Congress, despite Washington's recommendations for promotion to brigadier general; returned to duty after Gates's defeat at Camden and was promoted to brigadier general, 1780; served under Greene in south; most notable accomplishment was his classic double-envelopment victory over the British at the battle of the Cowpens; retired soon afterward because of ill health; served in U.S. House of Representatives, 1797-1799, from Virginia.

**Morgan, John.** 1735-1789. Physician, b. Philadelphia, Pa.

Medical director of the Continental Army, 1775-1777.

**Morris, Gouverneur.** 1752-1816. American statesman, lawyer, diplomat, landowner, b. Morrisania (now part of New York City), N.Y.

Member, provincial congress of New York, 1775-1776; with John Jay and Robert L. Livingston, drafted New York constitution; delegate to the Continental Congress, New York, 1777-1780; delegate to Federal Constitutional Convention, 1787; devised decimal system for U.S. coinage; commissioner to England, 1790-1791; minister plenipotentiary to France, 1792-1794; member, U.S. Senate, New York, 1800-1803; chairman of the Board of Erie Canal Commissioners; half-brother of Lewis Morris.

**Morris, Lewis.** 1726-1798. American statesman, militia officer (Brig. Gen.), farmer, jurist, b. Morrisania (now part of New York City), N.Y.

Delegate to the Continental Congress, New York, 1775-1777; signer of the Declaration of Independence; half-brother of Gouverneur Morris.

**Morris, Lewis, Jr.** Continental officer (Brevet Lt. Col.).

Aide-de-camp to Maj. Gen. John Sullivan; fought in the Rhode Island campaign, 1778; aide-de-camp to Maj. Gen. Nathanael Greene, 1779-1783; son of Lewis Morris.

**Morris, Robert.** 1734-1806. American statesman, merchant, b. Liverpool, England.

Morris settled in America at 13 and became a highly successful merchant; he was a delegate to the Continental Congress from Pennsylvania, 1776-1778, and a signer of the Declaration of Independence, although he had originally voted against it. He was chosen president of the Pennsylvania Assembly in 1776.

Morris signed the Articles of Confederation in March of 1778, and from August until November of 1778 he was chairman of the Congressional Committee on Finance. He was involved in a controversy surrounding the operations of Roderique Hortalez et Cie., the secret firm for French aid, and his own firm of Willing and Morris, and was attacked by Thomas Paine and Henry Laurens for allegedly dishonest dealings; he was exonerated after an investigation. Appointed Superintendent of Finance, 20 February 1781, he established the Bank of North America, obtained a loan from the Netherlands, and saved the United States from financial collapse. He is called the "Financier of the Revolution." Morris's own financial empire did eventually collapse and he died in 1806 after spending three years in debtors' prison.

**Morton, John.** 1724-1777. American statesman, surveyor, jurist, b. Morris Ferry (now Darby Creek Bridge), Ridley Township, Delaware Co., Pa.

Of Swedish descent; delegate to the Stamp Act Congress, 1765; delegate to the Continental Congress, Pennsylvania, 1774-1777; signer of the Declaration of Independence.

**Motte, Isaac.** 1738-1795. American statesman, b. Charleston, S.C.

Delegate to the Continental Congress, South Carolina, 1780-1782.

**Mottin de la Balme, Augustin.** 1736-1780. Continental officer (Col.), military writer, b. St. Antoine, Dauphiné, France.

French volunteer; killed in expedition against Detroit, 5 November 1780.

**Moultrie, John.** 1729-1798. Loyalist government official, physician, b. Charleston, S.C.

Lieutenant governor of East Florida, 1771-1784; brother of William Moultrie.

**Moultrie, William.** 1730-1805. Continental officer (Maj. Gen.), statesman, military historian, b. Charleston, S.C.

Brigadier general, 1776-1782; major general, 1782-1783; commanded Fort Sullivan (later Fort Moultrie) in successful defense of Charleston, 1776; successful at Beaufort, S.C., 3 February 1779; helped organize the defenses of Charleston, S.C., 10-12 May 1779; governor of South Carolina, 1785-1787, 1794-1796; brother of John Moultrie.

**Mowry, Daniel, Jr.** 1729-1806. American statesman, cooper, farmer, b. Smithfield, Providence Co., R.I.

Delegate to the Continental Congress, Rhode Island, 1780-1782.

**Mowat, Henry.** British naval officer (Capt.).

Led the expedition that burned Falmouth (now Portland), Me. (then part of Massachusetts), 18 October 1775.

**Moylan, Stephen.** 1737-1811. Continental officer (Col.), shipper, b. Cork, Ireland.

Secretary to George Washington, 1776; quartermaster general, 1776, succeeding Thomas Mifflin, and then being succeeded by him; Pennsylvania resident.

**Mugford, James.** d. 1776. Continental naval officer (Capt.).

Commanding the schooner *Franklin*, captured British transport *Hope* at Nantasket Roads, Mass., 17 May 1776; killed two days later in unsuccessful British attempt to capture his ship.

**Muhlenberg, Frederick A. C.** 1750-1801. Statesman, clergyman, b. Trappe, Pa.

Delegate to the Continental Congress, Pennsylvania, 1778-1780; member, U.S. House of Representatives, 1789-1797; first speaker of the House, 1789, served as speaker, 1789-1791, 1793-1795; brother of John P. G. Muhlenberg.

**Muhlenberg, John Peter Gabriel.** 1746-1807. Continental officer (Brig. Gen.), clergyman, b. Trappe, Pa.

Lutheran clergyman; Continental brigadier general, 1777-1783;

served at Brandywine and Germantown, and in the Yorktown campaign; member, U.S. House of Representatives, Pennsylvania, 1789-1791, 1793-1795, 1799-1801; member, U.S. Senate, 1801; brother of Frederick Muhlenberg.

**Mulligan, Hercules.** American spy.

New York City resident; suggested for intelligence work by Alexander Hamilton, who had earlier lived with the Mulligan family; remained in New York after British occupation, 1776, and sent out intelligence reports throughout the war.

**Murphy, Timothy.** 1751-1818. Continental soldier, rifleman, farmer, miller, b. near the Delaware Water Gap, Pa.

Famous marksman, most remembered for his feats at the action in Schoharie Valley, N.Y., 15-19 October 1780.

**Murray, James.** 1713-c.1781. Loyalist, merchant, planter, b. Scotland.

Prominent Massachusetts citizen; justice of the peace, 1768; left Massachusetts, 1776.

**Murray, John.** *See* Dunmore, John Murray, Earl of.

**Murray, Mrs. Robert.** Patriot heroine.

According to legend, this patriotic New York lady invited British General Howe and his staff for refreshments and delayed the British long enough for several thousand Continentals to escape safely after the defeat at Kip's Bay, New York, 1776.

**Musgrave, Thomas.** 1737-1812. British officer (Brig. Gen.).

Distinguished himself in the defense of Chew House at Germantown; quartermaster general at St. Lucia, West Indies, 1778; last British commandant of New York City, 1782.

# N

**Nash, Abner.** c. 1740-1786. Statesman, lawyer, b. Amelia Co. (later Prince Edward Co.), Va.

Settled at Halifax, N.C., 1762; supported eastern interests in Regulator disturbances; active in North Carolina Revolutionary activities; governor of North Carolina during period of military crisis, 1780-1781; delegate to the Continental Congress, North Carolina, 1782-1784, 1785-1786.

**Nash, Francis.** c. 1742-1777. Continental officer (Brig. Gen.), merchant, lawyer, b. Virginia.

North Carolina resident; made brigadier general, 1777; mortally wounded at Germantown.

**Neal, Thomas.** d. 1780. Militia officer (Col.).

Georgia resident; leader in victory over Tories at Williamson's Plantation, S.C., 12 July 1780.

**Nelson, Horatio.** 1758-1805. British naval officer (Lt.), b. Burham-Thorpe, England.

Assigned to the West Indies, 1777; commanded the brig *Badger* and the frigate *Hinchinbrook*; participated in the Nicaragua expedition of February 1780; later, hero of the battles of Aboukir Bay, Copenhagen, and particularly of Trafalgar, 1805, in which he was killed, but where his victory over the French and Spanish Fleets turned the tide of the Napoleonic wars.

**Nelson, Thomas, Jr.** 1738-1789. Statesman, militia officer (Brig. Gen.), Continental officer (Capt.), b. Yorktown, Va.

Delegate to the Continental Congress, Virginia, 1775-1777, 1779-1780; signer of the Declaration of Independence; appointed brigadier general in command of all state forces, 1777; governor of Virginia, 1781; played important role in defense of Virginia during last month of war; present at Yorktown and reportedly directed artillery fire against his own house.

**Neuville.** *See* Penot Lombart, Louis-Pierre, Chevalier de la Neuville.

**Neville, John.** 1731-1803. Continental officer (Col.), sheriff, landowner, b. Virginia.

Commandant of Fort Pitt, Pa., 1775-1777; saw action at Trenton, Princeton, and Germantown; commanded a regiment in the Monmouth campaign, 16 June–5 July 1778.

**Neville, Presley.** 1756-1818. Continental officer (Lt. Col.), merchant, b. Pittsburgh, Pa.

Aide-de-camp to Lafayette, 1778.

**Newall (or Newell), Simon.** American spy.

Resident of New York, near Peekskill; voluneer *agent provocateur*; on his own initiative, but with the approval of Brig. Gen. Oliver Wolcott, exposed and brought about the arrest of a group of secret Tory spies in the Peekskill area.

**Newman, Robert.** Patriot, church sexton.

Sexton of Old North Church, Boston; went with Paul Revere to the church the night of 18 April 1775 and probably placed the lanterns at the top of the belfry.

**Newman, Wingate.** Privateer captain.

Commanded the USP *Hancock* when it captured the HMT *Reward*, Portsmouth, N.H., 7 August 1776.

**Nicholas, George.** 1754-1799. Continental officer (Col.), statesman, pioneer, b. Williamsburg, Va.

Served as Continental officer, 1775-1778; entered Virginia House of Delegates, 1781; called for an investigation into the conduct of Governor Thomas Jefferson during Arnold's invasion, 1781, but later became a supporter of Jefferson; supported ratification of Federal Constitution; pioneered to Kentucky, 1790.

**Nicholas, Robert Carter.** 1728-1780. Patriot, colonial official, b. Williamsburg, Va.

Treasurer of Virginia, 1766-c. 1776; favored reconciliation during

pre-Revolution period; opposed Declaration of Independence; became conservative patriot.

**Nicholas, Samuel.** Continental marine officer (Capt.), b. Philadelphia, Pa.

Senior Continental Marine officer; led the storming of Fort Montagu, Nassau, 3-4 March 1776.

**Nicholson, James.** c.1736-1804. Continental naval officer (Capt.), b. Chestertown, Md.

Commanded the USS *Trumbull* when it was forced to strike its colors in an engagement with HMS *Iris*, 8 August 1781, in one of the more severe naval battles of the Revolution.

**Nicola, Lewis.** 1717-1807. Continental officer (Col.), merchant, editor, b. France (probably).

Probably educated in Ireland; settled in Philadelphia about 1766; edited *The American Magazine*; helped form American Philosophical Society; commanded Philadelphia "home guards," 1776-1782; commanded Invalid Regiment (made up of disabled veterans assigned to light duty), 1777-1783; wrote to Washington suggesting the country be made a monarchy with Washington as king.

**Nimham.** Indian leader.

Collaborated with the Americans; ambushed north of Manhattan, N.Y., 31 August 1778, by a British force under John Simcoe.

**Nixon, John.** 1727-1815. Militia officer (Col.), Continental officer

(Brig. Gen.), b. Framingham, Mass.

Veteran of French and Indian War; fought at Concord and Bunker Hill; Continental colonel, January 1776; brigadier general, 1776-1780; played a prominent role in the battle at Harlem Heights, N.Y., 16 September 1776; his brigade had relatively minor part in Saratoga battles, but led the ensuing pursuit; resigned, 1780, apparently because his vision and hearing had been impaired by a near-miss cannon ball at Saratoga.

**Nixon, John.** 1733-1808. Patriot, merchant, financier, b. Philadelphia, Pa.

Acting president of the Provincial Committee of Safety of Pennsylvania, 1775; served as a colonel in the Pennsylvania Associators, 1775-1777.

**Noailles, Louis Marie, Vicomte de.** 1756-1804. French officer (Col.).

Fought at Yorktown; represented the allies at the Yorktown surrender negotiations, 17 October 1781; member of prominent aristocratic family; cousin of Lafayette's wife.

**North, Sir Frederick (Lord North; after 1790, Earl of Guilford).** 1732-1792. British statesman, b. London.

Chancellor of the Exchequer, 1767-1770; Prime Minister, 1770-1782; developed a close relationship with King George III, with whom he shared the idea that the American colonies ought to be taxed by Parliament; stuck to his policies, despite attacks from others in Parliament and the out-

break of hostilities in America; after 1779, began to have doubts about the American war, but chose to continue supporting the King; did attempt to resign on several occasions, but was restrained by the King; finally, after the news of Yorktown reached London, succeeded in resigning, March 1782.

**Noirmont, Penot Lombart de.** *See* Penot Lombart de Noirmont, René-Hippolyte.

**Nutting, John.** Loyalist.

Massachusetts resident; cooperated with William Knox in the formation of a loyalist haven on the Penobscot River in Maine (Massachusetts).

# O

**O'Brien, Jeremiah.** 1744-1818. American naval and privateer officer, customs collector, b. Kittery, Me. (Massachusetts).

Leader of the lumbermen who captured the British schooner *Margaretta* off Machias Bay, Me., 12 June 1775; commanded privateer *Resolution*, 1777, with which he captured the *Scarborough*; was captured, along with his ship *Hannibal*, 1780; escaped from Mill Prison, Plymouth, England; returned to America, 1781, and commanded privateers for remainder of war; customs collector at Kittery, Me., 1811-1818.

**Odell, Jonathan.** 1737-1818. Loyalist agent, satirist, b. Newark, N.J.

Educated as a doctor and minister; antagonized the patriots

with his loyalist poetry and was arrested in 1776; escaped and joined the British as a secret agent; aided Joseph Stansbury in arranging the correspondence between Benedict Arnold and Major John André that led up to Arnold's treason; assistant secretary to Commander-in-Chief Guy Carleton, 1783-1784.

**Odell, William.** Loyalist officer (Maj.).

Commanded the Loyal American Rangers.

**Ogden, Aaron.** 1756-1839. Continental officer (Maj.), lawyer, statesman, steamboat operator, b. Elizabethtown (now Elizabeth), N.J.

Assistant aide-de-camp to Maj. Gen. William Alexander (Lord Stirling), 1778; aide-de-camp to Brig. Gen. William Maxwell, 1779; led the van when Hamilton's regiment stormed Redoubt No. 10 at Yorktown; practiced law and entered politics as Federalist; U.S. Senator from New Jersey, 1801-1803; governor of New Jersey, 1812-1813.

**Ogden, David.** 1707-1789. Loyalist, jurist, b. Newark, N.J.

Associate justice of the New Jersey Supreme Court, 1772-1776; author of a plan of government for the colonies "after their submission"; lived in England after the war.

**Ogden, Isaac.** Loyalist, lawyer.

Member, New Jersey Provincial Congress, 1775; sergeant of the Supreme Court of New Jersey; resigned in August 1775 from the Provincial Congress when he could not stop violent measures from being adopted; went to Canada and became a prominent judge; son of David Ogden.

**Ogden, James.** d. 1781. British spy.

Resident of South River (Willettstown), N.J.; member of British spy organization of John Rattoon; guided to Princeton John Mason, emissary sent by British General Clinton to the mutinous troops of the Pennsylvania Line, January 1781; hanged with Mason, 10 January 1781.

**O'Hara, Charles.** 1740?-1802. British officer (Brevet Brig. Gen.).

Served at Cowan's Ford, N.C., 1 February 1781; commanded the British reserve at Guilford Courthouse, and was instrumental in breaking the final resistance of Greene's army there; represented Cornwallis at the Yorktown surrender, 19 October 1781.

**Oliver, Andrew.** c. 1707-1774. Loyalist official, jurist, b. Boston, Mass.

Stamp officer under Stamp Act, 1765; threatened by mob and hanged in effigy; lieutenant governor of Massachusetts, 1770-1774; served under Thomas Hutchinson, his brother-in-law; author of some of the "Hutchinson letters" and involved along with Hutchinson in the controversy they caused.

**Oliver, Peter.** 1713-1791. Loyalist, jurist, b. Boston, Mass.

Chief justice of Massachusetts, 1771-1775; forced to flee to England in 1776; brother of Andrew Oliver.

**Oliver, Thomas.** Loyalist official.

Lieutenant governor and president of the Council of Massachusetts, 1774-1775; last royal lieutenant governor; not related to Andrew and Peter Oliver.

**O'Neal (or O'Neill), Ferdinand.** Continental officer (Capt.), b. France.

Defeated at Dorchester, S.C., by the British under a Captain Dawkins, 24 April 1782.

**Orvilliers, Louis Guillonet, Comte d'.** French naval officer (admiral).

Commanded French fleet threatening the British coast, 1778; fought inconclusive battle off Ushant, 27 July 1778.

**Osgood, Samuel.** 1748-1813. American statesman, militia officer (Col.), merchant, b. Andover, Mass.

Captain of company of minutemen, 1775; later aide-de-camp to Maj. Gen. Artemas Ward; delegate to the Continental Congress, Massachusetts, 1780-1784; Postmaster General, 1789-1791.

**Oswald, Eleazer.** c. 1735-1795. Continental officer (Lt. Col.), b. England.

Artillery officer; distinguished himself in Danbury (Conn.) raid, April 1777; published the *Independent Gazetteer* or *Chronicle of Freedom*, Philadelphia, 1782.

**Oswald, Richard.** 1705-1784. British diplomat, merchant, b. Scotland.

Conducted the final peace negotiations, beginning in April 1782; friend of Benjamin Franklin; authorized by Shelburne, the Prime Minister, to treat the American commissioners as representing the "13 United States".

**Otis, James.** 1725-1783. Patriot, pamphleteer, lawyer, b. West Barnstable, Mass.

Otis popularized the concept of "natural law" upon which the theory and rhetoric of the American Revolution were based, and was the leading writer and publicist for the demands of the colonies from 1761 until 1769; along with Samuel Adams, he produced the Massachusetts circular letters. In 1769 Otis was injured in a brawl, his reasoning was impaired, and he took no further significant part in the events leading up to the Revolution.

**Otto, Bodo.** 1711-1787. Continental Army surgeon, b. Hanover, Germany.

Received medical training in Germany; emigrated to America in 1755; practiced in Pennsylvania and New Jersey; member, Berks County (Pennsylvania) Committee of Safety and Pennsylvania Provincial Congress, 1776; senior surgeon, Middle Division, for Continental hospitals, 1776; established hospitals and treated wounded until end of significant hostilities, 1782.

# P

**Paca, William.** 1740-1799. American statesman, lawyer, jurist, b. near Abingdon, Queen Anne (now Hartford) Co., Md.

Active pre-Revolution patriot; delegate to the Continental Congress, Maryland, 1774-1779; signer of the Declaration of Independence; elected to first Maryland state Senate, 1776; governor of Maryland, 1782-1785.

**Page, John.** 1744-1808. American statesman, militia officer, b. Gloucester Co., Va.

Virginia militia officer in the Yorktown campaign, 1781; contributed funds to the Revolutionary cause; member, U.S. House of Representatives, 1789-1797; governor of Virginia, 1802-1805; brother of Mann Page.

**Page, Mann.** 1749-1781. American statesman, lawyer, landowner, b. Gloucester Co., Va.

Delegate to the Continental Congress, Virginia, 1777; brother of John Page.

**Paine, Robert Treat.** 1731-1814. American statesman, lawyer, b. Boston, Mass.

Associate prosecuting attorney at Boston Massacre trial; delegate to the Continental Congress, Massachusetts, 1774-1778; signed Olive Branch Petition, 1775; signer of the Declaration of Independence; attorney general of Massachusetts, 1777-1790; served on Supreme Court of Massachusetts, 1790-1804.

**Paine, Thomas.** 1737-1809. Writer, Continental soldier, b. Thetford, England.

Author of *Common Sense*, 1776, which urged immediate independence from England and had great influence, and *The Crisis*, 1776; enlisted in the Continental Army, 1776; served as secretary to the Committee on Foreign Affairs of the Continental Congress, 1777-1779; later active in the French Revolution; wrote *The Rights of Man* (1791, 1792) and *The Age of Reason* (1794, 1796).

**Palfrey, William.** d. 1780. Continental officer (Lt. Col.).

Massachusetts resident; aide-de-camp to General Washington, 1776; appointed U.S. consul to France, November 1780; lost at sea, December 1780.

**Palliser, Sir Hugh.** 1723-1796. British naval officer (Vice Adm.), b. Yorkshire, England.

Third-in-command of the Channel Fleet, 1778; at the battle of Ushant, 24-27 July 1778, failed to obey the commander, Admiral Keppel, allowing the French fleet to escape; he and Keppel were both court-martialed and acquitted.

**Palmer, Edmund.** d. 1777. Farmer, loyalist officer (Lt.), British spy.

Resident of Yorktown, Westchester Co., N.Y.; sent by his British superiors to his home county, early 1777, to carry out secret recruiting and spying missions; captured and tried by court-martial, July 1777; hanged at Peekskill, August 1777.

**Panin, Nikita, Count.** Russian diplomat.

Panin, Imperial Russian Foreign Minister, drew up the rules of neutrality on which the League of Armed Neutrality of 1780 was based. These rules, however, were those originally proposed by Bernstorff, the Danish foreign minister, and in the American "Plan of 1776". At first Panin had opposed such an approach, but he was persuaded by the Empress Catherine to agree to it.

**Parker, Sir Hyde ("Old Vinegar").** 1714-1782. British naval officer (Vice Adm.), b. Worcestershire, England.

Second-in-command in America, 1778-1781; repelled De Guichen's French fleet at St. Lucia, West Indies, 23 March 1780; defeated Dutch fleet in generally inconclusive battle of Dogger Bank, 3 August 1781.

**Parker, Sir Hyde, Jr.** 1739-1807. British naval officer (Commodore).

Led raid to Tappan Sea (now Tappan Zee), 12-18 July 1776, and was knighted for it; saw action at Long Island; convoyed expeditionary force that captured Savannah, Ga., 29 December 1778; made admiral in 1793; his irresolution at Copenhagen and in the Baltic, 1801, were offset by Nelson's aggressiveness; son of Sir Hyde Parker.

**Parker, John.** 1729-1775. Militia officer (Capt.), farmer, mechanic, b. Lexington, Mass.

Captain of the local company of minutemen at Lexington common, 19 April 1775.

**Parker, Sir Peter.** 1721-1811. British naval officer (Adm.), b. Ireland.

Knighted in 1782 for bravery at Charleston, S.C., during Clinton's expedition of 1776; supported the New York campaign, 1776, as a squadron commander; military commander at Jamaica, 1779-1781; later succeeded Lord Howe as Admiral of the Fleet.

**Parsons, Samuel Holden.** 1737-1789. Continental officer (Maj. Gen.), lawyer, frontiersman, b. Lyme, Conn.

Active pre-Revolution patriot; early advocate of intercolonial congress; brigadier general, 1776-1780; major general, 1780-1782; fought at Long Island and at Kip's Bay, 15 September 1776; conducted successful raid on Morrisania, N.Y., 22-23 January 1781; went to Ohio after the war.

**Partridge, George.** 1740-1828. American statesman, teacher, b. Duxbury, Mass.

Delegate to the Continental Congress, Massachusetts, 1779-1782, 1783-1785; member U.S. House of Representatives, 1789-1790.

**Paterson (or Patterson), James.** British officer (Brig. Gen.; local rank).

Adjutant general in America, 1776-1778; took Stony Point, N.Y., and Verplancks Point, N.Y., 1 June

1779; participated in the Charleston expedition of 1780; wiped out an American force at Salkahatchie, S.C., 8 March 1780.

**Paterson, John.** 1744-1808. Continental officer (Brig. Gen.), teacher, lawyer, b. Connecticut.

Moved to Massachusetts, 1774; member, Massachusetts Provincial Congress, 1774, 1775; as colonel, sent to Canada, 1775; retreated with Arnold's column; fought at Trenton and Princeton; after the war helped suppress Shays's Rebellion; member, U.S. House of Representatives, 1803-1805.

**Pattison, James.** 1724-1805. British officer (Maj. Gen.; local rank).

Commandant of New York City, 1777-1780; as brigadier general, assisted Brig. Gen. James Paterson at Stony Point, N.Y., and Verplancks Point, N.Y., 1 June 1779.

**Paulding, John.** 1758-1818. Militia soldier.

New York resident; a captor of Major John André, 1780; received a medal from Congress for this action, 1780.

**Pawling, Albert.** Continental officer (Col.).

New York resident; defeated the Tories at Wawarsing, N.Y., 22 August 1781.

**Paxton, Charles.** 1707-1788. Loyalist official, b. Boston, Mass.

Commissioner of Customs, Massachusetts; fled to England, probably in 1776.

**Peabody, Nathaniel.** 1741-1823. American statesman, physician, b. Topsfield, Essex Co., Mass.

Early patriot; participated in capture of magazines at Fort William and Mary, Portsmouth Harbor, N.H., December 1774; served repeatedly in New Hampshire State Legislature, 1776-1795; delegate to the Continental Congress, New Hampshire, 1779-1780.

**Peale, Charles Willson.** 1741-1827. Militia officer (Capt.), saddler, portrait painter, b. Queen Annes Co., Md.

Stamp Act patriot; forced out of saddler's trade by his creditors; became portrait painter; studied with Benjamin West in London, 1767-1769; served with Philadelphia militia in Trenton-Princeton campaign; made portraits of most Revolutionary figures, including several life portraits of Washington.

**Pearson, Sir Richard.** 1731-1806. British naval officer, b. Lanton Hall, near Appleby, Westmoreland, England.

Commanded the *Serapis* in its encounter with the *Bonhomme Richard* under John Paul Jones, 23 September 1779, off Flamborough Head; defeated in the hard-fought action.

**Pendleton, Edmund.** 1721-1803. American statesman, clerk, lawyer, jurist, b. Caroline Co., Va.

Conservative who opposed Stamp Act and later coercive acts, but worked for conciliation; chairman, Virginia convention of 1776; delegate to the Continental Congress, Virginia, 1774-1775; favored the Federal Constitution of 1789 and was president of the Virginia convention that voted ratification.

**Penn, John.** 1729-1795. Loyalist.

Grandson of William Penn, founder of Pennsylvania; governor of Pennsylvania, 1763-1771, 1773-1775; last royal governor of Pennsylvania; was allowed to keep his private estates and continued to live in Pennsylvania.

**Penn, John.** 1740-1788. American statesman, lawyer, b. Port Royal, Caroline Co., Va.

Delegate to the Continental Congress, North Carolina, 1775-1776, 1777-1780; signer of the Declaration of Independence.

**Penot Lombart, Louis-Pierre, Chevalier de la Neuville.** 1744-c.1800. French officer (Maj.), Continental officer (Brevet Brig. Gen.), b. France.

French volunteer; inspector general of the Northern Army, 1777; returned to France with Lafayette, January 1779.

**Penot Lombart de Noirmont, René-Hippolyte.** 1750-1792. French officer (Lt.), Continental officer (Brevet Lt. Col.), b. France.

French volunteer; aide-de-camp to Maj. Gen. Thomas Conway, 1777-1778; assistant inspector general of infantry in the Northern Army, May-July 1778; aide-de-camp to Lafayette, 1778-1779; served in Savannah, Ga., operations, 1779, as a lieutenant of infantry; killed in the massacre at the Abbaye prison, September 1792.

**Pepperell, Sir William the Younger.** *See* Sparhawk, William Pepperell.

**Percy, Hugh (Courtesy title, Earl Percy).** 1742-1817. British officer (Lt. Gen.).

Member of Parliament; led the relief column that saved Col. Francis Smith's command after Concord; division commander in the battle of Long Island and at the attack on Fort Washington, N.Y., 17 November 1776; served with Clinton in the occupation of Rhode Island, December 1776; assumed command of the Rhode Island post, 1777; became the Duke of Northumberland, 1778.

**Peters, John.** Loyalist officer (Lt. Col.).

Connecticut resident; raised and commanded the Queen's Loyal Rangers.

**Peters, Richard.** 1743-1828. American statesman, lawyer, judge, farmer, b. Philadelphia, Pa.

Secretary, and then member, of the Continental Congress's Board of War, 1776-1781; delegate to the Continental Congress, Pennsylvania, 1782-1783; member, Pennsylvania Assembly, 1787-1790, and Senate, 1791-1792, also serving as speaker of both bodies; judge of U.S. District Court, 1792-1828.

**Peters, Samuel.** c. 1735-1826. Loyalist, clergyman, b. Hebron, Conn.

Harassed by patriot mobs on two occasions; fled to England, 1774, and lived there until 1805; wrote *A General History of Connecticut* (1781).

**Phillips (or Philips), Frederick.** d. 1785. Tory militia officer (Col.).

Loyalist leader in Westchester County, N.Y., and an associate of Beverley Robinson.

**Phillips, William.** 1731?-1781. British officer (Maj. Gen.).

Commander at St. Johns, Canada, July-December 1776; second-in-command to General Burgoyne at Montreal, December 1776, and in Burgoyne's offensive, 1777; distinguished himself at the capture of Ticonderoga, 2-5 July 1777, and at the first battle of Saratoga; senior officer in the Convention Army that surrendered at Saratoga; exchanged, 13 October 1780; commander in Virginia, March-May, 1781; died at Petersburg, Va.

**Phripp, Matthew.** Merchant, b. Norfolk, Va.

From fear of Lord Dunmore, took an oath to the King; exonerated from being a loyalist, 1775; one of Virginia's leading merchants, Norfolk; later a leader in the Freemason movement.

**Pickens, Andrew.** 1739-1817. Militia officer (Brig. Gen.), farmer, justice of the peace, b. Paxtang, Pa.

Settled with parents in South Carolina as a boy; fought at Ninety-Six, S.C., November 1775; defeated the loyalists at the battle of Kettle Creek, S.C., 14 February 1779; distinguished himself at the Cowpens, and received a sword from Congress for this action; member, U.S. House of Representatives, South Carolina, 1793-1795.

**Pickering, Timothy.** 1745-1829. Militia officer (Col.), Continental officer (Col.), statesman, lawyer, b. Salem, Mass.

Adjutant general, Continental Army, 1777; quartermaster general, 1780; U.S. postmaster general, 1789-1791; Secretary of State, 1795-1800.

**Pigot, Sir Robert.** 1720-1796. British officer (Lt. Gen.), b. Patshull, Staffordshire, England.

Lieutenant colonel of the 38th Foot, 1774; distinguished himself at Bunker Hill in leading his regiment against the redoubt; commander in Rhode Island, 1777-1779; successfully defended Newport, 29 July–31 August 1778; became major general, 1777, and lieutenant general, 1782.

**Pinckney, Charles.** 1757-1824. American statesman, diplomat, militia officer (Lt.), lawyer, b. Charleston, S.C.

Participated in siege of Savannah, October 1779; captured when Charleston fell, 1780; delegate to the Continental Congress, South Carolina, 1777-1778; 1784-1787; delegate to the Federal Constitutional Convention, 1787, and prepared a draft of the Federal Constitution which contained over thirty provisions that also appeared in the final draft; governor of South Carolina, 1789-1792, 1796-1798; U.S. Senator, 1798-1801; minister to Spain, 1801-1806.

**Pinckney, Charles Cotesworth.** 1746-1825. Continental officer (Col.), lawyer, b. Charleston, S.C.

Held various South Carolina offices, 1769 to outbreak of Revolution; member, state legislature, 1778, and state Senate, 1779; participated in defense of Fort Sullivan, S.C., June 1776; aide to Washington, 1777; led his regiment in siege of Savannah, October 1779; later one of the special emissaries to France, 1797; involved in the "X-Y-Z Affair" at this time; Federalist nominee for Vice President in 1800; Federalist candidate for President in 1804, 1808; brother of Thomas Pinckney.

**Pinckney, Thomas.** 1750-1828. Continental officer (Maj.), lawyer, statesman, b. Charleston, S.C.

Served in various Southern campaigns, 1774-1781; governor of South Carolina, 1787-1789; minister to Great Britain, 1792-1796; negotiated "Pinckney's Treaty" of 27 October 1795 with Spain; brother of Charles Cotesworth Pinckney.

**Pitcairn, John.** 1722-1775. British officer (Capt., Royal Marines), b. Scotland.

Second-in-command at Lexington and Concord; killed in action at Bunker Hill.

**Pitt, William, the elder, Earl of Chatham.** 1708-1778. British statesman, b. Westminster, London.

Member of Parliament from 1735; as Prime Minister, 1757-1761, masterfully conducted the war against France; worked for repeal of the Stamp Act, 1766; raised to the peerage, 1766; again Prime Minister, 1766-1768; in poor health during much of this ministry, and not responsible for the Townshend Acts; made brilliant speeches in the House of Lords urging an end to hostilities against America and denouncing the use of Indians against the Americans, 1777; opposed, however, the immediate recognition of American independence that Rockingham favored; collapsed while speaking in the House of Lords on this subject, and died on 11 May 1778; father of William Pitt the younger (1759-1806), also brilliant and eloquent, who served as Prime Minister 1783-1801 and 1804-1806.

**Plater, George.** 1735-1792. American statesman, lawyer, b. "Sotterley," St. Mary's Co., Md.

Justice of the peace, 1757-1771; member, lower house of Maryland Assembly, 1757-1766; member, Executive Council, 1771-1774; delegate to the Continental Congress, Maryland, 1778-1781; governor of Maryland, 1791-1792.

**Plessis, Maduit du, Chevalier de.** d. 1791. Continental officer (Lt. Col.), b. France.

French volunteer; artillery officer; distinguished himself at the battles of Brandywine, Germantown, and Fort Mercer (Red Bank), N.J., 22 October 1777; won the thanks of Congress for his performance.

**Pollock, Oliver.** c. 1737-1823. Patriot, trader, planter, b. Ireland.

Commercial agent of the Continental Congress at New Orleans;

went into debt to send supplies up the Mississippi to George Rogers Clark.

**Pomeroy, Seth.** 1706-1777. Militia officer (Maj. Gen.), gunsmith, b. Northampton, Mass.

Raised and drilled troops in western Massachusetts, 1775-1776; brigadier general, 1775; major general, 1775; was offered, but declined, an appointment as brigadier general, Continental Army, 1775.

**Poor, Enoch.** 1736-1780. Continental officer (Brig. Gen.), trader, shipbuilder, b. Newbury, Mass.

Colonel commanding 2d New Hampshire Regiment, 1775; reinforced Arnold's retreating forces in Canada, 1776; fought at Trenton and Princeton, 1776-1777; brigadier general, 1777-1780; died of illness in 1780.

**Poor, Salem.** American soldier.

A Negro; Massachusetts resident; served so gallantly at Bunker Hill that Massachusetts officers signed a petition for a reward for him; was also at White Plains and at Valley Forge.

**Postell, James.** d. 1824. Militia officer (Col.).

Captured Capt. James De Peyster at Georgetown, S.C., 19 January 1781.

**Potts, Jonathan.** 1745-1781. Physician.

Gave medical care to wounded Pennsylvania troops in early 1776; served at Crown Point, N.Y., 1776; deputy director general of hospitals for the Northern Department,

1777, and for the Middle Department, 1778-1780.

**Potts, Richard.** 1753-1808. American statesman, lawyer, b. Upper Marlboro, Md.

Aide to Brig. Gen. Thomas Johnson, commander of Maryland militia, 1776; delegate to the Continental Congress, Maryland, 1781-1782; U.S. Senator, 1793-1796; judge of the Maryland Court of Appeals, 1801-1804.

**Pourre, Don Eugenio.** Spanish officer.

Commanded expedition that captured Fort St. Joseph, Michigan, January 1781.

**Prescott, Oliver.** 1731-1804. Physician, militia officer (Maj. Gen.), b. Groton, Mass.

Chairman of town committee to protest Stamp Act, 1765; pre-Revolution militiaman; major general commanding Massachusetts militia, 1778; helped suppress Shays's rebellion, 1787.

**Prescott, Richard.** 1725-1788. British officer (Maj. Gen.).

Colonel of his regiment and third-in-command at the occupation of Newport, R.I., November 1776; remained as garrison commander; captured, 1777; exchanged for General Charles Lee, 1778; commanded garrison at Newport, 1779, and evacuated the city, October 1779.

**Prescott, Robert.** 1725-1816. British officer (Maj. Gen.), b. Lancashire, England.

Participated in the New York campaign of 1776 and Philadelphia campaign of 1777; first brigadier general in General James Grant's expedition against St. Lucia, West Indies, 1778; major general, 1781; Governor of Canada, 1796-1798.

**Prescott, Samuel.** 1751-c.1777. Patriot, physician, b. Concord, Mass.

Rode from Lexington to spread the news that British troops were coming, 19 April 1775; was the only rider to reach Concord, as Paul Revere and William Dawes were stopped at Lexington.

**Prescott, William.** 1726-1795. Militia officer (Col.), farmer, b. Groton, Mass.

Commanded the redoubt on the hill (Breed's Hill) at the battle of Bunker Hill.

**Preston, Thomas.** British officer (Capt.).

Leader of the British unit responsible for the Boston Massacre, 5 March 1770; tried and acquitted, but discharged from the military service.

**Prudhomme de Borre, Chevalier Philippe Hubert.** Continental officer (Brig. Gen.).

French volunteer; served December 1776-September 1777.

**Prevost, Augustine.** 1723-1786. British officer (Maj. Gen.), b. Geneva, Switzerland.

Commanded British forces in East Florida, 1775; commanded all British forces in the south, 1778; performed outstandingly at Briar

Creek, Ga., 3 March 1779, and in the defense of Savannah, Ga., 9 October 1779.

**Prevost, James Mark (or Marc).** British officer (Lt. Col.).

Distinguished himself at Briar Creek, Ga., 3 March 1779, where his brother, Maj. Gen. Augustine Prevost commanded; appointed lieutenant governor of Georgia, March 1779, by British military authorities and served until July 1779.

**Pulaski, Casimir, Count.** c. 1748-1779. Continental officer (Brig. Gen.), b. Poland.

Volunteer aide-de-camp to Washington at Brandywine; "Commander of the Horse," commanding the Continental dragoons, 1777-1778; organized and commanded "Pulaski's Legion," 1778-1779; not a very effective commander; mortally wounded in a gallant but misguided cavalry charge at Savannah, Ga., 9 October 1779.

**Pulteney, William.** British statesman.

Member of Parliament; attempted to negotiate a peace settlement with Benjamin Franklin before Carlisle's peace commission left England, March 1778.

**Purviance, Samuel, Jr.** Patriot.

Chairman of the Council of Safety of Baltimore, Md.

**Putnam, Israel.** 1718-1790. Militia officer (Brig. Gen.), Continental officer (Maj. Gen.), farmer, tavern keeper, b. Salem, Mass.

Moved to Connecticut about 1740; won his military reputation in French and Indian War and Pontiac's War; member, Sons of Liberty; although present as a volunteer, shared command at Bunker Hill with William Prescott; major general, 1775-1783; participated in the New York campaign of 1776; commanded the forces defeated at the battle of Long Island; a fiery personality and inspiring symbol, but inept commander; cousin of Rufus Putnam.

**Putnam, James.** 1726-1789. Loyalist, lawyer, b. Salem Village, Mass.

Last attorney general of Massachusetts Bay under the Crown, 1777-1778.

**Putnam, Rufus.** 1738-1824. Militia officer (Lt. Col.), Continental officer (Brig. Gen.), engineer, surveyor, farmer, pioneer, b. Sutton, Mass.

Worked on military engineering at siege of Boston; acting chief engineer of the Army, 1776; worked on West Point defenses; made brigadier general, January 1783; drew up Newburgh Petition of officer grievances, June 1783; superintendent of the Ohio Company, 1788; first surveyor general of the United States, 1796-1803; cousin of Israel Putnam.

**Pyle, John.** Loyalist officer.

A North Carolina resident, Pyle was defeated by a detachment of General Greene's army at Haw River, N.C., 25 February 1781. This defeat ended Cornwallis's attempt to raise the North Carolina loyalists.

# Q

**Quincy, Josiah.** 1744-1775. Lawyer, jurist, b. Boston, Mass.

Active pre-Revolution patriot; with John Adams, defended the British soldiers involved in the Boston Massacre, 1770; went to England, 1774, to plead American cause; died of tuberculosis on the return voyage.

**Quincy, Samuel.** 1735-1789. Loyalist, lawyer, b. Braintree (now Quincy), Mass.

Solicitor general for Massachusetts, for the Crown; represented the Crown at the trial of Captain Thomas Preston in 1770, involving the latter's role in the Boston Massacre.

# R

**Rall, Johann Gottleib.** c. 1720-1776. Hessian officer (Col.), b. Hesse-Cassel.

Fought well at White Plains and at Fort Washington, N.Y., 16 November 1776; commander of the outpost at Trenton, N.J., overrun by Washington, 26 December 1776; mortally wounded in the battle.

**Ramsay, David.** 1749-1815. American statesman, physician, historian, b. Dunmore, Lancaster Co., Pa.

Delegate to the Continental Congress, South Carolina, 1782-1784, 1785-1786; brother of Nathaniel Ramsay.

**Ramsay, Nathaniel.** 1741-1817. Continental officer (Lt. Col.), statesman, lawyer, b. Lancanster Co., Pa.

Helped stop the retreat at Monmouth; delegate to the Continental Congress, Maryland, 1785-1787; brother of David Ramsay.

**Randolph, Edmund.** 1753-1813. American statesman, Continental officer, lawyer, b. Williamsburg, Va.

Aide-de-camp to George Washington, 1775; delegate to the Continental Congress, Virginia, 1779-1782; first Attorney General of the United States, 1789-1794; Secretary of State, 1794-1795; son of John Randolph and nephew of Peyton Randolph.

**Randolph, John.** 1727- or 1728-1784. Loyalist, b. "Tazewell Hall," Williamsburg, Va.

Father of Edmund Randolph; brother of Peyton Randolph, went to England at outbreak of Revolution.

**Randolph, Peyton.** c. 1721-1775. American statesman, lawyer, b. "Tazewell Hall," Williamsburg, Va.

Delegate to the Continental Congress, Virginia, 1774-1775; president of the Continental Congress, 1774, 1775; brother of John Randolph.

**Rankin, William.** Loyalist leader, landowner.

Pennsylvania resident; known by alias Mr. Alexander; organized loyalists in eastern Pennsylvania, Delaware, and Maryland.

**Rastel, Philippe François, Sieur de Rocheblave.** British officer, b. France.

Commandant of Fort Gage at Kaskaskia (in present-day Illinois) when it was captured, 4 July 1778, by George Rogers Clark.

**Rathbun, John Peck.** 1746-1782. Continental naval and privateer officer (Capt.), b. Exeter, R.I.

Served under John Paul Jones; promoted to captain, April 1777, and placed in command of sloop *Providence*; carried out daring and successful raid on Nassau, January 1778; captured at fall of Charleston, May 1780, and paroled; took command of the privateer *Wexford*, 1781; captured; died in Mill Prison, Plymouth, England.

**Rattoon, John.** British spy.

New Jersey resident; courier for British intelligence messages, including many to and from Benedict Arnold; organized group of spies for British; was never discovered to be spy in his lifetime and continued living in New Jersey after the war.

**Rawdon-Hastings, Francis (Lord Rawdon).** 1754-1826. British officer (Lt. Col.; Brig. Gen., local rank).

Served at Bunker Hill; aide-de-camp to General Clinton, 1778; adjutant general to Clinton, 1778-1779; distinguished himself in the Camden campaign (July-August 1780); was in command in South Carolina and Georgia, 1781; successful at Hobkirk's Hill, S.C., 25 April 1781, and Ninety-Six, S.C., May–June 1781; turned over his command to Col. Paston Gould, July 1781.

**Read, Charles.** 1715-1780. Militia officer (Col.).

New Jersey resident; deserted to the British in December 1776.

**Read, George.** 1733-1798. American statesman, lawyer, b. Cecil Co., Md.

Delegate to the Continental Congress, Delaware, 1774-1777; signer of the Declaration of Independence, which he originally had opposed; acting president (chief executive) of Delaware, 1777-1778.

**Read, James.** 1743-1822. Militia officer (Maj. or Lt. Col.), naval commissioner.

Delaware resident; major, Pennsylvania militia, 1777; secretary of the Navy Board, 1781.

**Read, Thomas.** 1740?-1788. Continental naval officer (Capt.), seaman, b. Newcastle Co., Del.

Became eighth-ranking captain in Navy, 5 June 1776; led a force on foot to help defend Assumpink Creek, near Trenton, 2 January 1777; scuttled his ship, the *George Washington*, to keep it from the British when they took Philadelphia, December 1777.

**Reed, James.** 1723-1807. Continental officer (Brig. Gen.), tailor, tavern keeper, landowner, militia officer, b. Woburn, Mass.

Led his men well at Bunker Hill; made brigadier general, 9 August 1776, but resigned soon after because recent illness, perhaps

smallpox, had left him blind and partly deaf.

**Reed, Joseph.** 1741-1785. American statesman, lawyer, Continental officer (Col.), b. Trenton, N.J.

Continental officer, 1775-1777; adjutant general in Washington's army, 1775-1777; distinguished himself at Harlem Heights, 16 September 1776; declined appointment as brigadier general in 1777; delegate to the Continental Congress, 1777-1778; exposed attempt of George Johnstone (of Carlisle's peace commission), to bribe him and others in Congress, 1778; president of the Supreme Executive Council of Pennsylvania, 1778-1781; kept Washington informed of affairs in the Continental Congress, 1777-1781; played a key role in settling the mutiny of the Pennsylvania Line, January 1781.

**Revere, Paul.** 1735-1818. Militia officer (Lt. Col.), silversmith, b. Boston, Mass.

Noted silversmith; active patriot before the Revolution; made the famous "midnight ride" on the night of 18-19 April 1775 to warn of the British advance on Lexington and Concord; courier to Continental Congress for Massachusetts Provincial Assembly; served in the Penobscot (Me.) expedition, July-August 1779; acquitted by court-martial of alleged misconduct in that expedition.

**Rhoads, Samuel.** 1711-1784. American statesman, carpenter, builder, b. Philadelphia, Pa.

Delegate to the Continental Congress, Pennsylvania, 1774-1775; mayor of Philadelphia, 1774.

**Riedesel, Baron Friedrich Adolphus.** 1738-1800. German officer (Lt. Gen., local rank).

Commander of the Brunswick contingent of German troops; took part in Burgoyne's offensive, 1777; distinguished himself at Hubbardtown, Vt., 7 July 1777, and in both of the battles of Saratoga; surrendered with Burgoyne at Saratoga, 17 October 1777; exchanged, 13 October 1780.

**Riedesel, Baroness Frederica von.** German writer.

Wife of Baron Friedrich Riedesel; accompanied her husband, with three young daughters, during his six years in America; wrote valuable memoirs of the experience.

**Rinker, "Mom".** American spy.

Resident of Germantown, Pa., where her family kept a tavern; received intelligence from Philadelphia, and passed it on by dropping a ball of yarn from a high rock, now part of Fairmont Park, where she sat knitting.

**Ritzema, Rudolph(us).** Continental officer (Col.), clergyman.

New York resident; assumed command of the 3d New York, 1775; went over to the British, November 1776.

**Rivington, James.** 1724-1802. Loyalist, American agent, bookseller, publisher, b. London.

Came to America, 1760; published *Rivington's New York Gazeteer*, 1773-1775; printing plant destroyed by patriot mob, November 1775; published *Rivington's New York Loyal Gazette* (later *The Royal Gazetter*), 1777-1783, virtually a daily newspaper and the first in America; sent secret British information to the Americans from 1781 on.

**Roberdeau, Daniel.** 1727-1795. American statesman, businessman (lumber), b. St. Christopher, West Indies.

Delegate to the Continental Congress, Pennsylvania, 1777-1779.

**Robertson, James.** 1742-1814. Frontiersman, b. Brunswick Co., Va.

Border leader against the Indians and Tories; called "Father of the State of Tennessee."

**Robertson, James.** 1720?-1788. British officer (Lt. Gen.), b. Fifeshire, Scotland.

Commanded a brigade at Long Island, N.Y., 27 August 1776; civil governor of New York, 1779; made lieutenant general, 1782.

**Robertson, James.** c. 1751-1818. Loyalist government official.

Helped in the attempt to reestablish royal government in Georgia, 1779, and became attorney general.

**Robinson, Beverley.** 1721-1792. Loyalist leader, landowner, loyalist officer (Col.), b. Middlesex Co., Va.

New York resident; attempted secretly and unsuccessfully to get Israel Putnam to agree to a peace settlement, November 1777; aided in making the arrangements for the Arnold-André meeting, 1780; raised Loyal American Regiment and a corps of Royal Guides and Pioneers; went to live in England, 1782.

**Robinson, John.** 1727-1802. British statesman, b. Appleby, Westmoreland, England.

Treasury Secretary to Lord North, 1770-1782; staunch supporter of North and the King on American affairs.

**Robinson, Thomas.** c. 1730-1789. Loyalist.

Most prominent of the Delaware loyalists; claimed to have raised 1,500 men, June 1776, and to have had to disperse them for lack of arms from the British; apparently in England during and after the war; was allowed to return to his home, c. 1786.

**Robinson-Morris, Matthew.** 1713-1800. British statesman, b. York, England.

A retired Independent Whig, he predicted disaster for Britain if it tried to suppress the American Revolution. He wrote *Peace the Best Policy, or Reflections upon the Appearance of a Foreign War* and *The Present State of Affairs at Home and the Commission for Granting Pardons in America.*

**Rochambeau, Donatien Marie Joseph de Vimeur, Vicomte de.** 1750-1813. French officer (Col.).

Assistant adjutant general to the French Expeditionary Force, 1779-1781; son of the Comte de Rochambeau; killed fighting as a division commander under Napoleon in the battle of Leipzig, 1813.

**Rochambeau, Jean Baptiste Donatien de Vimeur, Comte de.** 1725-1807. French officer (Lt. Gen.), b. Vendôme.

Distinguished himself during the Seven Years' War in the capture of Port Mahon, Minorca, 1756, at Crefeld, June 1758, and in saving the French from surprise attack at Clostercamp, October 1760; brigadier general, 1761, and also inspector of cavalry, in which post he carried out reforms in discipline, tactics, and troop welfare; promoted to lieutenant general and made commander of the French Expeditionary Force in America, 1780; played important role as diplomat and strategist; assisted Washington in planning Yorktown campaign; marched four regiments from vicinity of New York to Yorktown, and commanded French wing at siege of Yorktown; became a Marshal of France, 1791; arrested during the Reign of Terror and narrowly escaped execution.

**Rochester, Nathaniel.** 1752-1831. Militia officer, merchant, b. Westmoreland Co., Va.

North Carolina resident at time of Revolution; commissioner in charge of arms factory at Hillsborough, N.C., 1777-1778; founder of Rochester, New York.

**Rockingham, Charles Watson-Wentworth, 2nd Marquis.** 1730-1782. British statesman.

Whig leader and opponent of George III; Prime Minister, 1765-1776, March-July 1782; died in office; responsible for the repeal of the Stamp Act and for the Declaratory Act, 18 March 1766; favored reconciliation with America.

**Rodney, Caesar.** 1728-1789. American statesman, militia officer (Brig. Gen.), farmer, b. Dover, Del.

Local public official from 1755; delegate to Stamp Act Congress, 1765; delegate to the Continental Congress, 1774-1776, 1777-1778, 1782-1784; signer of the Declaration of Independence; president (chief executive) of Delaware, 1777-1782; brother of Thomas Rodney.

**Rodney, George Brydges.** 1718-1792. British naval officer (Adm.), b. London.

Commander-in-chief in the Leeward Islands, 1779; successful against the Spanish off Cape St. Vincent, 16 January 1781; defeated the French at the battle of the Saints, West Indies, 12 April 1782, where he captured Admiral de Grasse and his flagship; has been criticized for his failure to press pursuit of 20 other French ships after the battle.

**Rodney, Thomas.** 1744-1811. American statesman, militia officer (Capt.), jurist, b. near Dover, Kent Co., Del.

Fought at Princeton; delegate to the Continental Congress, Delaware, 1781-1783, 1785-1787; Delaware judge of admiralty, 1778-1785; brother of Caesar Rodney.

**Roe, Austin.** American intelligence courier.

Served as courier for the major American spy team of Robert Townsend and Samuel Woodhull ("the Culpers").

**Rogers, John.** 1723-1789. American statesman, lawyer, b. Annapolis, Md.

Delegate to the Continental Congress, 1775-1776.

**Rogers, Robert.** 1732-1795. Frontiersman, ranger leader, British officer (Col.), b. Methuen, Mass.

As leader of "Rogers' Rangers," hero of French and Indian War; imprisoned on orders from General Washington, 1776, on suspicion of being a spy; escaped and was commissioned by the British to raise the Queen's American Rangers, 1776; led his men in a skirmish at Mamaroneck, N.Y. (near White Plains), 22 October 1776; went to England soon after this action.

**Romans, Bernard.** c. 1720-1784. Surveyor, civil engineer, naturalist, cartographer, Continental officer (Capt.), b. Netherlands.

New York resident; mapmaker for Continental Army.

**Root, Jesse.** 1736-1822. American statesman, clergyman, lawyer, jurist, militia officer (Lt. Col.), b. Coventry, Tolland Co., Conn.

Delegate to the Continental Congress, Connecticut, 1778-1783; chief justice of the Connecticut Superior Court, 1798-1807.

**Rose, John.** *See* Rosenthal, Gustave Henri, Baron de.

**Rosenthal, Gustave Henri, Baron de.** 1753-1829. Continental officer (Lt.), surgeon, b. Livonia (Latvia), Russia.

Swedish nobleman whose home province, Livonia, had been ceded to Russia in 1721; volunteered for service in Continental Army, 1777; known as "John Rose"; returned to Russia, 1784, and became grand marshal of Livonia.

**Ross, Alexander.** 1742-1827. British officer (Maj.), b. Scotland.

Served throughout the war; aide-de-camp to General Cornwallis; represented Cornwallis at the surrender negotiations at Yorktown, 17 October 1781.

**Ross, Betsy.** 1752-1836. Seamstress, b. Philadelphia, Pa.

Mrs. Ross made flags, including American flags. According to a family legend, which appears certainly inaccurate, she made the first "Stars and Stripes."

**Ross, George.** 1730-1779. American statesman, jurist, lawyer, b. New Castle, Del.

Delegate to the Continental Congress, Pennsylvania, 1774-1777; signer of the Declaration of Independence.

**Ross, John.** Loyalist officer (Maj.).

New York resident; commanding 700 Tories and Indians, fought inconclusive action against Col. Marinus Willett and his 400 men at Johnstown, N.Y., 25 October 1781; apparently held advantage over the patriots when darkness ended the engagement.

**Rowley, Joshua.** 1730?-1790. British naval officer (Rear Adm.).

Served in the West Indies, 1778-1782; made Rear Admiral of the Blue, 1779; commanded rear in battle off Martinique, 17 April 1780; in command off Jamaica, 1782-1783.

**Rudolph, Michael.** b.c. 1754. Continental officer (Capt.), farmer, tax collector.

Maryland resident; served in Lee's Legion; breveted captain for conduct at Paulus Hook, N.J., 19 August 1779; outstanding officer in southern campaigns, 1780-1781.

**Rugeley, Henry.** Loyalist, British officer (Col.), landowner.

South Carolina resident; served in the British army, but with questionable loyalty; warned Governor Edward Rutledge in time for him to escape from Tarleton in the pursuit that ended at Waxhaws, S.C., 29 May 1780; made a humiliating surrender at Rugeley's Mill (or Mills), S.C., 4 December 1780, which ended his military career.

**Ruggles, Timothy.** 1711-1795. Loyalist militia officer, tavern keeper, lawyer, judge, b. Rochester, Mass.

Prewar justice of the peace and member of Massachusetts Assembly; fought as brigadier general in French and Indian War; formed Loyal American Association (loyalist volunteers), April 1775, and served as its commander; went to Nova Scotia, 1783.

**Rumsey, Benjamin.** 1734-1808. American statesman, jurist, b. Bohemia Manor, Cecil Co., Md.

Delegate to the Continental Congress, Maryland, 1776-1778.

**Rush, Benjamin.** 1746-1813. American statesman, physician, b. Byberry Township, near Philadelphia, Pa.

Best-known American physician of his day; made significant medical contributions, but also favored drastic bleeding and purging for all illnesses; delegate to the Continental Congress, Pennsylvania, 1776-1777; signer of the Declaration of Independence; served briefly as Continental surgeon general of Middle Department; involved in Conway Cabal; worked in antislavery, temperance, and penal-reform causes after the war.

**Rutherford, Griffith.** c. 1731-c. 1800. Militia officer (Brig. Gen.), b. Ireland.

Brigadier general of North Carolina militia, 1776-1783; served in many southern actions, 1776-1781; called out the militia to defeat the Tories in the decisive battle at Ramseur's Mill, N.C., 20 June 1780; moved to Tennessee after the war and became a leading citizen there.

**Rutledge, Edward.** 1749-1800. American statesman, lawyer, b. Christ Church Parish, S.C.

Delegate to the Continental Congress, South Carolina, 1774-1777; signer of the Declaration of Independence; along with Benjamin Franklin and John Adams, took part in a cordial but fruitless meeting with Lord Howe on Staten Island, N.Y., 11 August 1776, to discuss peace possibilities; brother of John Rutledge.

**Rutledge, John.** 1739-1800. American statesman, lawyer, b. Christ Church Parish, S.C.

Delegate to the Continental Congress, South Carolina, 1774-1777; 1782-1783; elected governor of South Carolina, 1779; nominated as Chief Justice of the United States, June 1795, and presided over the August 1795 term, but failed to be confirmed by the Senate, December 1795; brother of Edward Rutledge.

# S

**Sackett, Nathaniel.** Patriot.

With John Jay, headed patriot counterintelligence operations in New York, beginning in latter half of 1776; headed American espionage organization in Manhattan and New Jersey, 1777.

**St. Clair, Arthur.** 1737-1818. Continental officer (Maj. Gen.), landowner, statesman, b. Scotland.

Fought in French and Indian War; settled in Boston, 1762; moved to Pennsylvania frontier before the Revolution; brigadier general, 1776-1777; major general, 1777-1783; commanded a brigade in Canadian expedition, 1775-1776; became commander on Lake Champlain, 1777; forced to abandon Ticonderoga, 5 July 1777; held no further important commands during the Revolution; delegate to the Continental Congress, Pennsylvania, 1785-1787; President of the Continental Congress, 1787; first governor of the Northwest Territory, 1789-1802; as major general commanding the U.S. Army, suffered disastrous defeat by Miami Indians, 4 November 1791.

**Saint-Germain, Comte de.** French statesman.

Minister of War during American Revolution; approved of aid to the Americans.

**St. Leger, Barry.** 1737-1789. British officer (Col.).

Led expedition, June-September 1777, down the Mohawk Valley of New York as part of Burgoyne's offensive; principal engagements were those connected with the siege of Fort Stanwix, 2-23 August 1777, and the Oriskany ambush, 6 August 1777; famed for establishment of the St. Leger, English horse racing classic, 1776.

**Saint-Simon, Claude Henri de Rouvroy, Comte de.** 1760-1825. French officer, land speculator, writer, b. Paris.

Served at Yorktown, 1781; captured at battle of the Saints, West Indies, 12 April 1782; imprisoned during the Terror of the French Revolution; made a fortune in land speculation; became a founder of French socialism.

**Saint-Simon Montblern, Claude Anne, Marquis de.** French officer (general).

Commander of French troops that reached Yorktown with Admiral De Grasse.

**Salomon, Haym.** 1740-1785. Patriot, merchant, banker, b. Lissa, Poland.

Member of New York Sons of Liberty; a financier of the Revolution.

**Salstonstall, Dudley.** 1738-1796. Continental naval officer (Commodore), merchant captain, privateer, b. New London, Conn.

A leader in the ill-fated Penobscot (Me.) expedition, 22 July-14 August 1779; court-martialed and dismissed from the Navy for his poor leadership at Penobscot Bay; was later successful privateer.

**Salvador, Francis.** 1747-1776. Patriot, militia officer, b. England.

Came to South Carolina, 1773; first Jew elected to office in the Americas; delegate to the South Carolina Provincial Congress, 1775; killed in action at Essenecca, S.C., 1 August 1776.

**Sampson, Deborah.** 1760-1827. American soldier, teacher.

Massachusetts resident; masqueraded and enlisted in Army as a man under the name of Robert Shurtleff, 1782; twice wounded;

discovered and honorably discharged; pensioned.

**Sandwich, John Montagu, 4th Earl of.** 1718-1792. British statesman.

First Lord of the Admirality, 1748-1751, 1771-1782; generally blamed for the poor condition of British naval vessels and personnel at the outbreak of the Revolution; also blamed for mishandling naval affairs during the Revolution.

**Sartine, Antoine, Comte d'Ally.** French statesman.

Maritime Minister; assisted in aid to the Americans, 1775.

**Scammel, Alexander.** 1747-1781. Continental officer (Col.), surveyor, lawyer, b. Mendon (now Milford), Mass.

Adjutant General to George Washington, 1778-1780; killed at Yorktown, 30 September 1781.

**Schaffner, George.** d.c. 1795. Continental officer (Maj.).

Of Pennsylvania German ancestry; fought in Continental partisan legion of Colonel Charles Armand (Charles-Armand Tuffin, Marquis de la Rouerie); became Tuffin's personal friend, returned to France with him, and joined him in fighting and exercising diplomacy against the French Revolution; apparently died in the Vendée uprising.

**Schuyler, Philip John.** 1733-1804. Continental officer (Maj. Gen.), landowner, b. Albany, N.Y.

Commander of the Northern Department, 1775-1777; directed, but did not directly participate in,

the Canada invasion of 1775-1776; relieved of command, after a bitter feud with Maj. Gen. Horatio Gates, 4 August 1777; delegate to the Continental Congress, New York, 1775-1777, 1778-1781.

**Scott, Charles.** c. 1739-1813. Continental officer (Brig. Gen.), frontiersman, statesman, b. Goochland Co., Va.

Brigadier general, 1777-1783; prominent in the Monmouth campaign, June-July 1778, as part of Maj. Gen. Charles Lee's command; moved to Kentucky after the war, was active in Indian fighting there, and was elected governor of the state in 1808.

**Scott, John Morin.** 1730-1784. American statesman, lawyer, militia officer (Brig. Gen.), New York, N.Y.

Successful lawyer and prominent Whig before the Revolution; opposed Stamp Act; helped organize Sons of Liberty; leader of the radical group in the provincial congresses of 1775-1777; participated in battle of Long Island; New York secretary of state, 1778-1784; delegate to the Continental Congress, New York, 1780-1783.

**Scudder, Nathaniel.** 1733-1781. American statesman, physician, militia officer (Col.), b. Monmouth Courthouse, N.J.

Delegate to the Continental Congress, New Jersey, 1777-1779.

**Seabury, Samuel.** 1728-1796. Loyalist, clergyman, b. Groton, Conn.

Political theorist; considered one of the most able and learned clergyman in America; wrote *Free Thoughts on Proceedings of the Continental Congress*, 1774, and other pamphlets; first Episcopal bishop in America, 1785.

**Searle, James.** 1730-1797. American statesman, businessman, b. New York, N.Y.

Active pre-Revolution patriot; delegate to the Continental Congress, Pennsylvania, 1778-1780; sent by Pennsylvania to Europe to try to negotiate a loan, 1780, but was unsuccessful.

**Sears, Isaac.** 1730-1786. Patriot, seaman, b. West Brewster, Mass.

Leader in the New York Sons of Liberty; mob leader; after the news of Lexington and Concord, April 1775, Sears and the group he led had virtual control of New York City until the arrival of Washington's army a year later; later became a privateer.

**Senter, Isaac.** 1755-1799. Militia officer, surgeon, diarist, b. New Hampshire.

Kept a journal of Arnold's march to Quebec, 1775; surgeon general of the Rhode Island militia, 1779-1781.

**Sergeant, Jonathan D.** 1746-1793. American statesman, lawyer, b. Newark, N.J.

Delegate to the Continental Congress, New Jersey, 1776, 1776-1777.

**Serle, Ambrose.** British official.

Civilian secretary to Admiral Howe; wrote *The American Journal of Ambrose Serle, Secre-*

*tary to Lord Howe, 1776-1778* (ed. Edward Tatum, Jr., San Marino, Calif., 1940).

**Sevier, John.** 1745-1815. Militia officer (Col.), statesman, farmer, trader, surveyor, b. New Market, Va.

Colonel in the North Carolina militia; one of the leaders at the battle of Kings Mountain; led frontier militia in victory over the Tories and Indians at Lookout Mountain, Tenn., 20 September 1782; member, U.S. House of Representatives, North Carolina, 1789-1791, Tennessee, 1811-1815; first governor of Tennessee, 1796-1801.

**Sewall, Jonathan.** 1728-1832. Loyalist, attorney, b. Massachusetts.

Supporter of Governor Thomas Hutchinson; close friend of John Adams, who tried to convert him to the patriot cause.

**Sharpe, William.** 1742-1818. American statesman, lawyer, b. Rock Church, Cecil Co., Md.

Delegate to the Continental Congress, North Carolina, 1779-1782.

**Shaw, Samuel.** 1754-1799. Continental officer (Capt.), diplomat, b. Massachusetts.

Artillery officer; aide-de-camp to Maj. Gen. Henry Knox, 1782-1783; kept a valuable journal; first U.S. consul to China, 1796.

**Shays, Daniel.** 1747-1825. Continental officer (Capt.), b. Massachusetts.

Received sword from Lafayette for bravery; insurrectionist, responsible for Shays's Rebellion, 1786–1787.

**Sheftall, Mordecai.** 1735-1795. Patriot.

Chairman of the Parochial Committee, organized to regulate the internal affairs of Savannah, Ga., during the Revolution; participated in defense of Savannah, December 1778; captured by the British.

**Shelburne, William Petty, Earl of.** 1737-1805. British statesman, b. Dublin.

Secretary of State for the Southern Department (in charge of colonial affairs), 1766-1768, under Chatham; favored a conciliatory policy toward the American colonies, and was dismissed in 1768 after his policy was frustrated; Prime Minister, replacing Rockingham upon his death, 1782-1783.

**Shelby, Evan.** 1719-1794. Militia officer (Col.).

Virginia resident; successful against Chickamauga Indian villages in Tennessee, April 1779.

**Shelby, Isaac.** 1750-1826. Militia officer (Col.), statesman, b. Maryland.

Virginia resident at the time of the Revolution; one of the principal leaders at the battle of Kings Mountain; first Governor of Kentucky, 1792-1796.

**Sheldon, Elisha.** Continental officer (Brevet Brig. Gen.).

Connecticut resident; breveted brigadier general, 1780.

**Shell, John Christian.** Patriot.

Successfully defended his property from an assault of Tories and Indians led by Donald McDonald at Shell's Bush, N.Y., 6 August 1781.

**Shepard, William.** 1737-1817. Continental officer (Col.), farmer, selectman, b. Massachusetts.

Fought in French and Indian War; took part in 22 Revolutionary War engagements; helped put down Shays's rebellion, 1786-1787; member, U.S. House of Representatives, 1797-1801.

**Sherman, Roger.** 1722-1793. American statesman, cobbler, surveyor, lawyer, merchant, b. Newton, Mass.

Moved to Connecticut, 1743; pre-Revolution conservative Whig; delegate to the Continental Congress, Connecticut, 1774-1784; signer of the Declaration of Independence; with Richard Law, revised Connecticut statutory law, 1783; delegate to the Federal Constitutional Convention, 1789, where he worked for the "Connecticut Compromise."

**Shippen, Edward.** 1729-1806. Loyalist, jurist, b. Philadelphia, Pa.

Chief justice of Pennsylvania, 1799-1806; father of Margaret Shippen.

**Shippen, Margaret (Peggy; Mrs. Benedict Arnold).** 1760-1804. b. Philadelphia, Pa.

Married Arnold 8 April 1779; assisted and probably encouraged her husband in his treason; daughter of Edward Shippen.

**Shippen, William.** 1736-1808. American statesman, physician, teacher, b. Philadelphia, Pa.

Teacher of anatomy at College of Philadelphia medical school from 1762; medical director of Continental Army hospitals, 1777-1781; delegate to the Continental Congress, Pennsylvania, 1778-1780; cousin of Edward Shippen.

**Shreve, Israel.** d. 1799. Continental officer (Col.).

Commander of the 2d New Jersey Regiment, 1776-1781.

**Shuldham, Molyneux.** 1717?-1798. British naval officer (Vice Adm.).

Vice Admiral of the Blue; commander-in-chief on the North American coast, 29 September 1775-June 1776; superseded by Lord Howe.

**Silliman, Gold Selleck.** 1732-1790. Militia officer (Brig. Gen.).

Commanded a Connecticut regiment at Long Island and White Plains in the New York campaign of 1776.

**Simcoe, John G.** 1752-1806. British officer (Col.), b. Cotterstock, Northamptonshire, England.

British commander of the Queen's Rangers, a Tory regiment; took part in the battles of the Brandywine and Monmouth and in the engagements at Quintain's Bridge, N.J., and Hancock's Bridge, N.J., March 1778, and at Verplanck's Point, June 1779; routed the militia defenders of Richmond, Va., 5 January 1781, and the militia at Charles City Courthouse, Va., January 1781; be-

came lieutenant governor of Upper Canada in 1791; became lieutenant general, 1798; appointed commander-in-chief in India, 1806, but died before taking up duties.

**Simitière, Pierre-Eugène du.** 1736-1784. Artist, b. Geneva, Switzerland.

Made portraits of many of the American leaders of the Revolution.

**Sinclair, Patrick.** British government official.

Lieutenant governor at Michillimackinac; force he sent out was repulsed by Spanish expedition under Captain Don Fernando de Leyba, Spanish commandant of modern St. Louis, 26 May 1780.

**Skene, Philip.** 1725-1810. Loyalist, British officer (Brig. Maj.), British government official, b. England.

Vetern British officer; fought in French and Indian War; founded Skenesboro (now Whitehall), N.Y., 1759; governor of Ticonderoga and Crown Point, N.Y., 1775; principal official in new government the British were trying to establish on Lake Champlain to end New York–New Hampshire dispute over Vermont territory; principal loyalist advisor to General Burgoyne; imprisoned in 1775 and again in 1777; went to live in England after the war.

**Skinner, Cortlandt.** 1728-1799. Loyalist officer (Brig. Gen.), government official.

Attorney general of New Jersey, 1775; raised and commanded a body of loyalists called Skinner's Brigade.

**Skinner, John.** d. 1827. Loyalist, British officer.

New Jersey resident; joined the British Army, 1772; served in the south during the Revolution; commanded a troop of Tarleton's British Legion in the battles of Blackstocks, S.C., 20 November 1780, Cowpens, and Guilford Courthouse; remained in the British Army and eventually became general.

**Smallwood, William.** 1732-1792. Continental officer (Maj. Gen.), statesman, b. Charles Co., Md.

Fought in French and Indian War; delegate to Maryland Assembly, 1761; raised (1776) and commanded Smallwood's Maryland Battalion; wounded in effectively leading his men at White Plains; became brigadier general, 23 October 1776; sent south with De Kalb, 1780; did not distinguish himself at Camden, but succeeded to command of the remnants of De Kalb's Continental division after the battle; major general, 1780-1783; governor of Maryland for three terms beginning in 1785.

**Smith, Claudius.** d. 1779. Loyalist partisan fighter.

Known as the "Tory Cowboy of the Ramapos"; roamed the mountains of Rockland County, N.Y., in search of booty for the British; may have been part of James DeLancey's New York Volunteers.

**Smith, Francis.** 1723-1791. British officer (Maj. Gen.).

Lieutenant colonel and senior officer in Boston garrison in early 1775; commanded the expedition to Lexington and Concord, 19 April 1775; major general, 1779; lieutenant general, 1787.

**Smith, James.** c. 1719-1806. American statesman, lawyer, surveyor, b. Ireland.

Came to Pennsylvania as a child; lived in York; supported "back-country" Pennsylvanians politically against eastern interests; active patriot before the Revolution; delegate to the Continental Congress, Pennsylvania, 1776-1778; signer of the Declaration of Independence.

**Smith, Jonathan.** 1742-1812. American statesman, jurist, university trustee, b. Philadelphis, Pa.

Delegate to the Continental Congress, Pennsylvania, 1777-1778.

**Smith, Joshua Hett.** 1736-1818. Militia officer, lawyer, b. New York.

An active patriot, 1775-1779; directed the secret service for Maj. Gen. Robert Howe at West Point, 1778-1779, and also for Maj. Gen. Benedict Arnold, 1779-1780; discovered Arnold's treason and shared in the capture of John André; acquitted, 26 October 1780, of any involvement in the treason; imprisoned in 1780 on suspicion of being a loyalist, but escaped to the British, 1781; went to England, 1783, but returned to the United States in 1801; brother of William Smith II.

**Smith, Meriwether.** 1730-1790. American statesman, lawyer, b. "Bathurst," Piscataway Creek, Essex Co., Va.

Actively opposed Stamp Act, 1766; member, House of Burgesses, 1775, and of Virginia revolutionary conventions; delegate to the Continental Congress, Virginia, 1778-1782; served in Virginia House of Delegates; opposed ratification of the Federal Consitution.

**Smith, Richard.** 1735-1799. American statesman, b. Burlington, N.J.

Delegate to the Continental Congress, New Jersey, 1774-1776; kept detailed diary which is a valuable historical source.

**Smith, Samuel.** 1752-1839. Continental officer (Lt. Col.), militia officer (Maj. Gen.), merchant, b. Carlisle, Pa.

Moved with parents to Baltimore, Md., as a child; commander of the defense of Fort Mifflin, Pa., October-November 1777; voted a sword of thanks by Congress; commanded Maryland troops in Whiskey Rebellion suppression; member, U.S. House of Representatives, 1793-1803, 1816-1822; U.S. Senator, 1803-1815, 1822-1833; president pro tempore of the Senate, 1805-1808; major general of Maryland militia, 1812.

**Smith, Thomas.** 1745-1809. American statesman, jurist.

Delegate to the Continental Congress, Pennsylvania, 1780-1782.

**Smith, William, II.** 1728-1793. Loyalist, jurist, historian, b. New York, N.Y.

With William Livingston, prepared first digest of New York statutes (1752 and 1762); published a history of New York (1757), which he later expanded; later wrote valuable memoirs; chief justice of New York from 1763; lived in patriot-imposed "exile" in New York City, 1778-1783; lived in England, 1783-1786; Chief Justice of Canada, 1785-1793; brother of Joshua Hett Smith.

**Smith, William.** 1728-1814. American statesman, merchant, b. Donegal Township, Lancaster Co., Pa.

Delegate to the Continental Congress, Maryland, 1777-1778

**Smyth, Frederick.** d. 1815. Loyalist, jurist.

Chief justice of New Jersey, 1769-1776; appointed by Crown to assist British peace commisioners in America.

**Sower (or Saur), Christopher.** 1754-1799. Loyalist, publisher, b. Germantown, Pa.

Published the *Germantowner Zeitung* (Germantown, Pa.), which supported the loyalist cause; published the loyalist *Staats Courier*, 1777, in Philadelphia; served as a link between General Henry Clinton and the Pennsylvania loyalists, 1778-1781.

**Spalding, Simon.** 1742-1814. Continental officer (Capt.), b. Plainfield, Conn.

Moved to the Wyoming Valley of Pennsylvania, 1772; became lieutenant in Wyoming Valley Company, 1776; distinguished himself at Bound Brook, N.J., 13 April 1777; commanded a company in Sullivan's expedition, 1779.

**Sparhawk, William Pepperell.** Loyalist.

Massachusetts resident; successful colonial merchant; inherited the estate of his grandfather, Sir William Pepperell, upon adopting the latter's name, c. 1759; created baronet, 1774; fled to England in 1775.

**Spencer, Joseph.** 1714-1789. Continental officer (Maj. Gen.), statesman, b. East Haddam, Conn.

Fought in French and Indian War; brigadier general, 1775-1776; major general, 1776-1778; delegate to the Continental Congress, 1778-1779.

**Springfield, Loadices Langston.** Patriot.

Kown as "Dicey Langston"; Revolutionary heroine; served as a spy and a scout; South Carolina resident.

**Sprowle, Andrew.** d. c.1776. Loyalist, merchant.

One of Virginia's wealthiest men; for 36 years president of the Court of Virginia Merchants, a merchants' association.

**Stansbury, Joseph.** c. 1742-1809. Loyalist, poet, businessman, b. England.

Settled in Philadelphia, 1767; remained discreetly loyalist; was

go-between for Benedict Arnold and John André, 1779-1780.

**Stark, John.** 1728-1822. Militia officer (Col.), Continental officer (Brig. Gen.), farmer, b. New Hampshire.

Fought in French and Indian War; commanded militia regiment with distinction at Bunker Hill; victor of the battle of Bennington, 16 August 1777; cut off Burgoyne's last escape route, making certain complete American success at Saratoga, October 1777.

**Stedman, Charles.** 1753-1812. Loyalist, British officer (Col.), military historian, b. Philadelphia, Pa.

Served in the American Revolution in various campaigns from 1775 until 1781; wrote *History of the Origin, Progress, and Termination of the American War* (2 vols., London, 1794).

**Stephen, Adam.** c. 1730-1791. Continental officer (Maj. Gen.).

Veteran of French and Indian War; brigadier general, 1776-1777; major general, 1777; endangered Washington's Trenton operations by sending unauthorized patrol across the Delaware, 25 December 1776; defeated at Piscataway, N.J., 10 May 1777, in an attempt to surprise the 42d Highlanders; dismissed, 20 November 1777, after being convicted of misconduct at the battle of Germantown.

**Stephens, Philip.** 1725-1809. British official, b. Eastington, Gloucestershire, England.

Admiralty secretary, 1763-1795, serving under Lord Sandwich during the Revolution; member of Parliament, 1768-1806.

**Stephenson, Hugh.** Patriot, militia officer (Col.).

Raised and commanded the Virginia and Maryland Rifle Regiment; resident of western Virginia.

**Steuben, Friedrich Wilhelm Augustus von (or de).** 1730–1794. Continental officer (Maj. Gen.), b. Magdeburg, Prussia.

Foreign volunteer; major general, 1778–1784; Inspector General of the Continental Army, 1778–1783; adapting his Prussian training and indoctrination to American circumstances, developed and carried out highly successful training program for Washington's army at Valley Forge, early 1778; took part in Virginia operations of 1781; settled in New York after the war; a major contributor to American independence.

**Stevens, Edward.** 1745-1820. Militia officer (Maj. Gen.), b. Culpeper Co., Va.

Commanded a brigade of Virginia militiamen at Camden; served with greater distinction in command of a different militia force at Guilford Courthouse; commanded a Virginia brigade under Lafayette at Yorktown.

**Stewart, Alexander.** c. 1741-1794. British officer (Col.).

Commander of field forces at Orangeburg, S.C., 1781; in command of British forces at Eutaw Springs, S.C., 8 September 1781.

**Stewart, Anthony.** Ship's master.

Stewart paid duties on tea for his ship, *Peggy Stewart*, at Annapolis, Md., 1774. The resulting anger of a patriot mob caused him to burn his own ship (19 October 1774) in an effort to satisfy the mob and avoid greater violence.

**Stewart, John.** d. 1782. Continental officer (Lt. Col.).

Led an assault at Stony Point, N.Y., 16 July 1779; voted a silver medal from Congress; Maryland resident.

**Stewart, Walter.** c. 1756-1796. Continental officer (Col.), merchant.

Pennsylvania resident; aide-decamp to General Gates, 1776-1777; helped to settle the mutinies of the Connecticut Line, May 1780, and the Pennsylvania Line, January 1781; served in Yorktown campaign, 1781; organized the officers' movement that led to the Newburgh Addresses, March 1783.

**Stiles, Ezra.** 1727-1795. Educator, clergyman, b. North Haven, Conn.

Congregational clergyman; scholar; president of Yale College, 1778-1795; supported the Revolution and kept a valuable diary of events, enhanced by maps.

**Stirling, William Alexander, Lord.** *See* Alexander, William (Lord Stirling).

**Stockton, Richard.** 1730-1781. American statesman, lawyer, b. "Morven," Somerset Co., N.J.

Originally favored reconciliation and, in 1774, proposed a solution similar to what later became the Commonwealth system; delegate to the Continental Congress, New Jersey, 1776; signer of the Declaration of Independence; captured by the British and mistreated in prison.

**Stoddert, Benjamin.** 1751-1781. Continental officer (Capt.), businessman, statesman, b. Charles Co., Md.

Served early in the war as a cavalry officer and later ably as secretary of the Board of War, 1779-1781; successful shipper at port of Georgetown, Md., 1781-1798; first Secretary of the Navy, 1798-1801.

**Stokes, Anthony.** c. 1736-1799. Loyalist, jurist.

Last royal chief justice of Georgia, 1768-1778.

**Stone, Thomas.** 1743-1787. American statesman, lawyer, b. Poynton Manor, Charles Co., Md.

Delegate to the Continental Congress, Maryland, 1775-1779, 1784-1785; signer of the Declaration of Independence.

**Storer, Anthony Morris.** 1746-1799. British statesman.

Member of Parliament, 1774-1780, 1780-1784; member of Carlisle's peace commission, 1778.

**Stormant, David Murray, Viscount.** 1727-1796. British diplomat.

British ambassador to France; gained knowledge of the secret French operations to aid the Americans and lodged protests against them and against the use of French ports by American privateers.

**Strachey, Henry.** British diplomat.

Assisted Richard Oswald at the peace negotiations of 1782-1783.

**Stranger, Richard.** British privateer.

Commanded privateer *Admiral Duff*, which was captured by the Massachusetts Navy frigate *Protector*, under Capt. John Foster Williams off the Newfoundland coast, 9 June 1780.

**Stringer, Samuel.** 1734-1817. Physician.

Maryland resident; medical director of the Northern Army, 1775-1777; dismissed by Congress, 1777.

**Strong, Jedediah.** 1738-1802. American statesman, lawyer, b. Litchfield, Conn.

Delegate to the Continental Congress, Connecticut, 1782-1784.

**Stuart, John.** British government official, merchant, b. Scotland.

British superintendent of Indian affairs for the south, 1762-1779; southern equivalent of Sir William and Sir Guy Johnson; he attempted to prepare the Indians, notably the Cherokees and Seminoles, for effective hostilities against southern patriots, but these tribes took little part in the war; tried to prevent the Cherokee uprising of 1776 against frontier settlements; father of John Stuart, Jr.

**Stuart, John, Jr.** 1759-1815. Loyalist, British Army officer (Capt.), b. Georgia.

Served with the 3d Foot Guards, 1778-1783, at Ninety-Six, S.C. (May-June 1781), and at Eutaw Springs, S.C. (8 September 1781); later fought in the Napoleonic wars and became a lieutenant general in 1807; son of John Stuart.

**Sturges, Jonanthan.** 1740-1804. American statesman, lawyer, b. Fairfield, Conn.

Delegate to the Continental Congress, Connecticut, 1774-1787; member, U.S. House of Representatives, 1789-1793.

**Suffren de Saint Tropez, Pierre André de.** 1729-1788. French naval officer (Adm.).

Distinguished himself at Newport, R.I., August 1778; later defeated a British squadron at Porto Prayo in the Azores, April 16, 1781, en route to a successful naval campaign in the Indian Ocean; one of France's greatest admirals.

**Sullivan, James.** 1744-1808. American statesman, lawyer, jurist, b. Berwick, Me. (then Massachusetts).

Delegate to the Continental Congress, Massachusetts, 1782; governor of Massachusetts, 1807, 1808.

**Sullivan, John.** 1740-1795. Continental officer (Maj. Gen.), lawyer, statesman, b. Somersworth, N.H., or Maine.

A leader of a group of patriot volunteers that took Fort William and Mary, Portsmouth, N.H., 14 December 1774; brigadier general, 1775-1776; sent to reinforce the army invading Canada, 1776, and took command upon the death of Maj. Gen. John Thomas; defeated at Trois Rivières (8 June 1776) and replaced by Maj. Gen. Horatio Gates; major general, 1776-1779; was captured at Long Island, 27 August 1776, but immediately exchanged; played a significant role in the New Jersey campaign of 1776-1777, especially at Trenton; led unsuccessful assault on Staten Island, N.Y., 22 August 1777; fought at Brandywine and Germantown; was commander in Rhode Island, 1778, during unsuccessful Franco-American attack on Newport (29 July-31 August 1778); led expedition against the Iroquois Indians, May-November 1779; delegate to the Continental Congress, New Hampshire, 1774-1775, 1780-1781; governor of New Hampshire, 1785-1790.

**Sumner, Jethro.** c. 1735-1785. Continental officer (Brig. Gen.), planter, tavern owner, b. Virginia.

North Carolina resident; distinguished himself at Eutaw Springs, S.C., 8 September 1781; commanded Continental forces in North Carolina, 1781-1783; brigadier general, 1779-1783.

**Sumter, Thomas.** 1734-1832. Continental officer (Col.), militia officer (Brig. Gen.), storekeeper, statesman, b. near Charlottesville, Va.

Settled in South Carolina, 1765; fought as Continental officer in

Georgia and Florida, resigning in 1778; became partisan commander, 1780; noted for victories at Williamson's Plantation, S.C., 12 July 1780, and Hanging Rock, S.C., 6 August 1780; defeated by Tarleton at Fishing Creek, S.C., 18 August 1780; member, U.S. House of Representatives, 1789-1793, 1797-1801; member, U.S. Senate, 1801-1810; last surviving general of the Revolution.

**Sutherland, William.** British officer (Lt. Col.).

Took part in the Lexington and Concord expedition, April 1775; aide-de-camp and adjutant to General Henry Clinton; may have been the officer who was court-martialed for conduct at Paulus Hook, N.J., 19 August 1779; commanded a force comprising the 9th and 47th Foot in the final phase of Burgoyne's offensive, 1777.

**Swetland, Luke.** Continental soldier.

Early settler of the Wyoming Valley, Pa.; captured by Indians, he escaped a year later (1779).

**Sykes, James.** 1725-1792. American statesman, lawyer.

Delegate to the Continental Congress, Delaware, 1777-1778.

# T

**Tabb, John.** c. 1737-1798. Patriot.

Member of Virginia House of Burgesses; member of Committee of Safety, 1775-1776, and various Revolutionary conventions.

**Talbot, Silas.** 1751-1813. Continental naval officer (Capt.), Continental officer (Lt. Col.), b. Dighton, Bristol Co., Mass.

Settled in Providence, R.I., 1772; served early in Revolution as Army officer; his naval exploits, including the capture of HMS *Pigot* on the Sakonnet River, 28 September 1778, won him a commission as a Continental naval captain, 17 September 1779; no suitable Navy ship being available, he became a privateer; captured after taking one prize, he spent two years in prison; member, U.S. House of Representatives, 1793-1795; served in U.S. Navy, 1794-1801.

**Tallmadge, Benjamin, Jr.** 1754-1835. Continental officer (Lt. Col.), businessman, statesman, b. Brookhaven, N.Y.

Fought at Long Island, White Plains, Brandywine, Germantown, and Monmouth; manager of General Washington's secret service, 1778-1783; his initiative led to the exposure of Arnold's treason, 1780; commended by Congress and Washington for his work; leader of Lloyd's Neck, Long Island, N.Y., raid, 5 August 1779.

**Tarleton, Banastre.** 1754-1833. British officer (Lt. Col.), statesman, b. Liverpool, England.

Commander of the British Legion; won victories in South Carolina in 1780 at Monck's (Monk's) Corner, 14 April, Lenund's Ferry, 6 May, and the Waxhaws, 29 May; defeated Thomas Sumter at Fishing Creek, N.C., 18 August 1780; was defeated by Daniel Morgan at the Cowpens; conducted a raid on Charlottesville, Va., 4 June 1781, and another Virginia raid, 9-24 July 1781; was victor at Tarrant's Tavern, N.C., 1 February 1781; probably the British officer most hated by patriot Americans; after the war was member of Parliament, 1790-1806, 1807-1812; was appointed a full general, 1812, and created baronet, 1815.

**Tarrant, Sarah.** Patriot.

Heroine of Salem, Mass.; taunted and defied the British during the Salem raid of 26 February 1775.

**Taylor, Daniel.** British officer, British spy.

Carried message, concealed in small silver ball, from Lt. Gen. Sir Henry Clinton to Lt. Gen. John Burgoyne, October 1777; was captured near Newburgh, N.Y. and swallowed the "silver bullet"; it was recovered, however, and he was court-martialed and hanged, 16 October 1777.

**Taylor, George.** 1716-1781. American statesman, businessman, jurist, b. Ireland.

Settled in Pennsylvania about 1736; pre-Revolution patriot; supported western interests; delegate to the Continental Congress, Pennsylvania, 1776-1777; signer of the Declaration of Independence.

**Taylor, John, of Caroline.** 1753-1824. American statesman, Continental officer (Maj.), militia officer (Lt. Col.), lawyer, farmer, political theorist, writer, b. Orange Co. or Caroline Co., Va.

Continental officer serving in Virginia, New York, and Pennsylvania, 1775-1779; militia officer, 1781; member, Virginia House of Delegates, 1779-1785, 1796-1800; member, U.S. Senate, 1792-1794, 1803, 1822-1824; opposed ratification of the Federal Constitution; Jeffersonian Republican; wrote numerous works on political theory, the U.S. Federal system, and agriculture.

**Taylor, Thomas.** Militia officer (Col.).

South Carolina resident; surprised and captured British troops and supplies under Colonel Carey at Fort Carey (Wateree Ferry), S.C., 15 August 1780.

**Tazewell, Henry.** 1753-1799. American statesman, lawyer, b. Brunswick Co., Va.

Member of Committee to frame constitution and bill of rights for Virginia; member, U.S. Senate, Virginia, 1794-1799; president pro tempore of the Senate, 1795-1796.

**Teissedre de Fleury, François Louis.** b. 1749. French officer (Lt. Col.), Continental officer, b. Provence.

French volunteer; distinguished himself at Brandywine and at Stony Point, N.Y., 16 July 1779; awarded one of eight medals presented by Congress during war.

**Telfair, Edward.** 1735-1807. American statesman, merchant, landowner, b. Scotland.

Settled in Georgia, 1766, living mostly at Savannah; active pre-Revolution patriot; delegate to the Continental Congress, Georgia,

1777-1779, 1780-1783; governor of
Georgia, 1786, 1790-1793.

**Temple, Sir John.** British agent.

Came to America to act as a
secret agent for Carlisle's peace
commission, 1778.

**Ternay, Charles Louis d'Arsac,
Chevalier de.** 1722-1780. French
naval officer (admiral).

Commanded fleet that accompanied Rochambeau's expeditionary force to America, 1780; died at
Newport, 12 December 1780.

**Thacher, James.** 1754-1844. Surgeon, diarist, b. Barnstable, Mass.

Surgeon, Continental Army,
1775-1783; author of *A Military
Journal During the American
Revolutionary War*, a valuable historical source, and of many books
on medicine.

**Thatcher, Samuel.** 1732-1786.
Militia officer (Col.).

Member, Cambridge Commit-
tee of Correspondence, 1772; captain of Cambridge militia in 1775.

**Thayendanegea.** *See* Brant,
Joseph.

**Thomas, Isaiah.** 1749-1831. Patriot,
publisher, militiaman, printer, historian, b. Boston, Mass.

Founder (1770) of the *Massachusetts Spy*, a patriot newspaper;
took his press from Boston to
Worcester, 16 April 1775, to escape
the British occupation; served as
minuteman at Lexington and Concord; became successful printer,
publisher, and bookseller after the
war; spent last years as historian of
printing.

**Thomas, John.** 1724-1776. Continental officer (Maj. Gen.), surgeon,
b. Marshfield, Mass.

Was trained as a surgeon and
practiced medicine before the
Revolution; brigadier general,
1775-1776; major general, 1776; in
charge of the operation at Dorchester Heights, Mass., 2-27 March
1776; sent to take command of
disaster-ridden Quebec expedition,
March 1776; died of smallpox after
withdrawal to Sorel, 2 June 1776.

**Thomas, Tristam.** Militia officer
(Col.).

South Carolina resident; leader
in American victory at Hunt's
Bluff, S.C., 1 August 1780.

**Thompson, Benjamin; later Sir
Benjamin Thompson; Count Rum-
ford.** 1753-1814. Loyalist, physicist,
government official, British officer
(Lt. Col.), b. Woburn, Mass.

Appointed major of 2d New
Hampshire Provincial Regiment,
1772 or 1773; spied for British,
1775; went to England, 1776;
served in the British Colonial Office, 1776; was given a sinecure
position as secretary of the province of Georgia, c. 1776; under
secretary of state for the Northern
Department, 1780; fought as British officer in America, 1781-1783;
conducted scientific experiments;
known for studies on nature of
heat; knighted 1784; served as administrator for the Elector of
Bavaria, 1784-1795; count of the
Holy Roman Empire.

**Thompson, William.** 1736-1781.
Continental officer (Brig. Gen.), b.
Ireland.

Settled near Carlisle, Pa.; fought in French and Indian War; served on local committees of correspondence and safety; raised and commanded Thompson's Rifle Battalion (later 1st Continental Infantry), 1775-1776; commanded American counterattack on Lechmere Point, Mass., 9 November 1775; commanded disastrous attack at Trois Rivières, Canada, 8 June 1776.

**Thompson, William.** d. 1796. Continental officer (Col.).

Received thanks of Congress for his conduct in the defense of Charleston, S.C., 28 June 1776; South Carolina resident.

**Thomson, Charles.** 1729-1824. American statesman, teacher, merchant, biblical scholar, b. County Derry, Ireland.

Brought to Pennsylvania as a child; leading pre-Revolution Philadelphia patriot; secretary of the Continental Congress, 1774-1789; spent last years translating Bible from the Greek.

**Thornton, Matthew.** c.1714-1803. American statesman, physician, b. Ireland.

Came with his parents to New England as a child; active in New Hampshire politics from 1758; delegate to the Continental Congress, New Hampshire, 1776-1778; signer of the Declaration of Independence.

**Thornton, Presley P.** d. 1811. Continental officer (Lt. Col.), b. Northumberland Co., Va.

Aide-de-camp to George Washington, 1777.

**Thruston, Charles Mynn.** 1738-1812. Continental officer (Col.), clergyman, judge, statesman, b. Virginia.

Episcopal clergyman; raised a company at the beginning of the war; colonel of a Continental regiment, 1777-1779; wounded at Trenton; lost an arm at Amboy, N.J., 8 March 1777.

**Thurlow, Edward, first Baron Thurlow.** 1731-1806. British statesman, b. Bracon Ash, Norfolk, England.

Became Attorney General of Great Britain, 1771; became Lord Chancellor and was created baronet, 1778; an active Tory who remained as Chancellor when the Whig ministry of Rockingham took office.

**Thynne, Thomas, third Viscount Weymouth.** 1734-1796. British statesman.

Secretary of State for the Northern Department, 1768; Secretary of State for the Southern Department, 1768-1770, 1775-1779; Tory; strong supporter of the King.

**Tilghman, Matthew.** 1718-1777. American statesman, jurist, planter, b. "Hermitage," near Centerville, Queen Annes Co., Md.

Wealthy landholder; early patriot and advocate of independence; delegate to the Continental Congress, Maryland, 1774-1777, but absent when Declaration of Independence was voted on and when it was signed; president of convention that drafted the first

Maryland constitution, 1776; uncle and father-in-law of Tench Tilghman.

**Tilghman, Tench.** 1744-1786. Continental officer (Lt. Col.), merchant, b. Talbot Co., Md.

Aide-de-camp to George Washington, 1776-1783; given honor of taking news of Yorktown victory to Congress; nephew and son-in-law of Matthew Tilghman.

**Tonyn, Patrick.** 1725-1804. British officer (Maj. Gen.), government official.

Governor of East Florida, 1774-1783.

**Townsend, Robert.** Merchant, journalist, American spy.

Resident of New York City; used code name "Culper, Jr."; with Samuel Woodhull, formed highly successful Culpers spy team; sent intelligence reports from Manhattan to Woodhull on Long Island, usually by the courier Austin Roe; most impressive accomplishment was stealing and successfully transmitting the British Navy's signal book.

**Townshend, Charles.** 1725-1767. British statesman.

Chancellor of the Exchequer, 1766-1767; author of the Townshend Acts of 1767, a precipitating force in the American Revolution.

**Trapier, Paul.** 1749-1778. American statesman, b. Prince George's Parish, near Georgetown, S.C.

Delegate to the Continental Congress, South Carolina, 1777-1778.

**Trescott, Lemuel.** d. 1826. Continental officer (Maj.).

Massachusetts resident; led the raid to Treadwell's Neck, Long Island, N.Y., 10 October 1781.

**Trevett, John.** 1747-1823. Continental marine officer (Capt.).

Commanded shore party in Capt. John Peck Rathbun's raid on Nassau, January 1778.

**Tronson de Coudray, Philippe Charles Jean Baptiste.** 1738-1777. French officer (Chef de Brigade), Continental officer (Maj. Gen.), b. Reims.

As French officer, assembled French materiel and advisors for American use before the alliance; as a foreign volunteer, commissioned major general, Continental Army, 1777; appointment brought resentment and threats of resignation from senior American officers who had been passed over; drowned accidentally, 1777.

**Trumbull, Benjamin.** 1735-1820. Clergyman, historian, militia officer (Capt.), b. Hebron, Conn.

Pastor of Congregational Church, New Haven, Conn., 1760-1820; served as chaplain, June-December 1776; elected captain of company of volunteers, 1776; wrote several useful histories of Connecticut; cousin of the Jonathan Trumbull family.

**Trumbull, John.** 1750-1831. Poet, lawyer, jurist, b. Westbury (now Watertown), Conn.

Wrote the comic epic, *M'Fingal* (1775-1776), the narrative of a Tory squire's misfortunes; a leader of the literary group called the Hartford Wits in the 1780's and 1790's; Federalist in politics; held Connecticut state judgeships, 1801-1819; cousin of the Jonathan Trumbull family.

**Trumbull, John.** 1756-1843. Continental officer (Col.), painter, b. Lebanon, Conn.

Son of Jonathan Trumbull the elder; aide-de-camp to General Washington, 1775; brigade major, 1775-1776; saw action at Dorchester Heights, March 1776; served as colonel and deputy adjutant general under Maj. Gen. Horatio Gates at Crown Point, N.Y., and Ticonderoga, N.Y.; served under Brig. Gen. Benedict Arnold in Rhode Island; left army, February 1777, but served as volunteer aide-de-camp to Maj. Gen. John Sullivan, 1778; went to London, with British permission, 1780, to study painting with Benjamin West; after the Revolution made 250-300 paintings of Revolutionary battles and other scenes, notably "The Declaration of Independence," and of leading Revolutionary figures.

**Trumbull, Jonathan, the elder.** 1710-1785. American statesman, merchant, b. Lebanon, Conn.

Governor of Connecticut, 1769-1784; supported colonial protests and favored independence; made valuable contributions in supplying Continental troops with food, clothing, and munitions.

**Trumbull, Jonathan, the younger.** 1740-1809. Continental officer (Lt. Col.), statesman, b. Lebanon, Conn.

Paymaster general of the Northern Department, 1775-1778; comptroller of the treasury, 1778-1781; secretary to George Washington (succeeding Alexander Hamilton), 1781-1783; member, U.S. House of Representatives, 1789-1795; speaker of the House, 1791-1793; member, U.S. Senate, 1794-1796; son of Jonathan Trumbull the elder; brother of John Trumbull the painter and of Joseph Trumbull.

**Trumbull, Joseph.** 1738-1778. Continental officer (Col.), merchant, b. Lebanon, Conn.

Commissary general of Connecticut troops, 1775; commissary general of the Army, 1775-1777; delegate to the Continental Congress, 1774-1775; son of Jonathan Trumbull the elder; brother of John Trumbull the painter and of Jonathan Trumbull the younger.

**Tryon, William.** 1725- or 1729-1788. British government official, British officer (Lt. Gen., local rank), b. "Norbury Park," Surrey, England.

Royal lieutenant governor of North Carolina, 1764-1765; royal governor of North Carolina, 1765-1771; suppressed the Regulator movement, ultimately defeating the Regulators at the battle of Alamance, 16 May 1771; royal governor of New York, 1771-1775; served in Revolution as British officer commanding loyalist troops; as colonel, led the Danbury (Conn.) raid, April 1777; destroyed the patriot camp and supply depot called Continental Village, near Peeksville, N.Y., October 1777; led the Connecticut coast raid, July 1779; major general, 1778; lieutenant general, 1782.

**Tucker, St. George.** 1752-1827. Militia officer (Col.), lawyer, jurist, b. Port Royal, Bermuda.

Came to Virginia about 1770; distinguished himself at Guilford Courthouse; also served at Yorktown; professor of law at William and Mary from 1800; held several judicial posts from 1803, including Federal district judge, 1813-1827.

**Tuffin, Charles-Armand, Marquis de la Rouerie.** *See* Armand, Charles.

**Tupper, Benjamin.** 1738-1792. Continental officer (Col.), teacher, surveyor, pioneer, b. Stoughton, Mass.

Veteran of French and Indian War; led the highly successful raid on Great Brewster Island, Mass., 4 November 1775; attacked British ships that penetrated to Tappan Sea (now Tappan Zee), N.Y., 12-18 July 1776; participated in Saratoga and Monmouth campaigns; helped defend Springfield, Mass., against Shays's Rebellion, 1786; leader in formation of Ohio Company and settlement of Ohio.

**Turgot, Anne-Robert Jacques, Baron.** French official.

Comptroller General of Finances; disapproved of aid to the Americans.

**Turnbull, George.** Loyalist officer.

New York resident; commanded a battalion of DeLancey's New York Volunteers; sent out expedition to Williamson's Plantation, S.C., 12 July 1780; held out against Thomas Sumter's attack on Rocky Mount, S.C., 1 August 1780.

**Turner, George.** d. 1781. Militia officer (Capt.).

South Carolina resident; killed in "massacre" at Cloud's Creek, S.C., 9 November 1781, by a Tory unit under "Bloody Bill" Cunningham.

**Twiggs, John.** Militia officer (Brig. Gen.).

Brigadier general of Georgia militia; defeated British at Hickory Hill, Ga., 28 June 1779.

# V

**Van Buskirk, Abram.** Loyalist officer (Lt. Col.).

Served in the loyalist brigade of Cortlandt Skinner; attempted to halt Henry Lee's raid at Paulus Hook, N.J., 19 August 1779.

**Van Cortland, Philip.** 1749-1831. Continental officer (Col.), statesman, civil engineer, surveyor, b. New York, N.Y.

Commander of 2d New York Regiment, 1776-1783; breveted brigadier general (1783) for his performance at Yorktown, 1781; active in politics after the war; favored ratification of the Federal Constitution, but became an Anti-Federalist; served in the U.S. House of Representatives, 1793-1809.

**Van der Capellen tot den Poll, Johan Derck.** Dutch statesman.

Member of the provincial assembly of Overyssel; proponent of the American cause; maintained political correspondence with Governors Trumbull and Livingston.

**Vanderhovan, John.** American spy.

Effective spy who worked with the Hendricks brothers in the New York spy network headed by Col. Elias Dayton; directed the work of at least four assistants.

**Vay Dyke, Nicholas.** 1738-1789. American statesman, lawyer, b. New Castle, Del.

Moderate Whig before the Revolution; delegate to the Continental Congress, Delaware, 1777-1782; president (chief executive) of Delaware, 1783-1786.

**Van Rensselaer, Robert.** d. 1802. Militia officer (Brig. Gen.).

Brigadier general, New York militia; in action at Fort Keyser, N.Y., 19 October 1780.

**Van Schaak, Peter.** 1747-1832. Loyalist, lawyer, b. Kinderhook, N.Y.

Member, New York Committee of 51, 1774; member, Committee of 60, 1774; member, Committee of 100, 1775; elected to Kinderhook Committee of Safety, 1775; opposed taking up arms against Britain; was expelled from the committee and spent the war in England; returned to Kinderhook in 1785, and taught and practiced law.

**Van Schaick, Gosen (Goose).** 1736-1789. Continental officer (Col.), b. Albany, N.Y.

Active throughout war on the New York frontiers; led a successful raid on the Onandaga Indians, 20 April 1779, as part of Sullivan's expedition.

**Van Wart, Isaac.** 1760-1828. Patriot, farmer.

New York resident; a captor of Maj. John André, 1780; received a medal from Congress, 1780.

**Vardill, John.** 1749-1811. Loyalist, clergyman, educator, b. New York, N.Y.

Professor of natural law and moral philosophy at King's College (now Columbia University), 1773, at the age of 21; under the pseudonym "Poplicola" wrote several Tory pamphlets; served the British as a secret agent in Paris, and was able to examine correspondence between the American commissioners.

**Varick, Richard.** 1753-1831. Continental officer (Lt. Col.), statesman, b. Hackensack, N.J.

Private Secretary to George Washington, 1781-1783; mayor of New York City, 1789-1801.

**Varnum, James M.** 1748-1789. Continental officer (Brig. Gen.), militia officer (Maj. Gen.), lawyer, statesman, b. Dracut, Mass.

Served as colonel at siege of Boston, 1775, and in battles of Long Island and White Plains; brigadier general, 1777-1779; responsible for defense of Fort Mercer, N.J., and Fort Mifflin, Pa., 1777, at time of their loss; took active part in Monmouth campaign; delegate to the Continental Congress, 1780-1782, 1786-1787.

**Vaughan, John.** 1748?-1795. British officer (Maj. Gen).

Commander of the grenadiers in the battle of Long Island; captured Fort Montgomery, N.Y., 6 October 1777, during Clinton's expedition to the Hudson Highlands; returned to England, 1779, and became commander-in-chief of the Leeward Islands, West Indies.

**Vauguyon, Duc de la.** French diplomat.

Ambassador to the Netherlands during the American Revolution; worked successfully to have the Dutch maintain strict neutrality, as the French defined it (1779); this meant persuading the Dutch to protect with warships their merchant vessels carrying naval stores for French use.

**Vence, Jean Gaspard.** 1747-1808. French privateer, naval officer, b. Marseilles.

Operated in the West Indies during the Revolution; became an admiral, 1793.

**Vergennes, Charles Gravier, Comte de.** 1717-1787. French statesman, b. Dijon.

French Foreign Minister; instrumental in creating the alliance between the United States and France.

**Vernier, Pierre-François.** 1736- or 1737-1780. Continental officer (Maj.), b. Belfort, France.

Officer in Pulaski's Legion; mortally wounded at battle of Monck's Corner, S.C., 14 April 1780.

**Vigo, Francis (Joseph Maria Francesco).** 1747-1836. Italian trader, b. Mondevì, Piedmont.

Established his trading headquarters at St. Louis, c.1772; sympathized with patriot cause; gave George Rogers Clark information about the British defenses at Vincennes that led to its capture,

1779; also gave Clark much-needed financial help.

**Vose, Joseph.** 1738-1816. Continental officer (Col.), b. Mass.

Distinguished himself at the raid on Great Brewster Island, Mass., 21 July 1775.

# W

**Wadsworth, Jeremiah.** 1743-1804. American statesman, businessman, seaman, b. Hartford, Conn.

Commissary General of the Continental Army, 1778-1779, succeeding Joseph Trumbull; delegate to the Continental Congress, 1787-1788; worked for ratification of the Federal Constitution as member of the Connecticut convention on ratification; successful in the insurance and wool manufacturing business.

**Wadsworth, Peleg.** 1748-1829. Militia officer (Brig. Gen.), merchant, landowner, b. Duxbury, Mass.

Brigadier general, Massachusetts militia, 1777-1782; a leader in the Penobscot (Me.) expedition, 19 July–24 August 1779; member, U.S. House of Representatives, Massachusetts (representing Maine), 1793-1807.

**Walker, Benjamin.** Continental officer (Lt. Col.).

New York resident; aide-de-camp to George Washington, 1782-1783.

**Walker, John.** d. 1809. Continental officer (Lt. Col.).

North Carolina resident; aide-de-camp to George Washington, 1777.

**Walker, Thomas.** 1715-1794. Patriot, physician, soldier, explorer, landowner, b. King and Queen Co., Va.

Surveyor, explorer, and land speculator before the Revolution; commissary general for Virginia troops in French and Indian War; member, House of Burgesses, 1756-1761; from 1769 was active in patriot movement; member, Virginia Committee of Safety, 1776; member, State Executive Council, 1776.

**Wallace, Sir James.** 1731-1803. British naval officer (Capt.).

Commanded HMS *Rose* (20), 1771–July 1776; 1776-1779, commander of the *Experiment* (50); 20 August 1778, in order to escape capture by the French off Newport, took his ship through Hell Gate, Long Island Sound, a navigation feat considered impossible for a ship of its size; became an admiral, 1808.

**Wallis, Samuel.** d.1798. Loyalist, secret agent, shipper, speculator, b. Maryland.

Pennsylvania resident; drew up a false map of the Iroquois country for Sullivan's expedition, May-November 1779; dealt with John André and George Beckwith; his treachery was not known until the 20th Century.

**Walter, William.** 1739-1800. Loyalist, clergyman, b. Massachusetts.

Reactor of Trinity Church, Boston, 1763-1776.

**Walpole, Horatio (baptized Horace).** 1717-1797. British historian, statesman, b. London.

Member of Parliament; kept a very full diary; publications from it include *Memoirs of the Reign of King George III* (4 vols., 1845) and *Reminiscences* (1819); regarded as one of the great English letter writers.

**Walton, George.** 1750-1804. American statesman, lawyer, b. Farmville, Cumberland Co., Va.

Delegate to the Continental Congress, Georgia, 1776-1779, 1780-1781; signer of the Declaration of Independence; governor of Georgia, 1779, 1789; member, U.S. Senate, 1795-1796.

**Wanton, Joseph.** 1705-1780. Loyalist.

Royal governor of Rhode Island, 1769-1775; deposed by the Assembly, 7 November 1775.

**Ward, Artemas.** 1727-1800. Militia officer, Continental officer (Maj. Gen.), statesman, jurist, b. Shrewsbury, Mass.

Major general, 1775-1776; commander-in-chief of troops in Massachusetts, 1775; commander, from his post at Cambridge, of the battle of Bunker Hill; delegate to the Continental Congress, 1780-1781; House of Representatives, 1791-1795.

**Ward, Samuel.** 1725-1776. American statesman, farmer, b. Newport, R.I.

Royal governor of Rhode Island, 1762, 1763, 1765-1767; delegate to the Continental Congress, Rhode Island, 1774-1776.

**Ward, Samuel, Jr.** 1756-1832. Continental officer (Lt. Col), merchant, b. Westerly, R.I.

Served in various campaigns, 1775-1781; promoted to lieutenant colonel after serving at Newport, R.I., July-August, 1778; prominent merchant and businessman after the war.

**Warner, Seth.** 1743-1784. Continental officer (Col.), militia officer (Brig. Gen.), b. Woodbury (now Roxbury), Conn.

Moved to Bennington, Vt., 1763; a leader of the Green Mountain Boys, originally under Ethan Allen; aided in the capture of Fort Ticonderoga, N.Y., 10 May 1775; occupied Crown Point, N.Y., 12 May 1775; elected commander of the Green Mountain Boys when they became a Continental unit; led them in invasion of Canada, under Maj. Gen. Richard Montgomery, 1775; fought at Longueil, near Montreal, 25 September 1775; fought effective rear-guard action at Hubbardtown, Vt., 7 July 1777; played important role at battle of Bennington, 16 August 1777; brigadier general in the Vermont militia, 1778.

**Warren, James.** 1726-1808. American statesman, merchant, farmer, b. Plymouth, Mass.

Paymaster General of the Continental Army, 1775-1776; member of the Navy Board, 1776-1781; member of Massachusetts legislature repeatedly during 1770's; held various state offices after the war.

**Warren, John.** 1753-1815. Surgeon, b. Roxbury, Mass.

Continental Army surgeon; served as senior surgeon of the hospital at Cambridge, Mass.;

served as surgeon at the general hospital on Long Island, N.Y., 1776; leading New England surgeon of his day; a founder of the Harvard Medical School; younger brother of Joseph Warren.

**Warren, Joseph.** 1741-1775. Physician, writer, orator, militia officer (Maj. Gen.), b. Roxbury, Mass.

Active in Stamp Act protest, 1765; leading Massachusetts patriot; drafted Suffolk Resolves, September 1774; sent Paul Revere and William Dawes to warn patriots at Concord, 18 April 1775; president of the Provincial Council of Massachusetts, 23 April 1775, succeeding John Hancock; major general of Massachusetts militia; killed at battle of Bunker Hill; brother of John Warren.

**Warren, Mercy Otis.** 1728-1814. Historian, poet, dramatist, b. Barnstable, Mass.

Wrote a history of the Revolutionary War; wife of James Warren; sister of James Otis.

**Washington, George.** 1732-1799. Continental General and Commander-in-Chief, militia officer (Col.), statesman, surveyor, landowner, planter, b. Westmoreland Co., Va.

Washington, a successful surveyor and landowner at 21, was commissioned major of Virginia militia in 1753. He undertook a mission to the French commander at Fort Le Boeuf that winter for Governor Dinwiddie of Virginia, returning to alert the governor to French preparations for war (the French and Indian War). Promoted to lieutenant colonel, he was sent the following spring to reinforce frontier militiamen at the Forks of the Ohio (site of present-day Pittsburgh), but was forestalled by the French, who had established Fort Duquesne on the site. In the first action of the French and Indian War, he was overwhelmed by a much larger French force and surrendered Fort Necessity.

Serving with General Edward Braddock on the disastrous expedition of 1755, Washington helped rally the survivors of the battle of the Monongahela and bring them back safely. He was then promoted to colonel, made commander of all Virginia militia, and spent the rest of the French and Indian War protecting the Virginia frontier from Indian attack.

A member of the House of Burgesses, 1759-1774, Washington favored military preparations to protect colonists' rights as tensions grew in 1774. He was a delegate to the First and Second Continental Congresses (1774, 1775), and on 15 June 1775 was unanimously elected by Congress as "General and Commander-in-Chief of the army of the United Colonies."

After forcing the British to evacuate Boston (March 1776), Washington was ordered by Congress to hold New York, an impossible task. He made serious errors in defending Long Island (August 1776), but skillfully managed the withdrawal after that defeat, and the long retreat, punctuated by battles, up Manhattan and through Westchester and New Jersey. Particularly brilliant and daring were his strikes back across the Delaware

River against Trenton (25-26 December 1776) and Princeton (3 January 1777), triumphs of tactics, logistics, and morale maintenance under overwhelming difficulties. Recognizing the limitations of British seapower and the vulnerability of Burgoyne's army in 1777, Washington had many of his best units and commanders transferred to the Northern Theater. Because of this, and his own errors, he was defeated at Brandywine (11 September 1777), withdrew from Philadelphia (26 September 1777), and was defeated again at Germantown (4 October 1777). Washington then withdrew to winter at Valley Forge, Pa., where his men suffered severely but were effectively drilled by General von Steuben.

Meanwhile, thanks to his strategy, and the reinforcements he sent to Gates's command in the north, Burgoyne had been defeated at Saratoga by Gates and Arnold. Saratoga made certain France's entry on the American side and turned the tide of the Revolution. The next year Washington salvaged the battle of Monmouth Courthouse, after Maj. Gen. Charles Lee's mismanagement had caused near disaster. The main action of the war then shifted to the south, where Washington exercised overall strategic supervision after Gates's defeat at Camden.

In 1781 Washington again saw a strategic opportunity when French seapower briefly overbalanced that of Britain, and another British army appeared vulnerable. With the French,

Washington planned and executed a coordinated land and sea envelopment of General Cornwallis's British army at Yorktown, August-October 1781. The war was won, with major credit properly going to Washington's skillful strategic management of what was fundamentally a defensive, delaying conflict; to his superb tactics on crucial occasions; and to his inspirational leadership. The peace treaty was signed on 3 September 1783, and, resigning his commission (23 December 1783), Washington retired to Mount Vernon, his home near Alexandria, Va.

Washington was among those favoring a stronger federal union for the nation, was a delegate to the convention at Philadelphia that became the Federal Constitutional Convention (1787), and was chosen its presiding officer. When the new government was organized, in 1789, he was the electors' unanimous choice to be the first President of the United States. As President, he supported the financial policies of Alexander Hamilton and other measures aimed at strengthening the federal government. He firmly suppressed the Whiskey Insurrection of 1794; supported Jay's Treaty, 1794; steered clear of the European wars that had grown out of the French Revolution; developed the U.S. cabinet system; and tried to balance conflicting political views by having both Anti-Federalist Thomas Jefferson and Federalist Alexander Hamilton in his cabinet. Re-elected in 1792, he refused to stand for re-election in 1796, retiring to Mount Vernon. When war with France threatened in 1798, an increased army was hastily authorized by Congress and Washington was appointed, first, "Lieutenant General and Commander-in-Chief of all armies of the United States" (4 July 1798) and, later (3 March 1799), "General of the Armies of the United States."* The threat of war waning, he returned home again to his final retirement, dying late that same year.

**Washington, William.** 1752-1810. Continental officer (Col.), statesman, b. Virginia.

Wounded at Long Island; played significant role at Trenton; as a cavalry (dragoon) commander, fought Tarleton in South Carolina, 1780; won impressive victories at Rugeley's Mill (Mills), S.C., 4 December 1780, and in his Hammond's Store (S.C.), raid, 27-31 December 1780; fought well at Cowpens, Guilford Courthouse, and Hobkirk's Hill, S.C. (25 April 1781); wounded and captured at Eutaw Springs, S.C., 8 September 1781; a cousin of George Washington.

**Watson, Abraham.** 1729-1781. Surgeon, statesman.

Surgeon, Continental Army; member, Cambridge (Mass.) Committee of Correspondence and Massachusetts Provincial Congress.

*He never assumed this later title, authorized by Congress in the event of declared war with France.

**Wayne, Anthony ("Mad Anthony").** 1745-1796. Continental officer (Brig. Gen.), tanner, surveyor, b. Chester Co., Pa.

Brigadier general, 1777-1783; commander of the Pennsylvania Line at Brandywine; was surprised at Paoli, Pa., 21 September 1777, by Maj. Gen. Charles Grey, but was acquitted of negligence; prominent at Germantown; helped Washington salvage victory from defeat at Monmouth Courthouse; won impressive victory at Stony Point, N.Y., 16 July 1779; handled mutiny of the Pennsylvania Line, 1-10 January 1781; won further distinction, despite defeat by overwhelming odds, at Jamestown Ford, Va., July 6, 1781; served at Yorktown; member, U.S. House of Representatives, Georgia, 1791-1792; major general and commander-in-chief of the U.S. Army in the northwest, 1792-1796; victorious at the battle of Fallen Timbers, 20 August 1794.

**Webb, Samuel B.** 1753-1807. Continental officer (Col.), b. Connecticut.

Stepson of Silas Deane and his secretary in the patriot activist period before the Revolution; wounded at Bunker Hill; aide-de-camp to George Washington, 1776-1777.

**Wedderburn, Alexander.** 1773-1805. British statesman, b. Edinburgh, Scotland.

Member of Parliament, 1774-1778; British Solicitor General, 1771-1778; Lord Chancellor, 1793; drafted conciliatory bills, passed by Parliament, March 1778, that provided for repeal of the Massa-chusetts Act of 1774, prohibited Parliament from imposing any duty, tax, or assesment on any of the colonies, provided for a commissioner to meet with any body or assembly in America, and suspended all acts passed since 1763 that related to the American colonies.

**Weedon, George.** c. 1730-1793. Continental officer (Brig. Gen.), innkeeper, b. Fredericksburg, Va.

As colonel, took part in New York and New Jersey campaigns of 1776-1777; brigadier general, 1777-1783; acting adjutant general, 1777; played key role at Brandywine; fought at Germanton; participated in Yorktown campaign.

**Weissenstein, Charles de.**

Pseudonym of a person, probably a private meddler with no official connections, who surreptitiously communicated suggested peace terms to Benjamin Franklin in Paris in 1778.

**Wemyss, James.** British officer (Capt.).

Commanded the Queen's Tory Rangers at Brandywine; active in the south, 1780; much hated by southern patriots; defeated, wounded, and captured at Fishdam Ford, S.C., 9 November 1780.

**Wentworth, John.** 1737-1820. Loyalist, merchant, British government official, b. Portsmouth, N.H.

Last royal governor of New Hampshire, 1767-1775; lieutenant governor of Nova Scotia, 1792-1808; created baronet, 1795.

**Wentworth, John, Jr.** 1745-1787. American statesman, lawyer, b. Salmon Falls, Strafford Co., N.H.

Delegate to the Continental Congress, New Hampshire, 1778-1779; probably distantly related to Governor John Wentworth.

**Wentworth, Paul.** d. 1793. Loyalist, British agent, planter, stock jobber.

Probably member of prominent Wentworth family of New Hampshire; had large landholdings in West Indies; was chief loyalist secret agent in London during the war; was given a seat in Parliament, which he held only six weeks, as a reward.

**Weymouth, Viscount.** *See* Thynne, Thomas, third Viscount Weymouth.

**Wharton, Samuel.** 1732-1800. American statesman, merchant, land speculator, jurist, b. Philadelphia, Pa.

Engaged in land promotion enterprises in England at outbreak of war; returned to America in 1779 or 1780; delegate to the Continental Congress, Delaware, 1782-1783; served as justice of the peace and judge after the war.

**Wheatley, Phyllis.** c.1753-1784. Poet, b. Africa.

Miss Wheatley was a Negro living in Massachusetts. Among her many works was a poem written in tribute to George Washington, which she sent him and which he graciously acknowledged.

**Wheaton, Joseph.** b. c.1755. Patriot, b. New York.

At Machias, Me., 12 June 1775, along with Jeremiah O'Brien, captured the British armed cutter *Margaretta.*

**Whipple, Abraham.** 1735-1819. Continental naval officer (Capt., Commodore), seaman, b. Providence, R.I.

Leader of the patriot force in the *Gaspée* affair, 1772; one of first Continental naval officers; active and successful until captured at fall of Charleston, S.C., 1779; pioneered to Ohio after the war.

**Whipple, William.** 1730-1785. American statesman, seaman, merchant, b. Kittery, Me. (then Massachusetts).

Seaman and slave trader in youth; became merchant, 1760; early patriot; delegate to the Continental Congress, New Hampshire, 1776-1779; signer of the Declaration of Independence; served as member of state Legislature and judge after the war.

**Whitcomb, John.** 1713-1783. Militia officer (Maj. Gen.).

Participated at Lexington and Concord; commanded at Lechmere Point in battle of Bunker Hill; major general of Massachusetts militia, 1776.

**Whitcuff, Benjamin.** British spy.

Free Negro; resident of Long Island, N.Y., at beginning of Revolution; spied for the British in New Jersey, beginning in 1776 or 1777 and continuing for two years; reportedly was captured and hanged but cut down by rescuing British troops and not killed; his father served in the American Army.

**White, John.** Continental officer (Col.)

Fought at Medway Church, Ga., 24 November 1778; North Carolina resident.

**White Eyes.** d. 1778. American Indian chief.

Leader of Delaware tribe; conciliatory toward white settlers; maintained neutrality during Lord Dunmore's War, 1774; remained neutral in Revolution, almost alone among Indian leaders; guided Americans toward Detroit, 1778; murdered by American soldiers.

**Whitefoord, Caleb.** 1734-1810. British diplomat, b. Edinburgh, Scotland.

Friend of Benjamin Franklin; secretary to the British commission at the Paris Peace Conference, 1783; served as an intermediary between Franklin and the British Government, 1782.

**Wickes, Lambert.** c.1742-1777. Ship's master, Continental naval officer (Capt.), b. Eastern Neck Island, Kent Co., Md.

Given command of Continental brig *Reprisal* (16), 1776; took three prizes on his first cruise and defeated HMS *Shark* (16), off Saint Pierre, Martinique; conveyed Benjamin Franklin to France, October-November 1776, taking two prizes on the voyage; the first Continental naval officer to operate in European waters, he took five British prizes in the English Channel, January 1777; commanding three vessels, carried out successful raiding mission in Irish Sea, capturing 18 small merchant vessels; by brilliant seamanship, escaped British ship of the line *Burford* (74) on return voyage to France; lost at sea off Newfoundland, October 1777.

**Wilkes, John.** 1727-1797. British statesman, journalist, b. Clerkenwell, England.

Member of Parliament; a leader of the opposition to George III and Lord Bute, Prime Minister, 1763; helped found *The North Briton*, which printed strong criticism of the King; arrested and subjected to police action that raised issues of habeas corpus and search and arrest procedures; expelled from the House of Commons, 1764; later repeatedly reelected to Parliament and other offices; became popular hero and symbol of "rights of Englishmen"; also became a symbol of the American cause; remained opposed to the policies of George III throughout the Revolution; shares with Isaac Barré the honor both of having Wilkes-Barre, Pa., named for him and of being one of the two men most disliked by George III.

**Wilkinson, James.** 1757-1825. Continental officer (Brevet Brig. Gen.). trader, politician, b. Benedict, Md.

Participated in Quebec expedition, 1775-1776; served as aide-de-camp to Brig. Gen. Benedict Arnold, 1776; served as aide-de-camp to Maj. Gen. Horatio Gates at the second battle of Saratoga; brevet brigadier general, 1777-1778, a rank to which he was promoted solely because he carried to Congress Gates's dispatch reporting Burgoyne's surrender; re-signed, 1778; clothier general of the Continental Army, 1779; re-signed again because of financial irregularities; brigadier general and second-in-command to Maj. Gen. Anthony Wayne in Indian fighting, 1792; succeeded Wayne as senior officer and nominal com-mander-in-chief, 1796; governor of Louisiana, 1805; involved in Aaron Burr's conspiracy, but acquitted by a series of courts-martial; still commanding general of the army at the outset of the War of 1812, he was promoted to major general (1813) and served with his custom-ary lack of distinction; acquitted by a court of inquiry investigating charges of misconduct, 1815; honorably discharged, 1815; docu-ments in Spanish archives later revealed that he was an agent in the pay of the Spanish Govern-ment during the time he com-manded the United States Army; known as the general who "never won a battle and never lost a court-martial."

**Willett, Marinus.** 1740-1830. Con-tinental officer (Col.), merchant, landowner, b. New York, N.Y.

Served in French and Indian War; Son of Liberty; helped foil a Tory plan to take arms from New York City, 6 June 1775; served under Maj. Gen. Richard Mont-gomery in Canada invasion, 1775; led many campaigns in New York against Tories and Indians, 1776-1783.

**William V of Orange.** 1748-1806. Prince of Orange, Stadholder (chief executive) of the Dutch re-public.

Nephew of George III; per-sonally sympathetic toward British, but unable to keep the Netherlands from going to war against Great Britain, 1780-1784.

**Williams, David.** 1754-1831. Mili-tia soldier, farmer.

A captor of John André; received a medal from Congress, 1780; New York resident.

**Williams, James.** d.1780. Militia officer (Col.).

A leader at the battle of Kings Mountain; mortally wounded in the battle; South Carolina resident.

**Williams, John.** 1731-1799. Amer-ican statesman, lawyer, b. Hanover Co., Va.

Delegate to the Continental Congress, North Carolina, 1778-1779.

**Williams, John Foster.** 1743-1814. State naval officer, privateer, b. Boston, Mass.

Commanded ships of the Mas-sachusetts navy throughout the Re-volution; commanding the *Protec-tor* (26), sank the British privateer *Admiral Duff* (32) off the New-foundland coast, 9 June 1780; after the war, commanded a U.S. revenue cutter, 1790-1814.

**Williams, Otho Holland.** 1749-1794. Continental officer (Brig. Gen.), b. Prince Georges Co., Md.

Brigadier general, 1782-1783; served with distinction in southern campaigns under de Kalb, Gates, and Greene, 1780-1781; led Ameri-cans in skirmish with Cornwallis at Wetzell's (or Whitsall's) Mills, N.C., 6 March 1781.

**Williams,    William.**    1731-1811.
American statesman, militia offi-
cer (Col.), merchant, b. Lebanon,
Conn.

Held numerous local and state
offices; gave considerable financial support to the Revolution; resigned militia commission, 1776,
to sit in Congress; delegate to the
Continental Congress, Connecticut, 1776-1778, 1783-1784; signer of
the Declaration of Independence.

**Williamson,    Andrew.**    c.1730-
1786. Militia officer (Brig. Gen.),
cow driver, planter, woodsman,
b. Scotland.

Saw action at Ninety-Six, S.C.,
19-21 November 1775; led forces
responding to Cherokee uprising
in Cherokee War of 1776; state
brigadier general, 1778; with his
militia, refused to participate in
the Charleston campaign, 1780;
escaped to the British, after being
imprisoned; did, however, pass on
information to the Americans
through Colonel John Laurens;
was allowed to live in South Carolina after the war.

**Williamson,    Hugh.**    1735-1819.
American statesman, b. Oterara
Creek, West Nottingham Town-
ship, Pa.

Delegate to the Continental
Congress, North Carolina, 1782-
1785, 1787-1788; member, U.S.
House of Representatives, 1789-
1793.

**Willing, James.** Patriot.

Agent for Commerce Committee
of Congress; led a raid down
the Mississippi River, January-
May 1778, in a river boat called the
*Rattletrap*, striking at Tory planters

and British commerce; antagonized
many non-Tories by his men's
indiscriminate looting.

**Willing,    Thomas.**    1731-1821.
American statesman, merchant,
jurist, b. Philadelphia, Pa.

Business partner of Robert
Morris; delegate to the Continental Congress, Pennsylvania, 1775-
1776; voted against independence;
chosen president of the Bank of
North America, 1781; favored
adoption of the Federal Constitution; president of the Bank of the
United States, 1791-1797.

**Wilmot,    William.**    d.1782. Continental officer (Capt.), b. Maryland.

Defeated the British in one of
the last actions of the war at Johns
Island, S.C., November 1782;
killed in the action.

**Wilson, James.** 1742-1798. American statesman, Latin tutor, land
speculator, writer, lawyer, jurist,
b. Scotland.

Came to America, 1765; chairman, Carlisle, Pa., Committee of
Correspondence, 1774; author of
widely read pamphlet urging
American independence within
the British Empire, 1774; delegate
to the Continental Congress, Pennsylvania, 1775-1776, 1782-1783,
1785-1787; opposed Declaration
of Independence but signed it;
Associate Justice of the U.S. Supreme Court, 1789-1798.

**Winslow,    Edward.**    1745-1815.
Loyalist officer (Col.).

Muster-master-general of loyalist forces; Massachusetts resident.

**Winston, Joseph.** 1746-1815. Militia officer (Maj.), public official, b. Louisa Co., Va.

A leader in the battle of Kings Mountain.

**Wisner, Henry.** 1720-1790. American statesman, farmer, powder manufacturer, b. Orange Co., N.Y.

Delegate to the Continental Congress, New York, 1774-1776; at outbreak of Revolution owned one of only two powdermills in New York; expanded production and made strong ånd successful efforts, and financial contributions, to provide enough powder for the armies.

**Witherspoon, John.** 1723-1794. Clergyman, educator, statesman, b. Yester, near Edinburgh, Scotland.

Prominent clergyman in Scotland; came to America, 1768, to be president of the College of New Jersey (later Princeton); delegate to the Continental Congress, New Jersey, 1776-1779, 1780-1781, 1782; signer of the Declaration of Independence; president of Princeton College, 1782-1794.

**Woedtke, Frederick William, Baron de.** c.1740-1776. Prussian officer (Maj.), Continental officer (Brig. Gen.).

Brigadier General, Continental Army, 1776; died of illness at Lake George, July 1776.

**Wolcott, Erastus.** 1722-1793. Militia officer (Brig. Gen.), jurist, b. Connecticut.

Commanded the 1st Connecticut Brigade; brother of Oliver Wolcott.

**Wolcott, Oliver.** 1726-1797. American statesman, militia officer (Maj. Gen.), jurist, b. Windsor, Conn.

Delegate to the Continental Congress, Connecticut, 1775-1778, 1780-1784; signer of the Declaration of Independence; commanded Connecticut militia in several actions; governor of Connecticut, 1796-1798; brother of Erastus Wolcott.

**Wood, James.** Frontiersman, Indian agent, militia officer (Brig. Gen.), statesman.

Traveled 800 miles through Indian country, July-August 1775, to invite Indian leaders to conference held at Pittsburgh, September 1775; militia brigadier general during the Revolution; founder of Winchester, Va.; governor of Virginia, 1796-1799; after service as governor, led movement for emancipation of slaves in Virginia.

**Wood, Joseph.** 1712-1791. American statesman, planter, b. Pennsylvania.

Delegate to the Continental Congress, Georgia, 1777-1779.

**Woodford, William.** 1734-1780. Militia officer (Col.), Continental officer (Brig. Gen.), b. Caroline Co., Va.

Commander of Virginia troops at battle of Great Bridge, Va., 9 December 1775; Continental brigadier general, 1777-1780; fought at Brandywine, Germantown, and Monmouth; made prisoner when Charleston surrendered, 12 May 1780, and died a prisoner of war in New York.

**Woodhull, Nathaniel.** 1722-1776. Militia officer (Brig. Gen.), farmer,

b. St. George's Manor, Mastic, Long Island, N.Y.

Veteran of the French and Indian War; president of New York Provincial Congress, 1775-1776; brigadier general of state troops, 1775-1776; wounded and captured at Jamaica, N.Y., 28 August 1776, dying several weeks later.

**Woodhull, Samuel.** American spy.

Resident of Setauket, Long Island, N.Y.; used code name "Culper, Sr."; with Robert Townsend, formed highly successful Culpers spy team; received infomation from Townsend, who collected it on Manhattan Island, and transmitted it by Caleb Brewster and his whaleboatmen to Connecticut; also gathered military information from Long Island.

**Woodworth, Solomon.** Continental officer (Lt.).

Ambushed and killed by Indians at Fort Plain, N.Y., 7 September 1781.

**Woolsey, Melancthon Lloyd.** d. 1819. Continental officer (Lt.).

At Middleburg, N.Y., 15 October 1780, successfully repulsed 1,000 British, Tories, Hessians, and Indians, led by Joseph Brant and Sir John Johnson; New York resident.

**Wooster, David.** 1711-1777. Continental officer (Brig. Gen.), militia officer (Maj. Gen.), seaman, b. Stratford (now Huntington), Conn.

Veteran of King George's War (1744-1745) and the French and Indian War; brigadier general, 1775-1777; served in the Canada invasion, 1776; major general of Connecticut militia, 1776; killed in the Danbury (Conn.) raid, 2 May 1777.

**Wormely, Ralph.** 1744-1806. Loyalist, b. Middlesex Co., Va.

Member of the Virginia (Governor's) Council, 1771; remained a loyalist, but took no overt action during the Revolution; member, Virginia House of Delegates, 1787, 1789, 1790, 1793.

**Wright, Sir James, the elder.** 1714-1785. British government official, lawyer, b. Charleston, S.C.

Royal governor of Georgia, 1762-1771, 1773-1776, 1779-1782.

**Wright, Sir James, the younger.** d.1816. Loyalist officer.

Raised and commanded the Georgia Royalists, 1779; commanded a redoubt in the defense of Savannah, 9 October 1779.

**Wright, Turbutt.** 1741-1783. American statesman, farmer, b. "White Marsh," near Chester Mills (now Centerville), Queen Annes Co., Md.

Delegate to the Continental Congress, Maryland, 1781-1782.

**Wurmb, Ludwig Johann Adam von.** Hessian officer (Lt. Col.).

Commander of the Jäger Corps, which included (1777) all jäger (light infantry) troops of Hesse-Cassel, Hesse-Hanau, and Anspach serving in America.

**Wynkoop, Henry.** 1737-1816. American statesman, jurist, b. Northampton Township, Bucks Co., Pa.

Delegate to the Continental Congress, Pennsylvania, 1779-1783; member, U.S. House of Representatives, 1789-1791.

**Wythe, George.** 1726-1806. American statesman, lawyer, teacher, jurist, b. Back River, Elizabeth City Co., Va.

Member, House of Burgesses, 1754-1755, 1758-1761, 1761-1768; leading early patriot; delegate to the Continental Congress, Virginia, 1775-1777; signer of the Declaration of Independence; speaker, Virginia House of Delegates; with Thomas Jefferson and Edmund Pendleton, revised laws of Virginia, completing the work in 1779; professor of law, William and Mary College, 1779-1790; judge of Virginia high court of chancery, 1778-1806, serving as sole chancellor, 1788-1801; made important contributions to American jurisprudence, including an early statement of the doctrine of judicial review (*Commonwealth* vs. *Caton*, 1782).

# Y

**Yates, Abraham.** American statesman.

Leader in New York state Revolutionary affairs; member of New York Revolutionary convention of July 1776; chairman of committee to write new state constitution; member of six-man committee to plan organization of government after constitution was adopted; member of state Senate during Revolution; commissioner of New York state Continental Loan Office, set up to raise state funds by borrowing from citizens, 1780.

**Yorke, Sir Joseph.** 1724-1792. British officer (general), diplomat.

British Ambassador to the Netherlands, 1761-1780; announced that Britain would seize all Dutch goods bound for France; gave the Netherlands a formal and unsuccessful appeal (March 1780) to disavow sympathy for the French and reaffirm the old British-Dutch friendship; created Baron Dover, 1788.

# Z

**Zane, Betty.** Patriot heroine, b. Virginia (now West Virginia).

Brought gunpowder to fort at Wheeling during siege of 1782; sister of Ebenezer Zane.

**Zane, Ebenezer.** 1747-1812. Pioneer, militia officer (Col.), land speculator, b. Hardy Co., Va. (now West Va.).

Founded Wheeling, Va., 1770; disbursing agent for Virginia militia; opened road from Wheeling to Limestone, Ky., 1796-1797; brother of Betty Zane.

**Zedwitz, Herman.** Continental officer (Lt. Col.), British spy.

New York resident; lieutenant colonel in 1st New York Regiment of Continental Army; attempted to alert New York Royal Governor William Tryon, 1776, to efforts by the Continental Congress to bribe Hessian and German soldiers to defect; successfully escaped and avoided capture and punishment by patriots.

**Zoutman, Johan Arnold.** Dutch naval officer (admiral).

Encountered the British under Admiral Hyde Parker in the battle of Dogger Bank, a drawn battle, 5 August 1781.

**Zubly, John J.** 1724-1781. American statesman, clergyman, writer, b. St. Gall, Switzerland.

Came to America, 1744; Presbyterian minister at Savannah, Ga., from 1760; delegate to the Continental Congress, Georgia, 1775; opposed independence; banished from Georgia as loyalist, 1777-1779.

# Appendix A

## Revolutionary People Categorized

### *Signers of the Declaration of Independence*

John Adams, Massachusetts
Samuel Adams, Massachusetts
Josiah Bartlett, New
   Hampshire
Carter Braxton, Virginia
Charles Carroll, Maryland
Samuel Chase, Maryland
Abraham Clark, New Jersey
George Clymer, Pennsylvania
William Ellery, Rhode Island
William Floyd, New York
Benjamin Franklin,
   Pennsylvania
Elbridge Gerry, Massachusetts
Button Gwinnett, Georgia
Lyman Hall, Georgia
John Hancock, Massachusetts
Benjamin Harrison, Virginia
John Hart, New Jersey
Joseph Hewes, North Carolina
Thomas Hayward, South
   Carolina
William Hooper, North
   Carolina
Stephen Hopkins, Rhode
   Island

Francis Hopkinson, New
   Jersey
Samuel Huntington,
   Connecticut
Thomas Jefferson, Virginia
Francis Lightfoot Lee, Virginia
Richard Henry Lee, Virginia
Francis Lewis, New York
Philip Livingston, New York
Thomas Lynch, Jr., South
   Carolina
Thomas McKean, Delaware
Arthur Middleton, South
   Carolina
Lewis Morris, New York
Robert Morris, Pennsylvania
John Morton, Pennsylvania
Thomas Nelson, Jr., Virginia
William Paca, Maryland
Robert Treat Paine, Massa-
   chusetts
John Penn, North Carolina
George Read, Delaware
Caesar Rodney, Delaware
George Ross, Pennsylvania
Benjamin Rush, Pennsylvania

Edward Rutledge, South
  Carolina
Roger Sherman, Rhode Island
James Smith, Pennsylvania
Richard Stockton, New Jersey
Thomas Stone, Maryland
George Taylor, Pennsylvania
Matthew Thornton, New
  Hampshire

George Walton, Georgia
William Whipple, New
  Hampshire
William Williams, Connecticut
James Wilson, Pennsylvania
John Witherspoon, New Jersey
Oliver Wolcott, Connecticut
George Wythe, Virginia

## General Officers of the Continental Army*

### General and Commander-in-Chief

George Washington, 1775-1783

### Major Generals

William Alexander, Lord
  Stirling, 1777-1783 (brigadier general, 1776-1777)
Benedict Arnold, 1777-1780
  (brigadier general, 1776-
  1777)
Thomas Conway, 1777-1778
  (brigadier general, 1777)
John De Kalb, 1777-1780
Louis L. Duportail, 1781-1783
  (brigadier general, 1777-
  1781)
Horatio Gates, 1776-1783
  (brigadier general, 1775-
  1776)
Nathanael Greene, 1776-1783
  (brigadier general, 1775-
  1776)
William Heath, 1776-1783
  (brigadier general, 1775-
  1776)
Robert Howe, 1777-1783
  (brigadier general, 1776-1777)

Henry Knox, 1781-1784 (brigadier general, 1776-1781)
Paul J. G. de M. Lafayette,
  1777-1783
Charles Lee, 1775-1780
Benjamin Lincoln, 1777-1783
Alexander McDougall, 1777-
  1783 (brigadier general,
  1776-1777)
Thomas Mifflin, 1777-1779
  (brigadier general, 1776-1777)
Richard Montgomery, 1775
  (brigadier general, 1775)
William Moultrie, 1782-1783
  (brigadier general, 1776-
  1782)
Samuel H. Parsons, 1780-1782
  (brigadier general, 1776-
  1780)
Israel Putnam, 1775-1783
Arthur St. Clair, 1777-1783
  (brigadier general, 1776-
  1777)
Philip Schuyler, 1775-1779
William Smallwood, 1780-1783
  (brigadier general, 1776-
  1780)
Joseph Spencer, 1776-1778
  (brigadier general, 1775-
  1776)

*Names are as given on the rolls of the
Continental Army.

Adam Stephen, 1777 (brigadier general, 1776-1777)

Frederick W. A. Steuben, 1778-1783

John Sullivan, 1776-1779 (brigadier general, 1775-1776)

Philippe Charles Baptiste Tronson de Coudray, 1777

## Brigadier Generals

Charles T. Armand, 1783

John Armstrong, 1776-1777

George Clinton, 1777-1783

James Clinton, 1776-1783 (Brevet Major General, 1783)

Elias Dayton, 1783

Mathias A. R. de Fermony, 1776-1778

John P. de Haas, 1777-1783

Joseph Frye, 1776

Christopher Gadsden, 1776-1777

Mordecai Gist, 1779-1783

John Glover, 1777-1782

John Greaton, 1783

Edward Hand, 1777-1783

James Hogan, 1779-1781

Isaac Huger, 1779-1783

Jedediah Huntington, 1777-1783

William Irvine, 1779-1783

Ebenezer Learned, 1777-1778

Andrew Lewis, 1776-1777

Lachlan McIntosh, 1776-1783

William Maxwell, 1776-1780

Hugh Mercer, 1776-1777

James Moore, 1776-1777

Daniel Morgan, 1780-1783

Peter Muhlenberg, 1777-1783

Francis Nash, 1777

John Nixon, 1776-1780

John Paterson, 1777-1783

Enoch Poor, 1777-1780

Philippe Hubert Prudhomme de Borre, 1776-1777

Casimir Pulaski, 1777-1779

Rufus Putnam, 1783

James Reed, 1776

Charles Scott, 1777-1783

Jethro Sumner, 1779-1783

John Stark, 1777-1783

William Thompson, 1776-1781

James M. Varnum, 1777-1779

Anthony Wayne, 1777-1783

George Weedon, 1777-1783

Otho H. Williams, 1782-1783

Frederick W. de Woedtke, 1776

William Woodford, 1777-1780

David Wooster, 1775-1777

## *Some Other Categories of Revolutionary People\**

*Bankers and financiers*

Fitzsimmons, Thomas

Levy, Aaron

Mease, James

Nixon, John

Salomon, Haym

*For information on these people, see the *People of the American Revolution* section of this book. Certain categories have not been listed here because examples appear on almost every page of the *People* section, and lists would therefore not be useful. These include Continental officers (except generals, listed above), patriot militia officers (except generals), lawyers, farmers, and civilian loyalists.

*Bookstore proprietors*
Bradford, William
Knox, Henry
Rivington, James
Thomas, Isaiah

*Businessmen*
Bingham, William
Bradford, William
Cadwalader, John
Clinton, George
Duer, William
Fehiger, Christian
Gerry, Elbridge
Graham, Joseph
Greene, Christopher
Habersham, Joseph
Mersereau, Joshua
Roberdeau, Daniel
Searle, James
Stansbury, Joseph
Stoddert, Benjamin
Tallmadge, Benjamin, Jr.
Taylor, George
Wadsworth, Jeremiah

*Clergymen*
Agnew, John
Allison, Patrick
Andrews, John
Baldwin, Abraham
Beach, John
Belknap, Jeremy
Boucher, Jonathan
Browne, Isaac
Byles, Mather
Caldwell, James
Camer, Henry
Camm, John
Cooper, Myles
Duché, Jacob
Fairfax, Bryan
Gibault, Pierre
Gordon, William
Hall, Lyman
Hussey, Thomas

Inglis, Charles
Lee, Ann
Lotbinière, Louis
Madison, James (b. 1729)
Muhlenberg, Frederick A. C.
Muhlenberg, John Peter
    Gabriel
Peters, Samuel
Ritzema, Rudolph
Root, Jesse
Seabury, Samuel
Stiles, Ezra
Thruston, Charles Mynn
Trumbull, Benjamin
Vardill, John
Walter, William
Witherspoon, John
Zubly, John J.

*College presidents*
Camm, John
Cooper, Myles
Howell, David
Madison, James (b. 1729)
Stiles, Ezra

*Craftsmen*
Badge, Thomas
Baldwin, Loammi
Barton, William
Bigelow, Timothy
Cornell, Ezekiel
Crane, John
Crosby, Enoch
Dawes, William
Dayton, Elias
Honeyman, John
Huntington, Samuel
Ludwick, Christopher
Mowry, Daniel, Jr.
Peale, Charles Willson
Pomeroy, Seth
Reed, James
Revere, Paul
Rhoads, Samuel

Ross, Betsy
Wayne, Anthony
*Engineers*
Armstrong, John
Cambray-Digny, Louis
Antoine Jean-Baptiste,
Chevalier de
Erskine, Robert
Gouvion, Jean-Baptiste
Gridley, Richard
Laumoy, Jean-Baptiste
Joseph, Chevalier de
Montresor, John
Putnam, Rufus
Romans, Bernard
Van Cortlandt, Philip

*Foreign volunteers in the
Continental Army*

Armand, Charles
Cambray-Digny, Louis
Antoine Jean-Baptiste,
Chevalier de
Celeron de Blainville, Paul
Louis
Colomb, Pierre
Conway, Thomas
Kosciusko, Thaddeus
Derick, Jacob Gerhard
Dubuysson des Hays,
Charles-François,
Vicomte
Duportail, Louis, Chevalier
de
Fermoy, Matthias Alexis de
Roche, Chevalier de
Galvan, William de
Gimat, Jean-Joseph
Sourbader de
Gouvion, Jean-Baptiste
Holtzendorf, Louis-Casimir,
Baron de
Kalb, Johann ("Baron de
Kalb")

Lafayette, Marie Joseph
Paul Yves Roch Gilbert du
Motier, Marquis de
Laumoy, Jean-Baptiste
Joseph, Chevalier de
Malmady, Francis, Marquis
de
Maussac de la Marquisie,
Bernard
Mottin de la Balme, Augustin
Penot Lombart, Louis-
Pierre, Chevalier de la
Neuville
Penot Lombart de Noirmont,
René-Hippolyte
Plessis, Maduit de, Chevalier
de
Prudhomme de Borre,
Philippe Hubert, Chevalier
Pulaski, Casimir, Count
Rosenthal, Gustave Henri,
Baron de
Steuben, Friedrich Wilhelm
Augustus von
Teissedre de Fleury,
François Louis
Tronson de Coudray,
Philippe Charles Jean-
Baptiste
Vernier, Pierre-François
*Frontiersmen*
Boone, Daniel
Campbell, Arthur
Campbell, William
Christian, William
Clark, George Rogers
Clarke, Elijah
Cleveland, Benjamin
Crawford, William
Cresap, Michael
Donelson, John
Floyd, John
Harrod, James
Hicks, Gershom

Kenton, Simon
McGary, Hugh
Parsons, Samuel Holden
Robertson, James
Rogers, Robert
Scott, Charles
Walker, Thomas
Williamson, Andrew
Wood, James
Zane, Ebenezer
*Governors, royal*
Bernard, Sir Francis
Botetourt, Norbonne Berkeley,
    Baron de
Bull, William, II
Campbell, Lord William
Dunmore, John Murray,
    Earl
Eden, Robert
Franklin, William
Hutchinson, Thomas
Legge, Francis
Martin, Josiah
Tryon, William
Wanton, Joseph
Wright, Sir James, the elder
*Indian agents*
Hawkins, Benjamin
Johnson, Guy
Wood, James
*Indian leaders*
Brant, Joseph
Brant, Molly
Cornstalk
Guristersigo
Langlade, Charles Michael
    de
Logan
Nimham
White Eyes
*Inventors*
Bancroft, Edward
Belton, Joseph

Bushnell, David
Ferguson, Patrick
Franklin, Benjamin
Hopkinson, Francis
Jefferson, Thomas
*Journalists and political writers*
Bailey, Francis
Dickinson, John
Freneau, Philip
Goddard, William
Junius
Langworthy, Edward
Leonard, David
McDougall, Alexander
Mauduit, Israel
Otis, James
Seabury, Samuel
Townsend, Robert
Vardill, John
Wilkes, John
Wilson, James
*Manufacturers*
Cary, Archibald
Hill, William
Humphreys, David
Lacey, John
Lewis, Fielding
Wadsworth, Jeremiah
Wisner, Henry
*Mapmakers*
Bauman, Sebastian
Berthier, Louis Alexander
DeWitt, Simeon
Erskine, Robert
Romans, Bernard
*Merchants*
Alsop, John
Bache, Richard
Bayard, John B.
Bingham, William
Bowler, Metcalf
Brown, John
Clymer, George

Costigin, Lewis J.
Elbert, Samuel
Fitzsimmons, Thomas
Gadsden, Christopher
Galloway, Joseph
Gerry, Elbridge
Gervais, John L.
Gibson, George
Gorham, Nathaniel
Gray, Harrison
Habersham, James
Habersham, John
Harnett, Cornelius
Henry, Patrick
Hewes, Joseph
Higginson, Stephen
Hopkins, Stephen
Jackson, Jonathan
Kemble, Peter
Lamb, John
Langdon, John
Langdon, Woodbury
Laurens, Henry
Lee, William
Lewis, Francis
Livingston, Philip
Low, Isaac
McLane, Allen
Matlack, Timothy
Mazzei, Philip
Morris, Robert
Murray, James
Nash, Francis
Neville, Presley
Nicola, Lewis
Nixon, John
Osgood, Samuel
Oswald, Richard
Parker, John
Phripp, Matthew
Rochester, Nathaniel
Salomon, Haym
Smith, William

Sprowle, Andrew
Stoddert, Benjamin
Stewart, Walter
Stuart, John
Telfair, Edward
Thomson, Charles
Tilghman, Tench
Townsend, Robert
Trumbull, Jonathan, the
    elder
Trumbull, Joseph
Ward, Samuel, Jr.
Warren, James
Wentworth, John
Wharton, Samuel
Whipple, William
Willett, Marinus
Williams, William
Willing, Thomas
*Militia generals, patriot*
Allen, Ethan
Clark, George Rogers
Davidson, William Lee
Dickinson, Philemon
Enos, Roger
Folsom, Nathaniel
Forman, David
Hancock, John
Heard, Nathaniel
Heath, William
Henderson, William
Herkimer, Nicholas
Huntington, Jabez
Johnson, Thomas
Jones, Allen
Lacey, John
Lawson, Robert
Lillington, John Alexander
Lincoln, Benjamin
Livingston, William
Lovell, Solomon
Marion, Francis
Morris, Lewis

Nelson, Thomas, Jr.
Pickens, Andrew
Prescott, Oliver
Rodney, Caesar
Rutherford, Griffith
Scott, John Morin
Silliman, Gold Selleck
Smith, Samuel
Stevens, Edward
Sumter, Thomas
Van Rensselaer, Robert
Varnum, James M.
Wadsworth, Peleg
Warner, Seth
Warren, Joseph
Whitcomb, John
Williamson, Andrew
Wolcott, Oliver
Wood, James
*Millers*
Humphreys, Charles
Murphy, Timothy
*Monarchs*
Catherine II
George III
Louis XVI
*Negroes*
Attucks, Crispus
Banks, John
Caesar
Christophe, Henri
Dabney, Austin
Freeman, Jordan
Frost, Neptune
Hector, Edward
Jerry
Lafayette, James
Poor, Salem
Whitcuff, Benjamin
Wheatley, Phyllis
*Officers, American naval*
  *(state)*
Haraden, Jonathan
Williams, John Foster

*Officers, British army**
Abercromby, James
Abercromby, Robert
Acland, John Dyke
Auchmutz, Samuel
Balfour, Nisbet
Barclay, Thomas
Beckwith, George
Bernière, Henry De
Bliss, Daniel
Brown, William
Burgoyne, John
Campbell, Archibald
Campbell, John, Maj.
Campbell, John, Brig. Gen.
Carleton, Christopher
Carleton, Sir Guy
Carleton, Thomas
Cathcart, Sir William Schaw
Clarke, Alured
Clerke, Sir Francis Carr
Clinton, Sir Henry
Coffin, John
Coffin, Sir Thomas Aston
Cornwallis, Charles, Earl
Craig, James Henry
Dalling, John
Dalrymple, John
Dalrymple, William
DeLancey, Oliver, the
  younger
De Peyster, Arent Schuyler
Despard, John
Doyle, John
Drummond, Duncan
Dundas, Thomas
Eliott, Sir George Augustus
Erskine, William

*A number of these men were American
loyalists. However, most American
loyalists who fought for Britain served
in Tory militia units; see Officers,
Tory, below. In some cases it could not
be ascertained whether a man was a
British officer or a Tory militia officer.

Ferguson, Patrick
Fraser, Simon, Brig. Gen.
Fraser, Simon, Capt.
Gage, Thomas
Garth, George
Gould, Paston
Grant, James, Lt. Gen.
Grant, James, Lt. Col.
Grey, Charles
Haldimand, Frederick
Hamilton, Henry
Hanger, George
Holland, Stephen
Howe, Sir William
Jackson, Robert
Kemble, Stephen
Leslie, Alexander
McArthur, Archibald
MacLean, Allan
MacLean, Francis
Maitland, John
Marjoribanks, John
Mathew, Edward
Mawhood, Charles
Monckton, Henry
Moncrieff, James
Montresor, John
Musgrave, Thomas
O'Hara, Charles
Paterson, James
Pattison, James
Percy, Hugh (Earl Percy)
Phillips, William
Pigot, Sir Robert
Pitcairn, John
Prescott, Richard
Prescott, Robert
Prevost, Augustine
Prevost, James Mark
Rastel, Philippe François,
  Sieur de Rocheblave
Rawdon-Hastings, Francis
  (Lord Rawdon)
Robertson, James

St. Leger, Barry
Simcoe, John G.
Skene, Philip
Skinner, John
Smith, Francis
Stedman, Charles
Stewart, Alexander
Stuart, John, Jr.
Sutherland, William
Tarleton, Banastre
Taylor, Daniel
Thompson, Benjamin
Tonyn, Patrick
Tryon, William
Vaughan, John
Wemyss, James

*Officers, British naval*
Affleck, Edmund
Arbuthnot, Marriot
Barrington, Samuel
Byron, John
Coffin, Isaac
Collier, George
Cornwallis, Sir William
Despard, Edward Marcus
Digby, Robert
Elliot, John
Elphinstone, George Keith
Gambier, James, Vice. Adm.
Gambier, James, Lt.
Graves, Samuel
Graves, Thomas
Hallowell, Sir Benjamin
Hood, Samuel, Viscount
Hotham, William
Howe, Lord Richard
  (Viscount)
Johnstone, George
Kempenfelt, Richard
Keppel, Augustus, Viscount
Mowat, Henry
Nelson, Horatio
Nicholas, Samuel
Palliser, Sir Hugh

Parker, Sir Hyde
Parker, Sir Hyde, Jr.
Parker, Sir Peter
Pearson, Sir Richard
Rochey, George Brydges
Rowley, Joshua
Shuldham, Molyneux
Wallace, Sir James
*Officers, Continental marine*
Trevett, John
*Officers, Continental naval*
Barney, Joshua
Barry, John
Biddle, Nicholas
Chapin, Seth
Conyngham, Gustavus
Dale, Richard
Hopkins, Esek
Hopkins, John Burroughs
Jones, John Paul
Manley, John
Mugford, James
Nicholson, James
Rathbun, John Peck
Read, Thomas
Saltonstall, Dudley
Talbot, Silas
Whipple, Abraham
Wickes, Lambert
*Officers, French army**
Aboville, Comte François
Deux-Ponts, Guillaume,
    Comte de
Berthier, Louis Alexander
Blanchard, Claude
Broglie, Charles-François,
    Comte de
Chastellux, Chevalier de
Choisy, Marquis de
Corny, Dominique-Louis
    Ethis de

*Serving with French forces, not as
volunteers with American forces.

Crillon, Louis des Balbes de
    Berton
Cromot du Bourg, Baron de
Gribeauval, Jean-Baptiste
Noailles, Louis Marie,
    Vicomte de
Rochambeau, Donatien
    Marie Joseph de Vimeur,
    Vicomte de
Rochambeau, Jean-Baptiste
    Donatien de Vimeur,
    Comte de
Saint-Simon, Claude Henri
    de Rouvroy, Comte de
Saint-Simon Montblern,
    Claude Anne, Marquis de
Tronson de Coudray,
    Philippe Charles Jean-
    Baptiste
*Officers, French naval*
Barras, Louis de (Jacques-
    Melchior Saint-Laurent,
    Comte de Barras)
Bougainville, Louis Antoine
    de
Destouches, Charles-René-
    Dominique Sochet,
    Chevalier
Estaing, Jean-Baptiste
    Charles Henri Hector
    Théodât, Comte d'
Grasse, François Joseph
    Paul de
Guichen, Luc Urbain de
    Bouexic, Comte de
Landais, Pierre
Orvilliers, Louis Guillonet,
    Comte d'
Suffren de Saint Tropez,
    Pierre André de
Ternay, Charles Louis
    d'Arsac, Chevalier de
Vence, Jean Gaspard

*An attempt has been made to list here only loyalist militia officers, but it is possible that some of these men received the King's commission and thus were officers in the British Army.

Stranger, Richard
Vence, Jean Gaspard
Williams, John Foster
*Scientists*
Franklin, Benjamin
Jefferson, Thomas
Mazzei, Philip
Thompson, Benjamin
Romans, Bernard
*Shipbuilders*
Gilman, John Taylor
Mersereau, Joshua
Poor, Enoch
*Ship's masters*
Higginson, Stephen
Saltonstall, Dudley
Stewart, Anthony
Wickes, Lambert
*Shippers*
Conyngham, Gustavus
Moylan, Stephen
Stoddert, Benjamin
Wallis, Samuel
*Spies and secret agents,*
*American*
Bancroft, Edward
Bankson, Jacob
Barker, Isaac
Brewster, Caleb
Bruen, Caleb
Bryan, Alexander
Chambers, Stephen
Clark, John
Craig, Charles
Costigin, Lewis J.
Crosby, Enoch
Darragh, Lydia
Davis, Joshua
Gray, David
Hale, Nathan
Hart, Nancy Morgan
Hendricks, John
Hicks, Gershom

Honeyman, John
Hunter, Elijah
Lafayette, James
Lee, Andrew
Mersereau, John, the elder
Mersereau, John, the
younger
Mersereau, Joshua
Mulligan, Hercules
Newall, Simon
Rinker, "Mom"
Rivington, James
Roe, Austin
Springfield, Loadices
Langston
Townsend, Robert
Vanderhovan, John
Woodhull, Samuel
*Spies and secret agents, British*
André, John
Arnold, Benedict
Badge, Thomas
Bancroft, Edward
Bates, Ann
Beckwith, George
Berkenhout, John
Bernière, Henry De
Brown, William
Church, Benjamin
Church, Thomas
Ferguson, Robert
Heron, William
Howe, John
McFarlan, Robert
Marks, Nehemiah
Mergann, Maurice
Moody, James
Moody, John
Odell, Jonathan
Palmer, Edmund
Rattoon, John
Stansbury, Joseph
Taylor, Daniel

Maurepas, Jean Fredéric,
Comte de
Montmorin, Armand, Comte
de
Saint-Germain, Comte de
Sartine, Antoine, Comte
d'Ally
Vauguyon, Duc de la
Vergennes, Charles Gravier,
Comte de
*Statesmen and diplomats,*
*Russian*
Panin, Nikita, Count
*Statesmen and diplomats,*
*Spanish*
Almodovar, Marquis of
Aranda, Pedro, Count of
Floridablanca, José
Galvéz, Bernardo de
Galvéz, José de
Grimaldi, Jerónimo
Miralles, Juan de
*Surveyors*
Brodhead, Daniel
Crawford, William
Gridley, Richard
Heron, William
Hopkins, Stephen
Huntington, Benjamin
Morton, John
Putnam, Rufus
Romans, Bernard
Scammel, Alexander
Sevier, John
Smith, James
Van Cortlandt, Philip
Walker, Thomas
Washington, George
Wayne, Anthony
*Tavernkeepers and innkeepers*
Brewer, Jonathan
Jones, Isaac
Reed, James
Ruggles, Timothy

Sumner, Jethro
Weedon, George
*Teachers*
Bates, Ann
Hale, Nathan
Heron, William
Houston, William C.
Langworthy, Edward
Lovell, James
Lovell, John
Partridge, George
Paterson, John
Sampson, Deborah
Shippen, William
Thomson, Charles
Vardill, John
Wilson, James
Wythe, George
*Traders*
Butler, Richard
Cresap, Michael
Fanning, David
Girty, George
Girty, James
Gwinnett, Button
Huntington, Jedediah
Jamieson, Neil
Pollock, Oliver
Poor, Enoch
Sevier, John
Vigo, Francis
Wilkinson, James
*Women, British*
Acland, Lady Harriet
*Women, German*
Riedesel, Baroness Frederica
von
*Women, loyalist*
Bates, Ann
Ferguson, Elizabeth Graeme
McCrea, Jane
McDonald, Flora
Shippen, Margaret

*Women, patriot*
   Burgin, Elizabeth
   Corbin, Margaret Cochran
   Darragh, Lydia
   Hart, Nancy Morgan
   Hays, Mary Ludwig
   Murray, Mrs. Robert
   Rinker, "Mom"
   Ross, Betsy
   Sampson, Deborah
   Springfield, Loadices
      Langston
   Tarrant, Sarah
   Warren, Mercy Otis
   Wheatley, Phyllis
   Zane, Betty
*Writers\**
   Beaumarchais, Pierre
      Augustin Caron de
   Belknap, Jeremy
   Berkenhout, John
   Brackenridge, Hugh Henry
   Chalmers, George
   Chastellux, Chevalier de
   Ferguson, Elizabeth Graeme
   Franklin, Benjamin
   Freneau, Philip

Gordon, William
Hopkinson, Francis
Humphreys, David
Hutchinson, Thomas
Jefferson, Thomas
Jones, Thomas
Lamb, Roger
Locke, John
Moultrie, William
Odell, Jonathan
Ramsay, David
Riedesel, Baroness
   Frederica von
Saint-Simon, Claude Henri
   de Rouvroy, Comte de
Smith, William, II
Stansbury, Joseph
Stedman, Charles
Taylor, John, of Caroline
Thomas, Isaiah
Trumbull, Benjamin
Trumbull, John
Walpole, Horatio
Warren, Joseph
Warren, Mercy Otis
Wheatley, Phyllis
Zubly, John J.

\*Poets, playwrights, and historians.
*See also* Journalists and political
writers.

# Appendix B

## Major Battles of the Revolutionary War

Brandywine, Pa., 11 September 1777

Bunker Hill (Breed's Hill), near Boston, Mass., 17 June 1775

Camden, S.C., 16 August 1780

Concord, Mass., 19 April 1775

Cowpens, S.C., 17 January 1781

Germantown, Pa., 4 October 1777

Guilford Courthouse, N.C., 15 March 1781

Kings Mountain, S.C., 7 October 1780

Lexington, Mass., 19 April 1775

Long Island, N.Y., 27 August 1776

Monmouth Courthouse, N.J., 28 June 1778; Monmouth campaign, 16 June-5 July 1778.

Princeton, N.J., 3 January 1777

Saratoga, N.Y., 19 September 1777 (Freeman's Farm), and 7 October 1777 (Bemis Heights)

Trenton, N.J., 26 December 1776

White Plains, N.Y., 28 October 1776

Yorktown, Va., campaign, August-October 1781; siege, 30 September-18 October 1781; surrender, 19 October 1781.

# Appendix C

## "Color" Admirals in the British Navy*

During the Dutch wars of the 17th Century, the British fleet had been divided into three squadrons, with the ships of the center squadron flying red ensigns, those of the van squadron white ensigns, and those of the rear squadron blue ensigns. Although always considered officially to indicate specific posts, not ranks, the "colored admiral" titles did become *de facto* ranks. When an officer was promoted to flag rank, he became Rear Admiral of the Blue. He then rose to Rear Admiral of the White, Rear Admiral of the Red, Vice Admiral of the Blue, and so on up to Admiral of the White and then Admiral of the Fleet (the alternate and customarily used title for the Admiral of the Red). Since there were only nine officers of flag rank under this system, since there was no retirement for naval officers, and since strict seniority determined promotion, British naval thinkers in the 18th Century began to recognize a desperate need for a way to bring able younger men to flag status. In the 1740's the Admiralty began to appoint more than one man to the lower "color" posts and also to pass over the less able officers, making them flag officers but not assigning them to one of the hypothetical color squadrons. They were then said in the naval slang of the day to have been appointed to the Yellow Squadron, or to have been "yellowed."

The little American Navy had no admirals during the Revolution, nor until the Civil War. Commodore was its highest rank.

*This information on the "color" admirals is from Michael Lewis, *The Navy of Britain: A Historical Portrait* (London: George Allen and Unwin, 1948), pp. 265-270.

# Bibliography

Abbott, Wilbur C. *New York in the American Revolution.* New York, 1929.

Allen, Gardner W. *Naval History of the American Revolution.* 2 vols. 1913. Reprint (2 vols.). New York, 1962.

Andrews, Wayne, ed. *Concise Dictionary of American History.* New York, 1962.

*Annals of America,* Vol. II, 1755-1783. *Resistance and Revolution.* Chicago, 1968.

Armstrong, William C. *The Battles of the Jerseys and the Significance of Each.* Newark, N.J., 1916.

*Army Almanac,* Washington, D.C., 1950.

Bakeless, John. *Turncoats, Traitors, and Heroes.* New York, 1959.

Barrs, Burton. *East Florida in the American Revolution.* Jacksonville, Florida, 1949.

Bemis, Samuel F. *The Diplomacy of the American Revolution.* Bloomington, Ind., 1957.

Bill, Alfred H. *New Jersey and the Revolutionary War.* Princeton, N.J., 1964.

Billias, George Athan, ed. *George Washington's Opponents: British Generals and Admirals in the American Revolution.* New York, 1969.

*Biographical Directory of the American Congress, 1774-1949.* Washington, 1950.

Boatner, Mark M. *Encyclopedia of the American Revolution.* New York, 1966.

Bolton, Robert. *The History of Several Towns, Manors and Patents of the County of Westchester.* New York, 1881.

Boyd, William K. *A Syllabus of North Carolina's History, 1584-1876.* Durham, North Carolina, 1913.

Brown, Wallace. *The Good Americans: The Loyalists in the American Revolution.* New York, 1969.

Burt, Sturthers. *Philadelphia: Holy Experiment.* New York, 1945.

Callahan, North. *Flight from the Republic: The Tories of the American Revolution.* Indianapolis, 1967.

_____. *Royal Raiders: The Tories of the American Revolution.* Indianapolis, 1963.

Campbell, William W. *Annals of Tryon County, New York.* New York, 1924.

Carruth, Gorton. *Encyclopedia of American Facts*, 4th ed. New York, 1966.

Caruso, John Anthony. *The Appalachian Frontier: America's First Surge Westward.* Indianapolis, 1959.

_____. *The Southern Frontier.* New York, 1963.

Caulkins, Frances Manwaring. *History of New London, Connecticut.* New London, 1895.

Clark, William Bell. *George Washington's Navy.* Baton Rouge, 1960.

_____, ed. *Naval Documents of the American Revolution.* Washington, 1964-.

Clayton, Woodford W. *History of Union & Middlesex Counties, New Jersey.* Philadelphia, 1882.

Coggins, Jack. *Ships and Seamen of the American Revolution.* Harrisburg, Pa., 1969.

Coleman, Kenneth. *The American Revolution in Georgia.* Athens, Ga., 1958.

Commager, Henry Steele. *Living Ideas in America.* New York, 1951.

Commager, Henry Steele, and Richard B. Morris. *The Spirit of 'Seventy-Six: The Story of the American Revolution as Told by Participants.* New York, 1958.

Conn, Stetson. "An Army Chronology of the American Revolution" (preliminary draft). Reproduced photographically. Washington: Office of the Chief of Military History, Department of the Army, May 1971.

Dawson, Henry B. *Battles of the United States by Sea and Land,* Vol. I. New York, 1858.

DeMond, Robert O. *The Loyalists in North Carolina During the Revolution.* Durham, N.C., 1940.

Des Cognets, Louis, Jr. *Black Sheep and Heroes of the American Revolution*. Princeton, 1965.

Dictionary of American Biography. Allen Johnson and Dumas Malone, eds. Rev. ed. 22 vols. in 11, including supplements. New York, 1964.

Dictionary of National Biography. Sir Leslie Stephen and Sir Sidney Lee, eds. 22 vols. Oxford, 1917.

Dunaway, Wayland Fuller. *A History of Pennsylvania*. New York, 1946.

Duncan, Louis C. *Medical Men in the American Revolution, 1775-1783*. Carlisle Barracks, Pa., 1931.

Dupuy, R. Ernest, and Trevor N. Dupuy. *The Compact History of the Revolutionary War*. New York, 1963.

_____. *The Encyclopedia of Military History from 3500 B.C. to the Present*. New York, 1970.

Dupuy, Trevor N. *The Military Life of George Washington*. New York, 1969.

Dupuy, Trevor N., and Grace P. Hayes. *The Military History of Revolutionary War Naval Battles*. New York, 1970.

East, Robert A. *Business Enterprise in the American Revolutionary Era*. New York, 1938.

Eckenrode, Hamilton J. *The Revolution in Virginia*. 1916. Reprint. Hamden, Conn., 1964.

Ellet, Elizabeth F. *The Women of the American Revolution*. 2 vols. Philadelphia, 1900.

Flick, Alexander C., ed. *The American Revolution in New York: Its Political, Social, and Economic Significance*. Port Washington, Long Island, N.Y., 1926.

_____. *The History of the State of New York*, Vol. III. New York, 1933.

Force, Peter, ed. *American Archives: Fourth Series, Containing a Documentary History of the English Colonies in North America from the King's Message to Parliament of March 7, 1774, to the Declaration of Independence by the United States*, Vols. I-VI. Washington, 1847-1848.

_____. *American Archives: Fifth Series, Containing a Documentary History of the United States of America from the Declaration of Independence, July 4, 1776, to the Definitive Treaty of Peace with Great Britain, September 3, 1883*, Vol. I. Washington, 1848-1853.

Ford, Worthington Chauncey, ed. *Journals of the Continental Congress, 1774-1789*. 34 vols. Washington, 1905-1937.

Freeman, Douglas Southall. *George Washington: A Biography*. 7

vols. New York, 1949-1957.

Gabriel, Ralph, and William Wood. *The Winning of Freedom*. The Pageant of America, Vol. VI. New Haven, Conn., 1927.

Gipson, Laurence Henry. *The Coming of the Revolution, 1763-1775*. New York, 1962.

Godfrey, Carlos E. "Muster Rolls of Three Troops of Loyalist Light Dragoons Raised in Pennsylvania, 1777-1778," *Pennsylvania Magazine of History and Biography* 34 (1910): 1-8.

Gottschalk, Louis. *Lafayette Comes to America*. Chicago, 1935. 2nd impression. 1965.

Green, Frank B. *The History of Rockland County (N.Y.)*. New York, 1886.

Guthorn, Peter J. *American Maps and Mapmakers of the Revolution*. Monmouth Beach, N.J., 1966.

Hammond, Otis G. *Tories of New Hampshire in the War of Revolution*. Concord, N.H., 1917.

Hancock, Harold Bell. *The Delaware Loyalists*. Wilmington, 1940.

Harrell, Isaac S. *Loyalism in Virginia*. Durham, N.C., 1926.

Hatch, Charles E., Jr. *Yorktown and the Siege of 1781*. National Park Service Historical Handbook Series, No. 14. Revised ed. Washington, 1957.

Heitman, Francis B. *Historical Register of Officers of the Continental Army During the War of Revolution*. Rev. ed. 1914. Reprint. Baltimore, 1967.

*Historical Sketch to the End of the Revolutionary War of the Life of Silas Talbot*. New York, 1803.

Hufeland, Otto. *Westchester County During the American Revolution*. New York, 1926.

James, Sir William M. *The British Navy in Adversity: A Study of the War of American Independence*. New York, 1970.

Jensen, Merrill. *English Historical Documents: American Colonial Documents to 1776*. New York, 1955.

————. *The Founding of a Nation: A History of the American Revolution, 1763-1776*. New York, 1968.

Jones, E. Alfred. *The Loyalists of Massachusetts: Their Memorials, Petitions and Claims*. London, 1930.

————. *The Loyalists of New Jersey: Their Memorials, Petitions, claims etc. from English Records*. Newark, 1927.

Kallich, Martin, and Andrew MacLeish, eds. *The American Revolution Through British Eyes*. Evanston, Ill., 1962.

Kessey, Ruth M. "Loyalty and Reprisal: The Loyalists of Bergen County, New Jersey, and Their Estates." 1957. Mimeographed. Daughters of the American Revolution Library, Washington.

Ketchum, Richard M. *American Heritage Book of the Revolution.* New York, 1958.

Kull, I. S., and N. M. Kull. *Short Chronology of American History, 1492-1950.* New Brunswick, N.J., 1952.

Labaree, Leonard W. "The Nature of American Loyalism," *Proceedings of the American Antiquarian Society* 54 (1945), 15-58.

Lacy, Dan. *The Meaning of the American Revolution.* New York, 1964.

Langer, William L., ed. *An Encyclopedia of World History.* Boston, 1963.

Little, Charles E. *Cyclopedia of Classified Dates.* New York, 1900.

Lossing, Benson J. *Pictorial Field-Book of the Revolution.* 2 vols. New York, 1850-1852.

Lowell, Edward J. *The Hessians and the Other German Auxiliaries of Great Britain in the Revolutionary War.* Port Washington, N.Y., 1965.

McCall, Hugh. *The History of Georgia, Containing Brief Sketches of the Most Remarkable Events up to the Present Day.* Atlanta, 1909.

McCrady, Edward. *The History of South Carolina in the Revolution, 1775-1780, 1780-1783.* 2 vols. New York, 1901, 1902.

Mackenzie, George C. *Kings Mountain National Military Park.* National Park Service Historical Handbook Series, No. 22. Revised ed. Washington, 1956.

Malone, Dumas. *Jefferson the Virginian,* Vol. I of *Jefferson and His Time.* Boston, 1948.

Metzger, Charles H., S.J. *Catholics and the American Revolution.* Chicago, 1962.

Montross, Lyn. *The Story of the Continental Army, 1775-1783.* New York, 1967.

Morison, Samuel Eliot. *The Oxford History of the American People.* New York, 1965.

Morris, Richard B. *Encyclopedia of American History.* 2nd. ed. New York, 1961.

Nevins, Allan. *The American States During and After the Revolution, 1775-1789.* New York, 1924.

New York State Division of Archives and History. *The American Revolution in New York.* Albany, N.Y., 1926.

*Newspaper Extracts,* vols. I and III, in *Archives of the States of New Jersey, First Series, 1631-1800.* Newark, 1880-1941.

Noel Hume, Ivor. *1775: Another Part of the Field.* New York, 1966.

Noyes, Marion F. *A History of Schoharie County (N.Y.).* Richmondville, N.Y., 1964.

Ogg, Frederic. *Builders of the Republic.* The Pageant of America, Vol. VIII. New Haven, 1927.

Onderdonk, Henry. *Revolutionary Incidents of Suffolk and Kings Counties.* New York, 1849.

_____. *Documents and Letters Intended to Illustrate the Revolutionary Incidents of Queens County.* New York, 1846.

Peck, Epaphroditus. *The Loyalists of Connecticut.* New Haven, 1934.

Peters, Madison C. *The Jews Who Stood by Washington: An Unwritten Chapter in American History.* New York, 1915.

Peterson, Harold C. *Arms and Armor in Colonial America.* New York, 1956.

Quarles, Benjamin. *The Negro in the American Revolution.* Chapel Hill, N.C., 1961.

Quincy, Josiah F. *Reports of the Cases Argued and Adjudged in the Superior Court of the Province of Massachusetts Bay between 1761 and 1762.* 1865. Reprint. New York, 1969.

Rankin, Hugh F., and George F. Scheer. *Rebels and Redcoats: The Living Story of the American Revolution.* New York, 1957.

Rathbun, Frank H. "Rathbun's Raid on Nassau." *United States Naval Institute Proceedings* 96 (November 1970): 40-47.

Sabine, Lorenzo. *Biographical Sketches of Loyalists of the American Revolution with an Historical Essay.* 2 vols. Boston, 1864.

Smith, Paul H. *Loyalists and Redcoats: A Study in British Revolutionary Policy.* Chapel Hill, N.C., 1964.

Squires, James D. *New Hampshire: A Students Guide to Local History.* New York, 1966.

*Standard Jewish Encyclopedia, The.* Edited by Cecil Roth. 2nd ed. New York, 1962.

Stark, James H. *The Loyalists of Massachusetts and the Other Side of the American Revolution.* Boston, 1910.

Stevens, Sylvester K. *Pennsylvania's History in Outline.* Harrisburg, Pennsylvania, 1960.

Tercentenary Commission of the State of Rhode Island and Providence Plantations, *Rhode Island's Historic Background with a Rhode Island Historic Calendar,* 1936.

Tyler, Lyon Gardiner. *The Encyclopedia of Virginia Biography.* 5 vols. New York, 1915.

United States Bureau of the Census. *Historical Statistics of the United States, Colonial Times to 1957.* Washington, D.C., 1960.

_____. Department of the Interior. *Colonials and Patriots.* Washington, D.C., 1964.

_____. National Park Service. Handbooks: *Kings Mountain; Morristown; Guilford Court House; Yorktown.* Washington, D.C.

Van Alstyne, Richard W. *Empire and Independence: The International History of the American Revolution.* New York, 1965.

Van Doren, Carl. *Secret History of the American Revolution.* New York, 1941.

Van Every, Dale. *A Company of Heroes: The American Frontier, 1775-1783.* New York, 1962.

*Webster's Biographical Dictionary.* Springfield, Mass., 1957.

Wertenbaker, Thomas Jefferson. *Father Knickerbocker Rebels: New York City During the Revolution.* New York, 1948.

Wheeler, Richard A. *History of the Town of Stonington (Connecticut).* New London, Connecticut, 1900.

Whitridge, Arnold. *Rochambeau.* New York, 1965.

Wickwire, Franklin B. *British Subministers and Colonial America, 1763-1783.* Princeton, 1966.

Williams, Neville. *Chronology of the Modern World.* New York, 1967.

Wilson, Harold F., Chairman, New Jersey History Committee. *Outline History of New Jersey.* New Brunswick, 1950.

The Writers' Program of the Work Projects Administration of North Carolina. *Now North Carolina Grew.* Raleigh, 1941.

## Unpublished Materials

Letters from historical organizations of the following states and cities, on file in the offices of the Historical Evaluation and Research Organization, Dunn Loring, Va.: Cambridge, Mass.; Elizabeth, N.J.; Maryland; Raleigh, N.C.; Rochester, N.Y.; West Virginia. Additional data on Capt. John Peck Rathbun was given verbally by Mr. Frank Rathbun.

# Index

American Revolution*

Whipple, Abraham: 17, 62
Whipple, William: 113
White, Col. Anthony: 205
White, Col. John: 176
White Plains, N.Y., battle of: 121, 122
Whitehaven, England, raided: 163
Whitemarsh, Pa.: 150, 156
Whitsall's Mills, N.C.: 235
Wiboo Swamp, S.C.: 235
Wiggins' Hill, Ga.: 236
Willett, Col. Marinus: 59, 134, 143, 246, 255, 256
Williams, Capt. John Foster: 208
Williams, Brig. Gen. Otho: 232, 233, 235
Williams, William: 113
Williamsburg, Va.: 251, 253
Williamson, Brig. Gen. Andrew: 82, 112, 114
Williamson's Plantation, S.C.: 210, 227
Willing, Thomas: 29
Wilmington, N.C.: 231, 235, 239, 257
Wilson, James: 113
Windham, Conn., Resolution: 29
Winn, Capt. Richard: 132

Winnsboro, S.C.: 207, 222
Witherspoon, John: 113
Wofford's Iron Works, S.C.: 215
Wolcott, Oliver: 113
Woodford, Col. William: 81, 85
Woodhull, Nathaniel: 115
Woodworth, Lt. Solomon: 251
Woolsey, Maj. Melancthon Lloyd: 222
Wooster, Maj. Gen. David: 96, 99, 135
Wright, Sir James: 94
Wright's Bluff, S.C.: 233
Writs of Assistance: 1-2, 8
Wyoming Valley: 269; "Massacre," 170
Wythe, George: 113

*Yankee Hero*, USP: 103
*Yarmouth*, HMS: 161
York River, Va.: 247, 250
Yorktown, Va.: 247, 250, 253, 254, 255; siege begins, 253; surrender, 255
Young, Joseph: 178
Young's House, N.Y.: 178, 199

Zoutman, Rear Adm. Johann Arnold: 247